God's Scrivener

God's Scrivener

THE MADNESS AND MEANING OF JONES VERY

Clark Davis

The University of Chicago Press CHICAGO AND LONDON

The University of Chicago Press, Chicago 60637
The University of Chicago Press, Ltd., London

Published 2023
Printed in the United States of America

32 31 30 29 28 27 26 25 24 23 1 2 3 4 5

ISBN-13: 978-0-226-82868-8 (cloth)
ISBN-13: 978-0-226-82869-5 (e-book)
DOI: https://doi.org/10.7208/chicago/9780226828695.001.0001

The University of Chicago Press gratefully acknowledges the generous support of the College of Liberal Arts at the University of Denver toward the publication of this book.

Library of Congress Cataloging-in-Publication Data

Names: Davis, Clark, author.
Title: God's scrivener : the madness and meaning of Jones Very / Clark Davis.
Other titles: Madness and meaning of Jones Very
Description: Chicago ; London : The University of Chicago Press, 2023. | Includes bibliographical references and index.
Identifiers: LCCN 2023011328 | ISBN 9780226828688 (cloth) | ISBN 9780226828695 (ebook)
Subjects: LCSH: Very, Jones, 1813–1880. | Poets, American—19th century—Biography. | Mystics—Massachusetts—Biography. | American literature—19th century—History and criticism. | Transcendentalism (New England) | Religion and literature—United States. | LCGFT: Biographies.
Classification: LCC PS3128 .D38 2023 | DDC 811/.3—dc23/eng/20230407
LC record available at https://lccn.loc.gov/2023011328

♾ This paper meets the requirements of ANSI/NISO Z39.48-1992 (Permanence of Paper).

For Hillary

If it its Pen had of an Angels Quill,
    And Sharpend on a Pretious Stone ground tite,
And dipt in Liquid Gold, and mov'de by Skill
    In Christall leaves should golden Letters write
    It would but blot and blur yea jag, and jar
    Unless thou mak'st the Pen, and Scribener.

EDWARD TAYLOR, "Prologue" to *Preparatory Meditations*

Where, for example, shall we pause, and separate the sane from the insane, among those who believe themselves to be favored perpetually with special, particular, and ultra-scriptural revelations from heaven? The most modest enthusiast of this class, and the most daring visionary, stand together on the same ground of outlawry from common sense and scriptural authority; and though their several offences against truth and sobriety may be of greater or less amount, they must both be dealt with on the same principle; for both have alike excluded themselves from the benefit of appeal to the only authorities known among the sane part of mankind, namely, reason and Scripture: those who reject both, surrender themselves over to pity—or compulsion.

ISAAC TAYLOR, *Natural History of Enthusiasm* (1829)

And if another Messiah ever comes twill be in Shakespere's person.

HERMAN MELVILLE to Evert Duyckinck, February 24, 1849

Contents

II. "Flee to the mountains!"

III. God's Scrivener

IV. Man of Peace

Figures

FIGURES FOLLOW PAGE 130.

Introduction

In September of 1838, a few months after Ralph Waldo Emerson delivered his Divinity School Address, a twenty-five-year-old tutor and divinity student at Harvard named Jones Very stood before his beginning Greek class and proclaimed himself "the second coming." By the end of the week he had been relieved of his teaching duties and sent home to Salem, where he spent Saturday and Sunday repeating his claims to astonished and outraged religious leaders, some of whom were angry enough to throw him physically from their houses into the dusty Salem streets. The following Monday, Very entered McLean Hospital—or McLean Asylum for the Insane, as it was then known—where he stayed for a month, reading and writing and spreading his idiosyncratic interpretation of the Gospels to other patients. Over the next twenty months, he would write more than three hundred sonnets, many of them in the voice of a prophet like John the Baptist or of Christ himself—all, he was quick to claim, delivered to him, as though through dictation, by the Holy Spirit. His purpose or mission Very tried to explain to anyone who would listen, and his listeners included the major figures of Unitarianism and the emerging Transcendentalist movement. He was examined by the dean of romantic Unitarianism, William Ellery Channing, and strove to "convert," among others, Elizabeth and Sophia Peabody, Bronson Alcott, Nathaniel Hawthorne, and Emerson. For a short time Very haunted Salem like one of Hawthorne's obsessed characters, bright-eyed and feverish, an avatar of an individualism so complete that it erased all individuality. His demands were impossible, his intense faith unnerving and otherworldly. Some thought he had become a kind of walking corpse; others, that he had, in Channing's words, "obtained self annihilation & become an oracle of God" (EP 408). Probably no one believed that his poems came as directly from God as Very claimed or that the "other consciousness" he had detected inside himself was unquestionably divine. But many were moved by his presence and even more impressed by the quiet, controlled poetry that spilled forth during his season of spiritual ecstasy.

This brief but strange episode in the larger story of Transcendentalism constitutes the essence of Very's reputation as a significant, if curiously idiosyncratic, early American poet and a momentary refractor of the developing light of American individualism. But the full story of his life is much more than a footnote to the biographies of Emerson or the Peabody sisters. Born into the same politically riven, rich but recalcitrant Salem that produced Hawthorne, Very overcame repeated tragedies—the loss of two of his siblings and his father's traumatic death when he was still a boy—as well as a questionable family reputation, to become a star student at Harvard. While there, fired by the ambition to become an epic poet, he pursued a line of personal reading and development that took him, via his own path, toward similar ground as Emerson, whose *Nature* appeared just a few weeks after Very's graduation in 1836. In the months leading up to that famous September that saw the birth of the Transcendental Club, Very had begun his own revolutionary process, an attempt to remove all trace or tremor of personal will, to transform himself, anticipating the most famous passage in *Nature* itself, into "part or particle of God" (LA 10). Over the next two years, this increasingly stringent, internal demand to give up all, to surrender "every thought and affection" to God, would lead to his assumption of the role described by Emerson in the Divinity School Address: "a newborn bard of the Holy Ghost" (LA 89).[1]

Often misread as the story of a Salem eccentric more amusing than important, Very's life stands instead as a parallel history to Transcendentalism that casts a revealing and critical light on its central claims. For all of Emerson's dramatic language about the divinity of the true self, the logical implications of such a claim, as Lawrence Buell argued in *Literary Transcendentalism*, actually "disturbed" many who might otherwise consider such language symbolic.[2] Very came to embody both the full radicalism of Emerson's idealism and the dramatic effects of that disturbance. For some, and likely for Emerson in the end, he was simply an atavism, a pre-Enlightenment "stylite" who failed to address the problems of skepticism and epistemology. But to other eyes, Very's ecstatic "mission," his rejection of will and individual desire—his extension of radical individualism to its breaking point—revealed the trap of isolation and emptiness that lay in wait for those who sought complete "transcendence." Hawthorne's well-known description of Very, whom he knew and had observed personally, is deeper and more apt than has typically been appreciated. In "The Hall of Fantasy," a satirical sketch devoted in part to skewering Transcendentalists, Hawthorne placed Very in a corner, so to speak: "In the same part of the hall, Jones Very stood alone, within a circle which no other of mortal race could enter, nor himself escape from."[3] More than just another critique of monomania, this quick, precise portrait strikes at the core of the individualist dilemma: if the inner life is truly all that there is, the only reliable source of meaning or value, then the conclusion of its pursuit can be as much a form of melancholia as of ecstasy. The Emersonian "circle" or individual horizon, here subtly alluded to, may be (must be?) a cage of sorts; or, if we are willing to let this metaphor develop forward ten more years, not a cage but a claustrophobic Wall Street office where a once enthusiastic scrivener named Bartleby finds himself similarly "cornered."

As odd as it is, Very's life—at least during those heady months in 1838–39—suggests a kind of nodal point where the fullest development of romantic individualism meets one of the earliest expressions of modern isolation. Unlike Emerson, whose skepticism allowed him the saving space of irony, Very seems to have taken all of the implications of "inner light" spirituality seriously. Unwilling or unable to accept any version of subjectivity, he combined Anne Hutchinson's literal claim to "direct revelation" with the romantic notion of the vatic poet intent on developing a modern epic of inwardness. Closer in this sense to William Blake than to Wordsworth, Very forged his own idiosyncratic alloy of millennialist prophecy and soaring egotism, the latter defined, paradoxically, by its intense suppression of desire. That he believed all of it—believed in his union with the divine in a way that most other Transcendentalists did not—opened him to charges of madness. As much as anything else, such attacks mark him now as a peculiar amalgam of contemporary and premodern thought, a "brave saint," as Emerson called him, who nevertheless threw a gaunt, forlorn shadow over the mid-nineteenth century.

As a poet of inner divinity or the ventriloquism of divine voice, Very's unsettling of Transcendentalist assumptions marks a particularly important point in the story of American poetry. His anticipation of Whitman's prophetic persona has often been noted, but the radicalism of the claim that underpins his extraordinary flood of spiritual sonnets has seldom been appreciated. Out of a deep reading of Milton, Byron, Wordsworth, and Shakespeare, among others, Very developed a version of poetic embodiment that understood all bodily action of the will-less individual as a form of prayer—and all prayer as the incarnation of the divine spirit. The sonnets he copied onto foolscap sheets and folded into book-like squares were to him the direct communication of the Holy Spirit, much as Blake had spoken of the "immediate Dictation . . . without Premeditation & even against my Will" of his *Four Zoas*.[4] If Whitman could say in his poem "So Long" that "this is no book, / Who touches this touches a man,"

Very could claim the messianic basis of such a figuration almost twenty years before, assuming we understand that the "man" in question was also understood as "the son" of God. Prayer, he wrote in the extraordinary and vatic "Epistles to the Unborn," makes our bodies "the *true* body of Christ."[5] Language becomes flesh, in other words, but flesh that expresses divinity. As he explained to William Ellery Channing when asked about the intentionality of his everyday physical movements, Very believed that even so trivial a gesture as placing a hand upon a fireplace mantel was directed by the Holy Spirit. In his mind, by eliminating his personal will, he had become a physical extension and bodily expression of that Spirit within.

Yet so thorough a relinquishment of self and identity, as Hawthorne implied, was not without its costs. Again, the fullest result of an imagined collapse of the human into pervasive Soul might be ecstasy, but it could just as easily cause a dangerous loss of self. Very's passion may have shown the limits of Transcendentalist pretension and produced remarkable if idiosyncratic poetry, but it also left him open to what his contemporaries sometimes called "morbidity." In the later stages of his enthusiasm, Bronson Alcott thought Very near death, like a "spectre. . . . He is a voice from the tombs."[6] And Emerson, after one particularly odd social encounter, pronounced him "a corpse in the apartment" (*JMN* 7:213). The peril, in other words, of the poet-prophet's calling, of the flirtation with the dissolution of "mean egotism," is precisely the sort of isolation felt and expressed by Emerson himself in the opening to his great essay "Experience": "Was it Boscovich who found out that bodies never come in contact? Well, souls never touch their objects. An innavigable sea washes with silent waves between us and the things we aim at and converse with" (LA 10, 473). How Very found his way back from the peak of spiritual transcendence, which was also somehow the nadir of his young life, how he domesticated his "madness" and became something of a local legend of spiritual commitment and worldly detachment—these too are part of his story and part of the significance of his unusual life. If the divine isolato who once told his students to "flee to the mountains, for the end of all things is at hand!" can return to and recover the phenomenal world, there may be a hint in Very's life of something beyond the dead-letter office—a beatitude perhaps of the small and the still, a devotion to peace.

Over fifty years have passed since the last major biography of Jones Very, Edwin Gittleman's *Jones Very: The Effective Years, 1833–1840*, published in 1967. In that interval, scholarship on Very's life and work has developed considerably, producing a much clearer picture of his published and unpublished writing and a much fuller sense of the many details of his life. The work of Helen R. Deese, whose monumental edition of Very's complete poetry was published in 1993, has established a comprehensive, impeccably annotated text for all of Very's surviving poems. At the same time, Deese, David Robinson, Phyllis Cole, and others have brought to light a number of manuscripts, including selections from Very's sermons and important student lectures and other writings. These publications, along with the digitization of Very's commonplace books and other documents at Harvard, have made a reevaluation of the existing biographical evidence both necessary and particularly fruitful. While Gittleman's book has many strengths, including the invaluable collection and close examination of then unexplored sources, it also suffers from significant shortcomings. Seized by the theory that Very, in imitation of Hamlet, was intent on saving his mother from her reported atheism, Gittleman too often contorts the patchy evidence of Very's intentions to fit what is otherwise little more than a surmise. This distortion includes the depiction of Lydia Very, Jones's mother, as an angry, embittered widow intent on imposing her radical ideas on her children—a reductive, unsympathetic portrait so shadowed by the image of the stereotypical Salem "witch" as to suggest a lapse into prejudice. Other moments of overreach, such as the entirely fabricated scene in which Very was supposedly abducted from his home and taken to McLean Hospital, tend to overdramatize and underanalyze the sparse documentary trail that survives. New discoveries of essential personal records, including the official marriage record of Very's parents (long considered nonexistent) and the full probate documents from his father's estate, have helped clarify many of these crucial questions and allow us to reconsider Very's biography from a wider perspective.

God's Scrivener attempts to examine the entirety of Very's life, not just what Gittleman called "the effective years," in the hope of providing a more complete, carefully grounded biography true to the information now available. At the same time, it avoids the temptation to fill the gaps in that record through speculation not otherwise noted as such. One of the challenges of writing about Jones Very, whose life was both infamous and obscure, is to recognize the limits of what we can know and to respect those limits as constitutive of the person now available to us. The documentary record for Very's life is remarkably sparse. According to William Bartlett, well-meaning family retainers burned the vast majority of the Very family's papers in 1901, just after the death of Lydia L. A., Jones's last surviving sibling. Thus what motivated Very to claim his own status as "the second coming" remains, in its deepest sense, a mystery. Modern, clinical explanations offer little in the way of genuine understanding of character; too often they simply translate basic description into a specialized vocabulary. But a careful consideration of the facts as they now exist can take us closer to a clearer, more reliable account of the strange events of 1838–39 as well as their possible causes and effects. At the same time, a deep reading of the full range of Very's poetry, notebooks, and other personal writings allows us to see him less as a curiosity and more as a significant figure in the literary and intellectual history of the American nineteenth century. As extreme or simply peculiar as he could be at times, Very was neither an unhinged zealot nor a mindless mystic; he was, in fact, a highly developed intellectual who engaged intensely with the literary and religious culture of his era. The story of individualism, the history of messianic religious thinking, and the development of a distinctive American poetic tradition all depend upon the contribution of his unusual life and remarkable work.

PROLOGUE

1823

The boy was slight. It was May in Helsingør. The sea lavender, rust blue and purple, bloomed beside the Øresund.

It was the time of the storks, their spindle legs dangling as they swam beneath the clouds. Soldiers in blue and scarlet uniforms paced the castle works; the plumes atop their bearskins danced in the breeze.

A slender, three-masted barque—the *Aurelia*, Jones Very master—lay at anchor off the point of Kronborg Slot. It had sailed from Boston in January, carrying raisins and coffee, lead and candy, hops, rice, and almonds. Since 1582, ships passing this pinch in the Øresund had been required to pay a toll to the Danish crown. The registers record 776 ½ Daler, 18 Skilling charged to "Jones Very from Boston, Amr." (see fig. 1).[1] Or Salem, to be more precise: from a line of shipmen and sailors. Bridget Very, their ancestor, had immigrated from Salisbury in the 1630s and settled on a farm near Cedar Pond in what is now Peabody, Massachusetts. As Salem became a busy port in the eighteenth century, farmers turned sailors, and the Verys took to the tight streets of the growing town.

At thirty-three, Captain Very was a Freemason and master mariner who had commanded the trading brig *Concord* for three years before taking over the larger *Aurelia*. He had served as a privateer on the *Montgomery* during the War of 1812, taking prizes and fighting in deadly engagements against the British. In May of 1813, the *Montgomery* was taken by HMS *Nymphe* as it returned from the coast of Ireland, its crew imprisoned on Melville Island in Halifax. Only a few months before, in the intense aftermath of his bloodiest battle, Very had married his cousin Lydia Very (fig. 2). Their first son, also named Jones, was born the following August, while his father was still in prison.[2] Nine years later, both Joneses, father and son, looked out from the deck of their ship onto the legendary castle that was the setting for Shakespeare's *Hamlet*.

We have no way of knowing what the younger Jones Very looked like at this age. The one surviving portrait of his father (fig. 3), made before 1820 by a Parisian artist, reveals a pleasing face: long nose, steady jaw, small confident mouth. The almost tousled, wavy hair may have been enhanced by the clever portraitist; perhaps overall the sketch is handsomer than the reality. There seems little doubt, however, that the master of the *Aurelia* was a dashing figure, bold, brave, a fair specimen of the sort of New England trader who sailed the globe in the eighteenth and early nineteenth centuries. As a young man he had served on his own father's ships before working his way up from seaman to mate to master, sailing to ports as distant as Stockholm and Buenos Aires. When he returned to Salem after a voyage in 1822 and saw his skinny, shy, nine-year-old son with little experience of work or men, he knew it was time: the next route, to Russia, Kronstadt, the island port near St. Petersburg. The boy was slight. He needed stiffening.

If Jones Very (the younger) wrote anything about the legendary Russian port near St. Petersburg, with its isled fortresses and white cathedral spire, it hasn't survived. But he did speak of his early voyage to Kronborg castle and "Elsineur," as Ralph Waldo Emerson later recorded.[3] The visit left a profound though incompletely expressed impression on the boy who was to become the "mystic" poet of Transcendentalism. Fourteen years later, at the height of his messianic fever, he spent much of his time thinking not about Jesus but about Shakespeare. How could such a "phenomenon" exist without a true consciousness of Christ?[4] Like his romantic predecessor John Keats, Very understood Shakespeare as an almost impersonal force, "possessed by that which is before it," moved by the "Divine Will . . . as it does the material world."[5] And Hamlet, "the son of a dear father murdered," was not just a great character but the sensibility of the playwright himself: "We feel," Very wrote, "that Hamlet is rather such a son as Shakespeare would have made," not a weak or diseased mind but a young man prey to "that wild tumultuous sea of thoughts" at the "idea of death and the presence of things invisible" when they "stood sensible to sight and touch before him."[6]

Eighteen months after the two Joneses walked through the *hovedportal* into the courtyard of "Hamlet's Castle," Captain Very was dead. The tuberculosis contracted in the damp wards of Melville Island had never fully receded, and during his final voyages to New Orleans and the Continent his strength had begun to fail.[7] Young Jones, then eleven, could only watch as his thirty-four-year-old father aged horribly in just a few months.

There is no record of the fear and grief that must have gripped Lydia Very and her other children when her husband, relieved of his command and confined to bed, died three days before Christmas in 1824. Pain and loss had stalked her. She now had four children: two girls, Frances and Lydia Louisa Anna (Lydia L. A.); and two boys, Jones and Washington. A third son, Horace, had died within a year of his birth in 1820. A fourth, Franklin, was born blind and died of rheumatic fever the year before his brother Jones went to sea. Six months before her husband died, her own father, Samuel Very, was put to earth. The "idea of death and the presence of things invisible" must have stood starkly before the young Jones, back from the hardening the sea could provide but now the oldest male in a shattered, fragile household. Whether or not he had read or seen a performance of *Hamlet* at this age, his later conviction that the question of Being "is written over every scene" must have rooted here, sprung from the same dark bulb as the mysticism and "madness" that came to define him.

I

"There is something very strange in it all"

✷ 1 ✷

Cousins

In the Old South Cemetery in Peabody, Massachusetts, a tapered column of gray granite rises from a stepped plinth. Only a few feet from busy Boston Street, it stands just three miles from the glacial rock formation known as Ship Rock and from Cedar Pond, where Bridget Very, her two sons, Samuel and Thomas, and her daughter, Mary, started a farm in the 1630s. Less than a mile in the opposite direction Boston Street meets Essex at a wide and irregularly shaped intersection once known as Buffum's Corner. Formerly the entrance to Salem and the passage to common pasture, this crossroads became the origin point of the Salem Turnpike in 1803. In 1789 when he paid a celebrated visit to the region, George Washington paraded past in a ragged line of local dignitaries and militiamen.[1] The increasing traffic made it a good place for a mercantile store of the sort Lydia Very's father, Samuel, set up when he retired from the sea. The shop sold household goods such as molasses, cordials, cider, vinegar, and salt as well as scales, empty casks, brooms, and scythe handles.[2] On the narrow loop of May Street, just steps behind the shop and house, lived Samuel's brother Isaac, a master mariner and minor official at the Salem customhouse.

It was a close-knit world, an almost claustrophobic geography. The granite stone marks the grave of Jones Very, his father, mother, and five siblings. He was born at Buffum's Corner, probably in his grandfather Isaac's house, on August 28, 1813.[3] He lived most of his life—except for the two voyages with his father and his four years at Harvard—inside these few square miles at the edges of Salem and South Danvers. Gallows Hill is close by, and closer still Proctor's Ledge, the more likely site of the hanging of those convicted of witchcraft in 1692. From its brushy brink beside the North River (since diverted and buried at this spot), St. James Catholic Church is easily visible a few hundred yards away, on the slight ridge that parallels Bridge Street and overlooks what remains of the tidal inlet. At 154 Federal Street (fig. 4), now the church's chapel and parish office, stood the house where Very spent most of his life. Lydia moved her family here in the summer of 1833, after six years of raising her children in a small, run-down dwelling at what is now 13 River Street, a few blocks away. And at Federal Street she remained with all of her surviving children until her death in 1867; the last surviving sisters, Frances and Lydia L. A., continued to occupy the address until 1895 and 1901, respectively.

Large households and limited geographies were not unusual in early America. The older Very brothers went through six wives between them (four for Isaac, two for Samuel) and fathered twenty-one children in all. The numbers speak to the dangers of childbirth as well as to crowded living conditions, particularly when older children started their own families and grandchildren increased the count. (The 1810 census lists eleven total inhabitants in Samuel's house, eight in Isaac's.) We can imagine crowded beds and competition for space, a seemingly constant flow of brothers and cousins setting out for and returning home from voyages. Among the tussle and flow of everyday life there would have been quarrels, changing friendships, alliances for and against. And love affairs: innocent crushes perhaps of young girls on handsome older cousins. In most cases they amounted to little more than flirting, but once in a while a childhood friendship bloomed into something more. The marriage of first cousins was not uncommon under such conditions, common enough, that is, to cause no scandal.

And yet there was something scandalous or at least unusual about the union formed between Lydia Very and her cousin Jones some time before 1813. In December 1824, the day after her husband's funeral, Lydia sat tensely in the family parlor as her uncle and father-in-law, Isaac, demanded his son's property, specifically "a quadrant and sextant and spy glass" as well as $1,250 in gold that had been in a canvas bag in his writing desk when he died. Jones's will had provided for a small income of yearly interest on $1,500 for Lydia and $1,000 principal each for the four children, but she refused to hand over the personal property and denied that she had the gold. With her children around her and in what must have been a tremulous but defiant voice, she told Isaac that she was Jones's "wife and these were his children" and they "had the best right" to the property. But the old sailor was no pushover. He had one powerful card, and he played it: in front of her children he told her plainly that she had no proof she had ever been married. When she shot back that there was "a certificate" in her room, Isaac replied—with what measure of malice and naked calculation it's difficult to imagine—that she "should not find it there."[4] A quick search proved him correct, and yet this subterfuge and threat failed to produce Captain Very's effects or his gold. Instead, there was defiance.

Lydia, though a loving and solicitous mother, had a steely will of her own and would not be cowed: the stand-off continued for more than a year, until the legal estate of her husband sued Lydia Very in Essex County Probate Court.

The transcript of these proceedings reveals much about the family life of the Verys at the same time that it raises important questions about the younger Jones's adolescent psychology. The trial makes clear, for instance, just how strong and resourceful a woman Lydia Very really was, how quick and precise in her answers, every bit the match of her bullying uncle. Though questioned closely, she stood her ground so effectively that the court found her story convincing and ruled in her favor. We can also sense the depth of the conflict, the contest of wills with Isaac. If her husband's death was the flash point, how long had this feud been gathering heat? There are suggestions that Isaac's fourth wife had stirred up trouble with her daughter-in-law. If Lydia and her children were living in Isaac's house at this time, it wouldn't be surprising for small disagreements to have grown into larger battles, particularly when someone as blunt and forceful as Lydia was involved. In her testimony, she blamed the missing gold on Isaac's wife (did she suspect her of taking the certificate as well?), implying perhaps a history of snooping and other violations of privacy.

In fact the court case was only the last in a series of maneuvers that suggest a concerted attempt on Isaac's part to alter his son's wishes. Though the probate judge, Daniel Appleton White, approved Jones Very Sr.'s will just a few months after his death, Lydia challenged the decision, citing the lack of signatures, both her husband's and those of any witnesses, on a codicil written on a second page just a few days before he died. This added "P.S." appointed Isaac as executor of the will and listed a number of outstanding loans held by Jones on relatives and friends. A look at the original document confirms Lydia's suspicions: though the handwriting on the first page is clearly that of a shaky but lucid Captain Very, the almost illegible scrawl on the second page suggests a hand barely able to hold a pen.[5] If, as it appears, the second page was added when Lydia was absent, it's hardly surprising that she would object to its contents. Ultimately, she was able to force Isaac to withdraw from his appointment as executor, convincing the court that a more neutral representative was necessary to manage her husband's estate.

Though her victory in court may have provided some official sanction for Lydia's questioned marriage, the proceedings shed little light on what made it contestable in the first place. Previous biographers have worked from the assumption that Lydia and Jones were never officially married, seeing the apparent lack of an official Salem record as evidence of her radical opposition to traditional marriage. But the couple were in fact legally married in Providence, Rhode Island, on February 21, 1813. The union was announced in the *Salem Gazette* on March 5, 1813, making clear that there was nothing secretive or illegitimate about it in civic terms.[6] Even so, the probate case—particularly the struggle over the "certificate"—does suggest a whiff of disapproval, at least in the noses of some family members. Did the two cousins, who had grown up next door to one another, steal away to legitimize their relationship, perhaps in response to an unexpected pregnancy? Given that young Jones's birth took place at the end of August, six months after the marriage date, this scenario seems likely. Despite the fact that premarital sex was common in the late eighteenth and early nineteenth centuries, family criticism of such an affair could account for Isaac's behavior after his son's death.[7] Of the very few biographical details on record about Jones Very's paternal grandfather, a brief note in a family genealogy explains that, as a young man of ten, Isaac had experienced a "saving conversion" in response to "deep religious impressions" produced by the great earthquake of 1755.[8] Like his brother Samuel, he had been a member of the conservative Salem Tabernacle until 1792 (when he was excommunicated for what appears to be lax attendance) and may well have disapproved of Lydia's independent spirit and freethinking.[9] His niece, by contrast, appears to have been anything other than a meekly obedient child and daughter, and there is evidence to indicate that her uncle's church did in fact stigmatize behavior such as hers as early as 1751. As one historian records, the comparatively liberal Reverend William Bentley of Salem's East Church was sometimes called upon to perform baptisms for children "born or conceived" out of wedlock because local evangelicals "were not so forgiving [of such transgressions]. The Tabernacle required . . . that the applying parents confess to the congregation their 'breach of the seventh commandment' before being admitted to Communion and putting up the children for baptism."[10] It's possible of course that Isaac's maneuvers were motivated by little more than greed, but he did participate in a milieu that was determined to single out those who had failed to follow increasingly strict moral conventions. Whatever his ultimate motive, Isaac Very seems to have gambled on the possibility that, certificate or no, his son's marriage was irregular enough to be attacked as illegal or illegitimate.

Lydia's victory, satisfying though it may have been, failed to provide much security for her as a young widow: despite being the sole adult in her small family, she had little legal standing or parental authority. A few months after successfully petitioning the court to remove Isaac as executor, she agreed to accept Benjamin Cheever, a friend of the family and one of her husband's debtors, as guardian of the children and administrator of the estate. When it came to matters of money, including regular household expenses, Cheever served as the de facto head of the Very household for several years. Lydia was neither the legal guardian of her own children nor their chief provider; virtually all of the money in the estate was owned by the children. Probate records indicate that even the smallest decisions about her children's welfare had to be approved by Cheever and Judge White's Probate Court if they involved the estate's funds in any way. The suggestion hinted at by previous biographers that Lydia had hidden the disputed gold and used it to purchase the two houses the family later occupied is therefore incorrect. Both the River Street house and the Federal Street property were purchased by the estate in the names of the children, using roughly equal sums from the accounts of each.[11] Other than a few shares of railroad stock that rarely paid enough dividends to support her modest needs, Lydia Very owned little if any property during her lifetime.[12]

Such details are significant precisely because they give us a much more accurate picture of the position and psychology of the key figure in Jones Very's life. Any attempt to understand Lydia Very, whose presumed ideas and personality have been the linchpin of influential accounts of Very's life, must begin here: not with her purported atheism or her "tiger"-like defense of her son but with her clear lack of power and agency in the face of tragedy and family hostility. Years after her death neighbors remembered Lydia's "almost desperate" concern for her children and her equally intense devotion to plants and animals.[13] They explained that she "tenderly cared for wounded birds, and . . . offered a home to all the stray cats and forsaken kittens in her neighborhood."[14] In her memoir about the Federal Street house and garden, her youngest daughter Lydia L. A. Very affirms this connection between pain and caregiving: "The mother was passionately fond of flowers," she tell us. "They were her solace and delight in her cares and sorrows. When about her work she still had time to go into the garden and pluck a poppy flower, to turn the petals back, tie them with a bit of grass, leaving the round, green seed vessel to make a dolls' head while the petals formed the dress, for the little invalid who reclined on her elbows and knees on the carpet (for two years) till they were calloused."[15] What was important, in other words, was the maternal intent to lessen suffering, whether a child's, an animal's, or Lydia's own. Her life had been difficult. She had accumulated too many losses to bear them with ease or quiet, and now, though still a mother, she could neither provide for her children nor make important decisions about their welfare without court approval. Whatever intensity or defensiveness she might have shown during the events of her son's young life, whatever desperate care she lavished on her family and neighborhood, we can sense the emotional origin in the fierce response to her husband's death, her uncle's attack, and her tenuous status as a largely disenfranchised widow.

And what was the effect of all this on the young Jones Very? He was present in the room when his grandfather demanded his father's missing gold, accusing Lydia of a false marriage. He watched as his mother faced down the old, imposing captain, absorbing and possibly internalizing her scathing attacks on parts of his father's family. We can imagine a sensitive child overhearing such disagreements for much of his boyhood and knowing exactly what some in the extended family thought of his mother. It's also clear that throughout his life he loved the passionate, combative Lydia with at least some measure of the intense devotion she gave to her children. And yet, when he faced the great crisis of faith in his life, Jones Very found the solution to his inner conflict in a suppression of *will*. There was no more willful or powerfully determined presence in young Jones's life than his mother. There was no greater example of the power of the individual will to stand up to strife or overcome resistance. (There was likewise no more striking illustration of the cost of such defiance.) Did he, as some biographers have conjectured, object in some respect to Lydia's defiant personality and possible freethinking? Was he ashamed of her resistance to common pieties or practices? Did he know—and perhaps blame her for it—that his own conception had been premature or that some in the family may have considered his parents' marriage questionable? Or were his feelings about his mother a complicated mixture of pride and shame, an awareness of what she had suffered and borne for her children coupled with a need to push away, to find a path unmarked by her intense presence?

As the small, fragile family moved away from Buffum's Corner into the nearby neighborhood along the North River (fig. 5), how did the thirteen-year-old Jones Very reckon with the fact that his "difficult" mother was on her own with four children to care for? His father was gone. Like Hamlet, Very faced the "idea of death and the presence of things invisible." How long before he too confronted the mystery and began to "build deep down on the clear groundwork of being"?[16]

✸ 2 ✸

Federal Street

The scenery of Denmark and Russia, New Orleans and Portugal, makes few appearances in Jones Very's writings. Two poems, "The Moon Was Shining on the Deck" from 1836 and "The Barque *Aurelia* of Boston" from 1861, offer muted suggestions of the ship boy's experiences in the Baltic and among the tropical exotica of the lower Mississippi delta. The earlier student poem, untitled and possibly unfinished, emphasizes the emotional cost of leaving home for the first time. The speaker is a boy who takes comfort in hearing an older sailor's account of his own first voyage. The two—teller and listener, old and young, father and son?—blend together through the rhyming of experience: "and I was young my boy as thou / And all around seemed strange and new" (*CP* 50). The final lines register both the boy's pain at leaving home and the man's accumulated experience of loneliness: "I looked behind—my home had fled / And seemed afar like distant cloud / My mother all I loved seemed dead / I wept and sobbed aloud" (*CP* 50).

"The Barque *Aurelia* of Boston," by contrast, is a mature recollection of Very's trip to New Orleans in 1823–24. Addressed to William Hooper, another captain's son temporarily stranded in the busy port, it commemorates their friendship and "the winter time spent" exploring the city (*CP* 345). Though incorporated into the United States in 1803 via the Louisiana Purchase, New Orleans in the 1820s retained its Spanish and French colonial flavors and offered sights and experiences stranger and more various than the northern cities Very had visited. When not in school, the boys sat by the river and watched merchant ships sail up from the Gulf of Mexico and flatboats float livestock, flour, and other commodities down from the upper South and Northwest Territory. Behind them, in the original crescent of the city, lay the iron-fenced parade ground of the Place d'Armes, with its cross-shaped paths and flanking rows of large red maple trees. The three towers of St. Louis Cathedral, topped with bell-shaped tips, rose up between the almost identical Hotel de Ville (Cabildo) and Presbytère. In the early 1820s, slave pens were still common in the oldest part of the city, and the poem records an encounter with "Slaves, and Indians . . . ne'er seen before" (*CP* 345). But rather than dwell on the details of the city or the strange sights taken in by a boy from Salem, Very predominantly celebrates an old friendship and the memory of lost fathers. The poem's nostalgia is neither curious nor deeply informative about faraway places. In fact, as a poet Very himself seems little interested or able to conjure evocative details of his early years at sea.

What effect did these voyages have on the boy who lived the remainder of his adult life almost entirely within the narrow ways and surrounding fields of Salem? Adventure and travel to strange places were associated with his father, and the memory of Captain Very's final years must have been both cherished and painful, something to be held inside but rarely consulted. There is little doubt that Very retained proud memories of his father: he recalled him outrunning pirates off the coast of Florida during their voyage to New Orleans and later recorded an incident that occurred in 1818, when Captain Very transported 117 immigrants from Amsterdam to Philadelphia on the *Concord*. Frederick Schwickard, one of the passengers, published a tribute to the captain in the *American Daily Advertiser*, noting his attention to "the accommodation and comfort" of his passengers, in contrast to the typical "barbarous treatment" of immigrants by many captains.[1] (In the same article, Very explained that his father was responsible for bringing the first Royal Muscadine and White Hamburg grapevines into the country, these becoming the "parent vines" of these two varieties in the United States.) But the final voyage had killed the elder Jones, and for his son to have witnessed that loss at a young age, followed by family strife and Lydia's proud withdrawal, may have left him deeply averse to the world of maritime Salem and Buffum's Corner. His mother was certainly strong-willed, perhaps even unpredictable, but she offered—and needed—protection from the uncaring reach of Isaac Very and his wife.

The little family of five at first found some refuge in a small house on River Street, a huddled row of small structures that angled back to the edge of the North River. It was less than a mile from Samuel Very's house but closer to Jones's school and afforded breathing room unavailable in the contentious spaces of May Street. The property was purchased in the names of the four children for $925 from Stephen Fogg, an acquaintance of Jones Very Sr. (His name appears in a court-ordered inventory of the estate, having recently paid back $1,326.33 that he borrowed some time before Captain Very's death.)[2] Lydia and her four children lived in the house for six years, but there is little direct information about daily life there. Given the close proximity to their subsequent home on Federal Street, we can imagine that these childhood days of young Jones passed much like those described in Lydia L. A.'s memoir, *An Old-Fashioned Garden.* (As the youngest, Lydia L. A. was four years old when the family moved to River Street, and ten when they left for the larger property nearby.) The two addresses are no more than half a mile apart, and both are defined by their proximity to the river. Though Federal Street clearly offered improvements over the River Street house, which at the time of its sale was described as an ill-kept structure unsuitable for children, the neighborhood was substantially the same.[3] For children especially, daily activities took their shape and circumstance from the sparkling, lakelike arm of water that stretched enticingly close to the end of their street.

Now little more than a cement-lined drainage, the North River at the foot of River Street was once a wide inlet, the inner reach of estuarial waters from Salem Sound. Though even then partially polluted by whale oil factories and shops associated with the leather trade, it remained during Very's childhood a clear saltwater inlet with a clean sandy bottom that was sprinkled with cockles and other shells left by the tide. The larger properties along the shore kept small bathing houses at the bases of their gardens; from a small, wharf-like wall children could catch tomcod and other fish, float homemade boats, or swim in the shallow, salty water. In winter they skated on the frozen surface or sailed ice cakes out on the receding tide. The hill opposite the river was high enough for a thrilling sled ride back down toward the icy inlet. In her memoir Lydia L. A. remembers the neighborhood children calling this open land "Paradise," a wooded space where in the warmer months they collected nuts or went "A-Maying."[4]

Given her devotion to gardening, we can imagine Lydia Very maintaining a small plot at the River Street house and filling the cramped rooms with pots and seedlings. But not until the family moved in 1833, when Very was twenty and about to begin his first year at Harvard, was she able to exercise the full range of her horticultural talents. When the estate purchased the property for $1,500, this "old-fashioned" house at 154 Federal Street was not in the best of shape.[5] Moved from a nearby lot some forty years before, it had been in the possession most recently of a tanner who left the remnants of his trade both in and out of the house, including leather shavings piled up against the base for insulation.[6] But, despite the dirt and squalor, Lydia saw its potential. The unremarkable gambrel house with its central chimney and Beverly jog stood, like most houses in Salem, only steps from the dusty brick street, but the lot behind extended all the way down to the banks of the river, with roughly fifty yards of overgrown garden ready for working. The grassy slope that terraced down to the water was framed by ancient locust trees, several young apple varieties had taken root, and there was room for many more. If ever a place could seem ideal for Lydia Very and her children, it was this. The family set to work immediately, clearing away the tanner's leavings, digging new flower beds and paths, and gradually transforming the overgrown lot into an extensive private retreat.

Her daughter's memoir makes clear that in many respects Lydia *was* her garden, and for the younger children in particular its shady slope became the shelter where they played and worked and imbibed a dreamy self-sufficiency. More trees were planted: horse chestnuts at first, followed in later days and years by ashes, buckthorns, maples, quinces, plums, peaches, and cherries. Two square plots were laid out just behind the house and lined with boxwood. Here Lydia seeded her favorite flowers or transferred potted plants kept inside over the winter. On the woodsy terraces her children did chores—one of Jones's tasks when he was home from college involved tarring the trunks of the young apple trees to ward off cankerworms—or sketched and read in their individual bowers, little nooks in the bushes and branches with a bench and plenty of shade. Jones was the first to erect his "summer house," later christened "Inspiration Point" by his friends. Less interested than his mother or siblings in planting and weed-pulling, he enjoyed the quiet greenness and the chance to meditate and later work on poems. In the early verse "Nature" (1835), the speaker extols solitude and the soul-sustaining power of a "prospect wide" such as his bower could afford:

> Oh! grant me an hour, an hour like this,
> To drink from far purer streams of bliss,
> Than flow near the dusty paths of life,
> Uptost by madd'ning passion and strife;
> For my mind comes back with lighter spring,
> Than the bird from her weary wand'ring;
> With calm more deep than the still bright sea,
> Where the white sail sleeps so peacefully; (*CP* 28)

Though the Very family continued to live in the Federal Street house for over seventy years, accounts of the property are soaked from the beginning in nostalgia and loss. This wistful tone may be attributable to typical feelings of retrospection or the awareness that the environment along the river was rapidly changing. But there is a sense that family losses and Lydia's embattled personality may have intensified the children's natural awareness of the fleeting quality of cherished things. Life was obviously fragile, and only now, after years of increasing uncertainty, did they find some measure of solace in the old but comfortable house with the beautiful garden—all presided over by a fierce mother determined to protect not only her own children but all living things.

An important, youthful poem, written during Very's first years at Harvard, captures the combination of happiness and worry that haunts both his early poems and his sister's memories. It describes an incident from the life of his brother Franklin, who was born blind and died in 1822 at the age of four. This same anecdote is repeated in Lydia L. A.'s *An Old-Fashioned Garden*, suggesting that the memory had become a kind of family legend, repeated by their mother and by others with ritual regularity. Lydia L. A. was too young to have known Franklin, but Jones was eight when his younger brother died, and given the closeness of this small, beset family, he is likely to have registered not only Franklin's heartrending disability but his mother's helplessness at the loss of her most threatened child.

Untitled in its original publication in 1834, the poem begins with a haunting and direct memory of Franklin himself:

> I saw a child, whose eyes had never drunk
> The cheerful light of heaven; yet they were fair
> And beautiful, and oft those mild blue orbs
> Would turn, and seem to seek the forms of those
> He lov'd. (*CP* 17)

"I saw": this quick emphasis on the speaker's ability to see his brother's blindness is powerful and poignant, guilty and gently puzzled. Why can he see, and Franklin not? The weight falls on the younger brother's eyes, both blindly looking and looked at by the speaker, who tries to understand what "sight" might mean in the absence of light. The older eyes watch, charged perhaps with protecting the boy, who runs instinctively to his mother when unsure or scared:

> If stranger's voice,
> Or stranger's step obtruded on his ear,—
> Shrieking, he to his mother closer clung,
> And with his fair yet sightless eyes uprais'd
> Would seem from her, whom best he knew, to ask
> Protection. (*CP* 17)

The scene is important for thinking about Jones Very's early development. Franklin died before Jones's first voyage with his father, possibly while the captain was still away at sea. (It's worth asking whether the impact of this harrowing experience had something to do with his father's decision to take Jones on his next voyage.) During this time Lydia was largely alone, as she often was in childbirth, and in the care of her children; the apparent conflict within the Buffum's Corner households as well as her strong-willed independence made it unlikely that she had very many family allies. In the years after her husband's death, she became even more the locus of protection and object of concern for her intelligent and observant son: if she was the center of the household, to whom all the children clung in times of stress, could she really prevent catastrophe? Could she save them? The poem registers the intimacy of Lydia and her children but indirectly questions her ability to keep the strange and threatening world at bay.

The blind boy was "bless'd," the poem assures us, in spite of his inability to see the wonders of the world—except, that is, "but once, / For mother's fondest care prevented more." Only once, in other words, "ere he departed to the world, / Where all are bless'd with perfect sight," did his mother's protection fail (*CP* 18). This near contradiction—for it goes without saying that she also failed to keep him alive—introduces the story of Franklin trying to pick a flower but closing his hand instead on a bee and finding pain where he expected pleasure. The speaker then awkwardly moralizes on this image, suggesting that the sting is like the painful attack of "vice" and that this "dire foe" must be crushed "with firm, / Unsparing grasp" in order to achieve freedom (*CP* 19). The analogy suggests that in his Harvard years, as he approached his period of crisis, Very thought of his own spiritual struggle in terms of both his brother's blindness and his mother's weakness. As strong as Lydia was, in other words, as sheltering as the home on River Street or the bowered garden of Federal Street might be, these were tenuous strongholds, willed idylls constructed to keep the threatening world at a distance but built, nevertheless, on the knowledge that suffering and loss were inevitable.

✷ 3 ✷

Eldest Son

Roughly two blocks from River Street stands a clean-lined, rectangular building with a carved stone lintel identifying it as the location of the Hacker School. Often referred to as the West School, it began as a small, wooden structure built in 1785 but was reconstructed in 1820 in the red-brick Federal style of the time. Until 1843, when Jonathan Carlton received permission to build a bridge at this spot—then the end of Dean (now Flint) Street—the North River remained an open, navigable waterway, with only the North Street bridge as a crossing point until you reached Frye's Mills, the current Grove Street. When the seven-year-old Jones took his place with the other boys in the recently finished building, the smell of cut wood and fresh paint mingled with the freshness of the evergreen branches and summer flowers that decorated the new classroom. A row of eight windows looked out in the direction of what would later become the Very garden behind Federal Street. From his desk, Jones could stare off toward the rising land of Gallows Hill, perched greenly above the rippled, sparkling water.[1]

Though his time at the West School was interrupted by the voyages with his father, Very enjoyed academic work and was consistently a strong student. Despite his attraction to roaming the nearby fields and woods, he was remarkably mature and serious for his age, a capable, if reticent, boy who took pride in his work and was often at or near the top of his class.[2] (A notebook survives that shows his diligent practice in arithmetic, with inverse and compound proportions written out in an elegant cursive hand. The mathematical word problems reveal the school's proximity to the sea: one asks the student to calculate how long bread will last for a ship's company of fifteen, who then rescues a "crew of five persons in distress.")[3]

This drive for academic success may have intensified in the years immediately following his father's death. In 1826, coincidentally on his thirteenth birthday, the School Committee of the Town of Salem presented

Jones with a copy of *Biographia Americana; or a Historical and Critical Account of the Lives, Actions, and Writings of the Most Distinguished Persons in North America* for "diligence and proficiency in his studies" and "exemplary conduct and strict attention to the regulations of the School."[4] This was one of several awards he would receive during his academic career, notices of which were unfailingly printed in the local Salem papers. After the revelations about his parents' questionable marriage, the conflict with his grandfather Isaac, and the loss of connection to the maritime world of his father, it may be that a young man, even if already inclined to schoolwork, would find academic challenge both a relief and a reward, a way to push back against emotional turbulence and exercise some control over his life. Success as a scholar suggested a path, dimly perceived at such a young age, away from diminished status and economic dependency. Though clearly not a part of the wealthy upper echelon of Salem society, the larger Very family were still comparatively prosperous ships' masters and merchants; they owned property beyond their primary residences, traded in large consignments of goods, and possessed household items that indicated education and general prosperity. Samuel Very's will, for instance, lists additional real estate (two lots in North Salem and Danvers), a pew in the Tabernacle, and a considerable range of personal property, including books, crockery, pewter, silverware, a mahogany desk, and a brass fire set.[5] For his daughter to lose her husband and fall into the uncertain care of the probate courts after Samuel's own death was clearly a diminishment of status for her and her children. Even as a young man, Jones Very would have sensed this in the way all children instinctively grasp such changes in their lives. (A later poem records the common refrain in a family forced to pinch pennies: "When thoughtlessly two lamps were burned, / 'Twas in our poverty, / 'We need but one,' we oft were told, / 'We have no ships at sea'" [*CP* 499]). Though the sea had, in a sense, taken his father and the economic stability he provided, the classroom may have offered a way back to some form of respectability.

A useful comparison can be made here to the early life of Nathaniel Hawthorne, another Salem son of a sea captain (just nine years older than Very) who lost his father at a young age. The Hathornes, as they were known until the author changed the spelling, found themselves, after the death of Nathaniel Hathorne Sr., dependent upon their mother's family, the Mannings. Young Nathaniel went from being the son of a captain to one of many dependents in a crowded household of aunts and uncles. Fatherlessness and economic uncertainty were not unusual in a maritime town (the 1785 census records 419 widows in a population of just over 6,000), but the effects of such losses are difficult to gauge.[6] Though never the devoted scholar that Very became as a young man, Hawthorne did show signs of a similar reaction to life lived on the edges of Salem's opulent but fading prosperity. Hawthorne's biographers have long speculated about the mysterious leg injury suffered when he was nine. The wound (from a ball that hit near his foot) resisted medical treatment, and the sensitive, shy, aesthetically particular young man was lame for almost three years. What brought about his eventual recovery remains a mystery, but many have ventured that a loss of psychological stability caused by the death of his father—as well as the weakened, if not imperiled, condition of his mother—may have led to a half-conscious bid for attention and control that he finally outgrew. Such adolescent dramas are not unusual, of course, and Very's intense application to his studies may have been little more than ambition tied to ability. But there remains an air of masculine anxiety in both biographies that suggests a kindred reaction to Salem's potent social stare.

For so proud and successful a pupil, it must have been disappointing, then, when Very was told he would have to leave school and find work. He was only fourteen, but the family needed the money, and as the oldest he had a responsibility to do what he could to help his mother. In a children's story titled "The Year and the Four Seasons," Lydia L. A. Very may have recalled this moment when her older brother was forced to take his first step into the adult world. The book, for young readers, is built on the personification of the year as a mother who watches over her children, the seasons:

> The mother year stopped working (for she was mending the children's clothes,) called the oldest boy to her side and said, "Spring, my dear child, tomorrow you must go to work to help support your mother. Farmer Scantem needs a boy, and I have promised him you shall come. You are not very strong and I hate to have you go, but it must be so." And the poor mother year had as much as she could do to keep back her sobs.
>
> Spring laid his head caressingly on her lap. "Dear mother, don't grieve, it is time I did something to help you."
>
> So, next morning he set off to his new place.[7]

The "place" was a local auction house, perhaps one like J. A. Turrell's, which sold "glass ware, decanters, lamps, salts, pungents, and Palla pans" and advertised in 1825 for "[a] smart active Lad that writes a fair hand, and is acquainted with Arithmetic."[8] As an "errand and store boy" Very did help provide for his mother and younger siblings, but it seems clear from most accounts of these years that he had no intention of giving up his education. He studied avidly on his own and after three years found a local tutor, J. Fox Worcester, who specialized in preparing young men for Harvard, to train him for a job as a teacher.[9] While employed at the auction house, Very had often admired and read from the books that came in from local estate sales, and on one occasion persuaded the shop owner to let him buy a rare edition of Shakespeare at a steep discount. After what must have been a deep dive into the plays that would later dominate his literary and spiritual meditations, he traded the valuable books for the complete set of texts required of Harvard freshmen.[10]

Whether Very's path to higher study emerged as a series of fortunate opportunities and generous favors or was carefully plotted by a young man who refused to be sidelined by limited means, we should recognize that he found his way forward through diligence and unshakable dedication. We can already detect hints of a singular focus in the teenager who impressed teachers with his unruffled demeanor. It must have been clear to many that he was not only bright but strikingly self-directed, already capable of the idealistic behavior and self-discipline that would mark his mystic phase. Worcester, who may have helped Very for little or no pay, prepared him for a position as tutor at Henry Kemble Oliver's new Latin school, only a few blocks away on Federal Street. Oliver was just thirteen years Very's senior and at the beginning of an extraordinary career as a teacher, administrator, textile mill executive, and state officeholder. A graduate of Dartmouth who later lived just a few houses down from the Verys, he became mayor of Salem in his later years and was an accomplished and well-regarded musical presence in the city; for twenty years he served as organist and choir director at the North Church, of which Very was later a member, and wrote several popular songs, including the well-known "Federal Street." Very seems to have impressed this formidable and energetic young scholar-musician strongly enough that Oliver took the time to lead him through the Harvard first-year curriculum, making it possible for Very to join the sophomore class in Cambridge in 1833.[11]

Having just turned twenty, he would be notably older than most of his classmates, many of whom had entered at the more typical age of sixteen. He had also found his way to Harvard via a less conventional path. And yet despite the obstacles, he had made it after all, and his maturity had already played to his advantage: his entrance examination was conducted by A. P. Peabody, who later admitted that he "was particularly struck by a certain 'rapt' expression in the young man's face."[12] With money saved from work and support from one of his uncles, the skinny, solemn but determined young Salemite took to his new world and work with avidity and what must have been a heady blend of pride and relief.[13]

✷ 4 ✷
Biography (I)

The story of Very's Harvard years is one of transformation—from shy, serious student to religious purist, "mad" evangelist, and mystic poet. It consists of two primary strands: his development into a religious poet and thinker of idiosyncratic originality; and his spiritual journey from his mother's household on Federal Street to Emerson's parlor in Concord. Though inseparable and mutually reinforcing, these lines of growth offer a provisional map of the complicated and dramatic changes Very experienced from 1833 to 1838. Understanding how he became the striking and peculiar figure now associated with Transcendentalism depends upon a careful account of the sometimes fragmented, sometimes opaque network of evidence that has informed previous readings of his life. But before proceeding with the story of his growth and development over these essential college years, we should take a moment to investigate how other biographers have interpreted the existing evidence, particularly when it comes to the character and beliefs of Lydia Very. If, as I contend, it's impossible to understand Jones Very without a clear sense of who his mother was and what she believed, a deeper look at Lydia's personality and commitments is essential. As part of this digression, it will be necessary at times to look ahead to the dramatic moment in 1838 when Very clashed with the Salem ministers and Lydia Very rose defiantly to her son's defense.

There have been two substantial biographies of Very, each of which constructs a functional narrative of the key years of his development. William Bartlett's 1942 *Jones Very: Emerson's "Brave Saint"* was an important first attempt to offer a fully researched narrative of Very's life. It provided access to primary documents until then unexamined and unpublished, including the transcripts of Lydia Very's probate hearing and a significant cache of Very's religious sonnets not included in previous editions. Bartlett also conducted interviews with older residents of Federal Street who remembered the Verys and provided vivid accounts of Lydia's personality and general eccentricity. For Bartlett, the question of Very's development into the "brave saint" described by Emerson was simplified by the fact that he understood Lydia Very as a conventionally pious, if "fiery," New England woman.[1] He fails to account for—or even mention—the significant description of the events of 1838: the Transcendentalist and activist Elizabeth Peabody's letters to Emerson written just after her attempts to help Very in his struggle with the Salem ministers. It's likely that Bartlett simply never saw this correspondence; though he does cite some of Peabody's letters, he conspicuously omits any mention of her account of the events leading to Very's committal to McLean Hospital. Perhaps less likely but also plausible, Bartlett may have had some reason to discount Peabody's description, given his interviews with surviving neighbors and other members of the community. Whatever the explanation, his reading of Lydia's beliefs, accurate or not, remains important if for no other reason than that it reminds us of the paucity of available evidence and the fragility of narratives built on so few reliable pillars. Bartlett's Very shows a significant and plausible consistency. Subject to few signs of internal struggle, his version of Very's development reveals only a gradual intensification of an inborn spiritual nature: "He conceived of God as an all-enveloping, ever-present Spirit, thoroughly and actively alive, flooding and saturating all nature and all personality, and flowing into the receptive soul with continuous enrichment. He became more and more of a mystic, firm in his resolution to be pure and will-less because he felt that the Spirit communed only with him who was pure of heart and devoid of will."[2]

The absence of a clear psychological account of Very's transformation from conventional to idiosyncratic believer may have prompted Edwin Gittleman to seek out a more dramatic narrative of development. In his painstakingly researched *Jones Very: The Effective Years, 1833–1840* (1967) he constructed a much more thorough etiology for Very's eventual messianism, seizing uncritically on Peabody's report of Lydia Very's supposed atheism (and all it may have entailed for her eldest son) as the driving force behind Very's eventual "madness." Imagining a Hamlet-like conflict in which young Jones is shadowed by the ghost of his father while attempting to "save" his wayward mother, Gittleman mines Very's student commonplace books, poems, and essays for any potential evidence of opposition to his mother's "atheistic materialism" (EG 221, 66–67). The result is a compelling, though selectively schematic and often highly suppositious, reading of sparse or obscure evidence.

Gittleman's account of Very's development during his undergraduate years rests on a few indispensable claims: first, that Lydia Very was, as Elizabeth Peabody claimed in 1838, an avowed and aggressive atheist; second, that Very's commonplace books, poems, and essays show an intensifying criticism of his parents, particularly of his mother's lack of religious belief; and third, that this opposition, catalyzed by the recognition of his own strong sexual desires, drove Very to make a radical choice between his mother's ideas and a complete commitment of self to the Holy Spirit. In looking more closely at each of these arguments, it's essential to recognize how patchy the evidence for this internal struggle really is—and how any reading of Very's motives depends upon the extension of a few suggestive elements. To support Gittleman's reading of Lydia Very's philosophy, for instance, there is only the one surviving source: Elizabeth Peabody, whose two letters to Emerson are dated October 20, 1838, and December 3, 1838. (A third Peabody letter, written over forty years later to William P. Andrews, revisits the subject in much the same terms.) Written during the controversy over Very's attempts to "convert" Salem ministers to his new vision, Peabody's account has a kind of breathless immediacy that lends it credibility while at the same time highlighting her reliance on local gossip. In the first of these two descriptions, written after her visit to Federal Street on September 16, she describes Lydia as "a course materialist [who] pretends to believe [her son] & to think he is not sick &c—which is foolish." A few months later, Peabody describes a second—and, apparently, final—attempt to offer aid to Lydia: "I went to see Mrs. Very on Saturday [December 1]—and I think it will be the last time—though she considers me a friend & asked me to come again—but it is painful to see such a tiger of a woman—She is almost a maniac from the simple vehemence of passion—She has been long at war with the world for Atheism's sake—and now has adapted [*sic*] the other view—identifying her son with the God in whom she at last believes.—There is something very strange in it all" (EP 219). Here the initial understanding of Lydia as antispiritual collides with new, contradictory evidence: she believes her son's claim of spiritual identification with the Holy Spirit. Peabody's account is arresting, and yet the portrait seems partly composed of her earlier assumptions combined with her direct experience of Lydia's emotional defense of one of her children. Peabody's sense that the situation is "very strange" may indicate unplumbed psychological depths or simply an inability to make Lydia's reputation square neatly with her current spiritual fervency.

More than forty years later, in response to editor William P. Andrews's query about Very, Peabody recalled the same incidents in even greater detail, including the visit to the house on Federal Street:

> Hearing this [that the ministers wanted to forcibly commit Very] I walked directly up to his mother's house—She was a person of great

> energy—was said to have more than doubts of another world and of the existence of God—having had a severe experience of life, and being at odds with the existing state of society—a disciple of Fanny Wright—She did not receive me graciously at first, but I persevered till she recognized that I was opposed to all violent methods—and had the greatest reverence for her son. When she told me she was sure he was not insane, but more sane than others, that he was an *angel* whom God had inspired—and a proof that there was a God above us who was Infinite Love—, I cannot remember her exact words but I know that I was so struck with what she said, that it seemed to me that to produce such a result in her mind was reason sufficient for Providence giving her the wondrous sign—. (EP 406–7; original emphasis)

Again, the vividness of Peabody's account, especially after so many years, speaks to its value as a portrait of Lydia. Even so, its claims warrant close examination. This account makes clearer, for instance, that Peabody's understanding of Lydia's philosophy was based on local gossip: Mrs. Very "was said" to have had these thoughts because of her difficult life, and so on. This assumption in turn may color the account of Lydia's defense of her son's sanity, a reaction that Peabody takes to be a proof of Lydia's conversion rather than a reinforcement of earlier held beliefs.[3] The added detail, that Lydia was a "disciple of Fanny Wright," raises even more questions. Wright did cause a stir throughout the 1820s with her attempt to establish a settlement of freed slaves on land she purchased near Memphis, Tennessee. After its collapse, she joined Robert Owen's New Harmony socialist community and began editing its newspaper and lecturing widely as a radical freethinker. Her 1829 lecture in Boston was noticed in the Salem newspapers (according to one, she was "the subject of conversation in almost every circle") and her *Course of Popular Lectures* was published in 1829 and 1836.[4] Essentially an empiricist who believed that knowledge is "an accumulation of facts gleaned by our senses, within the range of material existence," Wright offered a radicalism clearly ahead of its time, even for those inclined to agree with her about social issues such as emancipation.[5] The local guardians of religion considered her both a dangerous atheist and a threat to the idea of domesticity that put women at the spiritual center of their households—but kept them from the lecture circuit. Not only did Wright speak in public to mixed audiences in a style considered inappropriately masculine; she questioned the value of marriage and openly praised sexual experience. As Celia Morris Eckhardt explains in her biography, Wright was "labeled 'The Red Harlot of Infidelity'" because she "attacked the churches, . . . endorsed miscegenation, and most of all, because she shunned the pedestal prescribed for women."[6] Consequently, "to be called a Fanny Wrightist in America in the 1830s was no less threatening than being called a communist in the 1950s."[7]

What did it mean then for Peabody to identify Lydia as a "disciple" of Wright? Was this simply a shorthand for a kind of basic radicalism, the tendency to question the pillars of belief and social conformity, particularly with respect to women? Was it a more specific reference to Wright's empiricism, commonly considered to be an atheistic materialism, her insistence that all knowledge derives from experience? Or was it a partially veiled reference to Lydia's marriage, possibly a subject of local gossip, and her supposed attraction to Wright's opposition to legal marriage and preference for the "open" relationships associated with the Owenites? Peabody's emphasis (in her original letter to Emerson) on the strangeness of the situation in which a supposed atheist has accepted the near divinity of her "angel" son touches the deeper reaches of these questions. If we accept Lydia as a thoroughgoing materialist, her embrace of her son's mission is indeed extraordinary, though it immediately raises the suspicion that her atheism may not have been as firm as reported. If she was willing to believe in her son's messianic role, perhaps her interest in Wright, if it existed, had more to do with critiques of conventional piety and associated religious institutionalism than with philosophical empiricism. Given that her apparent elopement with her cousin preceded even Wright's initial visit to the United States in 1818, Lydia may have found some emotional support in Wright's subsequent critique of conventions as she battled Isaac Very over the estate. As someone who, by all accounts, possessed a vigorous and combative spirit, the "bold blasphemer . . . and voluptuous preacher of licentiousness" from Scotland may have given Lydia the reinforcement she required to counter any snubs or whispers from officious neighbors.[8] Given Peabody's emphasis on this connection to Wright, it even seems plausible to suggest that Lydia's marriage could have been misunderstood as radical or unsanctioned, despite the fact that it had been legally recorded in Rhode Island and announced in a Salem newspaper.

What then can we say with any degree of confidence or certainty about Lydia Very's beliefs? There is little corroborating evidence that clearly supports either Peabody's account or the more conventional picture painted by Bartlett. In two letters written by Mary Peabody, Elizabeth's sister, in the days just before Elizabeth sent her second account of Very's condition to Emerson, we do get an indirect portrait of Lydia that complicates the picture of her opposition to the local ministry. Here she is not described as notably antireligious or atheistic; in fact, Mary reports that Jones is most concerned that a local figure like John Brazer, the minister of the North

Church and one of Very's most vehement critics, could persuade Lydia to allow her son to be arrested or committed. "What right have they to send you away?" Mary records her father asking: "He [Very] said they can do it by making my mother think it best—they are men in authority & she can invest them with an authority that will compel me to go."[9] Would Very have had so intense a worry (Mary reports that "his eyes [were] full of tears & his face & brow flushed") if his mother was solely the "tiger of a woman" Elizabeth depicts as the combatant of Salem orthodoxy?[10] His fear suggests that she might have been more respectful, at the very least, of the local ministry than we would expect from a "follower of Fanny Wright." And yet, the independent streak certainly shines through the indirect reporting of Mary Peabody's letters. For a moment we hear Lydia's voice in one of the few sources that echoes her testimony in her husband's probate case fifteen years before: "the fact is Mrs. Peabody[,] said [Lydia], that my son is better than Mr. Brazer, and he knows it and it makes him *mad*. . . . She [Lydia] declares that he shall not be taken away from her—that he has income enough to maintain him—& so has she—She calls upon no one for assistance & wishes no one's interference."[11] The note of stung pride in stating that her son is better than the local minister says a great deal about Lydia's character—and may account more clearly than other sources for her reputation for spirited independence. (A similar chord is struck in Very's poem "The Widow," a possible portrait of Lydia from 1847, where the figure in question is depicted reading the Bible "For light, and strength . . . what the boasting pride / Of minister-service promised her in vain; / Though late she seeks, she shall not be denied" [*CP* 242]). Whatever the ultimate nature of her religious or other beliefs—and they are likely to have been more complex and mercurial than we can ever know—Lydia was a mother first, protective, proud, wary. Perhaps it was this undeferential attitude, considered less than proper for a woman in her position, that kept fresh the rumors of her "atheism."[12]

In her youngest daughter's writings, Lydia once again emerges as a fairly conventional mother, deeply devoted to her garden, emotional but never extreme. The youngest of the Very children, Lydia Louis Anna worked as a teacher in the Salem Schools for many years and was a successful and widely active poet and prose writer. (She created the first shaped children's book published in the United States, a die-cut version of *Little Red Riding Hood*.) Like her brother's, her poems sometimes reference family members or make use of memories from the many years living on Federal Street. Even more revealing, her book *An Old-Fashioned Garden, and Walks and Musings Therein* (1900) provides limited but penetrating pictures of her mother during the time of Very's early adulthood. Though a nostalgic haze drifts over much of the life described, Lydia L. A. has a sharp eye and a mind firm enough to distinguish fact from false emotion. Too young to have a full awareness of the events of her father's death and the controversy that followed, Lydia L. A. nevertheless heard the stories and saw her mother use her garden as a "solace and delight" for her "cares and sorrows."[13] Though muted, the emotions hinted at suggest powerful forces partially redirected into a maternal care generously dispensed: "Another, and never-to-be-forgotten picture. The mother bending over her pot plants she had cherished all Winter and planting new ones with a never failing pleasure; or sowing seeds, saying she would see with what body they would be clothed. Her passionate love of flowers her children have inherited as a precious legacy and memory."[14]

Those religious or philosophical ideas that can be inferred from *An Old-Fashioned Garden* give no hint of an aggressive atheism. A conventional, if somewhat romantic and nondoctrinal, set of beliefs governs Lydia L. A.'s memories of her mother, from a general sense that heaven exists and the beloved dead wait there for their children to an exaltation of nature as a place of "miracles" that reaffirm the miracles of the Bible.[15] Several of Lydia L. A.'s poems, including "My Mother," "The Empty Nest," and "Her Flowers Bloom On," suggest the same kind of basic faith blended with a sense of the importance of nature as a place of continuance and memory. This nondenominational but less-than-radical set of beliefs is reinforced by indications that Lydia L. A. seems to have had an unremarkable, though perhaps not entirely orthodox, religious upbringing. She recalls carrying her mother's flowers to "meeting" on Sundays, relates an incident that occurred when she was a little girl and an "old deacon" gave her a flower to keep her occupied during a "long-winded sermon," and remembers her mother offering "tender prayer[s]" and singing a "holy psalm" while watching over a sick child.[16]

In *A Strange Recluse*, a novel for young readers that she dedicated to her two brothers, Lydia L. A. gives her main character, the quiet Philip de Mervale, many of her own views about the value of nature, the treatment of animals, and the importance of charity. When he first meets the local minister, de Mervale offers an Emersonian conception of worship that may very well have descended directly from Lydia Very to all of her children:

> "I would have wished," said his visitor, "to have seen you at our little church. It is small, but large enough to hold the Lord of Hosts; and I believe, where a few are gathered together, there is He in the midst of them."

"I believe it," answered Philip, "and some minister wrote recently, 'It is better to worship in a barn, than in a costly church built by lotteries, chances, etc.'"

"When I say I would have liked to see you at our church, I do not mean to imply that we cannot worship elsewhere and anywhere. There may be as true worship in these woods as elsewhere. And who could fail to worship when looking at God's wonderful creations from the first flower of spring 'when is the glorious resurrections time, when all earth's buried beauties have new birth,' to the fall of the ripened leaves, when the trees don their Joseph's coat of many colors? . . . ."

"Yes," responded Philip, "you are right; those who seek the heart of Nature are led to her by Nature's God."[17]

Like Lydia and her mother, de Mervale takes in strays, both animal and human, and chastises friends and locals for their cruelty to animals and attraction to hunting. His suspicion of organized religion and its connections to money and power, as well as his instinctive preference for nature as the site of spiritual experience, aligns comfortably with what we know of the general tenor of belief in the Very household. In her final "day dream" recollections in *An Old-Fashioned Garden,* Lydia L. A. expresses this family feeling in an idealized image that echoes her portrait of de Mervale:

The Muser in the Old-fashioned Garden. The mother bending over her plants, the elder sister beside her. The brothers examining their trees.

The mother talking of things present and things to come, leading the thoughts of her children, from Nature's works to Nature's God.[18]

Though it's certainly possible that the older Lydia L. A. could have glossed over or intentionally hidden her mother's darker thoughts, there is no direct evidence to suggest that Lydia Very imposed a fully materialist critique of religion on her children. That she was an emotional and emotionally dominant figure in her family circle seems true, and it's entirely plausible that her several children would have experienced her intensity in different ways. What seemed peaceful to one child may not have been to another, but the picture of her mother left by her youngest daughter should at least cause us to question the image of the atheistic "tiger" left in 1838 by Elizabeth Peabody.

✱ 5 ✱

Cornelia Africana

Given the complexity and uncertainty of Lydia Very's ideas and beliefs, we should not overlook one final remnant of her life: her needlework depiction of "Cornelia and the Gracchi" preserved in the collection of the Peabody Essex Museum (fig. 6). Dated 1808 and constructed of silk, paint, and metallic thread, it was most likely an assignment or project completed by the fifteen-year-old as part of her education. Other Cornelias made from similar materials survive from this era in New England, all associated with the schoolwork of older girls and all based on the same painting, Angelica Kauffmann's *Cornelia, Mother of the Gracchi* from 1785.

Kauffmann was a Swiss neoclassical painter who found particular success in England painting decorative interiors for houses designed by Robert Adam. She was one of only two women among the founders of the Royal Academy of Arts, and the fact of her success in a male-dominated field may have made her work a popular model for young women to copy. The subject, however, was clearly more significant for eighteenth-century audiences than the artist. Cornelia Africana was one of the children of Scipio Africanus, the Roman general who defeated Hannibal at the battle of Zama in 202 BCE. After her father's death she married and bore several children, though only three survived into adulthood. Her husband, Tiberius Sempronius Gracchus, died when the children were still young, and Cornelia devoted her time, energies, and fortune to their education. The two sons, Tiberius and Gaius, "the Gracchi," served as tribunes, and both died at the hands of political enemies while their mother was still living. Cornelia soon became an exemplar of the devoted wife and mother. According to ancient sources, she refused to remarry after her husband's death and was known to intervene in her sons' political careers when she thought it necessary. Plutarch describes an incident in which she used her influence to prevent Gaius from taking revenge on one of his brother's enemies, noting that the Roman people were so delighted by her generosity of spirit that they erected a bronze statue of Cornelia with the inscription "Cornelia, mother of the Gracchi."[1]

Kauffmann's painting depicts a different but no less legendary moment in the life of Cornelia, one that became a standard subject for painters and sculptors in the eighteenth and nineteenth centuries. In conversation with a Campanian woman who was boasting of her private collection of jewelry, Cornelia was said to have pointed to her surviving children and responded, "*These* are my jewels." Like so many of the legends about Cornelia, scholars are unsure how this story came into existence (and whether or not it's true), but the combination of maternal devotion and family values resonated for those who wished to promote neoclassical models for women in the late eighteenth century. According to this legend, Cornelia was an educated, sophisticated, and powerful woman, but she placed the highest value on her children, embodying republican virtues without sacrificing her aura of personal and intellectual independence.

Given the popularity of the subject for turn-of-the-century girls' school assignments, there is little reason to think that Lydia Very had anything to do with choosing this scene for her needlework. What makes it potentially significant is not what it may have meant to her when she sewed it but the fact of its preservation, presumably both by her and by her children. Of course the artwork may have been little more than a keepsake, a remembrance of childhood or, for her children, a way to recall their mother through something she herself had worked on. Samplers and other elaborate forms of needlework were often mentioned in wills as important legacies to be retained by the family. But its preservation and eventual donation by the family to the Essex Institute suggest that the work could have been associated with Lydia Very in a way that went beyond simple memento. Though she, even as a young woman, may have admired Cornelia's independence and found some inspiration in Cornelia for her own unyielding spirit, we can also see that Lydia's own life came to resemble the legend of the "mother of the Gracchi." Like Cornelia, she lost children; her husband died and left her with a family to raise; she did not remarry; she clearly put her children first and was fiercely protective of them into their adulthood. And through all of this, she remained her own person: unique, unwavering, even, in an idiosyncratic way, exemplary. Did Lydia consider Cornelia a true model, someone she perhaps admired at first but with whom she came, more and more, to identify? Did her children see her proud, emotional commitment to their happiness in this image of the Roman woman who transformed the idea of motherhood into something more powerful, political, more elevated and self-determined? And what effect, if any, might this devotion to a classical image of motherhood have had on her reputation for independence of mind—or on her older son's eventual embrace of an invasive, all-pervading concept of Spirit?

Some clarity of context may be found in an incident that occurred in Salem during Lydia's childhood. In 1800, when she was eight years old, a local scandal developed around the figure of a Salem teacher of young women, Abigail Rogers. A well-educated widow with progressive ideas about education, Mrs. Rogers attracted well-to-do students from both of Salem's entrenched political parties, the Federalists, who were associated with the established merchant class, and the Democratic-Republicans or simply "Republicans," whose Jeffersonian politics allied more with new wealth and the working classes. These groups rarely mingled their social circles, and when one of Abigail Rogers's students, Lydia Nichols (from a Federalist family), began to develop a romantic relationship with the young Joseph Story (a Republican from Marblehead who later became a United States Supreme Court justice), Lydia Nichols's parents objected and sought assistance from the minister of the North Church, Thomas Barnard. In response, Barnard attacked Abigail Rogers in the *Salem Gazette*, accusing her of encouraging the young women of Salem to form coed social groups that were suspected of discussing radical, potentially "Jacobinical" ideas, particularly those of the recently disgraced Mary Wollstonecraft.[2] Wollstonecraft's *Vindication of the Rights of Women* (1792) had a strong circulation in the United States during the 1790s and early 1800s (it was reprinted four times in the two years after its initial appearance), and her opponents among the more staid Federalists in Salem considered the English feminist a brazen advocate for atheism and immorality. Barnard suggested that Rogers had been "unsex'd" (removed, in other words, from the traditional role of woman) and had used her "wicked and seductive arts" to mislead the young women in her charge.[3] With the help of vigorous rebuttals from many of her students and others (including Story himself, whose relationship with Lydia Nichols foundered as a result), Rogers overcame in a few years what was clearly a traumatic set of events and, for a time, a public stain on her reputation.

Though short-lived, the incident casts a helpful light on the intellectual and social landscape of Lydia Very's youth. It's difficult to determine which schools Lydia attended, but we can draw a few conclusions about her education from her needlework.[4] First, the advanced nature of the Cornelia piece indicates that Lydia likely attended a school similar to Abigail Rogers's. As historians of early republican needlework indicate, instruction in elaborate projects like samplers or imitations of paintings, often with expensive metallic threading, was reserved for those who could afford education beyond the basic household tasks typically taught to young girls. The needlework itself implied wealth and status and was often held as a keepsake rather than just another student assignment. In other words, even if the Verys were not one of the recognized first families of Salem, Samuel Very was clearly wealthy enough to send one or more of his daughters to what was the equivalent of a finishing school. Second, Lydia Very clearly came of age in a transitional era riven by political and social tensions, and some of the "new thinking" may well have reached her, either directly or indirectly, in the period before her controversial marriage. We know of her reputation for atheism, registered by Elizabeth Peabody in 1838, and I have already sought to complicate this labeling in order to better understand what such a reputation might mean in the 1830s. But in the Abigail Rogers controversy we have hints of an earlier potential source for Lydia's independent thinking, a context potentially more generative than Peabody's allusion to Fanny Wright. If Lydia was exposed, either during or after this controversy, to the debate over Wollstonecraft's writings, this heady air of early feminism may have played a role either in her decision to marry or in her defiant stand against her uncle after her husband's death.

Whatever the direct impact on Lydia Very, the controversy over Abigail Rogers's school helps us see more clearly the various tensions that governed the Salem world of Lydia's youth. The most obvious of these—and most often discussed—was the political conflict between Federalists and Republicans. Lydia's father, Samuel, played a part in Republican politics at least as early as 1804, and Jones Very Sr. worked for most of his life for the powerful shipping merchant William Gray, a Republican once considered the richest man in New England.[5] In 1808, Gray, then a Federalist, supported the trade embargo imposed by the Jefferson administration to convince Great Britain to stop impressing American sailors. The Federalists in Salem and along the Atlantic coast vehemently opposed the law because they bore the brunt of the economic misery it entailed. There were insinuations that Gray was profiting from the embargo because he was already well-stocked with foreign goods to sell, but whatever the reason, his Federalist friends repudiated him (to such an extent that he felt compelled to move to Boston), and he effectively became a Republican from that point on.[6] In addition to serving as master on two of Gray's ships, Jones Very Sr. appears to have had close financial relationships with Gray or other members of his family. His will mentions "one note against William Gray" for $4,000. He was also a member of the local masonic lodge that included the East Church minister William Bentley, a prominent Republican, suggesting that at least some of the Verys aligned themselves with the "Jacobinical" party of Jefferson and its freethinking coalition of "the slightly empowered and the newly empowered . . . unified against Federalist hegemony in matters sacred and secular."[7]

But perhaps the most significant tension for the young Lydia was the kind of stresses produced by the Abigail Rogers affair. This introduction of—and reaction to—radical ideas about women's roles indirectly reflected the potent political divisions in Salem. (It was the seemingly omnipresent Reverend Bentley, for instance, who came to Rogers's defense, alongside Joseph Story, against Barnard's establishment attacks.) New ideas were in the air, and some of those new ideas suggested that young women should not be mere accessories to their husbands' lives but independent figures in their own right, regardless of their status as spouses or mothers. Was this part of what Cornelia, mother of the Gracchi, suggested? Though certainly a formidable and powerful figure, Cornelia and her representative gesture of pointing to her children as her "jewels" hardly seem to embody Wollstonecraftian ideas. She is archetypically maternal, if nothing else, despite her apparent political power. Was this subject, then, considered a suitable one for a rebellious young woman, who might have already developed other ideas? Could a vigilant teacher have decided that the spirited Lydia Very, coming of age in an era where new ideas had already stirred youthful souls, would benefit from the slow patience of the needle as well as the subject of devoted maternity? With no way of knowing the answers to these questions, we can at least appreciate the complexity of a young woman's life in this roiled atmosphere of economic and sexual politics. The woman who eventually accepted her son's account of his own spiritual transformation had not only lived a hard life, but had been subject to a remarkable array of potential influences, both secular and religious, and had shown a determined spirit to see and confront the world in her own way.

✵ 6 ✵

Biography (II)

Unlike his younger sister Lydia L. A., Very left no memoir or other form of prose description of his childhood or family. His Harvard notes and commonplace books offer useful evidence of his intellectual progress during his undergraduate years and just after, but traces of specific conflict with his mother's character or behavior, if present, are oblique and far from definitive. He did write at least one important poem about Lydia during the period just prior to his mystic phase, and before we return to the development of his intellectual and spiritual commitments as a college student, we should look closely at this complicated "tribute" to her together with the prevailing account of its place in Very's development.

"My Mother's Voice" was likely written during Very's senior year at Harvard. It was published initially in the student literary magazine and later, also in 1836, in the *Salem Observer*. (It was again reprinted in 1846 in the *Christian Register* and in 1868 in the *Salem Gazette*.) It can therefore be considered one of Very's more popular, if also conventional, poems:

My mother's voice! I hear it now,
I feel her hand upon my brow,
As when, in heart-felt joy,
She raised her evening hymn of praise,
And called down blessings on the days
    Of her loved boy.

My mother's voice! I hear it now;
Her hand is on my burning brow,
    As in that early hour;
When fever throbbed through all my veins,
And that fond hand first soothed my pains,
    With healing power.

My mother's voice! It sounds as when
She read to me of holy men,
 The Patriarchs of old;
And gazing downward on my face,
She seemed each infant thought to trace
 My young eyes told.

It comes, when thoughts unhallowed throng,
Woven in sweet deceptive song,
 And whispers round my heart;
As when, at eve, it rose on high;
I hear, and think that she is nigh,
 And they depart.

Though round my heart all, all beside,
The voice of Friendship, Love had died;
 That voice would linger there;
As when, soft pillowed on her breast,
Its tones first lulled my infant rest,
 Or rose in prayer. (*CP* 38–39)

Though it's entirely possible that this generalized, sentimental statement about motherhood could have no reference to his own experience, "My Mother's Voice" has been read as one of the few direct descriptions of Very's relationship with Lydia. As such, it immediately raises an important question about accuracy and intention. For instance, can we take this picture of a caring, sustaining figure who prays, reads scripture, and sings hymns as a forthright depiction of Lydia's practices and beliefs? If so, it roughly coincides with the image constructed by Lydia L. A. in her memoirs and poems (and commemorated by the Cornelia needlework) but clearly complicates, and possibly contradicts, the reputation of Lydia as an aggressive atheist recorded in Elizabeth Peabody's letters. We can entertain the possibility that Very is idealizing and slightly disguising his mother's behavior to fit with the conventions of the moral guide whose image or voice returns to keep the speaker on the path of righteousness. But such a reading requires us to imagine an atmosphere and family environment for which there is little definitive evidence.

This is the burden of Edwin Gittleman's account of the poem. Given his dependence upon Elizabeth Peabody's description of Lydia, Gittleman has no choice but to read the poem as a partial fantasy, "a mixture of near-accurate recollection and dreamlike reconstruction of the mother he yearned for but did not have, a God-loving and God-fearing woman of gentle and warm nature, with none of the intensity and near-hysteria with which the actual Lydia Very conducted her affairs" (EG 95). Positing a Jones Very conflicted by his own spiritual opposition to his mother, Gittleman claims that the poem distorts the past, blending memories of Lydia's "possessive love" with fabricated signs of overt piety. In this way he can state confidently that Lydia had "never sung" hymns, "never related" stories from the Bible, and "never uttered" a prayer (EG 95). In other words, for Gittleman the poem describes the mother Very wanted, not the mother he had: a caring woman, yes, but one who imposed a militant atheism on her young children, even in moments of crisis.

While we may not want to discount all aspects of the tension Gittleman finds here, there is no doubt that this subversive reading is presented with far too much certainty. The image of Lydia offered by her daughter, though also sentimentalized, is consistent with the poem's account of someone who cared deeply for her children and may not have been as antireligious as Peabody's account indicates. To claim that Lydia Very never said daily prayers, even over meals, for example, or that she never told Bible stories or sung hymns, invites skepticism, if for no other reason than that individuals are often more complex and contradictory than we imagine them to be. That someone with Lydia's difficult early experiences, possibly rushed marriage, and family conflict would have been suspicious of public piety is entirely plausible; that, as a mother, whose devotion to her children appears to have been unquestionable, she would consistently impose an aggressive and even cruel critique of spirituality—interdicting her children's religious education or refusing to offer prayers or other conventional signs of belief, even when they were sick or suffering—seems far less likely. Given what we know of Lydia Very, we may have to accept the possibility that her son's memories in "My Mother's Voice" are accurate, if generalized, and that her freethinking, such as it may have been, was less consistent or predictable than Peabody's anecdote suggests.

If we reject Gittleman's conspiratorial reading of the poem, what can the verse tell us beyond its basic description of maternal comfort and moral stability? Despite its conventional language, the poem does describe a kind of tension between the speaker and the mother, who is not merely a guide but a dominant presence in his life. She is an internal reality at all phases of his development, from infancy to moments of adult crisis, and though her voice is described as a comfort and protection, it also opposes the presence of others: "Though round [his] heart all, all beside, / The voice Friendship, Love had died," his mother's voice would remain as it had been in his infancy. This inescapability can be understood as a positive value, of course, but it reaffirms an asymmetrical relationship: the mother, who can bless and heal and even "trace" the thoughts of "young eyes," dominates the largely passive speaker, suggesting an inability on his part to establish a voice of his own. For a poet who will soon learn to ventriloquize the voice of Christ, the poem could be seen to set a kind of boundary, acknowledging an influence in order to distance it, examining the source of his own voice in order to displace or re-create it.

This concern over voice, a crucial element of Very's eventual poetics, points us to a poem written a year later in 1837 (and closer to the period of Very's crisis) that Gittleman productively treats as a companion to "My Mother's Voice." "The Voice of God" establishes a much clearer distinction and conflict between what the speaker was "told" in childhood and what he has come to learn: "a holier creed / Than what my infancy was taught." The "voice of God" in question is the thunder itself, which was frightening when the speaker was young but which he has come to understand as his "Father's voice," a pervasive, cheering tone that only the "heedless" fear. Now he hears God in all things, "In all that stirs the human breast, / That wakes to mirth or draws the tear."

The question of the biographical reading of the poem hinges upon the first stanza in particular:

> They told me—when my heart was glad,
> And all around but said rejoice—
> They told me, and it made me sad,
> The thunder was God's angry voice. (*CP* 58)

For Gittleman, this poem, unlike "My Mother's Voice," is an undisguised account of Very's movement away from Lydia's atheism. Here Very "more accurately depicted the tone and beliefs prevailing in his Salem home" by claiming that "he had been taught a sardonic doctrine, one which masked total disbelief by contemptuous references to Deity" (EG 150). In other words, the "They" in the opening stanza is meant to indicate Lydia, who does not believe in God but is telling her young son "in derision" that the voice of God was an angry voice, available "only when the thunder's terrifying crash could be heard" (EG 150). Though we may be able to imagine the fierce nonbeliever of Gittleman's reading saying something of this sort to a child, the harshness of this strategy is difficult to square with the image of Lydia as the sheltering mother and devoted gardener.[1] If she had been an atheistic follower of the materialist Fanny Wright, would she have pretended to a young boy that God exists so that she could convince him that this god was angry and not to be trusted? Wouldn't she have simply explained the natural forces behind the phenomenon of thunder and demystified a common superstition? A more plausible explanation is that the poem describes a typical saying the speaker heard when he was a child, something other children were likely to repeat: that when it thunders, God is angry. This idea he imbibed when young, but it's now supplanted by the realization that the "Father's voice" calls "in every tone that cheered / Those rosy hours of childhood's mirth." In this sense the poem more conventionally describes a maturing of the spiritual sense and the development of more personal communion with divine intention. (In fact, the poem follows a similar account in Jonathan Edwards's "Personal Narrative," in which Edwards indicates his new sense of "divine things" by noting the change in his attitude toward thunder: "And scarce anything, among all the works of nature, was so sweet to me as thunder and lightning. Formerly, nothing had been so terrible to me.")[2] To go even further, this maturation duplicates the movement from Calvinism to Unitarianism that may have more generally underpinned Very's childhood. He was likely to have heard admonitions from his grandfather or others about the more forbidding and fierce god of predestination and apocalyptic judgment. But by the time he reached Harvard the benign image of what William Ellery Channing called "a God worthy of our love and trust" had supplanted these common threats from "the false and dishonourable views of God" attributable to the Calvinists.[3]

Does "The Voice of God," as Gittleman's reading implies, replace "My Mother's Voice," indicating in some larger sense a movement from Lydia's influence to a spiritual vision more fully Very's own? The evidence for this general claim is much stronger and not dependent upon so labored a reading. If "My Mother's Voice" registers a sense of dependence or absorption in Lydia's personality or will, "The Voice of God" suggests that the speaker has become similarly taken by or with an alternate presence:

> God dwells no more afar from me,
> His voice in all that lives is heard;
> . . .
> In passion's storm or soul's calm rest,
> Alike the voice of God I hear. (*CP* 59)

There is no need to believe that Lydia imposed a harsh or abusive form of materialism on her young son to recognize that a mother's emotional dominance might push him to seek a form of freedom that mimics her presence while pulling him away from it. A young, developing poet, in particular, one concerned with how his personal voice is emerging from or merging with a spiritual source, might be particularly attuned to the ways God's voice has changed for him. The move from the traditional—perhaps even Calvinist—conception of God as a source of threat and fear to an immanent, romantic (Unitarian) God-in-nature prepares the way for the ecstatic sonnets Very began writing at precisely this moment in his career. That Lydia played a role in this transition can hardly be doubted; any mother, particularly one with so strong a personality, will inevitably become both a source of and a resistance to the development of a mature voice. That she herself embodied an extreme set of apostate views—and so harsh an application of them—is far less certain.

As we return to the story of Very's intellectual and spiritual development at Harvard we should resist drawing early conclusions about how Lydia Very influenced or affected her son's eventual transformation into the poet and prophet of will-lessness. Her presence and influence should never be underestimated, but how it took shape and what form Very's response to that influence ultimately assumed are difficult facts to establish in the absence of a range of corroborating evidence. One quality we can rely on, however: Lydia Very was fiercely proud of her accomplished son. She saw in him something unusual, someone extraordinary, a validation of sorts of the struggles she had endured, possibly even a proof to herself and others that her life, so often criticized by others, was her own to tend and nurture as she saw fit.

✷ 7 ✷

A Student's Notes, 1833–34

If the one daguerreotype of Jones Very that survives from his early years (fig. 7) is any indication, the twenty-year-old who arrived in Cambridge in September of 1833 had little of his father's dash and brio. The captain's forthright gaze is nowhere to be seen; his eldest son's eyes focus inwardly, as though in quiet possession of a deepening thought. The Very family features are certainly present: a long, thin face, somewhat narrow eyes, the sharp line of jaw that meets at a pointed chin. But unlike a later photograph of his younger brother, Washington—taken at around the same age and projecting more than a little of the father's confidence—Jones sheds no smile. Instead, the surprisingly small mouth is tightly drawn, almost pursed, a feature consistent in all surviving images of him. It would be wrong to say that he seems severe; he is not frowning. And yet there is a pervasive tightness, an inner self-stiffening only partially allayed by the general stillness of demeanor. With his high collar and dark cravat typical of the time, the young man in the image looks proud, but we might imagine that he is marginally more interested in proving his worth to himself than to others. If there is something to be overcome, something to achieve, he will have to please an inner tribunal more severe—but also more gratifying—than anything the outside world can threaten.

Accounts of Very's three undergraduate years at Harvard emphasize his pent-up ambition and maturity as well as his reticent, kindly yet intense demeanor. He was, first and foremost, an excellent student, devoted not only to classwork but to participation in studious extracurricular activities. (One indication of his seriousness was his immediate request to the college librarian that he be allowed to borrow more than the usual allotment of books.)[1] To his more worldly classmates he could seem a drudge; to others, a somewhat distant but admirable example of discipline and devotion. Samuel Gray Ward, son of the American agent for Baring Brothers bank, shared recitations with Very for three years and found him distant and mildly odd: "There was an ungracefulness about him—yet it was a solemn, not-to-be-trifled-with awkwardness."[2] The much younger Ward was not among Very's intimates, but he, perhaps like many others, was aware of his classmate's "intense" self-consciousness and the "hard, thin, anxious look" on his tightly drawn face.[3] On the other hand, J. T. G. Nichols, who was later to become a minister and who was temperamentally much closer to Very, admired his friend's "devout nature" and "solemn demeanor."[4] Writing years later, Nichols attempted to capture Very's almost otherworldly aura at Harvard in terms consistent with his later reputation as a "saint": "I can see him now, emerging with long, stately tread from his room in Holworthy for his daily walk, and with the regularity of the clock returning,—nothing tempting him to deviate from the given distance or direction. A sweet, natural smile upon the seemingly fixed staidness of his face, and a gentleness of tone in his guttural voice, were an agreeable surprise on first acquaintance with him, showing a depth of sweetness and tenderness in his nature, which it would be quite possible for a casual observer to overlook."[5] Self-possessed and prematurely dignified Very may have been on his solitary walks, but in other contexts, Nichols admitted, his friend could be "nervously sensitive and excitable," particularly when faced with some sort of disagreement or opposition, which would cause his "long face" and neck to redden.[6]

Ambition to succeed—to prove he belonged despite his late arrival—mixed paradoxically with an inborn otherworldliness. "His mind, even then," as one writer put it years later, "was in a state of poetical and spiritual exaltation. He was not a practical man at all. Everyone felt that he was living in and for a higher world."[7] And yet, there was discipline and practicality enough to become a star student who graduated second in his class (short of first only because he began as a sophomore) and never fell below third during his three years as an undergraduate. Twice he was recommended by the administration to receive scholarship funds ($60 in 1836) from the estate of Mary Saltonstall, reserved for students "of bright parts and good diligence" who intended to follow the ministry.[8] He received Bowdoin Prizes in 1835 and 1836, the first time the award had been given in the junior and senior years to the same student, and was asked to participate in the spring exhibition and commencement exercises for his class.[9] After graduation he was appointed tutor of Greek and allowed to begin studies in the Divinity School. But the accumulation of honors masked a dramatic change in his inner life. During his senior year he underwent what he himself called a "change of heart, which tells us that all we have belongs to God, and that we ought to have no will of our own."[10] Something in him pushed back against his worldly desires while, at the same time, leading him further toward a kind of elevation of purpose through the struggle to erase his own inclinations. How did this change come about, and what gave it so dramatic and intense a form? How did the son of Lydia and Captain Very—married cousins drawn perhaps to the passionate and unconventional—come to believe that his only path to happiness lay in the complete suppression of intention, of self, the liberating relinquishment of intimate and idiosyncratic desire?

Harvard in the 1830s was a small and comparatively bucolic campus, an irregular arrangement of mostly Federal-style buildings on a green sward. Some idea of the semirural atmosphere can be derived from a drawing by Eliza Susan Quincy, daughter of college president Josiah Quincy, that shows the alumni procession for the bicentennial celebration of 1836, held just a week after Jones Very's graduation. In the stylized landscape, a stream of well-ordered pairs flows out of the First Parish Meeting House on their way to the Pavilion. The college buildings are generously spaced, and the road or lane leading toward the church resembles nothing more than a country cart path. Though hundreds of alumni proceed in a line around the campus for this special occasion, the graduating class that year had consisted of only thirty-nine seniors. Three years before, Jones Very had entered this group as a sophomore some three to four years older than his typical classmate. Given his age and late arrival, it can be no surprise that he stood out, seemed odd or overly mature; nor is it difficult to understand how his ambition would have been keener, his desire more honed, than that of his younger peers.

He must have been alarmed and annoyed, therefore, when his first year ended in a general scandal from which he could not entirely extricate himself. The so-called Dunkin Rebellion began when a member of the freshman class refused his Greek teacher's command to continue translating aloud in front of the class. According to the student in question, the Greek tutor, Christopher Dunkin, only twenty-two at the time and inexperienced, assigned a text that included a long list of names with unusual case endings. As the student began reciting, Dunkin corrected him repeatedly. Seeing that the list went on to more than one page and the corrections would continue, the student then refused to recite, defying further orders with the phrase, "I do not recognize your authority." After the incident was reported to Quincy, already known for heavy-handed discipline, the student was required to apologize; instead he openly refused and withdrew from the university. For the next ten days the freshmen and other undergraduates engaged in a variety of destructive protests, including trashing Dunkin's classroom and hanging Quincy in effigy. But it was the sophomore class that was ultimately punished en masse when, after demanding that the Greek requirement be lifted, they collectively disrupted morning prayers by loudly shuffling their feet. In late May the entire second-year class, except three members who had been away from campus at the time, was dismissed from the college. Though Very, along with a few others, argued that they had not participated in any of the actions, their petitions to be reinstated were not approved, and none returned until the following academic year.[11]

Though it cut short his first year, the Dunkin Rebellion had little impact on Very's overall success as a student. However, it does help clarify the difference in maturity and attitude—as well as economic security—that must have prevailed between him and many of his classmates. His age meant that he carried with him not just the desire to succeed but that sense of delayed arrival that made any further interruption in his progress dismaying. His lack of wealth or status made it far less likely that he would risk expulsion over a bad teacher or two. As his surviving notebooks make clear, Very was intent upon proving himself and developing his abilities to the highest level. More than simply a conscientious student, he was deeply determined—it's tempting to say, quietly self-required—to be a success; he devoted himself not only to his course work but to his own efforts toward self-education through extracurricular reading. Even if he could be imagined as sympathetic to the younger students' impatience with Harvard's teaching methods, what we know of him suggests that he would have considered the disruption—not to mention the anarchic hijinks that fed it—a deplorable waste of time. For him, there was work to be done, much of it focused on acquiring the broad education of a man of letters who was at least as intent on becoming a great poet as a successful minister.

This emphasis is clear in the notebooks that survive from these early college terms. There are four bound manuscripts from Very's undergraduate years in the Harvard University Archives. Three are listed as "commonplace books" and a fourth as a "notebook." The first commonplace book (CB I), labeled in the catalog as "circa 1830s," begins before Very entered Harvard, probably in the first half of 1833 or toward the end of 1832, and moves up to the summer after the end of his first academic year.[12] The second (CB II), also referred to as the "Scrapbook," covers a large swath of time from early 1834, during his first year, to approximately 1839. And the third (CB III) begins in 1837, during Very's year as a Greek tutor and student in the Divinity School, and extends into the 1840s. All reinforce the picture of Very as a serious student and thinker devoted to mastering the Harvard curriculum while privately investigating and modeling the art of poetry and a deep understanding of literary history. His moral and spiritual life can be said to be a concern throughout, but the development of his unique conception of what might be called his spiritual work—and unique prophetic role—is rooted in the idea (or ideal) of the inspired poet.

This specific combination of interests and unstated goals can best be seen by sampling from the material Very chose to record before and during his first year. Though we have no account of the preparatory work he did in Salem with Henry K. Oliver, we can infer from his earliest commonplace book that much of it concerned the classical canon. During the summer of 1833, for instance, Very was reading Virgil, Cicero, Tacitus, and Horace as well as essays from the *American Quarterly* and *Edinburgh Review* on Latin language and culture. He was also absorbing the latest interpretations of Roman cultural practices found in Jacob Bryant's *A New System or Analysis of Ancient Mythology* (CB I, 23). Whether this reading was directed or the result of his own continued discoveries, we can detect hints of topics that will become essential to Very's later intellectual interests. His future concern with the historical role of the epic, for instance, appears in quotations from an *American Quarterly Review* article on Friedrich August Wolf's *Prolegomena ad Homerum,* specifically its list of arguments against the single-author theory of Homeric authorship. (This historical dimension to Very's thought can be easily overlooked in the understandable emphasis on his later mysticism, but his literary criticism—devoted in the late 1830s to the epic and to Shakespeare—rests solidly on an abiding interest in intellectual and cultural history rather than solely on the spiritual comportment of the individual.) The image emerges of a serious young student determined to be current on the latest critical thinking, particularly new ideas about the relationship between pagan and Christian history—and between writers, their work, and their culture.

Nevertheless, even as he primarily focused on classical authors to prepare for Harvard in August, the question of his own spiritual or moral life did assert itself, both in reaction to his studies and in his poetic practice. Reading Sir James Mackintosh's *Dissertation on the Progress of Ethical Philosophy,* for instance, Very recorded this basic distinction on an otherwise blank page: "'Physical science answers the question of What is? Moral What should ^ought to^ be'" (CB I, 11; original emphasis). A short time later, while immersed in James Stuart's just published *Three Years in North America,* Very wrote his first poem about slavery, a forty-line reaction to Stuart's description of the treatment of slaves in Charleston, South Carolina. Stuart was a combative Scottish politician and a frank stylist, and he focused part of his memoir on the time he spent in a Charleston boardinghouse where the enslaved were abused and beaten on the slightest pretext. When he was able, Stuart questioned some of them about their treatment and heard in response harrowing stories of family separations, murders, and other atrocities. These accounts he reinforced with published descriptions of slave auctions and unpunished crimes against "men of colour." Though not itself an argument for abolition, Stuart's clear-eyed testimony made an effective case for the inherent violence and daily cruelty of the slave system, and the strong imagery and emotion of the account stirred Very to respond.

"Lines, Written on Reading Stuart's Account of the Treatment of Slaves in Charleston," published in the *Salem Observer* in August 1833, only a week or so after it was written, expands Stuart's argument into a full-throated and general condemnation of slavery. Where Stuart had taken pains to commend the kind treatment of slaves by a few masters, Very establishes the pervasive moral repugnance of this "bane of human kind; / . . . To all that's just, to all that's right a foe" (*CP* 5). He is particularly appalled by the idea of the market, the exchange of "gold" for "the unhappy victim of thy crime," an emphasis that suggests a connection between Stuart's account and Very's boyhood memories of slave pens in New Orleans. We have no evidence that Very himself witnessed a slave auction of the sort common in 1820s Louisiana, but if he did, such an experience would give the poem a slightly different inflection, of recovered shame blended with youthful indignation: "Would that my lips the tale could never tell, / The tale of horror, known, alas! too well" (*CP* 5).

As the already successful local poet moved to Cambridge a few weeks later, he continued to copy large portions of his reading into his notebook. Some of it reflects the standard Harvard curriculum, which, in addition to Latin and Greek, included math, English composition, theology, natural philosophy, and, for Very, French. Long sections of notes on the study of Latin and Greek are supplemented by gatherings from his "general reading," some of the scope of which can be determined by his library charge lists for the year. Of the over thirty books taken out of the Harvard library by Very during his first year, about two-thirds are related to the study of Latin and Greek languages and literatures. Classical authors include Cicero, Horace, Homer, and Tacitus, with associated commentaries and various lexicons to aid in reading. A much smaller set might be attributable to personal reading: a history of Napoleon, for instance, as well as the works of Byron, Locke, and Milton.

Within the pages of the 1833–34 commonplace book a large section is devoted to the acquisition of a fluent and lucid prose style, likely in response to Edward Tyrell Channing's instruction in rhetoric. Channing influenced a generation of Harvard students, including Emerson, Thoreau, and the abolitionist Wendell Phillips, among many others. Very was especially fond of Channing and later dedicated his only published book of poems and essays to him. In his introduction to his cousin's collected lectures, Richard Henry Dana Jr. describes Channing's influence both inside and outside the classroom:

> His reputation for pure style, and for exquisite taste and judgment in English literature, has been long established; and all who have been his pupils know how faithfully and successfully he brought these gifts and acquirements to bear upon the duties of his office. They acknowledge, too, his dignity, justice and impartiality, and his insight into character. . . . He was their adviser and guide in their reading: that which develops the minds and so much forms the tastes and influences the opinions of the young. Not merely by his course lectures, and by private interviews, but also in the voluntary reading classes that met at his study, he drew them from the fascination of the superficial, brilliant favorites of the day, to the writers of deep thought, elevated sentiments and pure style.[13]

As Dana's description suggests, Channing emphasized a timeless clarity and personal grace that was balanced against faddishness. He was particularly drawn to the Scottish commonsense philosopher Thomas Reid, whose optimism and sense of equipoise between the "active and rational powers" underpinned Channing's general approach toward rhetoric and literary expression.[14]

Channing may have sent Very for stylistic advice to writers like Lord Monboddo, who advised translating Greek (not Latin) into English and back again: "In this way Milton, & Elizabeth formed their stile" (CB I, 55). Very dutifully records similar advice from Gibbon's memoirs (Cicero into French and back), who likewise recommends the Greeks, particularly Xenophon, for style and "admirable lessons for public and private life" (CB I, 55). And did Channing recommend his older brother's essay "Remarks on National Literature" to the quietly self-possessed young poet who may have been trying on styles and approaches based on his reading of contemporary verse? During his first few weeks at Harvard, Very copied out the following passage, with its whiff of proto-Transcendentalism, from William Ellery Channing's 1823 essay: "Literature depends upon individual genius, and this, though fostered, cannot be created by outward helps. No human mechanism can produce original thought. After all the attempts to explain by education the varieties of intellect, we are compelled to believe that minds, like other products of nature, have original and indestructible differences; that they are not exempted from that great and beautiful law, which joins with strong resemblances as strong diversities; and, of consequence, we believe that the men who are to be lights of the world, bring with them their commission and power from God" (CB I, 49). Whatever his spiritual condition at this auspicious moment in his academic career, Very's personal and literary goals appear to have been considerable; this passage marks an important moment when his desire to be a poet found support in a spiritual language that connected genius to its source in the divine.

Later, toward the end of his first year, Very included a rare personal entry in his first commonplace book. He wrote out his study schedule under the heading "Account of 3rd term of College 1834":

> April 18. Thursday. Horace's Conversation with Trebatius and satire on temperance. *Non in caro nidore voluptus summa, sed in te ipso est.* Sat, book 2. Sat 1st and 2nd Friday. Read book from Dr. Beck. bene should have got an optime. Aim at highest -- began Mechanics: recited 2 first lessons on matter and its properties. French ½ 6th book Fontaine not got very well. Saturday Miss from Themes. got lesson for Monday began Alcestis. easier than Sophocles. Resolved to live temperate next week and go to bed early si possem [if I could]. (CB I, 87)

In all of Very's surviving student notes, this is one of only a few moments when he actually describes his life or creates what we might think of as an ordinary journal entry. Almost always, he simply quotes, nothing more—a reticence that makes interpreting these collections dangerously difficult for incautious biographers. In this instance, the deviation seems significant: Why did Very change his practice? Why record this one week's labor? The entry could be a sign of slight anxiety, a needed correction to habits, like missing a class, that might have become less than "temperate." Even so, it provides us with a glimpse of his intense self-curation, both scholastic and spiritual. It may be particularly significant that he recorded his encounter with Horace's satires from book 2, the first about the poet's struggle to find new subjects and avoid the trouble that comes with writing about the powerful; the second about the virtues of living and eating simply, of letting hard work supply the appetite for plain food. "True pleasure doesn't derive from / the savor of expensive dishes. / It resides in yourself."[15] Is this just a typical platitude copied by a morally serious student, one who reminds himself to continue to be "temperate" in the future? Or has Very fallen off the wagon of high seriousness somehow, become self-indulgent and put his performance—or even his soul—at risk?

What is important in retrospect are the tensions in play: the high drive, the internal push toward academic achievement; the moral perfectionism that seems entangled with ambition to succeed in terms that will validate his delayed career; the suggestion that behind the "solemn demeanor" may reside a sensuality or, at the very least, a sensitivity to aesthetic pleasures; and the tendency to oppose these external desires with a self-satisfying inwardness. Jones Very may well have been a reserved, somewhat aloof older student, but he was also driven, passionate—and concerned that unfettered passion might lead to chaos rather than accomplishment. If, as Channing proclaimed, "men who are to be lights of the world, bring with them their commission and power from God," what is the proper path toward cultivating "individual genius"? How can we discipline ourselves and, at the same time, find the "true pleasure" that outlasts the temporary delights of this world?

8

A Poet's Notes, 1834

It's difficult to say with any precision exactly when Very began writing poetry. The absence of early notebooks or juvenile manuscripts leaves us completely dependent upon dates of first publication, and we can only speculate about when or how his writing began. An early biographical reminiscence suggests that both of his parents were known to have written poetry, and a few hints survive to suggest that Lydia Very left poems in manuscript after her death in 1867.[1] (Among Very's papers at Brown University is a blue notebook marked "Jones Very AE. 12" and containing a fair copy of "The Arab Steed," an early Byronic imitation. If the age listed is accurate—and not a later, wishful ascription—the performance would be remarkable [JHL 1.6]). It was apparently a creative or literary household; the fact of his sister Lydia L. A. Very's productivity as a writer and illustrator suggests as much, and both Frances and Washington Very (fig. 8) saw poems published. Perhaps Jones's teenage encounter with Shakespeare sparked his creative imagination: his subsequent interest—or near obsession—with Shakespeare as an example of genius, coupled with the adoption of the Shakespearean sonnet as his preferred verse form, indicates a potential desire to emulate strong models. But in whatever way the interest took hold, by the time he arrived in Cambridge Very was serious about producing and publishing poetry and soon became known as someone who could readily provide verse for college occasions. It's possible that his publications in Salem had given him a modest, local reputation. Between May of 1833 and August of 1834, fourteen of his poems appeared in the *Salem Observer*. During the same period he produced at least two significant but unpublished lyrics as well as a song written for the sophomore class supper of 1834. Quiet and dignified he may have been as an older undergraduate, but he showed no reluctance to take on the public role (or receive the public praise) of the designated poet.

This impression of seriousness combined with ambition is reinforced by a careful survey of his "Scrapbook" (CB II), begun in the middle of his first year, probably in January of 1834.[2] Here he set down model passages from contemporary and classic poets, sometimes commenting on efficacy of expression but for the most part simply recording moments that caught his eye for one reason or another. The tantalizing collage of possible influences suggests a young poet interested in large, contemporary works, perhaps ambitious to produce something similar, at the very least attracted to the poet's prophetic role as well as his practice. The question addressed by these selections seems to have been not only how to write but how to live in a way that would produce the fullest expression of a naturalized spirituality, both romantic and Christian.

Across his very broad reading in classical and contemporary poetry, three figures stand out as potential models during Very's first two years at Harvard: Robert Pollok, the Scottish Presbyterian who died in his twenties just after completing his major work, *The Course of Time* (1828); Lord Byron, arguably the most famous or infamous poet of his era, whose spectacular career began around the time of Very's birth; and the Scottish romantic Robert Burns, a biography of whom had been published in 1828 by John Gibson Lockhart, editor of the *Quarterly Review*. It should come as no surprise that Very became interested in Pollok, whose long apocalyptic poem was widely popular throughout the nineteenth century. (It was estimated to have sold over 70,000 copies by 1900).[3] A slightly more gentle version of Michael Wigglesworth's *The Day of Doom*, *The Course of Time* describes all of human history through to the resurrection and final judgment. Its theology is largely Calvinist, though with less emphasis on predestination and more on the readily available evidence of Christian revelation. Perhaps most significant for Very, the story is told by a heavenly "Bard," whose poetic purpose appears to align with the Miltonic ambition to "justify the ways of God to men." The intention is both epic and Christian, in other words, with the contemporary poet occupying the central role of prophet or seer.

Very's initial interest in *The Course of Time* may have been more technical than substantive. He both praises and describes the shortcomings of Pollok's fluid but unremarkable verse, reminding us that the scrapbook is first of all the tool of a working poet. He singles out for particular notice Pollok's comparison of a mother's moment of death to the way the "morning star . . . melts away into the light of heaven," setting it beside similar examples from Fitz-Greene Halleck and Virgil, before noting that Pollok's scene is more effective for being applied to "a dying Christian" (CB II, 2–3).

But as such a concluding comment indicates, the technical could easily slide into the thematic in Very's rare notations: he was drawn to those moments in *The Course of Time* that offered a model for the Christian poet, both in terms of appropriate subject matter and as a warning against secular individualism. Of the six passages copied from the poem, one describes the dangers of indolence to the "literary man," one paints Byron's "wretchedness" in death, and three picture the high purpose and inspired figure of the true poet or "anointed bard" (CB II, 1–5, 10). It's difficult to imagine a young poet recording lines such as the following without thinking of them as modeling a particular poetic identity:

> It was indeed a wondrous sort of bliss
> The lonely bard enjoyed, when forth he walked
> Unpurposed; stood, and knew not why; sat down,
> And knew not where; arose, and knew not when;
> Had eyes, and saw not; ears, and nothing heard;
> And sought—sought neither heaven nor earth—sought naught,
> Nor meant to think; but ran meantime thro' vast
> Of visionary things, fairer than aught
> That was; and saw the distant tops of thoughts.
> Which men of common stature never saw. (CB II, 5)

Sloth might be dangerous, but the "true, legitimate" poet is both the passive recipient of vision and "most severely thoughtful, most minute / And accurate of observation" (CB II, 6). The bard is also closely connected to nature, entering into "Her inner chamber" and beholding "her face / Unveiled" (CB II, 5). The truth of his "measures" flows from his attentiveness to "nature's rule of taste" and his openness to the "sacred living impetus divine" (CB II, 6).

In February of 1834, while still recording passages from Pollok, Very borrowed Lord Byron's works from the Harvard library. He copied passages from *Childe Harold's Pilgrimage* and "The Giaour" into his scrapbook and would continue to read Byron through the course of the following year. Though Very offers little technical comment on these selections, he does show a consistent interest in the role or personality of the Byronic adventurer, first as the isolated romantic immersed in nature and second as a monitory figure of excessive sensuality and self-concern. The image of romantic stillness and reception that Pollok offers in his ideal examples of the spiritualized poet finds a response in this passage from *Childe Harold,* though the tone of isolation in Byron is sharper and the engagement with nature more restless than passive:

To sit on rocks, to muse o'er flood and fell,
To slowly trace the forest's shady scene,
Where things that own not man's dominion dwell,
And mortal foot hath ne'er or rarely been;
To climb the trackless mountain all unseen,
With the wild flock that never needs a fold;
Alone o'er steeps and foaming falls to lean,—
This is not solitude; 't is but to hold
Converse with Nature's charms, and view her stores unrolled. (CB II, 6)

A long passage from "The Giaour" then follows, describing the dark "scowl" and divided self of the infidel ("But brighter traits with evil mixed") and concluding with a defiant statement of Byronic action in the face of despair:

The keenest pangs the wretched find
Are rapture to the dreary void,
The leafless desert of the mind,
The waste of feelings unemployed.
Who would be doomed to gaze upon
A sky without a cloud or sun?
. . . .
Better to sink beneath the shock
Than moulder piecemeal on the rock! (CB II, 10–13)

It may well be that Very recorded these excerpts as poetic exempla and nothing more. The passage from "The Giaour," for instance, is long enough to suggest that it stands as a strong example of vivid characterization and propulsive language. But the overall arrangement of the scrapbook implies that Very was using Byron most often as a negative example of isolation in the absence of traditional belief. The description of the Giaour, often understood as a stylized portrait of Byron himself, is set beside Pollok's moralistic summation of Byron's life of excess from book 4 of *The Course of Time*: "He died. He died of what? Of wretchedness. / Drank every cup of joy, heard every trump / Of fame, drank early, deeply drank, drank draughts / That common millions might have quenched; then died / Of thirst, because there was no more to drink."[4] And to another stanza from *Childe Harold*—one that describes the "quenchless" desire and "fever at the core" of the romantic hero—Very responds: "How many are, whose religion, at best, is an anxious wish like that of Rabelais, 'a great Perhaps'" (CB II, 13).

Though Byron clearly stood as a warning against insufficient faith, the image he projected of the solitary, romantic poet remained a powerful attraction to the young poet in Very. (He continued to copy passages from *Childe Harold* in particular well into 1836.) Pollok's Christian epic may have had the proper underpinning of belief, but its Miltonic approach to spiritual history left little overall imprint on Very's poetic practice.[5] The apparent need to graft the romantic veneration of nature onto a more sturdily Christian framework, while preserving the allure of the Byronic wanderer, may have led him to a kind of synthesis in the figure of Robert Burns. While continuing to record selections from *Childe Harold,* Very began reading Lockhart's biography of Burns, highlighting those moments when the Scottish romantic emphasized the importance of direct contact or immersion in nature as the key to poetic inspiration. In some respects, these excerpts place a particular weight on experience as the key to the poetic process, emphasizing those moments when Burns recorded his impressions as they occurred. For example, Lockhart describes Burns riding through a storm in Galloway, composing a poem that captures his delight in the wildness of the weather and its intimations of divine power:

> "There is hardly," says [Burns] in one of his letters, "any earthly object gives me more—I do not know if I should call it pleasure—but something which exalts me, something which enraptures me—than to walk in the sheltered side of a wood in a cloudy winter day, and hear the stormy wind howling among the trees, and raving over the plain. It is my best season for devotion; my mind is wrapt up in a kind of enthusiasm to *Him,* who, in the pompous language of the Hebrew bard, 'walks on the wings of the wind.'" (CB II, 17)

The vividness and validity of experience may provide a kind of authenticity to the verse, but they also allow access to a divine presence, and it's this blending of the moment of emotion with the perception of transcendence that Very seems most to value. In response to another of Byron's registrations of the sublime, he brings Burns's description of process to bear as an explanation for its effect. After copying a stanza from book 3 of *Childe Harold,*

> The high, the mountain-majesty of worth
> Should be, and shall, survivor of its woe,
> And from its immortality look forth
> In the sun's face, like yonder Alpine snow,
> Imperishably pure beyond all things below.

Very comments:

> The beauty which the sentiments in the last part of the above stanza have received from being composed while contemplating natural objects, is evident; and showes [*sic*] the advantage to be derived from this manner of composition. Burns says of himself when composing a song "My way is this: I consider the poetic Sentiment, correspondent to my idea of the musical expression; then chuse my theme; begin one Stanza; when that is composed, which is generally the most difficult part of the business, I walk out, sit down now and then, look out for objects in Nature around me that are in unison or harmony with the cogitations of my fancy and workings of my bosom; humming every now and then the air with the verses I have framed. When I feel my Muse beginning to jade, I retire to the solitary fireside of my study, and there commit my effusions to paper; swinging, at intervals, on the hind-legs of my elbow chair, by way of calling forth my own critical strictures, as my pen goes. Seriously, this, at home, is almost invariably my way.—What cursed egotism!" (CB II, 29)

Once again, the sequence is as important as the ideas expressed. The Byronic experience continues to attract, particularly the intoxicating but dangerous yearning for adventure, but it's Burns's example that provides the ballast, both procedural and theological, that keeps such desires in check. Here the search for ecstatic union with nature is balanced by the reflectiveness of the fireside, an almost dialectical process that seems to elicit an awareness of the self's own limits ("What cursed egotism!"). In what appears at times to be an internal debate, Very seems intent on reminding himself that the true function of nature's inspiration is to carry us up and through the personal experience of beauty toward a clear union with the divine. Byron suggests a dangerous adherence to personal experience for its own sake; Burns indicates how to balance and channel aesthetic wonder into theological confirmation. That this tension continued to play a part in Very's development is suggested by the persistence of his need to evoke and then deny the attraction of the Byronic figure. For instance, in the only such instance of repetition in his entire scrapbook, the stanza from *Childe Harold* that earlier provoked his response about the weakness of faith in many writers (Rabelais's "great Perhaps") appears a second time, its last four lines copied again, just after a comment that defines "true glory" as that which is "kindled from above" rather than from natural experience. Very may have disapproved in one sense of the desire that "once kindled . . . preys upon high adventure" and is a "fever at the core / Fatal to him who bears, to all who ever bore," but he takes pains to remind himself to disapprove. And in this respect he can seem at times both attracted to the romantic idea of inspiration such as Burns represents and critical of its need for natural sources of inspiration in the first place. In a comment responding to a passage from Francis Lieber's *Letters to a Gentleman from Germany* (1834), he takes the entire project a step further:

> The reason of people's requiring some great & powerful physical phenomenon to lead them from nature to nature's God, their adhering to matter and not elevating themselves to a contemplation of the principle of Life—results in my opinion from having their thoughts to [*sic*] much engaged in worldly pursuits so that they have no time for meditation—abstract their attention from these—lead them to contemplation, lead them to know the feeling infinite. (CB II, 25)

Though the phrase "from nature to nature's God" was an eighteenth- and nineteenth-century commonplace (best known from its place in Jefferson's Declaration of Independence), it's intriguing that the same language appears in Lydia L. A. Very's final image in *An Old-Fashioned Garden* of her mother "leading the thoughts of her children" in the remembered world of Federal Street. Was this a phrase associated with Lydia Very, something she herself said that might have registered with both her oldest and her youngest child? Was it an idea suggested by her devotion to her garden and to neighborhood strays, a general approach to a romantic theology that became the ground bass of the Very world? Perhaps both Jones in his younger years and his sister later in life are simply accessing a general concept that shows little more than that they were of like mind overall. Whatever the case, Jones was clearly drawn to these moments where nature inducts spirit but sensed the weakness of this material path toward "the feeling infinite." Perhaps he intuited that Byronic ecstasy could only be derived from risky sensualities. Perhaps even Burns's intensity chanced placing too great an emphasis on the tumult of the storm rather than devotion to the god that made it. At what point, in other words, was nature a help and at what point a hindrance to seeing "the distant tops of thoughts" that common men never see?

The final three phrases of this intriguing passage responding to Lieber suggest a developing methodological approach: if we understand them as three commands based on Very's sense of the limitations of the material path toward spirit, they suggest a way forward for thinking about the kind of poetry he intended to write. "Abstract their attention from these [worldly pursuits]—lead them to contemplation, lead them to know the feeling infinite." "Worldly pursuits" here include attentiveness to nature, from which his audience's attention is to be "abstracted," brought toward the contemplation of spirit and the feeling infinite through an evocation of thought, principle, or idea. The particular may still be valuable—and based on his continued attention to Byron, attractive—but it stands only as an occasion for its ultimate erasure.

✵ 9 ✵

Early Poems, 1833–35

Very began publishing poems in Salem newspapers in the late summer of 1833, just before he left for Cambridge. The earliest of these suggest imitations of eighteenth-century models, with an avowed interest in nature still fastened to rhymed couplets of iambic pentameter. But as his wide reading has already indicated, he was a writer hungry for exempla, and his published work throughout his first two years demonstrates a variety of formal interests, from the more flexible blank-verse line of James Thomson to variations on the rhymed quatrain that suggest the balladic forms of early romanticism. Thematically, the poems include topical treatments such as the antislavery lines in response to James Stuart's *Three Years in North America* and an elegy for General Lafayette as well as seasonal picturesques (e.g., "Sleigh Ride") and moralized observations of nature.

Among this last clutch of often ordinary lyrics we can detect the most consistent preoccupation of the work as a whole: a worrying of the tension between worldly attractions, particularly ambition and sensuality, and the claims of spirituality. It should come as no surprise that this anxiousness finds its most acute location in scenes of death or dying. In its conventional form these thoughts followed Very home from his daily walks in Mount Auburn Cemetery in Cambridge, still a novelty only two years old in 1833 as the first "garden" or rural cemetery in the country. The romantic landscape transformed the more familiar Puritan graveyard, like the venerable burying point in Salem, into a gentler reminder for visitors "to place their happiness on things not / Fleeting but eternal in the heavens" (*CP* 7). Its "thickets dark" and "flowers of spring" enabled a withdrawal "from worldly thoughts, and worldly cares" and a "communion . . . / With those long since departed . . . whose never ceasing goodness / Crowns our life" (*CP* 6). Nature, in its juxtaposed presence to death, provided a cyclical context, reinforced by a quotation from James Thomson's "Winter," that spring (that is, immortality) will "encircle all" (*CP* 7).

This concern that worldly entanglements, no matter how pleasant, might mislead or misdirect the striving soul is not always so comfortably expressed, however. In a sequence of poems that includes the lines on the death of his brother Franklin ("I saw a child"), we can sense the murmur of deeper currents of feeling, not always under full control. As though extending the Mount Auburn poem, "Lines Suggested by Seeing a Butterfly Sculptured upon a Tomb" seems a conventional explication of the familiar symbol of "th' immortal soul" freed from its "dark and loathsome mansion" (*CP* 13). But the rhetoric intensifies when the speaker lays out instructions for those who "hop'st to soar, when from this earthly / Coil thou'rt freed" (*CP* 14). These are told to "plume thy wings while here below, / Cast off what then may clog thy flight, and bear / Thee down":

> Passions fierce attack, attack most
> Direful; lust, poisoning the relish
> Of the soul for all that's pure; indolence,
> With slow yet ceaseless course eating its way,
> Like rust, into the mind, and deadening all
> Its energies: . . . (*CP* 14)

Given Very's continued evocations in his scrapbook of Byron's wayward sensuality, of the dangers of ambition as well as adventure, we may hear in this surprise repetition of "attack" a momentary admission of weakness or even panic. That in this small stampede of emotions "passions" and "lust" lead the way, followed by "indolence," suggests at the very least an awareness of the enervating lift and plunge of sensual pursuits.

Published later the same month (July 1834), "Pleasure" takes up this attraction to the "false flickering / Light" of the goddess who leads "astray o'er treach'rous bogs" and eludes the "eager grasp" of the wanderer (*CP* 16). But true pleasure resides "At home," which is to say, in the mind: "It is the mind, communing with itself, / That cast a sunshine on the paths of life" (*CP* 16). Inverting Satan's desperate boast from *Paradise Lost*, Very's speaker declares "The mind / Is its own home," and unlike the external, "active life," it is "the banquet of the mind" that is the "inward fount" of knowledge and contentment. Again, though the topic is conventional, the accumulation of continued reminders, like a string of personal mementos, points toward a persistent interest in self-regulation, particularly a desire to restate—or perhaps recover—the purity of an inner life uncompromised by external desires.

The possibility that these statements of familiar moral restraint might bear a more personal weight for Very is heightened by their proximity in time to the short lyric "Give me an eye" and the lines on his blind brother Franklin's unexpected bee sting. It's likely that both were composed in July or August of 1834 and together speak more personally and more directly than most of Very's early work to the fear of misplaced loyalties, of specifically mistaking (mis-seeing) the proper path to a moral life. As I suggested in my earlier account of "I saw a child," this poem is one of Very's most direct descriptions of a childhood experience that, though innocent in itself, must have eventually been wrapped in traumatic memories of Franklin's death. (Franklin died in 1822; the memory is therefore of long gestation, and its emergence at this point in Very's career is significant.) The emphasis on Very's own sight in the absence of his brother's suggests both a latent guilt and a subtle questioning of the nature of true vision, particularly as it relates to his mother's ability (or failure) to shield her most fragile son from suffering. In its registration of Lydia Very's inability to protect, the poem seems uncertain about the true source of virtue, and it imposes a moral solution to the scene that demands the violent suppression of desire:

> Oft as vice assails,
> Rememb'ring that it stings both soul and body,
> Let us cast it from us; but if within
> Us it has taken root and flourish'd long,
> Let us, like that sightless boy, though many
> A pang we suffer in the attempt, with firm,
> Unsparing grasp, crush the dire foe, and be
> Forever free. (*CP* 19)

His metaphor not fully under control, Very understands the bee as an emblem of vice that can "take root" in the self. But whether flower or bee, freedom derives from the painful suppression of something inside us, and even (or especially?) the blind boy, undistracted by physical sight, can "see" this. Does the image suggest that we would have a clearer grasp of what is virtue or vice if we were not distracted by the enticements of the senses?

The poem Very published immediately before this, "Give me an eye, that manly deeds," implies a similar interest in sight, though the eye asked for here belongs to a companion or possibly a lover. The speaker seeks the inspiring or responding gaze of a woman to "kindle up with living fire" his soul to the performance of heroic deeds, someone who responds emotionally to beauty, who is sympathetic to "misfortune," and who humbly takes "reproof" from a "friend." This expression of a basic desire for friendship or intimacy (as though the poem is a kind of dating profile) is complicated by the strange emphasis on "eye," both in the opening phrase, "Give me an eye" and in the repetition of "An eye" at the beginning of each stanza. Perhaps it's this singular "eye," with its suggestion of a way of looking (a judgment) or a kind of seeing that gives what should be a search for a sympathetic soul an inquisitorial feel. Perhaps the phrase itself, "Give me an eye," which in its first iteration suggests a demand for sight, echoes meaningfully with the following poem's opening, "I saw a child, whose eyes had never drank / The cheerful light of heaven." The combination of the two poems conflates sight as companionship, inspiration, and judgment while questioning the ability of physical sight to determine true from false. The poems intimate both loneliness and anxiety, a persistent worry that pleasure is a kind of trap and that those we love, even as examples of virtue, may not be able to save us from ourselves.

In a letter written at the height of his prophetic intensity a few years later, Very described his early days at Harvard and his eventual conversion experience toward the end of his undergraduate career. A fuller reading of this rare and crucial document will come in due course, but for now we should confine our attention to the brief account of his time before this "change of heart" that occurred during his senior year.[1] "From what you knew of me before," Very explained to his friend Henry Bellows, "you are aware that my effort was ever to purify my soul and that I was so led by suffering to make this my constant work."[2] Though imprecise as to time and detail, particularly in terms of what he meant by his "suffering," this brief account of a young man existing in a tension between purity and impurity, spurred on by some emotional turbulence to see his struggle in these terms, provides a valuable context for these early poems. The poems themselves help clarify the nature of this "effort," specifically their attentiveness to death as it defines and clarifies the value of human desire. Similarly, the scrapbook's continual revisiting of *Childe Harold* implies a resilient attraction to the pursuit of pleasure or, perhaps more precisely, a recurring interest in the ambiguous glamour of the Byronic model. Passion and suffering seem to register as key terms, and despite the fairly consistent avoidance of personal revelation in both his poems and his notes, the undergraduate Very never seems to achieve the peaceful resignation and moral security he so often tries to extol.

As "Give me an eye" suggests, loneliness and the desire for a romantic companion likely fed this persistent, inner restlessness. Among the observant and penetrating comments of his former classmate Samuel Ward, perhaps the most surprising observation was that the "solemn" and "intense" Jones Very was known to have visibly struggled with his attraction to women:

> I began to hear strange stories of him from others. At first that he considered himself born for a great poet; to restore epic poetry. Then of unbridled passions overcome by monkish austerity and self-denial. [But he was so given to women {*crossed out*}] that he made himself a law not to speak (or look at women, I forget which).[3]

Ward's recollection was recorded in 1839, not long after Very attempted to convert him, and its timing makes it far more trustworthy than the reminiscences of classmates published in 1880 at the time of Very's death. It also has the mixed benefit of coming from the businesslike Ward, who was suspicious of Very's personality but perhaps also susceptible to rumor. Though Ward's account may suffer from a kind of reductive generality, there is no reason to believe it inaccurate. Of Very's poetic ambitions we have already seen examples in the notebooks; the seriousness of a young poet's intentions can well seem (and sometimes be) the pretentions of a novice. What his "unbridled passions" may have involved is more difficult to determine, but it suggests one or more intense attachments to local women. Whether these flirtations amounted to actual relationships or merely distant crushes, they were obviously strong enough to attract the attention of his classmates. And if they were in fact secretive, Very's "austerity and self-denial" would have been observable enough to elicit explanations for his behavior.

The suggestion of an erotic turmoil that Very fought to suppress—even as these early poems reconsidered moments from his life in which death sharpened the struggle against "vice"—gives us our first real exposure to the thinking that ultimately led to his erasure of will. As in "I saw a child," Very returns to the idea that the pursuit of pleasure leads to pain; pain in turn clarifies our bondage to the senses, to desire. Therefore, true freedom comes from not only crushing "vice" but relinquishing or erasing desire itself. We must kill the bee, in other words, and, at the same time, crush the rose, forever aware that the pain of one issues from the beauty of the other.

"Lines to _______ On the Death of His Friend," published at the end of Very's second year at Harvard, may be read as an extension of this developing antagonism to pleasure. Though a conventional elegiac lyric consoling a friend for the loss of a loved one, the form gives Very the chance to put on the steadying voice of resignation and spiritual comfort for a young man much like himself. The device of the poem is to argue that the grave contains only the body, not the spirit of the deceased. "She sleeps not *there*," the speaker proclaims, because if she did, "the wild flower's blush / Would kindle up her closed eye" (*CP* 24). The dead are no longer the "children" of the "Earth"; the soul has abandoned pleasure ("her joyous strain") and left behind "the spirit's robe" (*CP* 24).

Simple and familiar though the imagery is, the poem gathers tension around the opposition between soul and sense. Everything pleasurable derives from nature: "the gladsome Earth . . . where the wind's low whispering mirth / Steals o'er the silent graves" (*CP* 24). The soul, the true identity of the dead, cannot be in the grave because such natural beauty, the "sweet music's gush" (*CP* 24), would be impossible to ignore; the pleasures of the world are so great, in other words, that the dead cannot be close to them lest they be drawn back into life. The soul in its purity must be *elsewhere*: "The soul that drank her joyous strain / Has fled, forever fled!" (*CP* 24). The reassurance here underlines the stark division Very seems to bring increasingly to his own sense of life's competing allegiances: the attractions of the world are potent and fully acknowledged, but they have no analogue in spirit. Rather than seek a symbol in nature of the purity or fixity of the soul (as he did in "Lines Suggested by Seeing a Butterfly" the year before), here the soul is simply untouched, unmarred by contact with the world. It has escaped the senses entirely, leaving behind its faintly erotic trace in the "the wild flower's cheek of bloom" (*CP* 24).

✷ 10 ✷

The Uses of Faith, 1835

A clear chronology of Very's intellectual and spiritual development at Harvard is more difficult to establish than previous accounts have implied. As I have indicated, the notebooks, both the scrapbook and the commonplace books, contain very few dated entries and can only be speculatively organized by correlating quotations to Very's library charge lists. The poems can at least be dated by initial publication, but how long they may have gestated or how many drafts may have been built up and later discarded we have little idea. The vast majority of Very's surviving manuscripts appear to be fair copies; the presence of at least some marked-up texts makes it unlikely that he was in the habit of producing finished texts that required little or no revision. As a consequence, any narrative of growth or change must be considerably more hypothetical than one supported by regular correspondence, for instance, or by journal entries that are more personal and revealing than copied passages from texts. Even (or especially) the poems, which might be considered the most personal of these surviving documents, cannot be considered simply revealing on the surface: their subjects often seem caught in a complicated web of motives, from a young man's basic desire to *be a poet* to the very real need to explore deeply private but nevertheless thickly shrouded questions of Very's past life and future purpose.

A third category of evidence that offers a similar set of interpretive difficulties includes the essays that Very wrote in and around his years at Harvard. Here again the relationship between "public" utterance and private revelation poses significant problems, and we should be suspicious of attempts to flatten the surface of a student essay, for instance, into a transparent revelation of fully developed intimacies. Of Very's essays that do survive, the student work is limited to the two Bowdoin Prize–winning essays and the pieces written for end-of-the-year or commencement celebrations. The circumstances of their original composition are difficult to clarify. Were they written simply for these competitions or exhibitions? Did they emerge from class assignments or exercises? There is little doubt that they were designed to show off his rhetorical skills to their best advantage, but in this tangle of motives—some practical, some personal, others surely half-formed—how do we distinguish the transitory from the permanent features of his mind? This question, no matter how interruptive to a smooth narrative of development, should be kept at the front of any reading of this material.

The first of these essays, Very's Bowdoin Prize–winning production from the spring of 1835, provides a useful test case for such challenges. "The Practical Application in This Life, by Men as Social and Intellectual Beings, of the Certainty of a Future State" was awarded first prize for the junior class in 1835, earning Very $40. (He would win the first prize again the following year as a senior, making him the only student in the history of Harvard at that time to do so. Not even Emerson, who won consecutive seconds in his final two years, had achieved such an extraordinary honor.) And indeed, the essay itself reads as though it were built to impress, not merely in its eagerness to demonstrate the superiority of Christian to pagan culture but in its slightly overstuffed construction, range of reference, and stylistic showiness. Such signs of ambition, however, should not be taken as proof that the subject matter was impersonal or chosen cynically in order to impress the jury. (The topics were set by the examiners, and all three prizewinners in 1835 opted for the same theme.) In fact, the essay seems to be a working out, in a more formal space, of some of the tensions Very had been gesturing toward in his scrapbook and poetry.

As its long title suggests, the 1835 essay focuses primarily on the difference a faith in the specifically Christian afterlife makes in the "practical" lives of ordinary people. The classical past, Very argues, lacked a sense of punishment or reward to give permanent value to human actions. As a result, people craved glory or fame above all else; from this supreme earthly value, they derived their only practical sense of immortality. Rulers or governments then grafted this desire for greatness onto useful, higher ideals such as patriotism or courage, but too often the celebration of individual prowess led to the abuse of power and the vaunting ambition of men such as Alexander or Caesar. Classical glory was possible for only a few; those lower on the social scale lacked the power to achieve this kind of fame and so were excluded from access to the one quality that gave life value.

The absence of a morally determinant afterlife also tended to produce an empty sensuality, with too great a reliance on the pleasures of the senses and no real way to explain or justify suffering: "To the mind ignorant of a future life misfortune had no friendly meaning" (BPI 5). If there was no sense of reward or compensation for earthly suffering, in other words, God's actions in allowing it could seem cruel or capricious. For Very, the Stoics provided a clear example of the limitations of human reason in solving this dilemma: they attempted to control their emotional reactions to suffering with a noble resistance but were limited by the lack of a higher conception to explain that suffering. Their approach was superior of course to the Epicureans, whose "fear of death" rendered their minds "effeminate and vicious" (BPI 6). For the Epicureans, the "noble sentiments of soul are consumed, and an intense selfishness burns in their stead" (BPI 6).

What difference then does the Christian conception of the afterlife make in our everyday lives? For one, it provides a sense of "the beauty and sublimity of the world of thought," permitting us "to rise from that which is seen and temporal, to that, which is unseen and eternal" (BPI 7). As evidence, Very cites what he considers to be the pagan failure to perceive or celebrate the glory of nature: "Then, as now, the pages of nature spoke of the love and power of nature's God; but the human soul had forgotten the language, and it was not till again divinely impressed with the consciousness of its immortality, that it could hold sweet communion with the Eternal through the works of his hand" (BPI 8). The classical world offered little praise of nature because it lacked the ability to recognize nature as a manifestation of spirit. Christianity, by contrast, not only allows us to see the spiritual value of the natural world; it offers this glorification to everyone, not just the privileged or the powerful:

> Something was wanting—some motive, which should act alike on all, and maintain a direct and steady influence on every action of life—something, which while it should impart to the mind the highest sense of its own dignity, should also correct it by a virtue unknown to the heathens, humility, something, which should reconcile man to the dispensations of providence, and expand his narrow love of country into universal benevolence—something, which, while it was founded, not on the shifting sands, some momentary appearance of the ever-varying condition of man, but on that eternity, in the image of which man's soul was created—should be equally adapted to the lowest, as well as the loftiest intellect—something, in fine, which, while it should mingle with and purify the fountains of social life, should present in the far prospect the boundless fields of wisdom, the ever-extending regions of the Eternal Mind. (BPI 9–10)

Such elevated thoughts and language should not suggest that high-mindedness of this sort is too otherworldly or impractical to be of use.

Faith in an afterlife promotes a full and complete life and is "the only true solvent of the enigma of existence" (BPI 12). It allows us to see our lives, both the good and the bad, in proper perspective and gives us a sense of clarity and purpose that prevents any Hamlet-like indecisiveness. Instead, Christian minds (and perhaps Christian poets?) produce what is great and lasting: "We look upon the structures raised by such minds with the same wonder that we view the gigantic proportions exhibited in the remains of the eternal city, which seem to have been raised by might, which thought itself beyond the reach of chance, and independent of time" (BPI 16). Again, Very returns to the idea that these structures—or other products of this eternalized perspective—gather all who accept them; they are, in some sense, both more democratic and more ameliorative, consonant with general education and the improvement of the status of those, like women, who were diminished in pagan cultures. Given that women are the source of these early intimations of immortality, it's significant that the broad application of Christianity has made their spiritual education possible, just as it has made possible the expansion of the individual and the towering achievements of such figures as Newton and Milton.

As an undergraduate performance, the 1835 essay is undeniably impressive. Its sweep, its ability to propose a broad reading of cultural history, its range of reference and illustration all suggest a deeply thoughtful erudition that may be grandiose in its way but is nevertheless highly controlled and, if you will, intensely sober. The writing implies depths of feeling, to be sure, but the strong emotional upwelling is effectively disciplined by the clear commitment to humanistic study. Whatever gesture the essay may be making toward the exaltations of a life of faith, it suggests nothing antirational or in any sense mystical. Its only excess is an understandable weakness for the periodic sentence that here or there comes close to exceeding Very's considerable grasp.

But beyond what the performance has to tell us about Very's abilities or his professional hopes, there remain several important strands of developing thought of which we ought to take note. First, and most significant, the essay clearly addresses the struggle between "pleasure" and the resistance to the erotic ("vice") present in the poems from this period. If there is, in fact, a *personal* aspect to this very public performance, it's the formalization of this internal, spiritual agon. Second, Very grafts this contest of allegiances between body and soul onto a historical reading of the relationship between pagan and Christian culture. As someone who was simultaneously reading heavily in both classical and contemporary works, he seems here consciously and publicly (but perhaps also internally) to declare his allegiance not merely to faith but to a Christian poetic and the idea of the Christian poet. Third, the essay claims some degree of emotional solidarity with the spiritual lives of the less privileged, possibly as an echo of romantic poetics but more probably as an expression of his own tenuous economic and social position growing up in Salem—and now, as an older, less advantaged student. And finally, we can see him begin to imagine William Ellery Channing's concept of individuality as "genius" through an expression of a Christian conception of history. In other words, the development of faith in a meaningful afterlife, according to Very, made possible the individual achievements of men like Newton and Milton. The "effect" of faith, therefore, is to allow the emergence of the individual as a prophetic, apotheotic figure, the singular person who represents the highest form of achievement via faith's transcendent effect on daily life.

In all of these respects the 1835 Bowdoin essay helps clarify Very's intellectual and spiritual development. But was it meant to do more? Was it, as Gittleman argues, "the first of a series of formal and reasoned arguments which were privately directed to Lydia Very, designed to impress upon her the errors of her disbelief in the Christian God and afterlife" (EG 66)? The question depends, of course, upon our accepting as fact the contention that Lydia Very was—and had been from Very's earliest years—as materialistic in her beliefs as Elizabeth Peabody's 1838 letter indicates; and that her opposition to a spiritual life had led her son to shape his intellectual and emotional concerns around the overwhelming desire to change her thinking. But as with his earlier argument that Lydia had "never sung" a hymn or "never uttered" a prayer, the evidence for such a reading is startlingly thin. Even if we accept Peabody's description as defining for the entirety of Lydia's adulthood, there is no additional evidence to suggest that Jones "tacitly addressed" his 1835 essay to her or that the essay's argument against the human reliance on reason in the absence of faith refers to his mother in any way (EG 66). Gittleman is on safer ground when he claims that the essay "was a covert confession of the direction [Very's] life was taking, and a forecast of what, emotionally and religiously, still awaited him" (EG 67). Clearly, the struggle between sensuality and a life of suffering justified by the "certainty" of a heavenly reward reflected Very's documented internal struggle with desire. And Gittleman is largely correct in his assertion that the essay projected "Very's own intricate personality, reflecting private fears and repressed urges" (EG 70). But that it revealed Very's "ambivalent feelings toward his unrepentant mother" and his imagination of "the communion of Jones Very (the Son) with Jones

Very (the Captain Father)" in the afterlife suggests a theory that has outrun the facts (EG 70).

What the available evidence does point to is a young man of the highest poetic ambition who was "given to women" and yet determined to counter this earthly tendency with an intense devotion to both intellectual and spiritual labor. This is the "suffering" Very noted to Henry Bellows in his 1838 description of his early years at Harvard, and it is plausibly the pain he discussed in the 1835 essay that the idea of an afterlife would help explain or alleviate. (In 1838, he would also admit to Elizabeth Peabody that his "difficulty"—the one cherished worldly attachment he fought to relinquish—was "love of Beauty" [EP 222].) The essay allowed Very to formulate an argument in support of this resistance to sensuality, a way to convince himself that the path of renunciation was worth the difficulties it imposed on him—or, more specifically, that his decision to avoid all contact with women was justified. Did Lydia Very have an influence on all of this? It would be foolish to say no, and yet what that influence was, how it worked, how it evolved and whether it was specific or general, conscious or unconscious for her son, is impossible to know. A more plausible suggestion, based on what we do have as evidence, is that Jones Very sought to quell his own desires in light of the turbulence such feelings (or their disappointments) had brought to his mother's life. We do know that he witnessed her struggles when he was a boy; we know that the family lived in straitened circumstances, that they were poor at times and were possibly shunned as unwanted relations; we know that he was forced out of school as an adolescent to earn money for the family; we know that it was highly likely, based on his grandfather's aspersions, that his parents' marriage, though legally sanctioned, seemed questionable or false. It may well be that Very resented all of this and blamed his mother for its associated shame, but it's equally possible that he sympathized with her condition and simply vowed to avoid the pain that her headstrong, passionate ways had brought upon her. Like any son, he may have felt compelled to make up for what the family had lost, both in the form of a father-provider and in terms of economic or social position. Very's ambition would likely have been entwined with such a desire to prove himself, and in this sense he may well have wished to "save" his mother and his siblings by rising to a higher station or taking on a more exalted and morally uplifting role. In this respect, Gittleman's suggestion that the 1835 essay "contained the seeds" of Very's future "heresy" seems both perceptive and justified: "Nothing was impossible to a passionate young man who was confident that facts might be transfigured by strength of will and imagination, and that the world of nature was literally continuous with eternity" (EG 70). Like Newton or Milton, if he could so discipline his desires, Very might become what a poet or visionary should be: an individual susceptible to "that vast and boundless ocean outreaching before him . . . which raised his soul, and bore it onwards on the pinions of sublimity toward the throne of the Eternal" (BPI 22).

✷ 11 ✷

"Change of heart"

Very's final year as an undergraduate at Harvard was crucial in determining his eventual course of life. As he explained just a few years later to Henry Bellows, "In my senior year in college I experienced what is commonly called a *change of heart*, which tells us that all we have belongs to God, and that we ought to have no *will* of our own. It was a great happiness to me to find this change yet I could not rest in it."[1] At what point during the academic year this experience occurred is difficult to tell; there is no specific moment in his scrapbook or commonplace books that signals a significant shift of belief, and though attempts have been made to link the poem "My Mother's Voice" to this moment of transformation, there are few convincing signs of a "conversion" of any sort in Very's poems until later in 1838. The "change" itself may in fact have been less a conversion in the traditional sense than an intensification of faith in response to his struggles against sexual desire. The individual will had become the target, its erasure the key to freeing himself from the potential traps of worldly ambition and "Epicurean" sensuality. Evidence of Very's more general Unitarian faith is plentiful from the time of his entry to Harvard, but he himself seemed to understand that what occurred during his senior year signaled something more: an elevated sense of purpose and a specific, perhaps even idiosyncratic, interpretation of the relationship between the individual and God.

Understanding how Very came to this point is of course the object of any biographical study of his early years, but before we turn back to the notebooks and poems for clues to this essential pivot point, we should clarify what we can say with certainty of Very's religious beliefs before 1836. If we can accept that Lydia Very was, at the very least, critical of organized religion, then it may follow that she refused to include her children in any sort of religious education. It's true that the memoirs of her youngest daughter contradict this assumption at times, and it may be that Lydia was neither as intently antireligious as others assumed or that her opposition to religious education over the roughly thirty years of her children's upbringing was inconsistent. We do know that Very himself belonged to the North Church by the summer of 1836. In descriptions of the construction of the new "stone church" building, dedicated June 22, 1836, Very is credited with having written a hymn for the occasion and is noted as "a member of the society."[2] Was he a relatively new congregant, joining after his "change," when he came home for the summer following his graduation? Or had he been attending for some time, possibly since his studies with Henry Kemble Oliver, who, in addition to running a school, was the North Church organist?[3] Oliver was a magnetic leader devoted to strong moral and intellectual commitment (his effusive biographer describes the great man's brow as "Websterian—a beetling crag, underneath which his large, full-set and luminous gray eyes looked out with keen and kindly glance"), and it's hard to imagine the comparatively diffident Very resisting his council.[4] In a late remembrance, James Freeman Clarke gives us one of the few images of the younger Jones at worship: "In those days the most distinct & lasting impression his personal appearance made upon me was when from our pew in the opposite gallery to his in the old North Church, I used to see his tall form [hap?] along regularly every Sunday to a corner pew that overlooked the pulpit."[5] Clarke's memory is undated, but it does suggest, however indirectly, that Very attended services more often by himself than in the company of his family.[6] Did he at some point take it upon himself to join the North Church either against his mother's wishes or in quiet opposition to his family's lack of interest in organized worship?

Unable to answer such questions, we find ourselves restricted to the image of a young man, ambitious to succeed at Harvard, making use of what local connections he had among the intellectual elite of Salem, possibly moving away from a marginal and eccentric household toward a more socially approved role as minister or poet or some combination of the two. At the point Very acquired the discounted edition of Shakespeare from the auction house where he worked as a teenager we can see the path: an excellent student, of literary bent, impresses his employer; hoping to encourage him, the employer allows the purchase; Latin school follows; study with Oliver; other role models (significantly male) encourage belief and recommend church attendance. The full force of respected opinion, in other words—particularly the opinion of masculine and intellectual role models outside the family—likely channeled Very's ambition toward the establishment world of Harvard. And though we cannot document such a development in a precise sense, the plausibility of this portrait rests in part on Very's lack of a father (and thus his need for surrogate role models) and the difference between his own ambitions and those of his seafaring relatives. A young man in his position, economically and socially disadvantaged, possibly estranged from elements of his extended family, would naturally be on the lookout for opportunities and patrons who could provide a way into the intellectual world to which he was clearly suited.

That Very eventually joined the North Church indicates that his faith prior to his senior year at Harvard was likely both liberal and conventional. The landscape of official religion in Salem in the early decades of the eighteenth century was remarkably complex and offered a range of sectarian choices to anyone newly fired with belief. As New England Congregationalism fragmented over the latter half of the eighteenth century, Salem reflected the proliferation of Protestant groups that sprang from all points of the doctrinal compass. With the first wave of the Second Great Awakening in the early 1800s, the already evident split between strict Calvinists and those more liberal Congregationalists classified as Arminian (those who believed that a person's choices could effect salvation) was widened by the arrival of Methodists, Baptists, and Universalists. At the conservative end of the spectrum in Salem stood the Hopkinsian South Church (its version of Calvinism, derived from Jonathan Edwards, claimed that God's will was so absolute that even one's own damnation should be celebrated as evidence of God's sovereignty) and the Tabernacle, the large evangelical congregation that his grandfathers attended and that had emerged from an early split in the original Salem First Church in 1735. On the liberal side, the prosperous North Church, founded in 1772 from a practical (rather than doctrinal) division of the First Church, was steadfastly Arminian. By the early 1800s, it held the bulk of Salem's merchant elite and was on the path to what would officially become Unitarianism in the 1820s. Other than various smaller, sectarian groups that continued to sprout across the region, this left only William Bentley's East Church, a gradually diminishing congregation led in Very's childhood years by one of the most intellectually adventurous and theologically scandalous minds in New England.

There is no evidence to suggest that Very or his family had anything to do with the East Church or its freethinking minister, and we should register the fact that Bentley died in 1819 when Very was only six years old. But Bentley's presence in Salem during these formative years of Very's life is part of the wider context in which Lydia Very and her children matured as a family. When we consider the later accusations of atheism against Lydia, we should recognize that this was the vocabulary commonly used at the turn of the century to attack Deists or, as in Bentley's case, those who refused both the Trinity and the divinity of Christ—sometimes known as Socinians.[7] Bentley was an immensely learned product of the Enlightenment who used his pulpit to promote not only a civic-minded emphasis on good works but a generally Jeffersonian politics in opposition to the Federalism of the greater part of the Salem merchant class. Like Jones Very Sr., he was a Mason and a Republican, and his views may have been closer to those of Very's father than were the more conservative religious convictions of Samuel or Isaac Very.

For the young Jones Very, such a range of commitments and convictions must have been evident, both through an awareness of the bad blood within his parents' family and, more subtly, through a perception of his family's distance from mainstream convictions and communal feeling. In this context his decision to join the North Church, whenever it occurred, may be clarifying. With two grandfathers, each of whom was or had been a member of the conservative Tabernacle, and a mother who was associated with heterodox thinking, Very moved—or was convinced to move—onto the broad middle ground of socially approved Unitarianism. Henry K. Oliver himself had done something similar in the 1820s when he abandoned his own father's strict Calvinism in favor of the newly organized liberalism of Channing and company. In an 1851 speech to teachers at the American Institute of Instruction, Oliver described the kind of generalized Christianity he considered essential to an educated society. It avoided the narrow distinctions of sectarian polemic in favor of a broad, moral vision that restrained and directed a restless society toward order and improvement: in other words, those "principles, which all classes of Christians, with one consent, believe and acknowledge to be wholly essential, about which there never has been and never can be any dispute, and which therefore every Teacher, in any school, however miscellaneous may be the religious creeds of the parents of the attending children, may and must inculcate."[8]

Before the shift of feeling and conviction during Very's senior year at Harvard, his own beliefs likely had a similar, generalized foundation. If his ambitions were as much literary as spiritual and if Oliver was a primary model for this kind of life, he would have followed the more measured steps of liberal Christians whose spiritual commitments were closely bound to mainstream social status and cultural prominence. In other words, he was clearly on the path of the Unitarian intellectual by the time he arrived in Cambridge. Though his early journals indicate an interest in and even a devotion to Christian tenets, his approach is more often intellectual than emotional. Even his later reminiscence that he was a member "of a small society for religious improvement, which held meetings once a week, during most of [his] college course" suggests nothing out of the ordinary for a sober student who saw himself as a candidate for the Unitarian ministry. (In a later reminiscence, Very described this little group of worshippers: "During the senior year, Mr. Chisholm, Mr. West, and myself occupied the whole upper story of the third entry, in Holworthy. James was fond of singing, and often on Sabbath evenings he would enter my room and say: 'Come, let us sing some hymns;' and we spent many Sabbath evenings in singing together.")[9] In fact, the only element of his early intellectual makeup that suggests a possible opening to a more intense and emotional religious experience is his poetic ambition, particularly his desire to, as Ward noted, "restore epic poetry." This sense of a possibly exalted role—the ancient prophet combined with the modern or romantic poet—is present from the beginning of his scrapbook in early 1834, almost as a counterpoint to the more dutiful, rationalist, and classically grounded commonplace books that follow his studies. By 1836, Very seems to have merged these disparate identities: by eliminating his will, he could control his emotions or desires and, at the same time, gather their intensity for an expression of spirituality that transcended the constrained rationalism of liberal belief. This is another way of saying that his famous "mystic" phase, whose stirrings we can see as his undergraduate years come to an end, was less about religion per se than it was about poetry. Without the romantic conception of the poet as prophet, as voice or "genius," his idiosyncratic vision of messianic will-lessness is unlikely to have formed.

✷ 12 ✷

Scrapbook, 1835–36

The intellectual intensity and probing intelligence of Very's scrapbook for his final year at Harvard bear out his gradual intensification of purpose and movement toward the idea of the poet-prophet. From the end of his junior year in the spring of 1835 to his graduation a year later, he remained committed to a course of reading that reflected his deep interest in both the technical possibilities of the modern epic and the kind of poet who might best produce it. Though perhaps concentrated in the romantic poets and writers, particularly Wordsworth, Coleridge, Southey, Byron, and Scott, the citations often juxtapose modern to classical models, particularly Virgil. And Very's range of reference frequently takes in philosophical or moral commentators, including Sir James Mackintosh (*Dissertation on the Progress of Ethical Philosophy* [1830]), David Hume (*An Enquiry Concerning the Principles of Morals* [1751]), and Samuel Bailey (*Essays on the Pursuit of Truth* [1829]), as well as the sermons of the Unitarians Joseph Buckminster and William Ellery Channing. Once into the early months of 1836 we see passages from Madame de Staël's *The Influence of Literature upon Society* (1799), Goethe's *Faust* (1808, 1831), and the works of Milton and Shakespeare. But in the midst of this strong and consistent investigation of the modern epic impulse—carried out, it should be noted, in addition to much of his formal academic work—Very gave the majority of his attention to three works in particular: Wordsworth's anti-Byronic epic, *The Excursion* (1814), Henry Taylor's closet drama, *Philip Van Artevelde* (1834), and Alphonse de Lamartine's effusive, orientalist travelogue, *A Pilgrimage to the Holy Land* (1835). These three works, each in its own way shaped by the seductive disturbance of the Byronic idea, offer clues to Very's thinking as he moved closer to his conception of the romantic poet as the voice of unfiltered Spirit.

Very may have read *The Excursion* as early as November of 1834, when he first borrowed Wordsworth's *Poetic Works* from the Harvard library. However, the first extracts in his scrapbook correspond more directly to a second loan in April of 1835.[1] The timing suggests that the poem could have influenced Very's first Bowdoin Prize essay, particularly insofar as both pieces stress the value of faith and a conception of immortality as an antidote to skepticism and despair. More significantly, from the evidence of the scrapbook it seems clear that Very was most interested in book 4 of Wordsworth's poem; all but one of the many quotations are taken from the section subtitled "Despondency Corrected," long considered to be a direct response to the fashionable cynicism and despair of the Byronic hero.[2] A part of *The Recluse*, Wordsworth's projected spiritual autobiography, *The Excursion* is divided into nine books that follow the poem's speaker and his moral and spiritual guide, the Wanderer, as they visit local sights and converse with their inhabitants.[3] After an introduction that includes the tale of a young wife abandoned to penury and loneliness, the pair journey into the mountains to seek out the Solitary, "One who lives secluded there, / Lonesome and lost" (322), a former military chaplain who lost his wife and two children to disease, was inspired by the French Revolution to preach "The cause of Christ and civil liberty, / As one" (324), lost his faith to Enlightenment skepticism, and after a period of bitter wandering settled into a "mountain fastness" (322) to waste "the sad remainder of his hours / In self-indulging spleen" (326). The debate that follows makes up the bulk of the poem, in which the Wanderer and others attempt to clarify the value of faith and hope, particularly as it flows from "The breeze of Nature stirring in [the] soul" (392).

Of the twelve individual excerpts Very recorded from *The Excursion*, all but one come from book 4. Given his interest in Byron, including his attention to Pollok's *The Course of Time* and its anti-Byronic arguments, Very was most likely attracted to the Wanderer's attempts to counter the skeptical darkness of the Solitary's "despondency." Significantly, however, the initial passages he recorded are less censorious than sympathetic to the challenges of maintaining a connection to spirit in the face of mortal limitations:

> 'Tis, by comparison, an easy task
> Earth to despise; but, to converse with heaven—
> This is not easy:—to relinquish all
> We have, or hope, of happiness and joy,
> And stand in freedom loosened from this world,
> I deem not arduous; but must needs confess
> That 'tis a thing impossible to frame
> Conceptions equal to the soul's desires;
> And the most difficult of tasks to 'keep'
> Heights which the soul is competent to gain. (CB II, 40)

The possibility of relinquishment, later central to Very's conception of will-lessness, is here broached as the easier of two tasks: letting go of individual desires and establishing a spiritual existence unqualified by traces of material want. But grief, from which the Solitary suffers in particular, underscores the fragility of earthly existence, and only a strong faith in an afterlife can overcome its elevation of pain into egotism:

> For who could sink and settle to that point
> Of selfishness; so senseless who could be
> As long and perseveringly to mourn
> For any object of his love, removed
> From this unstable world, if he could fix
> A satisfying view upon that state
> Of pure, imperishable, blessedness,
> Which reason promises, and holy writ
> Ensures to all believers? (CB II, 40)

The challenge of physical versus spiritual desire, as it often does during this period of Very's life, once again evokes Byron; after this pointed passage from *The Excursion* on the ineluctable pull of body and earth,

> Too, too contracted are these walls of flesh,
> This vital warmth too cold, these visual orbs,
> Though inconceivably endowed, too dim
> For any passion of the soul that leads
> To ecstasy; and, all the crooked paths
> Of time and change disdaining, takes its course
> Along the line of limitless desires. (CB II, 41)

Very placed this mournful example from *Childe Harold* (3.14):

> Could he have kept his spirit to that flight,
> He had been happy; but this clay will sink
> Its spark immortal, envying it the light
> To which it mounts, as if to break the link
> That keeps us from yon heaven which woos us to its brink. (CB II, 41)

While *The Excursion* can certainly be understood as a corrective to the Byronic mythologizing of despair, it's notable that Very has here emphasized the problem more than the solution. The Wanderer may provide the kind of orthodox wisdom that represents the firm of faith and their connection to nature, but Very in these selections seems more sympathetic to the struggle between flesh and spirit than to the efficacy of a supposed remedy. Though he certainly appears to have sought out anti-Byronic texts, we should avoid assuming that the tension registered had been resolved or that the order of the excerpts negates the condition they describe. Far from vanquishing the Byronic influence during his last year and a half as an undergraduate, Very continued looking for ways to diminish or contain its power without entirely sacrificing its considerable attractions.

After the initial passages from *The Excursion* and their juxtaposition to Byron, Very introduced what can seem to be a third voice into this "conversation." At the same time that he was reading (or rereading) Wordsworth, he turned his attention to the "dramatic romance" *Philip Van Artevelde,* a closet drama by Henry Taylor published in 1834. Taylor was a well-connected friend of Wordsworth's and a significant figure as a poet, critic, and political theorist for much of the nineteenth century. His two-volume play about the Flemish burghers' rebellion was considered his major achievement as a poet; it was reissued in numerous editions and included in anthologies into the early twentieth century.[4] Its action follows the rise and eventual defeat of the Flemish leader, Philip Van Artevelde, in fourteenth-century Ghent. Less a tragedy than a study of virtuous and heroic character, the play follows Philip's sudden transformation from the self-indulgent son of a former leader to the just but firm head of the "White Hoods." After defeating Louis II, so-called Louis de Male, a French ally whose taxation policies had pushed the cities of Ghent and Bruges into open rebellion, Philip became regent of Flanders. Less than a year later his rebellion was crushed, and he was killed fighting the French at the battle of Roosebeke.

As he had been with Pollok, Very may have been drawn to *Philip Van Artevelde* as a possible model of large-scale contemporary poetic achievement. If in fact his early ambition upon arriving at Harvard was to renovate and restore the epic, a lengthy verse drama could have been an attractive form, a way perhaps to avoid the egotism of the romantic poem of experience while recovering something akin to Shakespeare's negative capability. Then again, though he recorded no passages from it, Very may have found Taylor's preface to the play provided the sort of anti-Byronic critique he had already begun to trace in *The Excursion.* In an effort to defend his "Historical Romance" against the potential "disappointment" of "the admirers of that highly coloured poetry" currently "popular," Taylor offered an extended attack on Byron's appeal to the "excitabilities of mankind" rather than to the "philosophical intellect."[5] Taylor was particularly interested in Byron's failure, as he saw it, to accurately portray human character: "There is nothing in them [Byron's 'portraitures'] of the mixture and modification,—nothing of the composite fabric which Nature has assigned to Man. They exhibit rather passions personified than persons impassioned. But there is a yet worse defect in them. Lord Byron's conception of a hero is an evidence, not only of scanty materials of knowledge from which to construct the ideal of a human being, but also of a want of perception of what is great or noble in our nature."[6] Taylor describes Byron's heroes as "creatures abandoned to their passions" and "beings in whom there is no strength, except that of their intensely selfish passions,—in whom all is vanity."[7]

This anti-Byronic focus on character offers the clearest connection to *The Excursion*, particularly to book 4, and gives us a firmer sense of Very's interest in the play as a study of a Van Artevelde's maturation and eventual firmness in the face of death. The many passages he copied into the scrapbook—more than from any other single work—closely track the arguments in Wordsworth's poem, with occasional added comments from Very linking Taylor's scenes to moments from book 4. For instance, after a brief extract from the second act of part 2 of *Philip Van Artevelde*,

> What then remains
> But in the cause of nature to stand forth,
> And turn this frame of things the right side up?
> For this the hour is come, the sword is drawn,
> And tell your masters vainly they resist.
> Nature, that slept beneath their poisonous drugs,
> Is up and stirring, . . . (CB II, 46)

Very glossed: "This passage may I think be traced to one of Wordsworth's . . . *Excursion*." He then copied the following from "Despondency Corrected":

> Therefore, not unconsoled, I wait—in hope
> To see the moment, when the righteous cause
> Shall gain defenders zealous and devout
> As they who have opposed her; in which Virtue
> Will, to her efforts, tolerate no bounds
> That are not lofty as her rights; aspiring
> By impulse of her own ethereal zeal.
> That spirit only can redeem mankind;
> And when that sacred spirit shall appear,
> Then shall our triumph be complete as theirs. (CB II, 46)

Van Artevelde may exemplify "what is great or noble in our nature," as Taylor implies in his preface, but he does so in notably romantic terms, standing "in the cause of nature," a phrase that echoes, as Very recognized, Wordsworth's "sacred spirit."[8] Indeed one of more remarkable moments in Taylor's play comes in the middle of part 2, act 5, when Van Artevelde, facing death, provides a brief intellectual autobiography more appropriate to the late eighteenth than to the fourteenth century. He describes a "philosophic youth" that makes no mention of Christianity or organized religious thought but instead follows a Lucretian or Enlightenment interest in "unmethodised matter" that results in a conception of the "circulating principle of life" and "Eternal mutability" (*PVA* 257–58). Very copied Van Artevelde's affirmation of organic continuance:

> But how far I may hold
> An interest indivisible from life
> Through change (and whether it be mortal change,
> Change of senescence, or of gradual growth,
> Or other whatsoever 't is alike)
> I question not of argument, but fact. (CB II, 47–48)

He then paired it with a passage from *The Excursion* (392) and the comment "The following remarks of Wordsworth are beautiful and true":

> Who thinks, and feels,
> And recognises ever and anon
> The breeze of nature stirring in his soul,
> Why need such man go desperately astray,
> And nurse 'the dreadful appetite of death'?
> If tired with systems, each in its degree
> Substantial, and all crumbling in their turn,
> Let him build systems of his own, and smile
> At the fond work, demolished with a touch; (CB II, 48; 392)

The distrust of "systems" is akin to Van Artevelde's relinquishment of individuated identity: both are products of the self divided from nature. What Very continues to underscore in his ongoing internal argument with Byronic sensuality is the possibility that thinking and feeling can lead him (back) to the recognition of the "breeze of nature stirring in his soul." Heroic and virtuous conduct in the face of death—to draw from Van Artevelde's example—flows not from the egotistical cultivation of despair and grief but from the recognition of change as a form of connection. Perhaps the self itself—with all its cherished but vain desires and particularities—can be discarded, can crumble at a touch, allowing thereby a union with spirit that enriches and liberates.

✷ 13 ✷
Lamartine

There is one other major presence in the scrapbook that has been overlooked in previous accounts of Very's development. At the beginning of 1836, in the midst of his final undergraduate year—the year of his "change of heart"—he began reading Alphonse de Lamartine's *A Pilgrimage to the Holy Land* (1835). Between the deep engagement with Wordsworth and Taylor several months before and this similar encounter with the author of *Harmonies poétiques et religieuses,* Very continued to read widely in romantic era texts, including Coleridge's *The Friend,* Sir Humphrey Davy's *The Consolations of Travel,* Edward Bulwer-Lytton's *England and the English,* Charles Lamb's *Essays of Elia,* and Goethe's *Faust.* But no work dominates the scrapbook of his senior year to the extent of Lamartine's *Voyage en Orient,* as it was originally titled. Only Taylor's *Philip Van Artevelde* yielded a similar number of extracts, and yet the play's consideration of romantic heroism in the face of death offers a less pointed model of poetic personality than does Lamartine's florid travelogue. If Very had indeed been on the hunt for a exemplar of the poet who combined Byronic sensuality with near-mystic, Christian-inflected romanticism, Lamartine must have been an exciting discovery. Only a year before the appearance of Emerson's *Nature,* the French poet's travelogue dramatized the sensibility of the poet-prophet as the site of a tremulous unity with the divine.

By the mid-1830s, Lamartine's reputation as a spiritually ecumenical poet who avoided overt moralizing was well established in the United States. The nonconformist Methodist minister Timothy Flint had praised Lamartine's *Méditations poétiques* in the *Western Monthly Review* in 1829, and Park Benjamin had published a translation of Lamartine's "Réponse aux adieux de Sir Walter Scott" in the *American Monthly Magazine* in 1833, referring to its author as "a living poet of France, perhaps the most popular, in our opinion the most inspired of his countrymen."[1] This inspiration included Martinist mysticism as well as a healthy dose of romantic sensationalism, concentrated around the idea of the poet as the destined voice of spiritual experience. According to Charles M. Lombard, Lamartine constructed his "Romantic notion of the poet's lofty mission" in part from Louis-Claude de Saint-Martin's idea that a "select group, the *hommes de désir* (men of desire), possessed extraordinary insights into the divine will and plan."[2] Lamartine would enact the role of the "poet-priest" who "communicates with a deity who transcends sectarian bounds."[3]

Though there are no references to Lamartine's earlier poetry in Very's notebooks, he may have been aware of the French poet as yet another figure who had engaged critically with Byron's fashionable cynicism. In his influential early collection, *Méditations poétiques,* Lamartine had scolded the scandalous but admired poet for his dark-eyed antiheroics:

> Thou, Byron, fill'st thy heart with sad despair:
> Thy perspective—evil, and thy victim—man;
> Thine eye, like Satan's, the deep abyss scans.
> Thy wandering soul from Heaven has strayed,
> Of Hope's bright charms thou seem'st afraid;
> In shades of darkness dost for ever dwell,
> For funeral dirges oft thy bosom swell.[4]

Similarly, the year after Byron's death Lamartine imagined him in "Le Dernier Chant du Pèlerinage d'Harold" as Childe Harold encountering Christ after death and failing to enter heaven. Like Pollok, Wordsworth, and Taylor, Lamartine, whatever else he may have offered Very in terms of acceptable sensuality, suggested a faith carefully wiped of most denominational fingerprints, a Christianity of sensibility rather than doctrine. More so than any of the others, however, Lamartine preserved an element of Byronic sensuality and self-indulgence, a relish of the exotic coupled with a soaring egotism that was limited, if at all, only by the faith implied in its Martinist mysticism.

Very's extracts from *A Pilgrimage to the Holy Land* suggest an interest in just such moments. He first copied two lines (with translation) from Lamartine's "Adieu: Tribute to the Academy of Marseilles," a poem composed as Lamartine and his family sailed "between the Isles of Pomegue and the coast of Provence":[5]

> Du bard voyageur le pain c'est la pensée,
> Son cour vie des ouvres de Dieu!
> The poet traveler—his bread is thought:
> His heart doth live upon the works of God. (CB II, 76)

Here is set an alternative in clear opposition to the Byronic wanderer: Lamartine will travel as a pilgrim of both "heart" and mind, but his emotions, rather than leading him toward cynicism, will form a direct connection to the divine. In a passage a few pages later that Very recorded, Lamartine elaborates on his version of romantic Christianity, noting that the "Christianity of sentiment" had become the "sweet soother of [his] thoughts": "If [truth] exists anywhere, it is in the heart, it is in the conscious evidence against which no reasoning can prevail." This "religion of the heart which associates so well with all the infinite sentiments of the soul" is what allows him to avoid "both doubt and endless dialogues which reason holds with itself" (CB II, 77).

As though in demonstration of this emphasis on feelings, Lamartine rarely misses an opportunity in his narrative to elaborate, often to excess, on experiences both significant and trivial. Underlying all is the assumption—more often implied than expressed—that as a poet his own sensibility acts as the focal point for spiritual illumination. In several passages copied by Very, the importance of instinct, genius, and the special role of the poet—language and thematic material that anticipates Emerson's soon-to-be famous *Nature*—provides clear evidence of Very's interest in the idea of a poet-prophet who sees into the spiritual architecture of creation:

> There are harmonies between all the elements, as there is a general one between material and intellectual nature. Each idea has its similitude in a visible object which repeats it like an echo, reflects it as in a mirror, and renders it perceptible in two ways—to the senses by the image, to the mind by the thoughts: it is the infinite poetry of double creation! Men call it combination:—combination is genius—creation is but thought under a thousand forms—to combine is the art and instinct of discovering words in this divine language of universal analogy which God alone thoroughly understands, but of which he permits certain men to discover a portion. This is the reason why, in the early ages, the prophet, or sacred poet, and the poet, or prophet profane, were everywhere regarded as divine beings. They are, at the present day, looked on as madmen, or, at least, as useless beings—that is logic! . . .
>
> We ask ourselves, What is instinct? and we find it to be reason itself—innate reason, reason unreasoned upon, reason such as God made such as man finds it. . . . Genius also is instinct, and not logic or labour. The more we reflect, the more we find that man has nothing great or beautiful appertaining to him that comes from his own power or will; but that all that is supremely beautiful comes from nature and

> from God. Christianity, which embraces all, has comprised it from the beginning. The first apostles felt in them that immediate action of the divinity, and exclaimed at once, "Every good and perfect gift cometh from God." (CB II, 78 [Lamartine's original emphasis; the final sentence is scored by Very in pencil in both margins])

In terms of romantic thinking, there is nothing unique or necessarily new in Lamartine's ideas. By 1835, this vision of the poet as, in Wordsworth's formulation in *The Prelude,* "a chosen son" who "had come with holy powers / To apprehend all passions and all moods" had largely run its course in Europe.[6] In the United States, however, such a post-Kantian emphasis on instinct and inner divinity had to wait for full attention until September 9, 1836, when James Munroe and Company released the anonymous book *Nature,* and what came to be called Transcendentalism sprang from the head of liberal Unitarianism. For Very, who may at this point be said to be on the same trail as Emerson, Lamartine offered a way to think about the prophetic spirit that was romantic but still identifiably Christian; his "sacred poet" is both elevated as the chosen vehicle of the "divine language of universal analogy" and absorbed into the role of apostle who feels "the immediate action of the divinity."[7] Such "divine beings" can of course be "looked on as madmen," but this is the price of the poet's prophetic identity, which is, it bears repeating Lamartine's phrasing, will-less: "The more we reflect, the more we find that man has nothing great or beautiful appertaining to him that comes from his own power or will; but that all that is supremely beautiful comes from nature and from God."[8]

Of the many remaining passages Very took from *A Pilgrimage to the Holy Land,* more than a few reflect the French poet's thoughts on the sites of Greece, Lebanon, and of course the Holy Land itself. In some instances, these encounters lead to wider considerations of history and the development of cultures, similar to the kind of analysis we see Very's 1835 Bowdoin Prize essay and the essays of his senior year, particularly the essay on epic poetry. For instance, Lamartine critiques modern "realist" biblical scholarship in an ecumenical argument that Very preserved: "What matters it whether the Jordan be a torrent or a river?—whether Judea be a steril [*sic*] rock or a delicious garden ?—whether this mountain be only a hill, or the whole kingdom only a province?—Men who combat and quarrel on such questions are as insensible as those who fancy they have overthrown a creed of two thousand years, when they have laboriously sought to give the lie to the Bible, and a blow to the prophecies" (CB II, 80). In a similar vein, he takes on the Homeric Question, siding with those who see the poet as "a single man" rather than a "race of Homeric men" responsible for the poems. And, most significant, he offers a version of the historical inevitability not only of Christianity but of an increasingly abstract, nonsectarian Christianity that is temperamentally close to Unitarianism:

> The idea of the unity of God impressed on the human mind is a better thing than these dwellings of marble [the Parthenon], where only his shadow was adored. . . . All nature her self presents a worthier temple. As religions become spiritualized, religious structures fall; Christianity itself, which peculiarly claims the Gothic, leaves its venerable cathedrals and churches to sink almost into ruins. The thousands of statues of her saints and demi-gods descend by degrees from their aerial niches round the cathedrals. Christianity, in fact, itself undergoes transformation, and its temples become more naked and simple as it throws off the superstitions of the dark ages, and resumes more fully the grand idea which it propagated upon earth—the idea of the one God, manifested by reason and adored by virtue. (CB II, 92)

This emphasis on the gradual occupation of the "grand idea" does not exclude the role of Christ, however. In a remarkable episode that Very read but did not copy, Lamartine describes his conception of a modern Messiah to the eccentric fortune-teller and English mystic, Lady Hester Stanhope.[9] Deliberately following in Byron's footsteps, Lamartine had arranged a visit to the once-wealthy and decidedly eccentric Stanhope at her "grotesque assemblage of ten or a dozen small cottages" near the Lebanese town of Joun.[10] Dressed in a "white turban" with a "purple colored woolen fillet," a "yellow cashmere shawl, and an immense Turkish robe of white silk, with flowing sleeves," the somewhat decayed but sibylline Stanhope declared that Lamartine had been guided to her by "good, powerful, and potent stars" so that God could "enlighten [his] soul."[11] "Do you believe that the reign of the Messiah is arrived?" she asked the French poet.[12] The dialogue that follows this dramatic question is both exalted and absurd, a contest of egos in which Stanhope prophesies the advent of a modern "redeemer" for the "social, political, and religious world," and Lamartine (im)modestly implies his fitness for the role:

> I believe then in a Messiah, not far distant from our epoch, but in this Messiah I do not see Christ, who has nothing to add to the wisdom, the virtue, and truth that he has already taught us; but I see him whom Christ has said should come after him. That holy spirit always acting, always assisting man, always revealing to him, according to the time, and his wants, what he ought to know and do. Whether this divine

> spirit becomes incarnate in a man or in a doctrine, in a fact or in an idea, matters little; I believe in it, I hope in it, and more than you, my Lady, I invoke it.[13]

The episode as a whole has the effect of anointing Lamartine—via however doubtful a source—as the romantic poet-prophet he already believes himself to be. Stanhope prophesies that her visitor will play a significant role in the future of a great drama: "France alone has a great mission still to accomplish, in which you will participate"—a prediction about as accurate as any vague forecast can be, given Lamartine's eventual role in the events of 1848.[14]

For Very, this scene may or may not have been important to his own developing ideas about the role of the poet or the possibilities of romantic spirituality. But just as Lamartine's language at times anticipated Emerson's so does the French poet's description of "divine spirit" here foreshadow Very's eventual accounts of his own will-lessness. "That holy spirit always acting, always assisting man," as Lamartine claims, "always revealing to him, according to the time, and his wants, what he ought to know and do" is only a step away from what Very will soon claim is the speaking force that governs not only his words but his impulses and even his physical movements. Believing that this "divine spirit" can be "incarnated in man" may have been an airy gesture of sorts to Lamartine, but it would soon become a life-altering, even life-threatening article of faith to the young man in the midst of a "change of heart."

✷ 14 ✷
Poems, 1835–36

Very's poetic output between the summer of 1835 and his graduation a year later is limited but important. The erotic turmoil of "Lines Suggested by Seeing a Butterfly Sculptured upon a Tomb" and "Pleasure" (from late 1834) had yet to dissipate and indeed may have intensified as Very pushed diligently toward the conclusion of his undergraduate studies. As he himself later admitted in his letter to Henry Bellows, his conversion experience during his senior year convinced him to renounce his personal will, but this ardent resolution was merely the beginning of a three-year war: "It was a great happiness to me to find this change yet I could not rest in it. The temptation I always felt to be in thought and as long as I had a thought of what I ought to banish I felt that some of my will remained. To this I was continually prone and against it I continually strove."[1] For this reason in part it's difficult to date with any precision Samuel Ward's account of Very's "unbridled passions" and his subsequent renunciation of women, except to posit that the spiritual resolution likely came in response to the problem of sexual desire during or after the summer of 1835. The poems of the following year show clear evidence of Very's continued attempts to overcome (or perhaps release) the lingering presence of the sensual. They also help solidify the sense that for Very the term "will" meant more than mere inclination; it was his general sign for the life of desire, particularly as it evoked sensual beauty or the prospect of personal romantic fulfillment.

This notation of desire's presence runs through many of the poems of this year, even when the ostensible subject seems to point in a different direction. "North River," for instance, written in July 1835, suggests the sort of poem a student might write on a summer home from school. From the backyard garden of the house on Federal Street Very could meditate upon the quiet waters of the tidal river and measure his changed response to a familiar scene. But the view offers less nostalgic consolation than a disquieted metaphor: the calm surface of the water is akin to the stillness of the spiritual self, but that "glassy breast" whose reflection blends "leafy groves" with the "blue expanse of upper skies" vanishes in turmoil when the wind kicks up (*CP* 25). In the poem's final stanza, the delicacy of spiritual sight is no match for intense emotion:

> But if upon the soul's calm face
> Dash the rough blasts of passion wild,
> Oh! then how soon is fled each trace
> Of all that in that vision smil'd. (*CP* 25)

Similarly, "Eheu! fugaces, Posthume, Posthume, Labuntur anni," written shortly after, pushes a fairly conventional imitation of Horace's famous ode ("Ah Posthumus, they fly away our years") toward one of the very few overt registrations of the erotic in all of Very's verse. While Horace's poem offers no consolation to the all-destroying power of death and time, Very exempts "Love's sweet voice" that lingers in the soul past the loss of "All that here may charm the heart" (*CP* 26). Time cannot erase the imprint of the penetrating gaze:

> As the years are gliding by me,
> Fancy's pleasing visions rise;
> Beauty's cheek, Ah! still I see thee,
> Still your glances, *soft blue eyes.* (*CP* 26; original emphasis)

Passion's strife may scatter the smoothness of the surface of the river/ soul, but here the memory of desire's moment stops the "gliding" of time. The verse itself slows, and the repetition and pun on "Still" indicates that what lasts, what stops as if frozen, is the timeless intervention of eros itself. "*Soft blue eyes,*" each word not only underscored but metrically stressed—these three charged sounds suggest the kind of passion held in by Very's tremulous self-control.

Similar, if less intense, moments occur in "A Withered Leaf—Seen on a Poet's Table" and the two versions of "Memory," both from the late autumn of 1835. The "brown and wither'd scroll" (*CP* 29) of the leaf might suggest a conventional meditation on death, but this memento mori becomes instead a remembrance of greener seasons: "Voices sweet of Summer hours, / Spring's soft whispers murmur by, / . . ." (*CP* 29). Like the "*soft blue eyes*" of "Eheu! fugaces," such "soft whispers" suggest a feminine presence even when attributed to the earlier month's birds ("Feather'd song from leafy bowers" [*CP* 29]). "Memory" too recognizes time's passage but insists on the heart's holding to "Words it cannot hear again— /

Echoes of remember'd pleasure, / Torturing there for aye remain" (*CP* 32). If "soft" can be understood as a shorthand for feminine beauty in Very's verse, the remembered "look" may stand for the experience of a desire that resists fading:

> Ling'ring looks around it hover,
> Mock with thoughts of former joy;
> Visions it can ne'er recover,
> Looks that time can ne'er destroy.

The heart may be mocked by these memories, but the memories themselves, these moments of seeing and being seen, are powerful enough to outlast the "too soon" fading that the poem otherwise describes. In the second version of "Memory," the subject matter is the same but the tone less tentative: the uncertain "may" of "the *heart* too fond may treasure" yields to "But the heart,—how fond 'twill treasure" (*CP* 33), and the mockery of the first version is cast aside for a greater definiteness: "There still dwell the looks that vanish, / Swift as brightness of a dream" (*CP* 33). While the first version is more poignant and effective, the second seems intent to master the feelings it reveals. Between the two we can sense the continued tension Very registered in his letter to Bellows: how to banish the temptation of a thought (or memory) when the thought itself recovers the moment of temptation?

Fortunately, so clenched a poetic could be relieved at times by more occasional or public-facing subjects. During the same period, Very wrote poems on the popular subject of King Philip, the Wampanoag sachem Metacomet, who became the figure for the heroic, "vanishing" Indian; and on the log recovered in 1775 by one Captain Warrens, "the master of a Greenland whale ship" (*CP* 36). Neither offers much beyond the expected pathos of its subject, though together they add interesting notes of silence and constraint to these months when Very appears to be looking for ways to speak of or still those "thoughts" he connected to willfulness. The inability of Philip to recover his lost family or silence their voices that "rise / In murmurs soft as summer's stream" falls into the same register as the lost ship's bodies "mailed in ice," a stillness unbroken by the speaker's repeated demand that the dead "Speak," or "Say!" what led to their icy voicelessness (*CP* 34, 36).

These notations of impotent or failed utterance are all the more suggestive for their proximity to the important poem "My Mother's Voice," written during the same month or so in the spring of 1836. I have discussed the biographical implications of this poem earlier, and though I disagree with Gittleman's contention that it presents a knowingly false portrait of Lydia Very as a conventional believer, I do find its emphasis on the intervention of a maternal voice into moments of desire deeply meaningful at this point in Very's development. The question of the mother's beliefs here is less important than its simultaneous disruption of and compensation for the erotic:

> It comes, when thoughts unhallowed throng,
> Woven in sweet deceptive song,
> And whispers round my heart;
> As when, at eve, it rose on high;
> I hear, and think that she is nigh,
> And they depart.
>
> Though round my heart all, all beside,
> The voice of Friendship, Love had died;
> *That* voice would linger there; (*CP* 38; original emphasis)

The "thoughts unhallowed . . . / Woven in sweet deceptive song" suggest precisely the sort of "temptation" Very refers to in his letter to Bellows. These attractions are "sweet" but "deceptive" and associated with "the heart," with "Friendship, Love." The poem suggests that because the speaker's mother represents an original purity or holiness connected to childhood, her voice disperses these immoral desires and leads him back to that earlier innocence. But the lines also, and somewhat more disturbingly, imply that the mother prevents friendship and love from forming. The mother's voice "whispers round my heart," not only supplying a comfort against loneliness but supplanting the thought of those who might become friends or lovers. Is there some faint echo of the ice-bound lives and "cold lips" of the dead sailors on "The Frozen Ship"? Are the "*soft blue eyes*" of "Eheu, fugaces" or the "soft whispers" of "A Withered Leaf" here banished by the mother's enfolding presence?

✳ 15 ✳

"The Torn Flower"

Among Very's surviving manuscripts, unpublished until 1980, is a small set of poems from 1835–36 that provide a less veiled, more dramatically complete image of his attempts to register and suppress his erotic or romantic desires. One of these, "Lines to _______ on the Death of His Friend," I have discussed above (it has been speculatively dated as early as June of 1835), but the remaining three may have been written at any time during Very's final year as a Harvard undergraduate or just after. The poems came to the Houghton Library in 1972 via the collection of Charles Stearns Wheeler, a poet and friend of Very's, who, along with Samuel Tenney Hildreth and Charles Hayward, was an editor of *Harvardiana*, the student magazine begun in 1835.[1] Though one year older than these classmates of Henry Thoreau, Very counted them among his few close friends, particularly Hildreth, whose poems Very copied into his own scrapbook in the spring of 1836 and to whom Very dedicated his 1836 Bowdoin Prize essay. Hildreth grew up in Gloucester, and at Exeter and Harvard seems to have followed a trajectory of poetic interests similar to Very's. A memorial article written in response to Hildreth's early death in 1839 notes that he "spent much time in studying the works of the great masters of song. Byron was at one time the 'god of his poetical idolatry,' and undoubtedly exercised a great influence in the formation of his intellectual habits. More lately Coleridge, and Wordsworth, charming him by the healthy and natural tones of their music, won him a great degree from the fevered page of Byron."[2] How the poems associated with Very's romantic life ended up with Wheeler is impossible to say, but their presence among his papers (as well as Very's own copying of Hildreth's work) indicates Very's participation in this small circle of poets more clearly than anything else in his archive. In fact, it seems likely that had these poems not remained among Wheeler's papers, they would not have survived the vigilant pruning of manuscripts most likely carried out by Very's sisters after his death in 1880.

The three poems, "I murmur not though hard the lot," "The Torn Flower," and "The Portrait," taken together suggest a simple dramatic plot: the speaker in each, through some failure of faith or excess of passion, has lost (or foresees losing) the affections of a beloved. In the first, he mutes his complaint at seeing "that fond smile" given to "another" (*CP* 47) and refuses to request relief from his pain:

> I would not ask those eyes to turn
> And shed their light upon my woe;
> To cool these throbbing veins that burn
> With passion's hottest maddest flow. (*CP* 48)

The speaker's burden of "sorrow" and "grief" is a "mountain weight" he will not impose on the joyous life of his lost love, though there is no "purer love" or "holier flame" than his:

> 'Twill burn, when yon bright beaming star
> With kindred light has ceased to glow,
> As pure in yon blue heaven afar,
> As in its earthly shrine below. (*CP* 48)

In a poet more accustomed to using this kind of language, such images would be neither surprising nor particularly effective. For Very, however, who so rarely admits to or releases the enormous energies that drove his academic and poetic ambitions, this "throbbing" passion seems all the more powerful and genuine. Here Ward's recollection that Very, despite being "monkish," was "so given to women" gains an added clarity. The renunciation in the poem, the dramatized refusal to speak (itself a kind of speaking), brings us to a familiar point of tension: the purer the passion, the "holier" the flame, the less likely it can be embodied in an "earthly shrine." Sublimation is not merely a result of such a passion; it is requisite.

"The Torn Flower" continues this elongation of the moment of loss by adding the threat (if not the actual fact) of destructive violence as a result of passion. Ostensibly a description of the speaker regretting his angry destruction of a path-side flower, the poem registers a metaphorical "tearing" of the loved one's "sweetness," suggesting again a relationship now past redemption:

> I tore thee—thou who looked so sweet,
> And shed thy fragrance at my feet;
>   I tore thee in my wrath;

Scattered thy sweetness to the wind,
Nor left one look of love behind
    To smile upon my path. (*CP* 48–49)

For a personality as apparently passive as Very's, the opening line is remarkably brutal: whatever scene, real or imagined, the poem describes, it registers the potential for an uncontrollable outburst of violence and its irreparable result: "I mourn too late! Ah! ne'er again / Shall visit thee the small-dropped rain" (*CP* 49). The speaker regrets his outburst of willful passion, more destructive than the "storms that filled the troubled sky" (*CP* 49). Twice, he registers this emotional outburst as a form of madness ("I madly crushed thee as I past"; "My heart's mad passion tore" [*CP* 49]), thereby establishing the harmful effects of impulse stirred by emotions seemingly less natural than those of the more forgiving storm: "Then I would learn me of the storm / To spare thy bright and tender form" (*CP* 49).

Very's response to such rare, violent outbursts is less often the mourning expressed in "The Torn Flower" than it is a kind of reactive stillness. In "The Portrait" this impulse emerges first as a formal constraint; it's only the second sonnet printed in *The Complete Poems*, after "The Winter Bird," though the dating of these poems is not precise enough to determine which was written first. Given the eventual importance of the sonnet to Very's ecstatic poetics, we should note what is clearly an overall tightening of poetic form from early 1836 through the autumn of 1837, from which point he writes nothing but sonnets for roughly two years. "The Portrait" suggests that at least part of his attraction to the form was its ability to constrain or bound his unruly emotions; if the will was to be erased or eliminated, as Very later claimed, it had first to be gathered, contained, calmed.

As in "The Torn Flower," "The Portrait" records a moment of regret, a sense of loss caused by the inability of the speaker to love purely and thereby merit "That smile whose sweetness words in vain would tell" (*CP* 53). Having lost that attention, he imagines stopping time itself, holding a moment in which the loved one is reflected in a mirror:

Would that I might stay those features as they pass,
Where beauty seems as if she loved to dwell;
And chain that smile upon the fickle glass,
. . . .
Or fix thy glance with all its heaven of blue,
The evening star that floats its azure through! (*CP* 53)

With echoes of the "*soft blue eyes*" of "Eheu, fugaces," the speaker responds to loss with an intense effort to "stay," "chain," and "fix" that "heaven of blue" upon himself, as though by stopping the movement of events he can thereby still his excessive passion. But his implied unfaithfulness makes such emotional repose impossible: "But no—the spot where I would bid them rest / Is all unworthy they should linger there" (*CP* 53). Because his "bosom" is not "The faithful mirror of a loving heart," it cannot provide a permanent "home" for this blue, fugitive glance (*CP* 53). It's as though the energy of desire is too mobile, too volatile to provide the restful presence that "a loving heart" should offer.

The failure in "The Portrait" to find a solution to the problem of passion—to combine love and desire with "rest" and faithfulness—returns us again to the final stanzas of "My Mother's Voice." Here it's the mother's voice that sounds "when thoughts unhallowed throng, / Woven in sweet deceptive song, / And whispers round my heart" (*CP* 38). Is it the mother's looming presence that makes the lover in "The Portrait" "unworthy" of the sweet smile and blue eyes (the glance associated with Venus, "the evening star" [*CP* 53])? We know very little of the actual biographical events that may have underpinned Very's turn against his own attraction to women. (Bartlett relates a family rumor that Very had been engaged to "a young woman of Salem" who backed out because of his "illness"—a possible but wholly unconfirmed story that seems at odds with the timeline of Very's "madness.")[3] But given Lydia's powerful and strongly emotional connection to her children, it's certainly plausible that her son found it difficult to supplant her affections with romantic attachments of his own. Enough evidence exists to tell us that the young Lydia had been a woman of passions and that her son had observed the effects of these turbulent emotions, both good and bad. "My Mother's Voice" may give an early sign of a retreat from Very's own desires, a way to calm his inner storm by declaring his faith to Federal Street rather than to "The voice of Friendship, Love" (*CP* 38). His ultimate renunciation of will, slowly clarifying during this period, included more than a sacrifice of romantic desire to spirituality. No matter how instinctively, Very may have hoped to escape his mother's emotionally troubled life by sublimating his erotic desires (for were these not the source of such trouble?) into a higher, quieter devotion—both to Lydia ("*That* voice" that lingers there) and to the inhabiting voice of the Holy Spirit.

✷ 16 ✷

Spiritual Freedom

Graduation ceremonies for the class of 1836 took place on August 31. The Dunkin Rebellion expulsions had reduced the cohort to thirty-nine; the average class size for the 1830s was fifty-six. The program was nevertheless long and heavy on scholarship and high-mindedness. There were over a dozen speeches, including a "salutation" delivered in Latin, a discussion on the comparative virtues of the "enlightened and ignorant classes," a lecture on the poetry of Milton, a "dissertation" on famous literary places, and, next to last among the undergraduate presentations, Very's "English oration" on the topic of "individuality."[1] Though there is little evidence to suggest his state of mind at the time, his high level of achievement and prominent part in the ceremony speak for themselves. He had already delivered an oration entitled "The Heroic Character" at that year's student exhibition and had won for the second year in a row the coveted Bowdoin Prize for his essay "What Reasons Are There for Not Expecting Another Great Epic Poem?" Members of his family from Salem would certainly have been present at the commencement exercises, and Very's pride in his academic achievements, an important ingredient in his general self-conception, was likely reaffirmed by the day's ceremonies.

The speech itself indicates significant developments in his emerging conception of the role of the poetic or prophetic self. Unlike "The Heroic Character," which did little more than condense the 1835 Bowdoin essay's argument for faith in immortality, "Individuality" begins with a direct critique of worldly "ambition" and selfishness.[2] True individuality, Very argued, is not expressed by the desire for wealth or power but by the internal, moral resistance to desire: "The heroism of Christianity is not so much in the outward act, as in the struggle of the will to control the spring of action."[3] To this end he cites *Paradise Lost,* arguing that both Adam and Satan can be considered heroic characters by virtue of their "free agency, which Christianity has developed": "But that which renders

Adam the hero of the poem makes Satan still more so; for Milton has opened his breast of flame, and bid us gaze on passions of almost infinite growth burning with intensest rage."[4] This internal struggle is the fight for "spiritual freedom": "Men should learn to contend for it as their fathers did for civil rights. Let them look upon it as something to be won by their own free exertions—something which no fathers [*sic*] hand can bequeath."[5] Freedom thus becomes a liberation from material or worldly desire, while "individuality" is that liberty wrested from the human will (impulse, urge) and given over to the "great law of our moral nature"—"the law of duty."[6]

The commencement audience may have heard little more than a conventional plea for Christian self-regulation in the twenty-three-year-old's quiet exhortation. But the text suggests that Very allowed himself to release at least some of the pressure that had been building in his thinking and writing during his final year. If indeed, as he later explained to Bellows, he had hoped during his senior year to eliminate his own will but struggled to do so, then "Individuality" may well be the most public revelation of his spiritual conversion and its attendant struggles. The description of Satan in particular suggests a glimpse of the "breast of flame" and "passions" of "intensest rage" that simmered behind Very's tight and conscientiously smoothed exterior. Would family members in the audience, if they were listening, have guessed the connection? Would they have found the reference to fathers who contended for "civil rights" to evoke the senior Jones Very, whose active life and death as a result of war made such a contrast to the son who was now battling his own desires to reach a purer sort of freedom? The occasion offers at the very least the added weight of significance for a young man who had pushed so relentlessly to achieve this moment. If Very did intend to give an account of himself to those who meant most to him, what better moment than in a speech that otherwise consecrated his success and marked him as a member of the Harvard establishment?

As important as "Individuality" is to Very's development, its relative brevity suggests that it too was compressed out of more expansive material and thinking. In fact, both of Very's senior speeches owe a great deal (to the point of repeating specific passages) to the much longer and more fully developed Bowdoin essay "What Reasons Are There for Not Expecting Another Great Epic Poem?" As with his 1835 prize essay, the topic was set by the college (all three winners wrote on the same theme), but the subject also seems fortuitously tailored to Very's pressing interests. The sophomore who, as Ward later reported, thought himself destined to "restore epic poetry" was now an astonishingly well-read and sophisticated senior who had spent a great deal of time considering not only the essence of the classical epic but its relationship to a modern, Christian culture devoted to an opposing set of values. His close attention to the larger works of Dante, Milton, Byron, Pollok, Taylor, and Wordsworth had convinced him that the classical epic's emphasis on heroism and worldly fame had yielded to the modern drama of the internal, spiritual crisis. This genre of "Christian epic" had reached its apex in *Paradise Lost,* which had transferred "the scene of action from the outward world to the world within" where the "modern poet" contends "with motives of god-like power."[7] As in "Individuality," what was now important was the internal struggle of the singular self; to whatever extent the modern poem could be "epic," it would seek to record or respond to this spiritual agon. It would be about "individuality."

Aside from the impressive range of Very's reading and his sometimes penetrating historical sense, "What Reasons" suggests a writer still reaching for a way around or through the models he has so carefully examined and at least partially discarded. Without directly promoting the work of any modern poet, Very concludes his historical contrast of classical and Christian epic with an indirect brief for the romantic, "sentimental" (in Friedrich Schiller's sense of self-reflective), and egocentric poetry of inwardness.[8] He quotes Coleridge to remind his audience that even Milton's apparently externalized moral battle could be gathered into the romantic conception of self: "'In the *Paradise Lost*—indeed in every one of his poems—it is Milton himself whom you see; his Satan, his Adam, his Raphael, almost his Eve—are all John Milton, and it is a sense of this intense egotism that gives me the greatest pleasure in reading Milton's works. The egotism of such a man is a revelation of spirit.'"[9] More appropriate to the age, however, is Lamartine's complaint that the traditional epic is now impossible; the "only epic poem the mind, in its present stage, is capable of giving," Very explains, is "the expression of [Lamartine's] feelings" about this impossibility.[10] For Very this inability to produce a modern epic along classical lines is not a failure but a victory: "We rejoice in this inability—it is the high privilege of our age—the greatest proof of the progress of the soul—and its approach to that state of being where its thought is action, its word power."[11]

This conclusion to what is arguably the most important essay Very wrote as an undergraduate at Harvard suggests a personal declaration. He may not have been able, as he told Bellows, to "rest" in his conviction that the personal will must be eliminated, but he had formed a conception of poetry and its relationship to action that could express this restless self-contention. We can perhaps hear a strange reverberation both backward and forward in the final line of this essay, with its subtle echo of *Hamlet* and its paradoxical celebration of the passive. The transformation that

Very experienced during his senior year has led him up to the idea that the only kind of heroism possible, indeed the only true form of action, is stillness. It's impossible to know whether he had yet formed some sort of plan for the writing of over four hundred sonnets; indeed, for someone who came to Harvard with the idea to restore the epic he left little evidence of ever attempting a long work of any sort. But his thinking about the modern epic opens the possibility that his astonishing production of spiritual sonnets could be said to fulfill its requirements as he has described them, to show not only the epic of true individuality, as Very defined it, but the approach of the soul to that "state of being where its thought is action and its word power."

But before he reached these years of crisis and exaltation, there was a future to be addressed and entered. After the festivities of commencement, followed even more dramatically by the elaborate celebrations for the Harvard bicentennial one week later, Very had time to visit Salem and take perhaps a more permanent sense of leave from his mother's garden on Federal Street. He had been appointed tutor of Greek and would begin studies in the Divinity School with an eye toward the ministry. The various roles of scholar, poet, and student would now blend with teacher, minister, and moral or spiritual adviser. His pace of reading, writing, and study would only intensify, married to higher purposes and deeper pursuits. In two poems ("Home of my youth!" and "Haunts of my youth farewell!") likely written during this period of transition, he effectively says goodbye to Salem and to his youthful past. Neither work is remarkable, though it is notable that they equally express strong feelings for everything touched by or associated with "home." There are no tensions, no subtle criticisms; he admits that others might find more beautiful places or fail to appreciate Salem's quieter loveliness, but "yet all to me are / Beautiful, round all alike O home thy / Charm is thrown I love you all" (*CP* 51). Again, he places himself beside the North River, comparing the pull of its current to his "love of home." The feelings are conventional, if always underlined by Very's characteristically soft vehemence. For all his intellectual and spiritual intensity in his final year as an undergraduate; for all his private notation of a moral crisis, his struggle against desire, against the urgency of a formidable will; for all his complex sense of purpose and ambition (both spiritual and literary), the high-minded conception of his potential as a poet, a visionary—Very remained attached, emotionally and imaginatively, to his mother's world.

The complexity of this entanglement should not be underestimated. It cannot be plausibly argued that he simply opposed Lydia and her Federal Street passions. Within an extraordinarily strong devotion to what she was and what she had been through, there is, however, an uneasiness and ambition to wriggle free from her embrace. His strong attraction to women had somehow been checked, not only by his own sense of emerging purpose but, quite plausibly, by the shadow of Lydia's intense attachments. These passionate impulses he had begun to translate into something safer, higher, stranger: a desire to overstep desire, somehow to remake his poetic ambition into a kind of spiritual ladder that would lift him above Lydia's turbulence and grant him an internal stillness. The strategy he had already partially determined was a kind of paradox: through an act of extraordinary, conscious will he would erase volition itself; impulse, so dangerous when guided by eros, would become solely an expression of spirit, a stainless inspiration breathed through his every movement. In this sense his mother's own "breast of flame" might be sanctified, redeemed in a sense but even more so quieted, made safe from its moral brinkmanship.

11

"Flee to the mountains!"

⁕ 17 ⁕

"Part or particle of God," 1836

A few days after its publication date of September 9, 1836, Jones Very purchased a copy of Ralph Waldo Emerson's *Nature*. Inside the dark blue cover embossed with the texture of vines, he wrote his name and beneath it "Sept. 1836 / Salem." Having graduated from Harvard at the end of August, he had likely seen the author of this anonymous little book walking in the long procession of alumni that snaked across the campus during the bicentennial celebration on September 8. That evening Holworthy Hall, where Very had lived for the past three years, glowed with celebratory lighting, the number "200" shimmering in the central windows while around it the luminous shapes of stars, diamonds, and pyramids cut through the leafy shadows.[1] A few hours before at Willard's Hotel in Cambridge, Emerson had met Henry Hedge, George Putnam, and George Ripley and formed what became known as the Transcendental Club. Determined to counter the perceived stultification of intellectual life at Harvard, the group devoted itself to the "new ideas" emerging from the blend of German philosophy and English romanticism. More of an intellectual "clearinghouse, full of yeast and ferment," according to Robert Richardson, than a "social clique," within a few years the club would include—alongside Henry Thoreau, Margaret Fuller, Bronson Alcott, Orestes Brownson, and others—the newly emerged poet, essayist, and visionary Jones Very.[2]

For the moment, however, Emerson's freshly printed essay was the most overt signal that something new was in the air. Very probably purchased it while he was back in Salem enjoying a break before he returned to Cambridge as the newly appointed tutor in Greek. That he seized upon the volume so soon suggests an awareness of the already controversial figure from Concord and the possibility that Very could have attended one of Emerson's many lectures that year in Salem or Cambridge.[3] Given the relatively small student and faculty body at Harvard and the even smaller community of Unitarian intellectuals in the area, it would hardly be surprising for someone as steeped in contemporary philosophy and poetry as Very to be eager to plunge into the heady, oracular prose of *Nature*. His own progress toward a conception of the poet-prophet had brought him to what might seem the perfect pitch of readiness, almost as though he and Emerson had been following the same set of signs or hidden signals that led to this momentarily shared vista.

Very's copy of what became known as the manifesto of Transcendentalism shows signs of damage from years of storage but still retains the now faint pencil marks of his reading.[4] His engagement with the text was serious and intent: there are over thirty-five scorings or comments, and they cumulatively confirm the impression made by his student notebooks that he was among the more sophisticated and well-informed readers of his era. But what more specific conclusions can we draw from these generally spare marginalia? As with the selections recorded in his commonplace books, it is possible to infer areas of interest, perhaps of agreement or subtle critique. Very recorded no obvious objections to Emerson's ideas (only a few corrections to a misprint and a misquoted poem), and for the most part he appears merely to reaffirm or partially rephrase some of Emerson's main points. The essay's central concern—that a unifying, divine spirit runs through all of nature and is available to the solitary, perceptive individual—would be congenial to the young man who had imbibed his mother's passion for flowers and gardens. And there are moments, such as this lightly scored passage from chapter 5, where we can sense a strong sympathy for Emerson's ascending vision in the terms of Very's Federal Street experience: "The river, as it flows, resembles the air that flows over it; the air resembles the light which traverses it with more subtile [*sic*] currents; the light resembles the heat which rides with it through Space" (LA 30).

In chapter 6 ("Idealism"), Emerson's attempt to address the "noble doubt" of skepticism (our "impotence to test the authenticity of the report of [our] senses") appears to have stretched or slightly troubled Very's sympathies (LA 32). He responded to the definition of the skeptical dilemma by writing at the bottom of the page, "We do not doubt the senses or the authenticity of their report, but we reject and refuse [their?] impression which they take." Very seems unwilling to recognize or engage with the controversial formulation of Bishop Berkeley (that all we can know is made up of the ideas formed from experience rather than experience itself) in the way that Emerson clearly did; he also seems less interested than Emerson in developing a full-throated expression of the spiritual possibilities of philosophical idealism. Instead, he reaffirms an underlying point of Emerson's overall project: that what is important is how we fail to "see" what we see; that we pull away from the divine source of experience and retreat into the shelter of custom.

The emphasis in chapter six on perception drew more attention from Very's pencil than any other part of the essay. He tracked Emerson's description of the ways point of view changes the world we experience, and marked the essay's reassurance that "whilst the world is a spectacle, something in [man] himself is stable" (LA 34). Recognizing this distinction between the spiritual and the perceptual brings with it, according to Emerson, "a pleasure mixed with awe; . . . a low degree of the sublime," a delight communicated "in a higher manner" by "the poet" (LA 34). In other words, the visionary with the "imperial muse" (in this example, Shakespeare) can show us particulars in a variety of unusual lights, but he preserves the unity of experience somewhat like the physicist whose single formula, in another passage marked by Very, "carries centuries of observation" condensed from the "cumbrous catalog of particulars" (LA 34, 37). While attempting to retain a childlike love of experience (Very underlined the immersive "I expand and live in the warm day like corn and melons"), Emerson offers a balance between "watching" and "doing," to which Very responded in the margin beneath: "The greatest men always believe in the stability of Nature and truth of its law" (LA 38).

What could be considered the culmination of Very's response to *Nature* appears in chapters 7 ("Spirit") and 8 ("Prospects"), where his markings suggest a reaffirmation of divine unity and its power to inspire. In response to the opening paragraph of chapter 7, where Emerson reaffirms that nature, no matter its uses or effects, in the end "always speaks of Spirit," Very echoes, in the margin beneath: "God is one. There is but one good" (LA 40). Concerns about philosophical skepticism now cast aside, Very marked a series of passages that seem to fall neatly into his well-established interests in the will and its relation to the influx of spirit:

> As a plant upon the earth, so a man rests upon the bosom of God; he is nourished by unfailing fountains, and draws, at his need, inexhaustible power.
>
> . . .
>
> The world proceeds from the same spirit as the body of man. It is a remoter and inferior incarnation of God, a projection of God in the unconscious. But it differs from the body in one important respect. It is not, like that, now subjected to the human will. Its serene order

> is inviolable by us. It is, therefore, to us, the present expositor of the divine mind.
>
> . . .
>
> It [the fallen world] is kept in check by death and infancy. Infancy is the perpetual Messiah, which comes into the arms of fallen men, and pleads with them to return to paradise. (LA 41, 42, 46).

Given that Very was at the beginning of his roughly two-year struggle to control and eventually eliminate his will, these annunciatory sentences from what can be considered the highest expression yet of the "new thought" may have helped shape his eventual self-conception. The sense of stillness in the first passage, of the elimination of effort that solicits an "inexhaustible power" from the "bosom of God," picks up the ideas of inspiration and incarnation in the second, where the connection between will-lessness and divinity finds expression in nature ("a projection of God in the unconscious"). Because nature is not "subjected to the human will," it is the "present expositor of the divine mind," a declaration whose implications are not here fully explored by Emerson but are possibly suggestive to Very of a redemptive state of being. It can be difficult then not to feel the link to Emerson's summative description in chapter 8 of "infancy" as "the perpetual Messiah," a reiteration of his earlier praise of childhood ("In the woods too, a man casts off his years, . . . is always a child.") but with the added hint that the messianic state (the role of the prophet-poet Very has been pursuing) is one that approximates a childlike oneness with nature (LA 10).

For some, *Nature* may have seemed to burst suddenly from the comparative torpor of New England Unitarianism, but it's unlikely that Very found it altogether surprising. The young poet who had read Lamartine's *A Pilgrimage to the Holy Land* would have guessed at the links between the French poet's Martinism and Emerson's soon-to-be notorious "transparent eye-ball." *Nature*'s first sentence would have tipped him off to the strong similarities: just months before, he had marked Lamartine's declaration that "past time is the sepulcher of generations that are gone; we should respect it, but we should not wish to bury ourselves and live in it." Now he opened the book to read in Emerson's ringing prose: "Our age is retrospective. It builds the sepulchers of the fathers" (LA 7). Having walked each day for most of the last three years through the quiet graves and gardens of Mount Auburn Cemetery, Very would have had no difficulty visualizing the contrast between the tombs of the past and the natural oneness of the present nor would he have been likely to balk at Emerson's momentary play at mysticism:

> Standing on the bare ground,—my head bathed by the blithe air, and uplifted into infinite space,—all mean egotism vanishes. I become a transparent eye-ball; I am nothing; I see all; the currents of the Universal Being circulate through me; I am part or particle of God. The name of the nearest friend sounds then foreign and accidental: to be brothers, to be acquaintances,—master or servant, is then a trifle and a disturbance. (LA 10)

For the senior who had discovered in the months before reading this that "all we have belongs to God and that we ought to have no *will* of our own," this moment of replete nothingness, of absorption into the "currents" of a divine stream, may well have confirmed his deepest intuition about his future (*CP* lvi). Did Emerson intend this scene of ebullient mysticism as a knowing exaggeration verging on satire? It hardly matters; irony made no part of Very's constitution. As though in anticipation of just this moment, he had highlighted Lamartine's assertion that "man has nothing great or beautiful appertaining to him that comes from his own power or will; but that all that is supremely beautiful comes from nature and from God" (CB II, 78). If Very did not yet think of himself as "part or particle of God," he certainly understood what Emerson likely meant by "mean egotism." Intent on shedding just this slough of petty desire, of leaving behind the wanting self, Very had only to find what might be considered both the language and the discipline of Emerson's "nothing."

✷ 18 ✷

The Messianic Moment

Despite the detailed record of his later, personal encounters with Emerson, we have only Very's marked copy of *Nature* to indicate how important the essay and its author may have been to his development prior to 1838. When he met Emerson for the first time in April of that year he carried the little blue book with him to request an autograph. On the blank page just beneath his own signature, Emerson wrote: "Har[mony] of Man with Nature must be reconciled with God." Whether this aphorism was meant to be a summation of the essay or a gloss on Emerson's first conversations with his intense younger friend, we can sense a certain consecration of Very's sympathy with the intellectual moment Emerson had come to embody.

That moment, caught and condensed in Emerson's poetic prose, marked the American conjunction of several strands of thought: Continental philosophy and theology (particularly German), translated and Anglicized by writers like Coleridge and Carlyle; the ideas of the Swedish theologian Emanuel Swedenborg, specifically his doctrine of correspondences between nature and spirit; the discontent of liberal Unitarians with what they considered their denomination's tepid spirituality and devotion to empiricism; and various threads of reformist thought, including new ideas about education and social improvement sometimes incongruously mixed with a powerful drive toward individualism. This mildly intoxicating brew made up most of what later came to be known as Transcendentalism, but in 1836 it was still a loose set of ingredients straining toward a synthesis that, arguably, it never completely achieved.

For Very, Transcendentalism was less a movement to which he belonged than a development of thought parallel to his own. Both could be said to have split, by varying degrees, from the Unitarian stem, sharing deeper roots that tapped European as well as early American soils. *Nature* itself, as many commentators have explained, brings into conjunction not only

German idealism, English romanticism, and liberal Unitarianism but a deeper line of American radical belief, beginning with the antinomianism of Anne Hutchinson and including those mystic traces that run through Quakerism, the Great Awakening sensationalism (and panentheism) of Jonathan Edwards, and the millenarian prophecies of early nineteenth-century sects like the Shakers, the Millerites (Adventists), and the Mormons. Even as early as 1836, Very could be said to have both direct and indirect relationships to this same radical tradition.

As he explained to Henry Bellows in 1838, Very's "change of heart" in 1836 came to him as the realization that "all we have belongs to God and that we ought to have no *will* of our own" (*CP* lvi). The terms may have been synthesized from his wide range of reading: in addition to his deep engagement with romantic and epic poetry, Very borrowed books on theology, moral philosophy, and biblical exegesis from the Harvard library. During his senior year he checked out Robert Southey's *The Book of the Church,* Isaac Taylor's *Natural History of Enthusiasm,* Charles Tilstone Beke's *Origines Biblicae,* the works of the seventeenth-century Anglican divine Jeremy Taylor, Richard Whately's *On Some of the Difficulties in the Writings of St. Paul,* and the tracts of William Ellery Channing. Though Channing was then and continued to be an important source for Very's understanding of his Unitarianism, it's Taylor's account of unusual or heretic "enthusiasms" that stands out from this somewhat eclectic selection of texts. Given Very's description of his own deeper conversion experience during these months as well as his eventual movement into what many considered the "madness" of his claims of divine influence, Taylor's careful account of what constitutes "healthful" or "heretical" versions of spiritual intensity offers a fascinating guide to the era's understanding of potentially mystic experience—and a tantalizing source for tracing Very's connections to the radical prophetic tradition.

Originally published anonymously in 1829, *Natural History of Enthusiasm* had a sudden and unexpected success; it went through multiple editions rapidly, perhaps an indication of just how common religious intensity and claims of special revelation had become as the Second Great Awakening began to wind down. Somewhat in the spirit of Jonathan Edwards's accounts of revivalist conversions in *A Treatise Concerning Religious Affections* (1746), Taylor's analysis is less interested in debunking spiritual transformation than in separating true from false manifestations of divine influence. "The belief," Taylor wrote in his preface, "that a bright era of renovation, union, and extension, presently awaits the Christian Church, seems to be very generally entertained. The writer of this volume participates in the cheering hope; and it has impelled him to undertake the difficult task of describing, under its various forms, that FICTITIOUS PIETY which hitherto has never failed to appear in times of unusual religious excitement, and which may be anticipated as the probable attendant of a new development of the powers of Christianity."[1] Though clearly sympathetic to the millenarian spirit of the times, Taylor implies a general suspicion of claims to special revelation, perhaps even a weariness at the proliferation of sects and apocalyptic predictions—a tone that could help clarify the eventual reaction, in Salem and elsewhere, to Very's messianic pretensions.

Despite this critical stance, Taylor's descriptions of genuine spiritual enlightenment are remarkably close to Very's language in the letter to Henry Bellows. In section 3, "Enthusiastic Perversions of the Doctrine of Divine Influence," Taylor begins by establishing a vision of divine sovereignty reminiscent of Jonathan Edwards: "Apart from the divine volition, perpetually active, there can be no title to existence; and in the moment which should succeed to the cessation of the efficient will of the First Cause, all creatures must fall back to utter dissolution."[2] This conception of unqualified divine power or sovereignty over all creation forms the central claim of Edwards's Calvinism, and versions of it can be found throughout his work, particularly *Freedom of the Will*, on which Taylor published a detailed essay in the *Presbyterian Review* in 1831.[3] Though there is no direct evidence that Very read Edwards, his encounter with Taylor's version of these ideas at the beginning of his senior year is important. Taylor's clear exhortations often anticipate Very's later language of will-lessness: "There can be therefore no particle of virtue or of happiness in the universe, any more than of bare existence, of which God is not the author. . . . But the healthful action of the soul consists in love to God, and free subjection to his will. Virtue is nothing else in its substance, nothing else in its cause. As in him we live and move and have our being, so also it is he who 'worketh in us to will and to do' whatever is pleasing to himself."[4] Very's eventual struggle not only to "banish" his will but to overcome even the awareness of that banishment by 1838 led him to speak, in his poetry, of a "new birth" and in his oracular "Epistles to the Unborn" of a genuine, "natural" birth "by which you recognize God as a parent."[5] Though conventional to a degree, the particular intensity of Very's application of this concept of conversion may have come from similar claims in Taylor: "The return to virtue and happiness is termed a resurrection to life; or it is a new birth; or it is the opening of the eyes of the blind, or the unstopping the ears of the deaf; or it is the springing up of a fountain of purity. . . . . On the one hand, it is evident that a change of moral dispositions, so entire as to be properly symbolized by calling it a new birth, or a resurrection to life, must be much more than a self-effected reformation; for if it were nothing more, these figures would be preposterous, unnecessary, and delusive."[6]

Though Very's unique conception of will-lessness should not be reduced to Calvinist or even Edwardsian terms, Taylor's simplification (or domestication) of Edwards's concept of divine sovereignty provides a useful link between Very's developing thought in 1836 and the radical tradition of direct revelation and "inner light" that reaches back to Anne Hutchinson. During the First Great Awakening it was common for so-called Old Light critics of New Light revivalism to connect what they considered the emotional excesses of the moment to earlier antinomian heresies. As Philip Gura explains, the English evangelist George Whitfield was consistently attacked as "antinomian" for his "insistence on the necessity of a 'New Birth'" through conversion.[7] The charge allied with what Gura calls "another of the most frequent complaints about the revivalists: that they encouraged antinomian behavior—that is, a belief that Christ actually lived in and guided the saint."[8] Very would eventually be assailed in much the same terms when he began to make his startling claims of direct influence via the Holy Spirit—all of which points to the shared conception of direct revelation that threaded its way through this radical tradition as well as the familiar counterargument that such extreme individualism in spiritual experience disrupts and potentially destroys not only civil order but religious community.

As David D. Hall has explained, the Quaker "inner light" tradition in America emerged from the same soil as this more general form of antinomianism: both stressed the absolute primacy of direct spiritual revelation, the Quakers moving ever closer to a true American mysticism.[9] Very's attraction to and admiration of the Quakers is well established in his surviving papers. A notebook entry from the 1840s contains an extract from the dying speech of James Nayler, a seventeenth-century English Quaker who once reenacted Christ's entry into Jerusalem on Palm Sunday by riding horseback into Bristol while his followers unfurled garments on the muddy ground in front of him. (Nayler was subsequently convicted of blasphemy and branded with a *B* on his forehead.) Very also copied out in full "The Remarkable Vision of Thomas Say," an account of the illness of a young Episcopalian who had joined the Quakers in Philadelphia and subsequently underwent what would now be called an out-of-body experience. Stricken with pleurisy, Say fell into a coma and later claimed to have seen heaven and witnessed the deaths of three men, two white and one black, the latter an enslaved person named Cuffee "who belonged to the widow Kearney," one of Say's neighbors (CB III, 146). "Though the negro's body was black," Say explained, "yet his soul was clothed in white. This filled me with greater joy than I had felt before; as it appeared to me a token of his acceptance. I was not, however, permitted to see him fully enter into rest; for as I was about to enter in myself, I came back into the body again" (CB III, 144–47).

Very read Say's story in the *National Anti-Slavery Standard*, the abolitionist paper founded by Lydia Maria Child and her husband, David Lee Child. Given his own abolitionist convictions, the choice of reading is not a surprise, but it and the extract from Nayler cast light on the shared ground between Very's will-less spirituality, Quaker aspirations to inner divinity, and the politics of American antislavery activism. If we add to this potent mixture the sporadic but widespread tendency toward millenarianism characteristic of the Second Great Awakening, we can begin to capture in wider view the context in which Very's unique version of direct revelation developed. Though messianic pretension is to some extent built into prophetic Christianity, the period of Very's youth and early adulthood bristled with sects devoted, in one way or another, to the idea of the end of the world or the return of the Messiah. Shakers, Mormons, Millerites (Adventists), and the Society of Universal Friends, among others, each proffered some version of the messianic idea, and even those more secular groups devoted to social reform and utopianism could be said to participate in related hopes of a millenarian age of righteousness.

In her study of late eighteenth-century women preachers, Catherine A. Brekus notes the frequency of messianic claims in the years leading into the Second Great Awakening: "In the 1790s, for example, a man named Nat Smith [from Medfield, Massachusetts] made the startling announcement that he was God. According to Ezra Stiles, 'Nat Smith proceeded to assume & declare himself to be the Most High God and wore a cap with the word GOD inscribed on its front. His Great Chair was a Holy Chair & none but himself must sit in it.'"[10] Similarly, a pipefitter named Shadrach Ireland from Charlestown wore his own God cap and told his followers he was "perfect and immortal," a claim not entirely disproved, some believed, by Ireland's own death.[11] New Light figures who emerged out of Quakerism, like Mother Ann Lee and the self-styled "Public Universal Friend" Jemima Wilkinson, were less blunt in their pretensions to divinity, but they allowed their adherents to believe something close to it at times. In 1808, two decades after her death and five years before Very's birth, Lee's followers openly proclaimed her to have been the "second incarnation of the spirit of Christ," the Messiah specifically reborn in the form of woman and mother.[12] And Wilkinson, after a near-death case of typhus, began telling people that she had died and was now reborn as pure, prophetic spirit, no longer the young woman Jemima Wilkinson but a genderless instrument of God to be called the Public Universal Friend.

Though there is no evidence to suggest that Very was influenced by either of these women, their unusual claims of transcendence do share elements with his eventual conception of self-erasure and immersion in the divine. In her embrace of a rigid doctrine of celibacy, Lee was likely responding to her harrowing experiences with childbirth, while Wilkinson's attempt to move beyond the binaries of gender has often been read as an escape from all forms of sexuality. Very's struggle to renounce his will (and overcome his attraction to "Beauty") suggests a familial connection of sorts, a desire to follow the antinomian or New Light embrace of inwardness as an antidote to sensuality. Isaac Taylor was clearly correct: there was a need to distinguish false from true prophets, but such skepticism as might have been applied to the Shakers, for instance, was clearly not enough to prevent others from finding their own sanction for individual divinity in an era of spiritual saturation.

In other words, revivalism, perfectionism (including moral self-regulation), and sectarianism were in the air, if not in the water and soil as well, from the "burnt-over region" of upstate New York, throughout New England, and into parts of the South and West. And though most of Very's contacts with such ideas may have come through antislavery publications or religiously affiliated reform groups, he likely brushed against adherents of one or more of these groups in Salem or elsewhere. The area of north Salem where he grew up, including the intersection of Boston and Essex streets known as Buffum's Corner, held a number of Quaker families. In fact, Caleb Buffum was among the earliest Quaker settlers in Salem, and his descendant David Buffum built a new Quaker meetinghouse on Essex Street in 1847. And of the two family members, outside his sisters, that Very mentioned in his will, his cousin Nancy (Manning) Southwick was a longtime member of the Second Advent Society, a Millerite congregation organized in 1848.[13]

"I am part or particle of God," Emerson had written in 1836.[14] In whatever way he conceived such a union of self and spirit, this declaration contains a trace of the same impulse that drove other prophets of the time to reimagine the return of Christ, the reincarnation as a form of individual perfectionism. For Very, whose "effort was ever to purify [his] soul," the language of romantic self-exaltation in *Nature* thrummed with the deeper bass of biblical prophecy, as though the secularized Christology of someone like Lamartine (the Christianity of sentiment and subjectivity) could clench itself to an objective miracle, a true apotheosis. Very was still, and would continue to be, a poet, but it was left to him to imagine a kind of poet who could entwine the romantic individualism of Byron or Wordsworth with the self-erasure of the divinely possessed prophet or the quiet waiting of the Quaker.

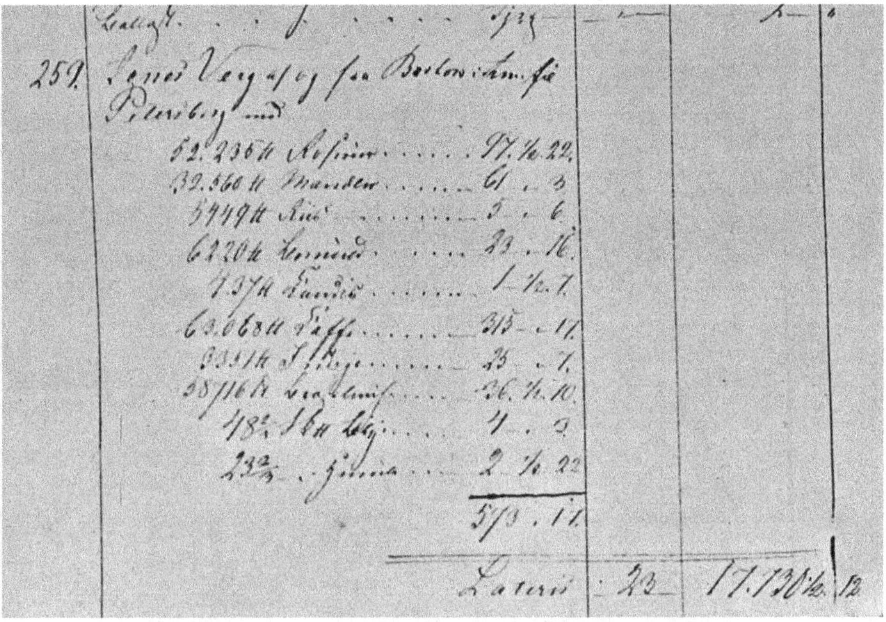

FIGURE 1. Sound toll register for the *Aurelia* (May 1823).
Danish National Archive. Photograph: Sound Toll Registers Online.

FIGURE 2. Unknown photographer, *Portrait of Mrs. Jones Very* (1844). Daguerreotype. Gift of the Estate of L. A. Very (1906). Photograph: Courtesy of the Peabody Essex Museum. Photography: Ani Geragosian and Chris Stepler.

FIGURE 3. Unknown artist, *Portrait of Captain Jones Very* (early nineteenth century [likely pre-1820]). Pastel. Gift of the Estate of L. A. Very (1906). Photograph: Courtesy of the Peabody Essex Museum. Photography: Ani Geragosian and Chris Stepler.

FIGURE 4. 154 Federal Street, Salem, Massachusetts. Home of Jones Very (ca. 1890). Photograph: Courtesy of the Phillips Library at the Peabody Essex Museum.

FIGURE 5. North River, Salem, rear view of Federal Street (ca. 1860). The Very house is at the far right. Photograph: Courtesy of the Library of Congress.

FIGURE 6. Lydia Very, *Cornelia and the Gracchi* (1808). Metallic thread, silk, and paint. Gift of the Estate of L. A. Very (1906). Photograph: Courtesy of the Peabody Essex Museum.

FIGURE 7. Jones Very (1837). Photograph: Courtesy of the Phillips Library at the Peabody Essex Museum.

FIGURE 8. Unknown photographer, *Portrait of Washington Very* (mid-nineteenth century [likely pre-1853]). Daguerreotype. Photograph: Courtesy of the Peabody Essex Museum. Photography: Ani Geragosian and Chris Stepler.

FIGURE 9. Barrell Mansion, McLean Hospital (ca. 1850). Photograph: Charlestown Lantern Slides, Boston Public Library.

FIGURE 10. Jones Very (ca. 1860). Photograph: Photography Collection, The New York Public Library.

✵ 19 ✵

Mr. Tutor Very

The Divinity School at Harvard was founded officially in 1816. Though the college had long been the primary training ground for Congregational ministers, there was no specific, professional program for ministerial training until Congregationalism split into orthodox (Calvinist) and liberal (proto-Unitarian) camps in the first decades of the nineteenth century. When Henry Ware, the liberal minister in Hingham, Massachusetts, was appointed Hollis Professor of Divinity in 1805, the lines in an already long and muffled dispute began to harden. To counter what they saw as the pernicious threat of anti-Calvinist theology, the conservative faction, led by Harvard overseer and Charlestown minister Jedidiah Morse, founded a new, orthodox seminary at Andover in 1807. The Harvard school, though it conferred no degrees until 1870, became the second professional school (after the medical school) at the university. By 1819 it had a faculty of four professors plus the president of the university, but its small size belied its impact: it was the Unitarian stronghold for years to come and played a central role in defining liberal Christianity in America for most of the nineteenth century.[1]

Though Very had let it be known when he came to Harvard that he wished, in Samuel Ward's phrase, to "restore epic poetry," it's hardly surprising that he saw the ministry as either an adjunct to or a substitute for that ambition. Even without his deepening piety during his senior year, the life of the minister was likely to have seemed the most welcoming and most appropriate to someone of Very's skills and sensibility. By the autumn of 1835, the path may have become even clearer when he received his first award from the Mary Saltonstall fund, an endowment designated specifically for promising students who intended to enter the ministry. The honor suggests not only that Very had decided by then to work toward admission to the Divinity School but that the college administration had identified him as a particularly worthy—as well as financially challenged—candidate.

At the spring exhibition of 1835, Very had been chosen to show off his Greek skills by presenting his translation of passages from Daniel Webster's popular oration at Plymouth from the 1820 celebration of the "First Settlement of New England."[2] The honor marked Very as one of the better candidates for a position as tutor of Greek after his graduation, but it seems at least as likely that his maturity and often-remarked seriousness of manner helped settle the question. He would be allowed to pursue the Divinity School curriculum while drawing a salary as a part-time tutor, perhaps offering two lines of preparation (teaching and ministry) for a potential career without creating a financial hardship. The devout twenty-three-year-old scholar would provide a clear role model for the boisterous Harvard freshmen (then commonly no older than sixteen or seventeen), and the Divinity School would find itself with one of the more accomplished and well-read Harvard alumni in many years.

Though considered by some to be unusual or even strange, Very did in fact prove to be a remarkable teacher for the two years of his appointment to the Harvard faculty.[3] The pedagogical style of the time, as is clear from the incident that sparked the Dunkin Rebellion, was dry, authoritarian, and heavily dependent on memorization and recitation. Though Very himself had encountered a few teachers, Edward Tyrell Channing in particular, who pushed against the type, the vast majority of the faculty showed, at best, a cool and, at worst, an Olympian indifference to their students. Very was clearly different. Not only did he lead the three sections of freshmen through the standard curriculum (the fifth, six, and seventh books of Herodotus's *Histories*; the first two books of Thucydides's *History of the Peloponnesian War*; as well as Charles Dexter Cleveland's *A Compendium of Grecian Antiquities* and J. Parker Buttman's Greek grammar), he took an interest in their intellectual and, especially, spiritual development.[4] This latter, more personal style of engagement may have been slow to develop; most of the reminiscences of Very's unique qualities as an instructor come from students in his second year, 1837–38. But his approach was nevertheless remarkable for its time, as the following testimonial from an unnamed student of that year suggests:

> You were my teacher of Greek . . . , and your manner of instructing made a favorable impression on my mind, and produced a leaning to that language which still lasts. You were unwearied in drawing our attention to tenses, and making us translate literally—two important points in learning languages, of which, however, Mr. Felton quite lost

> sight. The charm with which you surrounded Greek vanished from Harvard with you. You felt the spirit of the Greek people, and were ready to communicate it to such as had ears to hear. I often used to regret your departure, and think how different it could have been could we have continued under your guidance, instead of undergoing that superficial and heartless course under the professor.[5]

Student memories can often be clouded with nostalgia, but the surviving reports in this case tend to echo this point: Very was both a practical and an inspirational teacher. He offered more than a fresh grounding in a subject: his seriousness, intensity, kindness, and attention suggested what the best teachers often embody—a way of living. Many of his students, particularly those with similar interests and temperaments, found him immediately fascinating. The Salem native Samuel Johnson, who was Very's student in the fateful autumn of 1838, immediately warmed to him. "Mr. Very's conversation in the recitation room turns wholly on religious & moral subjects," he wrote to his father, "& he seems to labor hard for the good of his class: some of them, however, are rather impatient of this."[6] The young Thomas Wentworth Higginson, now best known as the friend and correspondent of Emily Dickinson, came to consider his former tutor "a man of genius."[7] In his journals, Higginson recorded his first dinner with Very: "Mr. Very supped here. He has been to Europe twice, studied two trades, been in an auction room three years, began to fit for college at seventeen, graduated at twenty-three."[8] The unusual resume must have impressed Higginson, whose later life was notable for its varied political engagement and determined action. Within a few months he had joined a small group that met in Very's room on Sundays to study the New Testament in Greek. At the end of the year, Higginson noted that among his teachers only Very made a point of saying farewell: "He made us a speech, read a chapter in John and made a prayer."[9]

Very's reputation as an eccentric followed him and likely became more pronounced among the younger students over whom he had some degree of authority. Edward Everett Hale remembered him as the slightly peculiar but reverenced presence in the residence hall at Harvard:

> Very's room was in the same entry [as Hale and Samuel Longfellow's rooms], and he was regarded as the proctor of that entry. He was evidently desirous to be on good terms with the boys in the entry and always saluted us cordially and invited us into his room. I was but a boy, but Sam Longfellow [the younger brother of Henry Wadsworth Longfellow] and I had sense enough to see the genius and insight of the

> man. We had a very great respect for him, though we knew he was odd, and was called a crank. But a sort of diffidence prevented him from taking in the least towards us the tone of an instructor or a leader.[10]

This brief sketch is more revealing than most. It makes clear that while some, perhaps many, of his students thought him a "crank," a few (and among them, some of the more distinguished Harvard graduates of the time) found his refusal of typical authority refreshing. Very's "diffidence" had been noted since he was young, but it was unexpectedly combined with a strong, if unique, adherence to inner conviction. His attitude toward teaching suggests cultivation rather than domination, the sort of attentiveness and care that he likely learned from watching his mother move about her garden. (It was commonly related that he was prone to writing inspirational poems as messages on the back of his students' assignments.) Given the many botanical metaphors in his poetry, we can safely imagine that Very knowingly built upon this basic but meaningful connection. Such a poem as "The Torn Flower," though redolent of failed romance, suggests an admonition to teachers as well. He may not have been a leader in the typical sense, but he was able to elicit respect by refusing harshness, fostering instead a uniquely reverential atmosphere in no small part by the example of his living.

Of course not everyone appreciated the quiet, morally tinged presence of Mr. Tutor Very. The future lawyer and Transcendentalist James Elliot Cabot was an amateur ornithologist during his undergraduate years at Harvard and with his like-minded friends tramped the woods and marshes along the Charles River shooting birds to skin as specimens. To escape punishment for what was a forbidden activity, the boys broke down their shotguns and hid them under their student cloaks. As Cabot explains, their "chief (or only) danger was meeting Jones Very before we had reached the shelter of the woods and remote fields, for he (alone of the college Faculty) was a great walker."[11] Very's disapproval extended beyond the mere breach of rules; like his mother and, notably, his younger sister Lydia L. A., he abhorred hunting or indeed any activity that disturbed the natural flourishing of plant or animal. "When he met us in this rig," Cabot explains, "(as he often did), he looked at us sorrowfully, no doubt penetrating our disguise, but was too high-minded to call us to question."[12]

✷ 20 ✷

Temptation and Peace

The curriculum of the Divinity School had by 1836 settled into five main areas: natural religion, Hebrew, biblical criticism, ecclesiastical history, and pastoral theology. The faculty was small, with the four professors covering all subjects for roughly thirty to forty students altogether. Many of the "resident graduates," like Very, received some form of financial assistance, though most were discouraged from teaching while following the course of studies.[1] To what extent Very's own appointment as tutor of Greek reduced his time in Divinity Hall is difficult to gauge, but his library charge lists and notebooks show no remarkable shift of interest toward theological topics. In his first year, out of over forty books borrowed, only two relate directly to religious subjects: Robert Southey's *The Book of the Church* and Richard Whately's *On Some of the Difficulties in the Writings of St. Paul*. This inventory includes books taken out from the collection of the Institute of 1770, whose library Very began to frequent in September of 1836. The majority of loans, by contrast, were of literary works, including the essays of Charles Lamb, a number of books of Shakespeare criticism, the letters of Heinrich Heine, and the philosophical writings of Victor Cousin. Of the eighteen items on his main library charge lists between September and June, half are devoted to Greek literature or culture, including several studies of Herodotus and Thucydides as well as Karl Otfried Müller's *The History and Antiquities of the Doric Race* and *The Athenian Letters*, the fictional correspondence of a Persian spy during the Peloponnesian War.

The commonplace book entries for 1836–37 reflect a similar set of priorities. The range is still considerable and more often than not literary or philosophical rather than purely theological, with passages copied from, among others, Goethe's *Faust*, Robert Southey's *The Doctor*, John Penrose's *An Inquiry, Chiefly on Principles of Religion, into the Nature and Discipline of Human Motives*, Henry Chorley's *Memorials of Mrs. Hemans*,

Madame de Staël's *Germany*, and the memoirs of Sir James Mackintosh. In contrast to his final years as an undergraduate, Very's literary interests at this point suggest less concern with poetry or poetic practice per se than with the role of the poetic or spiritual personality. Though he recorded considerably fewer examples of admired poetic performance, he continued to think about the nature of the artist's relationship to inspiration. In passages drawn from part 1 of *Faust*, we can hear potentially both the student who delivered orations during his senior year and the more experienced would-be tutor glancing back at recent experience. Very copied Wagner's concern that scholarly confinement ill suits him to "lead [the world] by persuasion" (CB II, 91). Wagner craves instruction in rhetoric, but Faust contends that such skill can never substitute for genuine emotion: "If you do not feel it, you will not get it by hunting for it," he responds, "—if it does not gush from the soul, and subdue the hearts of all bearers with original delight" (CB II, 91). Sincerity, "reason[,] and good sense" (CB II, 91) are the virtues underlined here, poised against other passages copied by Very that detail Faust's illusions and susceptibility to temptation. As though to redouble this protoromantic emphasis on feeling over strategy, Very then reaches back to the play's prelude to record the Poet's indignant response to the crowd-pleasing Director: "Begone and seek thyself another servant! The Poet, forsooth, is wantonly to sport away for thy sake the highest right, the right of man, which Nature bestows upon him! By what stirs he every heart? By what subdues he every element? Is it not the harmony? which bursts from out his breast, and sucks the world back again into his heart" (CB II, 92). The emphasis here on inner purity as a source of expression, on the natural as the spring of the genuine, is not remarkable at this point, particularly after the appearance of Emerson's *Nature*, but it is notable that Very has extracted this ideal from within a drama of temptation. Very understood all too well the life of the scholar working in isolation, but he had come to realize that for the "heart" of the poet to harmonize with the deeper currents of living, it must escape the pull of Faustian desire.

Some version of this dilemma may well have simmered in Very's mind for much of the school year, drawing him toward the remedy of spiritual stillness. From John Penrose's *Inquiry* he extracted a passage that defines "true religion" as "the least bustling and noisy" and "always most visible . . . in the peaceful influence which it exerts on the manners and sentiments of society" (CB II, 95). He underlined Penrose's further comment that literature "partakes also of that worst defect for which the page of history is notorious, that it says little of the pious and humble tenor in which good men often walk noiselessly on their way" (CB II, 95). The combination of the literary pursuit of simplicity and the spiritual comportment of stillness or peacefulness appears likewise in the close juxtaposition of passages from Felicia Hemans's memoirs and *The Martyrdom of St. Ignatius*, a play by the Moravian bishop and quietist John Gambold. After a set of extracts devoted to the complexity and turbulence of artistic personality (including the "all-absorbing . . . passion" of Paganini [CB II, 99]), Very records Hemans's statement that "nothing really worthy and permanent in literature . . . is ever built up except on the basis of simplicity," as well as this account of spiritual growth that suggests the contours of Very's own development: "I have now passed through the feverish, and somewhat visionary state of mind, often connected with the passionate study of art in early life;—deep affection and deep sorrows seem to have solemnized my whole being, and I now feel as if bound to higher and holier tasks, which, though I may occasionally lay aside, I could not long wander from without some sense of dereliction" (CB II, 100). As though to cement this desired movement from intensity to calm (and its related purity of voice), Very subsequently underscored the last two lines of this passage from Gambold:

> But who must talk? Not the mere modern sage,
> Who suits the softened gospel to the age:
> Who ne'er to raise degenerate practice strives,
> But brings the precept down to Christian lives.
> Not he, who maxims from cold reading took,
> And never saw himself but through a book:
> Not he who, hasty in the morn of grace,
> Soon sinks extinguished as a comet's blaze:
> Not he, who strains in scripture-phrase t' abound,
> Deaf to the sense, who stuns us with the sound:
> <u>But he, who silence loves, and never dealt</u>
> <u>In the false commerce of a truth unfelt</u>. (CB II, 101; Very's emphasis)

In the second half of the school year the evidence of Very's personal reading comes primarily from two substantial texts: Madame de Staël's *Germany* and James Mackintosh's *Memoirs*. This may not have been Very's first reading of *Germany*. His library lists show him borrowing the works of de Staël in the spring of 1836, and both his senior Bowdoin Prize essay and his oration "Individuality" show signs of her influence. The broad distinction Very draws between the classical era's emphasis on worldly fame and the Christian turn to the drama of inwardness tracks closely to de Staël's well-known contrast between "pagan" (classical) poetry and Christian (romantic) literature. Now, several months later, he returned to collect similar extracts but with a sharpened interest in questions of the will. From de Staël: "The fatality of the ancients is the sport of destiny; but fatality, in the Christian doctrine, is a moral truth under a terrifying form." To which Very responded: "The fatality of the ancient tragedy was a power without the human will which directed as it were all actions to some great end. Man & his objects were but its materials[.] This view came from their objective view—they must have some great result of corresponding to the direction of their own impulses & that was fate—" (CB II, 104). But the modern, "Christian" experience is fundamentally subjective, a drama of consciousness and time:

> [de Staël:] The description of the Alps, and of their vast solitude, is extremely beautiful; the abode of the culprit, the hovel in which the scene passes, is far from any other habitation; no church bell is heard there, and the hour is announced only by a rustic clock. . . . We ask, what has time to do in a place like this; to what purpose the division of hours that no interest varies? And when that dreadful hour of crime is heard to strike, it recalls to us the fine idea of the missionary who imagined that in hell the damned spirits are incessantly asking, "What's o'clock?" and that they are answered, "Eternity." (CB II 104)

> [Very:] Let us tremble at the approach of that day when time for us shall be no longer. You whom the follies & passions of time save from awhile from [*sic*] a crushing ennui—tremble least when the idea of eternity opens upon your minds it may not crush you with a weight of heaven than the burthen of piled up mountains on your breasts! (CB II, 105)

The drama of this Miltonic, psychological hell was made clear in Very's senior essays, particularly "Individuality," with its stark description of Satan's "breast of flame."[2] But in this later engagement with de Staël, Very seems to be moving toward, if not entirely reaching, a more daring formulation. As de Staël promotes romantic sincerity and simplicity ("One of the first characteristics of simplicity is to express what is felt or thought, without reflecting on any result, or aiming at any object" [CB II, 106]), Very notes the truth of her statement while nevertheless responding: "But this is but the simplicity of infancy, one to which *will* has lent no power nor given any virtue—" (CB II, 106; original emphasis). In other words, the "modern" experience of inwardness, the locus of Christian drama, is a moral struggle that requires the involvement of the will. And yet the romantic attraction to simplicity suggests that the will can be erased, that "infancy," as Emerson himself wrote in *Nature*, can be recovered "in the woods." Given Very's retrospective description of this period of his life as a struggle to remove his individual will, his response to de Staël seems especially significant. Can the romantic return to nature, to a state resembling childhood, be a way to eliminate the individual will without returning to a "pagan" conception of fate? Would such an attempt simply be an escape from responsibility, a failure to face the drama of Christian consciousness? Or could it be a way to combine, however paradoxically, the interior agon of individual salvation central to Christianity with the powerful simplicity of classical heroism? Could the individual, in other words, become a kind of hero by simultaneously engaging and eliminating the will?

Sir James Mackintosh, the Scottish Whig politician and lawyer who tangled with Edmund Burke over the meaning of the French Revolution, might seem an odd choice to follow Madame de Staël—and perhaps an odd choice for Very in general. But Mackintosh was frequently assigned at Harvard, and, whether guided to them or not, Very was often drawn to the sturdier moral and personal philosophies of Scottish thinkers, including Thomas Reid, Robert Burns, and Walter Scott.[3] He had read Mackintosh's *Dissertation on the Progress of Ethical Philosophy* more than once during his undergraduate years, and now he mined the newly published memoirs with an eye for aphoristic gems. But the problem of the will was still very much on his mind. After collecting a few of Mackintosh's observations on ancient history and the "oppressive grandeur" of "dark and unmeasurable antiquity" (CB II, 107), Very recorded the following thumbnail analysis of the French revolutionary Mirabeau: "A fair recital of his conduct must always have the air of invective. Yet his *mind* had, *originally*, grand capabilities. It had many irregular sketches of high virtue; and he must have had many moments of the noblest moral enthusiasm" (CB II, 107; Very's emphasis). And then responded: "However bright they may be they are but revelations which the will alone can render permanent." Still concerned about the relationship between will and virtue, Very seems attuned to the failure to convert momentary "enthusiasm" into higher conviction. The will here is essential, inescapable, a higher, regulatory function able to translate fitful emotion into moral structure. The romantic movement toward simplicity and spontaneity would implicitly disavow any such reflective correction. How then to coordinate this opposition between intensity of spiritual experience and the moral arrangement of "emotions recollected in tranquility"?

In general, the extracts Very chose from Mackintosh (and there are almost as many from the *Memoirs* as from any other source in his notebooks) suggest a respect for the Scottish jurist's worldly good sense and devotion to practical questions of human morality. Very recorded, for instance, Mackintosh's opinion, here related by a friend, on why "self-mortification" was prevalent in religions: "[Mackintosh] suggested two different accounts or explanations of the thing. One sufficiently reasonable, and therefore, probably, not the true reason; namely, that as most of the vices, and many of the crimes, among men, proceeded from the excess of sensual gratification, the line of virtue and acceptance to the Deity would come to be regarded in a direction the farthest from this extreme. The other explanation was likely to be the true one, as more analogous to the general cast of the human mind. Men regarded self-mortification in the light of a sacrifice" (CB II, 107). For someone engaged in a process of self-containment, Very may well have found Mackintosh's understanding of the "general cast" of the mind useful. Self-denial may indeed take him closer to the spiritual, but the idea of a heroic surrender of self would transform that loss into a gain. In responding to the extract, Very understood the impulse as a deep-seated sense of a higher purpose: "Men cannot resist the impression that they are made for Duty—not seen in animals—and men as we see when most embruted still differ in this—but the civilized voluptuary even worse than the savage" (CB II, 108).

For Mackintosh, human nature was inherently flawed, though in ways more often than not obscured by self-delusion. He recorded (and Very copied) examples of the Crusaders butchering women and children in Jerusalem and then weeping at the sight of the Holy Sepulchre (CB II, 108); the tendency of the powerful to convince themselves that they are building monuments to "the prevalent principle" rather than in the service of their vanity and "passion" (CB II, 111); and the inability of fear or threats to create virtue (CB II, 113). To Mackintosh's defense of "fictitious narrative" as "one of the grand instruments employed in the moral education of mankind," however, Very adds his own drop of contempt for the fragile goodness of humanity: "What a world is this," he notes disappointedly, "where men must have their duty served up in dainties" (CB II, 112). Though we might hear such a comment as little more than censorious, its tone deserves deeper consideration. As someone who had engaged deeply with "fictitious narrative" of all types, Very can be understood to include himself in this weary criticism of pleasure. The need to understand the quality and content of duty was pressing. If moral improvement were indeed understood as sacrifice, what else must be given up but the desire for "dainties," that is, the need for pleasure itself?

✵ 21 ✵

"My heart in life's winter"

Toward the end of his first year as tutor, Very officially joined the First Parish church in Cambridge, the Unitarian congregation associated with Harvard.[1] Though he had been a member of the Salem North Church since at least the summer before, he may have considered Cambridge his more permanent home for the foreseeable future. Despite studying for the ministry, he had demonstrated through a very successful academic career that his talents and inclination ran more toward the life of the writer-scholar than the pulpit orator. Evidence suggests that he thought of teaching as a kind of ministry, more personal and more powerful perhaps for its chance to shape developing minds. His move to the First Parish suggests a satisfaction in his current position along with a determination to follow the approved path of belief and practice for Harvard faculty.

But it was as a poet that Very first came to Harvard, and though the ambition to "restore epic poetry" may have fallen away during his final year as an undergraduate, he continued to write important and highly personal verse. Sorting out the compositional order of Very's poems remains a difficult task, and many of the poems listed tentatively as late 1836 or early 1837 in Deese's edition may have been written earlier. Some of the set found among Charles Stearns Wheeler's papers ("I murmur not though hard the lot," "The Torn Flower," and "The Portrait") likely preceded Very's time as a tutor, given their apparent engagement with his passion for women noted by his undergraduate classmate Samuel Ward. (There is no similar evidence, for instance, from those testifying to his behavior and comportment as a teacher.) The poems more securely dated to the autumn of 1836 and later share a tone of quiet loss and isolation in the contemplation of nature's seasonal symbolism. Emerging in the wake of Very's reading of Emerson's *Nature*, the meditative and experiential lyrics "The Autumn Leaf," "The Winter Bird," and "The Canary Bird" share a plaintive if gentle resilience against feelings of disappointment and loneliness.

"The Autumn Leaf" is certainly the most substantial of these, a meditation on decay and the need to turn inward in response to nature's paradoxical attractions. The speaker addresses the "fair yet lifeless leaf! on whom decay / Seems beautiful" (*CP* 45). Puzzled by the contradiction between the negative effects of age and the "red glowing" of the dead foliage, he looks for a meaning available to "the heart that loves its God." The leaf is "[a] thing of outward sense," "born to live but on the eye" (*CP* 45). Without a soul to cultivate, it seemingly celebrates its physical death as the fulfillment of its being. It also serves to clarify by contrast the demand on the speaker "To light a hidden soul with brighter hues / Than wait upon the colored dawn and hang / Upon the dying leaf" (*CP* 45). This is the task given to those born of more than sense: "To shape like him, from out a world of change / A spirit into those eternal forms / Of Love, Majesty, and Beauty" (*CP* 45).

The tension between the time-bound pleasures of sense and the higher calling of "eternal forms" takes on Very's continuing struggle against sensuality seen in such emotionally turbulent poems as "Eheu! fugaces." But the tone here is quieter, more resigned, as though less susceptible to storms of passion even when the problem of sensual attraction reasserts itself in other contexts. A clearer note of loneliness and dedication to the single soul's cultivation sounds in these poems, suggesting a return and rededication to the interior drama of the self. In this context "The Winter Bird" is particularly difficult to hear as something other than a veiled self-portrait. After noting that the bird sings "alone on the wintery bough / As if Spring with its leaves were around thee now," the speaker urges it to "Sing on—though its sweetness was lost on the blast / And the storm has not heeded thy song as it passed" (*CP* 46). With its hint of self-encouragement, this couplet sonnet (form and subject reminiscent of the English romantic John Clare) suggests resilience of the self and its song, despite the "frozen" silence of an unresponsive world. The winter bird's voice has not only recovered "Spring" for the speaker; it has inspired him to the renewal of his own: "Still I felt as my ear caught thy glad note of glee, / That my heart in life's winter might carol like thee" (*CP* 46).

The "heart in life's winter" implies not only isolation but dormancy, the hibernation of feeling. This sense of emotional mutedness can be detected not only in "The Canary Bird," a revealing if conventional treatment of the caged singer's pain and isolation, but in the small group of poems with springtime settings written in the first half of 1837. Thus "The Tree" begins with the recuperative appearance of "swelling buds" and "tender leaves" but ends with a stark image of emotional deprivation:

And when the autumn winds have stript thee bare,
And round thee lies the smooth untrodden snow,
When nought is thine that made thee once so fair,
I love to watch thy shadowy form below,
And through thy leafless arms to look above
On stars that brighter beam when most we need their love. (*CP* 54)

More expansively, "The Fossil Flower" takes up a similar image of "shadowy form" and works through its connections to loneliness and obscurity. A modest variation of sorts on Gray's famous "Elegy Written in a Country Churchyard," this blank verse address to a "[d]ark fossil flower" on a piece of coal evokes for the speaker "thoughts of distant time . . . like billows of the sea" (*CP* 55). After imagining a number of possible histories for the flower when in "the colors of [its] prime," the speaker then locates the fossil's value in the continued resonance of its "form":

For HE who to the lowly lily gave
A glory richer than to proudest king,
He painted not those darkly-shining leaves,
With blushes like the dawn, in vain; nor gave
To thee its sweetly-scented breath, to waste
Upon the barren air. E'en though thou stood
Alone in nature's forest-home untrod,
The first-love of the stars and sighing winds,
The mineral holds with faithful trust thy form,
To wake in human hearts sweet thoughts of love,
Now the dark past hangs round thy memory. (*CP* 55)

The idea that the shape of the flower can continue to evoke feelings in its observer is less powerful or significant here than the poignancy of the petrified object that serves to "wake" dormant human hearts. That God would use an emblem of death (or, more precisely, death-in-life) to symbolize a resurrection of self comports with the emphasis of "The Autumn Leaf," but it also reinforces the suggestion that Very was attracted to these images of frozen or muted emotions as well as to the promise of a return to feeling. His feelings, whether in response to nature or to moments of personal desire, were powerful. They evoked an equally forceful attempt to constrain or formalize their energies, converting emotion from sense to spirit. How then to rise above the need for constraint? How to understand form as a function of God's, rather than his own, voice?

✷ 22 ✷

The White Mountains, 1837

With his first year as a tutor behind him, Very returned to Salem in the summer of 1837 to rest and enjoy the shaded recesses of the garden on Federal Street. Given the track of his reading and writing, we might expect to see symptoms of the internal struggle he later described to Bellows, but the surviving evidence, particularly his short diary of a trip to the White Mountains in August, exhibits few obvious signs of spiritual turmoil. That he was able and willing to take such a trip largely for pleasure and relaxation suggests something of his state of mind for the moment. He may have been, more often than not, the intense tutor and Divinity School student who often struck observers as strange or otherworldly, but his diary makes clear that he was not so far removed from everyday enjoyment as to reject the pleasures of a summer tour.

In the moist stillness of an early August morning, he and a friend set out to walk from Salem to Cambridge, a roughly fifteen-mile trip that took about four hours.[1] By the time they arrived midmorning the sun was up and hot, but Very found some refuge catching up with his Harvard friends Charles Scates and Edmund Burke Whitman, both rising seniors of the class of 1838.[2] Later that evening they were joined by Horace Morrison, a graduating senior who, like Very, had entered as a sophomore in 1834. The plan was for Very and Morrison to head north, join up with other Harvard friends and classmates along the way, and spend two weeks tramping through the hills and vales of southern New Hampshire.

To get a quick start they decided to take the train from Boston to Lowell, a trip that took an hour and forty-five minutes, including stops, to cover the twenty-six miles. The little, cab-less, "John Bull" engine (the engineer stood behind it, open to the elements) with its light, coach-like carriages reached speeds of up to twenty miles per hour. Very was amazed—and afraid: "At first I felt a fear at the rapidity with which we moved," he recorded, "but this gradually yielded to the thought that I every moment stand amid movements far more worthy of alarm yet with perfect safety, for I am His care who gave me life" (CB III, 114). Though this surrender to divine presence is suggestive of Very's ideas about the individual will, his basic reaction to the feeling of speed was not extraordinary. He fails to say whether or not this was his first time on "the cars," as they were commonly called, but it probably was. The Boston to Lowell line was one of the earliest New England railroads and had been running for only two years. For many, the initial experience of movement faster than a brisk buggy ride could be unnerving, and Very's account is little different from any traveler's first time on a large machine over which the individual passenger has no control. After reassuring himself, he relaxed and began to marvel at the new technology: "As that fear gave way the sense of man's power and gifts came over me and I felt how sublime were the workings of that mind that could send us on our winged flight with such fearful accuracy" (CB III, 114). At Lowell, this exposure to "progress" was confirmed by his astonishment at "the great number of Factories" (CB III, 114) dominating the once sleepy confluence of the Concord and Merrimack rivers.

Once past Lowell, Very spent the next two weeks at a slower pace, walking or finding coach or wagon rides from Peterboro, New Hampshire, through Concord, Conway, Franconia, Hanover, and Brattleboro, Vermont. He was joined for most of the way by several Harvard friends, including (in addition to Morison) Charles Mason, Nathaniel Holmes, and Bernard Bemus Whittemore. Since this is one of the few moments in the archival record where we can see Very in the company of his peers, it's worth considering what sort of young men he found most congenial and what his chosen company can tell us about him. Horace Morison had a background remarkably similar to that of his friend from Salem. His father died when he was nine, and as a result he was "put out" to work on a nearby farm to support himself.[3] Despite a lack of formal education, he eventually apprenticed himself to a cabinetmaker in Peterboro who allowed him to attend school during winter. With local support, Morison was then able to attend Philips Exeter Academy and prepare to enter Harvard along with Very in 1834. The sketch of him in the Harvard Memorials could easily apply to Very: "He had the maturity of manhood when he entered, and his college associations were largely influenced by this fact. He was grave and somewhat reserved in his demeanor, earnest in his work, with no time and no inclination, probably, for the pranks of his younger associates."[4]

Charles Mason, the oldest of the group, was from Dublin, New Hampshire, and like Morison had spent time at Philips Exeter Academy to prepare for college. Though his path had fewer obstacles than Morison's,

Mason's early schooling was interrupted, as was often the case for farmers' children, by field work. He later "kept a public school" before, like Very, entering college at twenty-one.[5] After a year at Dartmouth, he moved to Harvard and graduated with the class of 1834. Mason briefly studied in the Divinity School, but likely came to know Very better during his time as tutor of Latin at Harvard, one year of which overlapped with Very's teaching appointment. Nathaniel Holmes, from Peterboro, was a year younger than Very, a member of the Harvard class that included Henry Thoreau and Richard Henry Dana Jr. Another product of Philips Exeter, he worked as a tutor, a schoolteacher, and later a lawyer, member of the Missouri Supreme Court, and professor in the law school at Harvard. In midlife he published a widely read book on Shakespeare in which he argued for the Baconian theory of authorship.[6] And finally, Bernard Bemus Whittemore, class of 1839, became a lawyer and local politician in New Hampshire and subsequently, with his brother, edited and published the *Nashua Gazette*.

What emerges from these brief biographical sketches is not only the similarity of the young men's backgrounds—good students, first-generation sons of farmers, sea captains, or skilled workers—but also their connection or devotion to the literary life. The majority of Very's close friends at Harvard were fellow poets, like Hildreth or Wheeler, or classics scholars who went on to become lawyers. Far fewer found their way to the ministry, even if, like Mason, they spent time in the Divinity School. Despite what seems Very's intense spiritual battle within himself, despite his visible sanctity and frequent recourse to the reassurances of faith, his friendships reinforce the impression given by his reading: his primary approach to questions of belief and the practice of that belief was through literature. He was less a Christian learning how to express his faith through poetry than a poet slowly developing a unique, writer-centered conception of Christianity.

The travel notes and descriptions he left bear out this slightly more worldly emphasis. Despite his momentary reaction to the speed of the train ride to Lowell, Very recorded few if any moments of anxiety on his tour through the hills, valleys, and notches of southern New Hampshire. He did attend church regularly when possible, in one case going to the "third service" at a church in Franconia with someone he met along the way, "Mr. Philemon Portman of Danvers—Superintendent of the Iron Works—Catholic or 'liberal practicing'" (CB III, 116). But he also swam in the Merrimack and in one of the lakes near Mount Washington, played games "very pleasantly" to pass the evenings, argued Christianity with a local wagon driver, and indefatigably hiked and climbed through rain and darkness to "see the lions" (take in the sights) of seemingly every cascade, floom, oxbow, or mountain vista in the area. At one point he seems amazed that he had walked "nearly forty miles . . . this day" (CB III, 116). He may even have flirted just a bit: at Centre Harbor he noted that "the party was increased by Mrs. S daughter and niece—very agreeably" (CB III, 116). The overall impression left by this brief diary is of a kind of quiet boisterousness, not a wild release certainly but an almost extroverted embrace of experience. The diary as a whole serves as a useful corrective to the idea that Very was increasingly isolated, strange, and otherworldly.

After fifteen days on the move, Very left by coach from Brattleboro at four in the morning on August 18 and made his way to Lowell by six o'clock that afternoon. From there he took the train back to Boston (with no comment this time on the speed) and walked home to Salem, arriving close to midnight. At the end of his diary he wrote: "We hap [through] [in] life through many places, as here were some, of which we can only in our haste hear of or call by their names. In our travel we forget to note the day of the month or week and hap on for a while as without time. In regard to proper names we feel their true force being actually in the place. And the real way of pronouncing them learned" (CB III, 117). So much movement after so long a period in the relative stasis of Salem or Cambridge seems to have generated a kind of half-formed dialogue between time and place, travel and stillness. The speed of the train had evoked a divine stasis, a "standing amid movements" shielded by a timeless hand. To surrender to this lack of control was to give up, for a moment, the illusion of will or self-direction. The two weeks' movement from hilltop to hilltop strangely suggested an escape from time rather than a surrender to its flow. Was time a necessary accompaniment to the will? Or was it merely consciousness that allowed us to imagine that we were in control of our lives? The implications of Very's "reflections" remained undeveloped and unpursued for the moment. But his comment about names is nevertheless instructive: only by "being actually in the place" do we feel their "true force" and learn to pronounce them properly. Of course this is not a new insight. Very likely absorbed the thought from Emerson's *Nature* ("Words are signs of natural facts") just as Emerson did from the works of Emanuel Swedenborg.[7] But it is a *poetic* insight, and as such suggests a permanence in language that extends beyond individual experience. Time and self may leak away, turn to mist in the blur and rush, but there remains a connecting energy, linking word to all-pervading spirit. From his travels, Very edged closer to his own conception of this higher language.

✷ 23 ✷

Arrival

Near the base of Church Street in Salem, tucked in among houses and livery stables, the clapboard-sided Salem Lyceum Hall posted lists of speakers and meetings on the wall beside its tall, porticoed front doors. Founded in 1830, the society hosted lecture series beginning in November and running through the spring each year. The plain-faced building, built along the lines of a Shaker dormitory, offered graduated seating and admission for the price of one dollar for "Gentlemen" and seventy-five cents for "Ladies." Many of the speakers were locals like the lawyer John Pickering or the energetic Henry K. Oliver who spoke on such subjects as "Pneumatics" and the "Solar Eclipse of 1831." Others included the great names of New England literary, cultural, and political life. Even if we confine ourselves to those series through 1840, the list is impressive: Emerson, Daniel Webster, Horace Mann, Oliver Wendell Holmes, George Bancroft, George Catlin, John Quincy Adams. It was an age of near mania for education and self-improvement. The religious impulses of New England revivalism and the Second Great Awakening fed the push for moral perfectionism and social reform. The American drive for betterment made people want to learn about the latest developments in science and industry. A mix of high-mindedness, secularized religious energy, and class striving assured the Lyceum's continued popularity and importance for roughly fifty years.

When Very was asked to speak in the ninth series (1837–38) it was a confirmation of his academic successes as well as an opportunity to develop his literary ambitions in a promising direction. There is no direct evidence for how the invitation came about, but for a young poet (and celebrated local student) who had frequently published verse in local papers the offer to speak is hardly surprising.[1] Nevertheless, it must have felt sharply meaningful to a clearly ambitious young man who had lost his father and grown up on the shabbier side of River Street with a mother who had a reputation for eccentricity and freethinking. For a subject Very chose to read his senior Bowdoin Prize essay, "What Reasons Are There for Not Expecting Another Great Epic Poem?," listed in the series simply as "Epic Poetry." Forty-three years later Elizabeth Peabody remembered the thin figure standing "alone on the platform" that late December evening as the applause for his lecture died down. To her he seemed "uncertain, shy, and embarrassed," and she turned to her father and suggested inviting Very back to their house on Charter Street, next to the Old Burying Point (EP 404). "He grasped my outstretched hand like a drowning man," she remembered, "and accepted the invitation" (EP 404).

It was a significant handshake. The thirty-three-year-old Peabody was not yet widely known as the promoter and industrious intellectual who ran the West Street Bookstore in Boston, but she had worked as Bronson Alcott's assistant at the controversial Temple School and published her journal of that work in *Record of a School: Exemplifying the General Principles of Spiritual Culture* in 1835. Very may have had a sense of her connections. He had been attending the Salem North Church, where the Peabody family owned a pew, since at least June of 1836. Perhaps his enthusiasm in accepting their invitation arose more from entering a new circle of associations in Salem than from the awkward isolation that Peabody later remembered. (If her account is accurate, for instance, why was Very alone after what must have been a signal event in the history of his family? In this his native town were there really no friends or relatives at the Lyceum to congratulate him or offer some form of celebration?) Later that evening, Peabody wrote to Emerson, who was in charge of inviting speakers to the Concord Lyceum. She urged him to get in touch with Very, knowing that the invitation to lecture included "the hospitality of Mr. Emerson's house" (EP 405). With her sharp eye for new talent and "spiritual culture," she had seen in Very qualities Emerson would admire and approve.

By the fireplace at the Charter Street house that evening, Very spoke of Shakespeare. Having revisited his essay on the epic, his mind was on literary subjects, and Peabody remembered him laying out his theories about the relationship between Shakespeare the man and his plays as well as the contrast between the playwright's all-encompassing "consciousness of Nature" and the "morally redemptive" power of Christ (EP 405). It's reasonable to suspect that by 1880 Peabody had telescoped her memory of Very's conversation that evening with her later reading of his 1838 essays on Shakespeare and *Hamlet*, but some version of these arguments was surely taking shape in the autumn of 1837. After his time in New Hampshire, Very had returned to Harvard to prepare for the new academic year and once again made extensive use of the Harvard library. In addition to books that helped him prepare for more Greek instruction (studies of Herodotus,

Homer; Edward Dodwell's *A Classical and Topographical Tour through Greece*), he had moved heavily into Shakespeare criticism, borrowing half a dozen books on the plays between September and the end of the year. These included William Richardson's *Essays on Shakespeare's Dramatic Characters*, William Hazlitt's *Characters of Shakespear's Plays*, the 1667 version of *Hamlet*, Nathan Drake's *Shakespeare and His Times*, and Maurice Morgan's *Essay on the Dramatic Character of Sir John Falstaff*. Once again for a part-time Divinity School student, the reading was remarkably literary, though Peabody's account indicates that Very had taken up a spiritual question that was to preoccupy him through the crucial months leading up to his crisis: How could a genius like Shakespeare function effectively *outside* of the Christian drama of salvation Very had identified as the successor to the classical epic? If, as he had argued in "What Reasons," it was Milton who had moved "the scene of action from the outward world to the world within," thereby creating the modern, Christianized drama, what to make of Shakespeare, who, with a play like *Hamlet*, had turned the action inward but without reference to salvation?[2] Strongly influenced by Coleridge and Hazlitt, Very's answer was to imagine Shakespeare as a "natural phenomenon" whose mind was moved by "the Divine Will in its ordinary operations . . . as it does the material world."[3] As the product of an almost romantic innocence, Shakespeare's genius flowed like a bright stream without the complications of will created by an awareness of the Fall and the need for salvation.

Over the course of the coming year, Very would work this argument into the essays "Shakespeare" and "Hamlet," both of which took final form in the crucial autumn of 1838, but it's clear that by the time of his first encounter with Peabody his thinking about the problem of the will had entered a new phase. Though less frequently quoted or referenced in his notebooks, Shakespeare had been a touchstone for him at least since his acquisition of the complete works during his teenage auction-house days. As it did for many romantic commentators, *Hamlet* seemed to him not only the most important of Shakespeare's plays but the most revealing of its author. Shakespeare was like Hamlet, and Hamlet's inner life was the prototype for the romantic concern with complex and constrained emotional experience. Very remembered walking the ramparts of Elsinore with his father, and his deep attraction to the play—whether through identification with the prince or through a feeling of resonance with his life—is undeniable. That in the middle of his attempt to subdue his own will, to achieve a kind of elevated purpose and moral vision, he turned to this play and this author suggests a deeper, more personal source of his struggle. How could he meditate on the nature of Hamlet as a character and not evoke the image of his own lost father? How could he confront the challenge of suppressing his own, often romantic or erotic desires without thinking about his parents' passionate but hasty marriage and his own quasi illegitimacy?

"I think that what [Shakespeare's] characters wanted [that is, lacked]," Very copied into his notebooks that autumn, "is purity & loftiness of Will, and that almost all the faults of his Plays, and, above all, his exceedingly bad jokes belong to this defect" (CB II, 115). The line is from an essay on *Hamlet* in Nathan Drake's *Memorials of Shakespeare* (1828). It reflects the familiar complaint in much of earlier Shakespeare criticism that the mixture of high seriousness and low comedy reveals a weakness in the author's character and a flaw in his art. Very's sense of Shakespeare's almost childlike reflection of reality can be found here alongside his own aversion to earthiness. But it likewise establishes a kind of escape: purify the will, lift it above the sublunary concerns of body and desire, and you liberate the soul to an unalloyed expressiveness. Immediately on the next of his notebook pages Very set down this passage from Carlyle's "Signs of the Times": "One man that has a higher Wisdom, a hitherto unknown spiritual Truth in him, is stronger, not than ten men that have it not, or than ten thousand, but than all men, that have it not; and stands among them with a quite ethereal, angelic power, as with a sword out of Heaven's own armoury, sky-tempered, which no buckler, and no tower of brass, will finally withstand."[4] With its connection to similar claims by Emerson and later Thoreau, this passage can seem in retrospect a Transcendentalist commonplace, but in Very's 1837 notebooks it functions both as a revolutionary tocsin of sorts and a specific outcome of his thinking about Shakespeare's limitations. Carlyle's angelic, messianic image answers the question posed by Very's concern over Shakespeare's (and possibly his parents') commitment to the passionate cords of desire that fasten us to an unredeemed experience. Those tragic ties led to death, as Very had seen and suffered early on. "Higher wisdom" and "spiritual Truth," in Carlyle's image, suggest strength, unconquerable defense, the "sky-tempered" steel of a life beyond folly.

✷ 24 ✷

"Beauty"

But was such a life achievable? This remained the question that seems to have eaten steadily at Very's core. If his mother's intense care and concern could not prevent these searing losses, could he avoid her depth of suffering by relinquishing his claim to what Melville would later call the "low enjoying power"? The turn to Shakespeare suggests that the question was becoming more acute, but in 1880 Peabody remembered specifically that at her first meeting with Very he was not strange or agitated, "excited or mystical" (EP 405). He must have impressed her at first as a talented young scholar and thinker, one who might make a useful recruit to the new thinking. But there was more to it than that, and her subsequent investigations turned up not only his interesting family history but his reputation as a teacher thus far at Harvard, his "habit of preaching" to his students and inviting "two or three to walk with him every day" in Mount Auburn Cemetery "for he always spoke of the deepest spiritual subjects . . . yet so free from cant as to command their reverence" (EP 405). There is more than a hint of prophetic purpose in Peabody's account of Very's thought and behavior, and it energizes her reaction to what might otherwise seem a modestly interesting young intellectual.

Retrospectively, of course, Peabody understood what was to become of Very, and some of the tremor in her account derives from the recollected emotion of those dramatic events of the following autumn. Still, it can be difficult to escape the conclusion that Very impressed many as paradoxically both calm and excited, reserved and expressive. Even before its formulation in such later sonnets as "The Hand and the Foot," his affect combined disparate elements of passivity and urgency, a conflict resolved, if at all, only after he had erased (as he understood it) all trace of the personal. During the autumn and early winter of 1837, however, no such radical resolution had yet taken place; he remained in the painful throes and occasional exhilarations of the "constant work" of purifying his soul.[1]

Some of this effort, as well as its cost, can be sensed in the poem "Beauty," written most likely during September of 1837. Originally titled "Love," it's one of the earliest English or Shakespearean sonnets in Very's collected poems, linking it to the enormous outflow of spiritual sonnets in the same form that began a year later. (There will be more to say about this form in the coming chapters, but for the moment it's enough to note Very's turn to compression and formal containment as the emotional stakes of his writing increased.) Like another of Very's more significant and personal poems, the meditation on his brother Franklin's blindness that begins "I saw a child," "Beauty" opens with the act of looking:

> I gazed upon thy face—and beating life,
> Once stilled its sleepless pulses in my breast,
> And every thought whose being was a strife
> Each in its silent chamber sank to rest; (*CP* 58)

Rather than emotional turmoil, the sight of the beautiful face produces calm in the speaker's body and mind. "Beating life," the pulse that would typically increase during such an encounter, stills, as though the moment, instead of arousing desire, enfolds the self, no longer "sleepless." Perhaps love or aesthetic transcendence can provide a remedy to the unnamed "strife" within the speaker, a solution even to the problem of being:

> I was not, save it were a thought of thee.
> The world was but a spot where thou hadst trod,
> From every star thy glance seemed fixed on me,
> Almost I loved thee better than my God. (*CP* 58)

Could love for another human being so subsume the self that the personal "I" ceases to exist? For a moment, at least, the answer is yes, as the world looks back at the speaker through the eyes of the beloved. But by the final line of the quatrain, the threat emerges. A distinction and a choice are established: the experience of passion threatens to supplant the higher object of devotion. The final lines imply both a withdrawal and a self-rebuke.

Here the sonnet turns, in effect after already beginning its volta, but also lingering in the emotional overflow of its initial moment:

> And still I gaze—but 'tis a holier thought
> Than that in which my spirit lived before,
> Each star a purer ray of love has caught,
> Earth wears a lovelier robe than then it wore,

And every lamp that burns around thy shrine
Is fed with fire whose fountain is Divine. (*CP* 58)

The mixture of emotions between the realization of the speaker's near-blasphemous adoration of the beautiful face and his "still" rapt attention to that vision is not entirely dissipated by the converting "but" that follows the dash. The caesura after "gaze" seems to hold all the poem's tensions: a silence in the presence of beauty that stops thought, even after the recognition that what is happening to the speaker may threaten his soul. In this sense, the poem's subsequent conversion of earthly affection into spiritual love seems less successful than it intends to be: the speaker remains devoted to the "shrine" of this now transcendent face, and the strength of his desire remains implied in the image of the fiery "fountain" of God's love.

"Beauty" may constitute one of the clearer examples of the difficulties Very faced in attempting to eliminate not only personal preference but the self-consciousness that seemed to smuggle the will back into power. As he later explained to Bellows, his senior year change had led him to see that "we ought to have no *will* of our own," but awareness of the problem seemed to make this elimination impossible: "The temptation I always felt to be in thought and as long as I had a thought of what I ought to banish I felt that some of my will remained."[2] A similar ghost of desire haunts the second half of the poem, as the speaker hopes by sheer determination to squeeze his passion into a form of faith. The effort resonates with a passage from Novalis's *Heinrich von Ofterdingen* that Very copied into his notebooks that autumn: "Poetry must, especially, be pursued as a *severe* art. As mere pleasure—amusement—it ceases to be poetry. . . . A pure open spirit, a habit of reflection and of observation, and skill in putting all his powers into a reciprocally quickening activity, and in holding them therein,—such are the qualities demanded of a poet" (CB II, 120; original emphasis). "Beauty" inaugurated, in its way, Very's dedication to this severity. It opened what would be a long and intense engagement with the sonnet form, the structures of which were to play a crucial role in the shaping of his messianic ventriloquism. It also forecast the role of constraint and restriction—not only of poetic form but of thought and even consciousness itself—in his movement toward a supposedly will-less existence.

25
Concord

In early April, Very carried his copy of *Nature* as he walked from Cambridge to Concord. At the lyceum there he repeated his lecture on epic poetry and had his first personal meeting with Emerson. It was to prove, in some respects, the most consequential encounter of Very's life. Despite its unique background and increasing spiritual intensity, Very's subsequent trajectory as a poet and self-made visionary is difficult to imagine without Emerson's influence. Only three months after this meeting, Emerson would deliver his controversial Divinity School Address and arguably move Very toward the final stages of his spiritual agon. That spring each was in a position to see the other as a way toward something more: in Emerson's case a higher, wilder calling that would deliver him from the torpor of Unitarianism; in Very's, a spiritual window out and above emotion and desire. Emerson's inscription in Very's copy of *Nature* suggests that he understood his new friend's approach (or possibly, reproach) right away. The experience of nature was not, for Very, purely subjective; there was a God, not just godlike experiences. Emerson found his new friend refreshing and stimulating, and he thanked Peabody for sending him "such wise men as Mr. Very, from whose conversation and lecture I have had a true and high satisfaction."[1] Lidian Emerson, writing to her sister the day after Very's visit, was even more enthusiastic: "This morning Mr. Very—a young Cambridge Tutor—took his departure from our castle where we had entertained him a day and a night—But as Carlyle said of mine own *angel*-man—he left us not as he found us; but rejoicing in the existence of so high souled—pure—loving—and lovely a being. . . . Mr. E loves him as well as I do."[2]

At thirty-four, Emerson was only ten years Very's senior, and though yet to achieve the kind of status that would enshrine him fully as the "Sage of Concord," he was widely known as a lecturer, writer, and sometimes unsettling thinker. After the death of his first wife in 1831, he had surrendered his appointment as junior minister at Boston's Second Church, citing an unwillingness to administer the sacrament of Communion. Drawn by temperament to stand apart from orthodoxies, Emerson was a hungry reader and assimilator of new ideas. His growing conviction that "religion in the mind is not credulity and in the practice is not forms" pushed him to fall back on what Robert Richardson calls "a major key to his strength," the ability "to reach for his own resources and to go it alone."[3] By 1838, Emerson had almost freed himself entirely from the ministry and was best known as the poetic (or to his critics, misty, obfuscating) speaker who had recently dazzled audiences with the Phi Beta Kappa lecture known as "The American Scholar." To the Unitarian establishment he was a worrying presence, undoubtedly brilliant, still perhaps in the fold to an extent—but risky. It was not uncommon for the very orthodox among New England Protestants to consider Emerson an atheist, just the sort of overreaching attack to excite the younger generation.

In the spring of 1838, Emerson found himself caught up, partly against his wishes, in the controversy over the Cherokee removals in Georgia. He was deeply sympathetic to the cause of the Cherokee nation in their resistance to the federal policy of relocation begun by Andrew Jackson and continued by his successor, Martin Van Buren. Emerson had heard the Cherokee leaders John Ridge and Elias Boudinot speak at the Federal Street Church in Boston in 1832 and came away impressed, particularly by Ridge's "fair fine Indian eloquence."[4] When Van Buren moved to enforce the removal act in 1838, Emerson participated in a series of lectures offered by the American Peace Society and later wrote a public letter to Van Buren, which he read at a protest meeting in Concord. Uncomfortable with political activity, Emerson had little hope that his "shriek," as he called it, would do any good: "But sometimes," he admitted, "a scream is better than a thesis."[5]

The unsettled mood of that April was reinforced by Emerson's continued unhappiness with Unitarianism. Though he regularly attended his local meeting in Concord, he found the minister, Barzillai Frost, to be "a young man who has not yet learned the capital secret of his profession namely to convert life into truth. . . . He smiles & suffers & loves yet, all this experience is still aloof from his intellect; he has not converted one jot into wisdom."[6] As others have argued, Emerson may have felt an internal need to justify his own decision to leave the ministry, and Frost's admittedly tepid preaching became a convenient symbol of everything Emerson hoped to escape when he left his position at Boston's Second Church.[7] When on March 21 Emerson was invited to deliver the address to the graduating class of the Harvard Divinity School in July, he began thinking about how to contrast "the ugliness & unprofitableness of theology & churches at this day" with "the glory & sweetness of the moral nature out of whose pale they [the churches] are shut."[8] If he could have little or no practical effect on the Cherokee controversy, perhaps he could change the way ministers at Harvard were being trained.

It was in this context that Emerson first encountered Very. A few weeks after that first visit and lecture, they met again, this time in the company of Cornelius Felton, the Eliot Professor of Greek Literature at Harvard, Henry Thoreau, Frost, and Rockwood Hoar, a recent Harvard graduate and the son of the Emersons' close friend Elizabeth Sherman Hoar.[9] Very and Felton had walked over from Cambridge, and the others, all locals and on hand, were invited to join the impromptu circle. After tea and dinner, Very and Felton stayed the night. In a journal entry that evening, Emerson grouped Very with other "aspiring and heroical young men" he had recently encountered who helped him "to conceive hopes of the Republic" (*JMN* 5:475). These included the poet William Cullen Bryant and the Unitarian minister Orville Dewey, as well as Harvard seniors Edward Washburn, Edward Augustus Renouf, and Henry Lawrence Eustis. All represented, to Emerson's thinking, a kind of energy and openness of thought missing in the unfortunate Frost—and, by extension, the Unitarian ministry in general. The influence of Very and those like him on the development of the Divinity School Address is thus clear, though it's possible that Very himself was more Emerson's model for the new prophetic "true man" than the others (LA 80). Later that same year, during Very's strange and eventful visit to Concord after his expulsion from Harvard, Emerson exulted in the way this "brave saint" routed the "local minister" (Frost) during another afternoon meeting (*JMN* 7:127). A spirit of rebellion, even mild rudeness, was building in Emerson's thinking throughout this period; contact with younger, at times bolder figures like Very gave it fuel. It was this quickening, the recovery of unorthodox energies, that led Emerson to imply to Elizabeth Peabody his need for—and profit from—such contacts: "I heartily congratulate myself on being, as it were, anew in such company."[10]

For Very, interaction with the Emersons was clearly life-altering, though the exact nature of their influence on him is more difficult to recover than his initial effect on them. There are no surviving accounts in Very's hand of these meetings, and though we do have his somewhat cryptic correspondence to Emerson and others from later in the year, there are no surviving letters to provide context for the earlier encounters in Concord. There are hints in Very's library records of Emerson's influence. Immediately following their first meeting, Very borrowed a collection of

Montaigne's essays and later in May J. S. Cardale's edition of Samuel Fox's translation of Boëthius. But the more discernible results may have been the publication of Very's lecture on epic poetry in the *Christian Examiner* in May and his invitation to join a meeting of the Transcendental Club that same month. At Caleb Stetson's house in Medford a group that included Emerson, George Ripley, Converse Francis, Frederic Henry Hedge, John Sullivan Dwight, Cyrus Bartol, and Theodore Parker met to discuss the question "Is mysticism an element of Christianity?"[11] According to Alcott, the discussion was "animated" and took up most of the afternoon "till twilight":

> On the main topic of conversation, much was said. Was Jesus a mystic? Most deemed him such, in the widest sense. He was spiritual. He spoke in parable. He drew images from nature: he spake in figure: nature was a language: he saw through its facts: these were transparent to his divine eye. All things were marvels: all things were mysteries. He used the universal tongue, and was intelligible to all men of simple soul.
>
> Yet technically he was not a mystic. He did not impose his own special view of things on others, by means of special symbols. His was not a special mind. He saw nothing special in nature, or soul. All was universal.[12]

This discussion was clearly important for the arguments Emerson would make in July at the Divinity School; the first part of Alcott's summary has the specific sound of Emerson's voice. There is also a preview of the so-called miracles controversy soon to flame up in response to Emerson's address: "All things were marvels" contains, in essence, Emerson's argument against supernaturalism and implies his vision of a Jesus who understands and reveals the miracle of "the blowing clover and the falling rain" (LA 80).

And what was Very thinking as the daylight dimmed and this daring vision of a modern Jesus was built up before him? He may have already explained and explored with Emerson and others his own desire to eliminate his personal will. The idea of a Christ understood as the pattern for (or after) the modern poet-prophet must have been thrilling in its way, as though all of his own reading of Milton, Byron, Pollok, Lamartine, and Wordsworth had brought him to this point of surprising resonance with the latest thinking. Even so the second part of Alcott's summary hints at what might have been a countercurrent in the meeting—a warning of sorts that seems to contain some of Very's own contradictions. Jesus was not a mystic in the sense of a "special" self or "mind"; there was no egotism, no cult of personality that might attach to a saint or prophet. How then could the modern notion of the image-maker who saw through the symbolic structure of nature (a kind of poet) be someone without distinction, without a "special view"? How was it possible to speak with prophetic authority, that is, and have no self?

There is no doubt that Very was excited by this new company. In June he again attended a meeting of the Transcendental Club, this time at Cyrus Bartol's house in Boston, and discussed, among other topics, personal identity, memory, and Goethe's character as an artist.[13] Since his meeting with Elizabeth Peabody in December, Very had entered a new circle of associations, and their interest in him and his work must have confirmed his long-held ambitions at the same time that it encouraged him to think of himself as important. To speak openly and frankly with such a figure as Emerson in the spring of 1838 put Very at the center of one of the more important moments in the development of New England thought, but it may have been the attention of women such as Peabody and Lidian Emerson that had the most impact. For a young man who had been, in his own terms, working to overcome a strong, erotic attraction to women—to translate desire into spiritual terms—the extraordinary response of someone like Mrs. Emerson likely both confirmed and confused his perfectionist impulses. From her first meeting, she seems to have understood him as a kind of guiding spirit: "But I feel the richer that I have seen him," she wrote to her sister, "and hope now never to lose sight of him through all my being."[14] Was such a strong, emotional response from a woman just eleven years his senior a confirmation or complication of his efforts to eliminate his will? Or did this kind of attention supply a degree of understanding otherwise missing from the world of his upbringing? A commonplace book entry from this period seems to suggest as much:

> The names and all connected with our kindred remain in our hearts as if possessed of some secret undefined power the witnesses of some covenant broken with the Lord—we all should have been good & each family spread out its arms naturally & locked its shade with others but such alas! has not been the case and here and there we see a single solitary rose on other stalks than our own paternal one which although foreign seems of nearer kindred than the blighted flowers at our own side. (CB II, 126)

Based on Very's library charge lists, this entry can plausibly be dated to April or May of 1838.[15] Its importance has been noted by previous biographers, but its meaning is by no means transparent. It suggests a young man's typical recognition that his biological family may not provide the true home for his deepest self. Some whiff of the family strife from Very's early years, perhaps especially his mother's court battle with his grandfather, lingers here, opposed to his attraction to the "solitary rose" that grows fresh on some "foreign" stalk. There is no evidence, even circumstantial, that Very is referring specifically to his parents as "blighted flowers" in this entry, but there is certainly a recognition that his new friends, possibly even new female friends, offered a more fertile field for his own development than the cloistered world of Salem and Federal Street.

Published the same month in the *Salem Observer*, one of Very's earlier sonnets relies on the same imagery:

> Thy beauty fades and with it too my love,
> For 'twas the self-same stalk that bore its flower;
> Soft fell the rain, and breaking from above
> The sun looked out upon our nuptial hour;
> And I had thought forever by thy side
> With bursting buds of hope in youth to dwell,
> But one by one Time strewed thy petals wide,
> And every hope's wan look a grief can tell:
> For I had thoughtless lived beneath his sway,
> Who like a tyrant dealeth with us all,
> Crowning each rose, though rooted on decay,
> With charms that shall the spirit's love enthral,
> And for a season turn the soul's pure eyes
> From virtue's changeless bloom that time and death defies. (*CP* 61)

Perhaps the strongest evidence to support the rumor that Very was once engaged, this poem speaks both to the notebook entry and to such earlier verses as "The Torn Flower." Here the speaker's love withers with the fading of the beloved's beauty because both are the product of a "thoughtless" devotion to the time-bound, sensual world. Time cheats us, the poem suggests, by seducing the spirit "With charms" that "for a season turn the soul's pure eyes / From virtue's changeless bloom." Here we have both the "solitary . . . foreign" rose of the notebook entry, attractive as a possible escape from family history, and the damaged or withered flower that is Very's preferred figure for time and death, the recurrent reminder that love and human passion, though powerful, are finally unreliable. There are moments when this argument can seem little more than an excuse to justify a failed romance, but the emotional core of the speaker's withdrawal from life is more than merely nervous—it is traumatic. What Very laments as lacking in his family is essentially a type of shelter: "We all should have been good & each family spread out its arms naturally & locked its shade with others." As in the poem on his brother Franklin's blindness, it becomes clear to the speaker of these verses that these earthly ties of love and affection cannot save the vulnerable or prevent the pain of their loss. The specter of a father's early death and a mother's long grievance casts its pall over all attachments, old or new.

✷ 26 ✷
Miracles

The history of New England Protestantism is often told through its controversies. For much of the seventeenth and eighteenth centuries, major sectarian differences could be attributed to the problem of grace versus works. Traditional Calvinists held, with some variances, that God's grace in choosing those to be saved preceded and essentially nullified any actions an individual could take to earn salvation. God's "sovereignty" was so complete that good works could only be evidence of a predetermined election. (And even this interpretation was subject to question, more propositional than reliable—a hypothetical preparation for a hypothetical salvation.) The doctrine produced two "heretical" responses: antinomianism, which argued that actions truly are irrelevant, even as evidence of salvation; and Arminianism, which allowed for some degree of choice or self-determination for those seeking salvation. By the late eighteenth century these divisions had produced a dizzying number of individual sects, each with slightly different approaches to this debate, though most by that point had made concessions to the Arminian critique. A country at least nominally devoted to increased individuality and democratic sentiment in its politics—to the ideals of self-making and self-determination—was unlikely to retain Calvinism's spiritual determinism into the industrial era.

At root, such a debate over the extent of God's power to know and to choose contained elements of a secondary argument about the nature of God himself. Among the more liberal congregations in New England during the eighteenth century, the forbidding and absolute God of the Calvinists had at times moved closer to a figure who, though still a divine being, embodied the practical virtues of rationality and order. The "supernatural rationalism" of such ministers as Charles Chauncey, the redoubtable leader of Boston's First Church who excoriated the excesses of the Great Awakening, shaped the eventual Socinian Christology of Salem's own William Bentley.[1] And though Bentley's beliefs were unusual for his time and place, they were part of a trajectory that pointed clearly toward the formation of the Unitarian church in the years just after his death. Both Bentley and the Unitarians rejected the doctrine of the Trinity, understanding Jesus as a human figure chosen by God for a divine purpose. As such, the Unitarians held that Christ could and did perform miracles as supernatural evidence of his role and purpose. In his foundational "Baltimore Sermon" in 1819, William Ellery Channing made clear the relationship between man and method:

> We believe, that [Jesus] was sent by the Father to effect a moral, or spiritual deliverance of mankind; that is, to rescue men from sin and its consequences, and to bring them to a state of everlasting purity and happiness. We believe, too, that he accomplishes this sublime purpose by a variety of methods; by his instructions respecting God's unity, parental character, and moral government, which are admirably fitted to reclaim the world from idolatry and impiety, to the knowledge, love, and obedience of the Creator; by his promises of pardon to the penitent, and of divine assistance to those who labor for progress in moral excellence; by the light which he has thrown on the path of duty; by his own spotless example, in which the loveliness and sublimity of virtue shine forth to warm and quicken, as well as guide us to perfection; by his threatenings against incorrigible guilt; by his glorious discoveries of immortality; by his sufferings and death; by that signal event, the resurrection, which powerfully bore witness to his divine mission, and brought down to men's senses a future life; by his continual intercession, which obtains for us spiritual aid and blessings; and by the power with which he is invested of raising the dead, judging the world, and conferring the everlasting rewards promised to the faithful.[2]

In line with the liberal tradition of the eighteenth century, Channing's Christ is largely a teacher, prophet, and moral exemplar; there is little emphasis here on the vernacular Jesus who turned water into wine. But the resurrection remained a supernatural event. Even if Christ himself was not understood as part of God, he had been granted the power over death essential to his "divine mission."

This limited supernaturalism helped early Unitarians fend off accusations that they were little more than Deists, a term that often implied a thinly disguised atheistic materialism. Emerson, of course, was hardly a Deist; as Robert Richardson puts it, "If anything, he believed too much, not too little."[3] But Emerson had come to the point of rejecting supernaturalism as an affront to the astonishment of Nature itself. He had distanced himself from the Eucharist, as he told his aunt, Mary Moody Emerson, because he was not prepared "to eat or drink religiously."[4] In other words, he considered the form of the service too material to produce a spiritual redemption. By the summer of 1838, partly in reaction to the tepid preaching of Barzillai Frost and others, Emerson was prepared in his Divinity School Address to go further—or at least to make explicit his objections to anything he considered unnatural in the common understanding of the Gospels. He prized immediacy of spiritual experience above all. In the revolutionary opening to *Nature*, he had wondered aloud why those in the present could not "enjoy an original relation to the universe" (LA 7). Supernaturalism in the form of ancient miracles seemed part of those "sepulchres of the fathers" that interfered with the wondrous perception of nature (LA 7).

The audience in Divinity Chapel that warm Sunday evening of July 15, 1838, was not entirely homogeneous. In addition to the six attending graduating students, their families and friends, there was the Divinity School faculty (the two Henry Wares, senior and junior, and the professor of biblical literature, John Gorham Palfrey) and some, like Elizabeth Peabody and Theodore Parker, who could be called, at least retrospectively, Transcendentalists. The students who invited Emerson may have been expecting something unusual from the still young speaker who had left his ministerial post, but most of the establishment figures were soon shocked by what they heard. After an opening hymn to summer and "the perfection of this world, in which our senses converse," Emerson spoke of the human spirit's desire to understand, to know what moves beneath or through these experiences. The "intuition of the moral sentiment," he insisted, allows all to recognize "the laws of the soul" through an instantaneous and instinctive ability to see the truth. Aligning ourselves with this internal directive, whose source is divine, manifests our own inherent divinity: "If a man is at heart just, then in so far is he God; the safety of God, the immortality of God, the majesty of God do enter into that man with justice" (LA 76).

Despite echoing the now well-known opening of *Nature* in which the speaker becomes "part or particle of God," this line may have caused the first real stiffening of disapproval for some in the audience. But it was soon to get worse. Having established intuition and immediacy as essential for spiritual experience, Emerson then attacked what he called "historical Christianity" as failing to cultivate this natural, "primary faith." Instead it had offered a time-encrusted, folkloric version of Jesus, too focused on "the *person*" (LA 81; original emphasis) to recognize his role as one of the "true race of prophets":

> Alone in all history, he estimated the greatness of man. One man was true to what is in you and me. He saw that God incarnates himself in man, and evermore goes forth anew to take possession of his world. He said, in this jubilee of sublime emotion, 'I am divine. Through me, God acts; through me, speaks. Would you see God, see me; or, see thee, when thou also thinkest as I now think.' But what a distortion did his doctrine and memory suffer in the same, in the next, and the following ages! . . . He spoke of miracles; for he felt that man's life was a miracle, and all that man doth, and he knew that this daily miracle shines, as the character ascends. But the word Miracle, as pronounced by Christian churches, gives a false impression; it is Monster. (LA 80)

Given the dependence among Unitarians on miracles to maintain their distance from materialism, this could only be understood as a provocation. Emerson had, in one stroke, transformed Channing's Christ, who had the power to raise the dead, into a modern messiah of perception. In other words, Jesus had no supernatural abilities, only the insight to recognize his own divinity—and, by extension, the divinity of all who are able to allow the instinctive force of virtue and godliness to flow through them.

This startling revision of Unitarian Christology would open Emerson to the accusation that he was simply turning Jesus into a Transcendentalist. That may have been cause enough for the firestorm that followed, but it was his insistence on eliminating all supernaturalism from the Gospels that tripped the loudest alarms. A Jesus who could not raise the dead—or, indeed, rise from the dead—would be no Messiah at all, as far as many in the audience were concerned. As Channing had indicated, this one supernatural occurrence was central to the idea of Christ's "divine mission," and Emerson had not merely argued against it, he had proclaimed it "Monster." For Emerson, whose faith was grounded in the idea of God's presence in nature, there could be no violation of natural processes. Nature was itself the miracle; we had only to change our perception to see it. To reach outside the natural order to locate God was a betrayal of the creation itself and a repudiation of each person's ability to locate the "current of Universal Being" within (LA 10.) In this sense, Emerson, though not a materialist, had aligned his understanding of Christianity with the materialist critique of metaphysics. He would have a Jesus who was a real person, like "you and me," who provided an example of how to recognize and release our inner God.

Emerson's criticism of conventional preaching grew easily from this revision of the messianic idea. Without naming the unfortunate Frost, he provided a memorable example of how nature (in the form of a snowstorm) outshone in eloquence the "formalist" in the pulpit: "The snow storm was real; the preacher merely spectral; and the eye felt the sad contrast in looking at him, and then out of the window behind him, into the beautiful meteor of the snow" (LA 84). This kind of preaching lacked immediacy, presence, life. It came "out of memory, and not out of the soul," and aimed at "what is usual, and not at what is necessary and eternal" (LA 86). He again blamed "historical Christianity" for reverencing tradition rather than exploring "the moral nature of man, where the sublime is, where are the resources of astonishment and power" (LA 86). The only cure was for the young ministers "to go alone, to refuse the good models, even those which are sacred in the imagination of men, and dare to love God without mediator or veil" (LA 88–89).

For those in the crowd already vibrating to Emerson's string, the speech was a triumph. Theodore Parker wrote in his journal: "[Emerson] surpassed himself as much as he surpasses others in the general way. I shall give no abstract, so beautiful, so just, so true, & terribly sublime was his picture of the faults of the church in its present position. My soul is roused."[5] And Convers Frances, minister at Watertown and brother to Lydia Maria Child, "found it crowded with stirring, honest, lofty thoughts. I don't know that anything of his has excited me more," he wrote to Frederic Henry Hedge a month later.[6] Others were appalled. Frances described the roiled waters as well as anyone in his report to Hedge: "The discourse gave dire offence to the rulers at Cambridge. The dean & Mr. Norton have pronounced sentences of fearful condemnation, & their whole *clique* in Boston & Cambridge are in commotion. The harshest words are not spared, & 'infidel' & 'atheist' are the best terms poor E. gets."[7] The graduating students, who normally saw to the publication of the address, waffled, eventually deciding to print three hundred copies but not have them distributed. Significant figures like Henry Ware Jr. and Andrews Norton responded, the first respectfully, the second with palpable venom. In his counter-lecture a year later, Norton released all the pent-up anger of the traditionalists: "The latest form of infidelity is distinguished by assuming the Christian name, while it strikes directly at the root of faith in Christianity, and indirectly of all religion, by denying the miracles attesting the divine mission of Christ. . . . The argument is founded on atheism."[8] Similar critiques were rehearsed in periodicals like the *Christian Examiner* and the *Biblical Repertory and Princeton Review*. Even liberal-leaning publications like Orestes Brownson's *Boston Quarterly Review* were largely critical, if more balanced in their assessments. And Emerson's Aunt Mary, often the whetstone to his thinking, found it all too much, saying in later years that the address "should be oblivion's, as under the influence of some malign demon."[9]

Emerson, though quiet and firm in his decision to avoid public dispute, was nevertheless disturbed by it all. He could hardly have been surprised at the reaction but was taken aback somewhat by the violence unleashed. Even if some, like Channing, were quietly receptive to the tenor of his views, Emerson increasingly understood that speaking his own truth was likely to evoke what he later called the "sharp salts" of social disagreement (*JMN* 9:311). Social conformity, he now realized with greater force, was thus the enemy of instinct, a point he would develop in "Self-Reliance" a few years later. For the moment, however, he had stirred the passions of many, both for and against his messianic individualism. Roused himself by the energy and unconventional behavior of such younger men and new acquaintances as Very and Henry Thoreau, he had excited an atmosphere of high emotion and passionate commitment that would remain charged for months to come.

✷ 27 ✷

"Newborn bard of the Holy Ghost"

Jones Very was in the audience for Emerson's address that summer Sunday. Though no direct mention of his attendance appears in any available source, the circumstantial evidence for his presence in Divinity Chapel is strong enough to make this claim with confidence. Very was present in Cambridge two days earlier, on July 13, when he borrowed four books, including James Fenimore Cooper's *The Spy*, from the Institute of 1770 library at Harvard. As a Divinity School student, he was sure to be aware of the commencement event scheduled for July 15, and as a new friend, but frequent listener, of Emerson's who had himself just joined the Transcendental Club, he would hardly have missed a chance to hear Emerson speak on the Harvard campus. Finally, a letter from Lidian Emerson to her sister both places Very in Emerson's company the night of the speech itself and implies excitement or urgency in Very's reaction. Referring to the "bold speech" her husband gave "to the Cambridge Div." students "last Sunday eve," Lidian worried that Emerson's radicalism may have "revolted" Reverend George Ware Briggs, the recently installed pastor at Plymouth, her hometown.[1] She notes that she saw Briggs "after the discourse" and wished to invite him to Concord but knew Emerson would be busy with a speech for Dartmouth's literary societies planned for July 24. She continues: "Mr. Very said to Mr. E that eveg. that he should be here Thursday but was told he *must not* till another week."[2] Put simply, Very not only spoke to the Emersons the night of the address but was eager to walk to Concord a few days later to spend more time with them both. The inference is clear: Very was there, he heard the address, and like Parker's, his soul was roused.

If his commonplace books are any indication, Very was increasingly receptive both to Emerson's message and to his prophetic, annunciatory tone. Even under the additional weight of the Divinity School curriculum combined with his Greek preparations, he remained a wide and active reader. Between March and July of 1838 he made extracts and took notes on a range of texts from Alessandro Manzoni's *The Betrothed* to John Gibson Lockhart's biography of Sir Walter Scott and John Wesley's life of the early Methodist John Fletcher. Increasingly, Very did more than just record passages; he responded often at length with analysis and opinion of his own. Reacting to a sentence (from Henry McCormick's *Philosophy of Human Nature*) about the promise of an afterlife free from misfortune, for example, Very responded with unusual vigor:

> We too often apply to the *next* world for a remedy wh[ich] was intended to be found in *this*. . . . We have but just begun to learn the sublime doctrines of our Religion. Why these separation [*sic*] of father from son brother and sister, friend from friend with which space and time are filled why loss upon loss disease upon disease decay upon decay was it merely that we might sigh for their loss or that a love might be newer born embracing life death and decay in its arms? That we might be born again widening our love from that of an earthly parent to that of a spiritual one who is without form whose love cannot but be universal for it is that of a Spirit. Grief at separation comes not merely that it may urge us on to a union with departed friends like that we have had here for if it is this we seek it cannot be found there. (CB III, 3–4; original emphasis)

As in the sonnet "Thy Beauty Fades," Very is here concerned with losses or failures that can lead to spiritual success—in life rather than afterlife. Grief can make room for an unexpected love, a new birth that delivers transcendence before rather than after death. A degree of emotional impatience pushes him forward: writing at speed, not punctuating, he seems intent on accumulating all of his personal losses—the deaths of his father, brother, friends, and others; the loss of romantic possibility—in a pained rush. What could they all mean except the possibility of a connection to "a spiritual one who is without form," a new life that admits of no loss?

A sense of immortal immanence, or at least its possibility, began to take hold of Very in the week preceding the Divinity School Address. Reacting to a passage from Scott's diary that registers how "a body under the influence of a violent emotion" cannot be stopped but may be redirected, Very again meditated on possible remedies for grieving:

> There is ever a deeper question than how to cure our grief or trouble—it is why are we disturbed or sorrow at all? Why is it that Time and Space and Death have this dominion over us at all? Is it not that we are living with our friends in the flesh and not in the spirit? We are not approaching Him who alone is good. Living with them and Him

> in that state of mind where there is no separation that is felt to be such for if it is in spirit alone we live the absent is near with a warm reality the soul still holding near it that which is not seen and living with a life deeper than death—It is the earthly feelings we cherish that causes [*sic*] our grief. (CB III, 8–9)

Given what we know of Very's intense but often constrained emotions, it comes as no surprise that he continued to look for ways to control his feelings. The focus on personal loss does inevitably raise the image of Lydia Very and her long-standing grievances, but it may well be that her eldest son needed to find ways to mitigate the kind of sorrow she could evoke *in him*. Again the writing is hurried, as though to capture the thought before his feelings can wash it away, but the paradoxical ecstasy of erasure is powerfully imagined. To live in "spirit alone" is to feel the "warm reality" of the absent; the word "near" echoes, bringing the missing and invisible ever closer in a "a life deeper than death." A strange, ecstatic vision emerges, one that acknowledges the limits of "Time and Space and Death" but imaginatively overwhelms them through a confluence of "earthly feelings" and spiritual transcendence.

This intense wrestling with the "grief" caused by emotion continued at least until mid-July. Responding to a passage from *The Life of Sir Thomas More* that criticizes priests who offer the comfort of a stress-free afterlife, Very began to redefine death as the failure to follow a spiritual path within earthly life:

> We are very apt living with our friends after the flesh and having our life and conversation in this world to look upon death as having some great power of change, but the death of the body has no such power. The sting of death is sin. We are dying or living daily till we leave this world and then the spirit has already died or through Christ found life. This each minute of this life that must prepare us for the next we live deadly much of the time and are not laying up treasures in heaven there is no hand given by us to the promptings of spiritual life and we rest in the physical—"let the *dead* said our savior bury their dead." (CB III, 13; original emphasis)

To "live deadly" echoes, in more traditional religious terms, Emerson's complaint in *Nature* that we fail to "enjoy an original relation to the universe" (LA 7). As Very attempted to renounce or erase his personal will, he sought not merely an escape from the pain caused by emotion but a way to infuse everyday life with an immortal vitality, a spiritual power that would vanquish death and all its sorrows *prior to* the death of the body. What he shared with Emerson and other Transcendentalists at this crucial moment was a critique of established religion's failure to seek or transmit this immanent ecstasy. A spiritualized existence was not meant to be attained only after death; for Very, it was a product of removing those obstacles (the willful desires of the earthbound) that kept him in thrall to vulnerable feeling.

What then was going through his mind as he listened to Emerson's attack on "historical Christianity" and Unitarian preaching? We cannot say with any certainty, of course, but we can infer sympathies and potential points of difference. Emerson's grounding of virtue in Nature was congenial to Very; we know from Very's reading of *Nature*, from the central role of the natural in his poetry, and from his own family history of immersion in his mother's garden that his spiritual sense was deeply connected to the movements of the river, the tides, and the seasonal flora. For Very, as it was for Emerson, nature was the locus of the spiritual, and if their conceptions of its substance diverged in subtle ways, the formulations were close enough for Very to be roused to attention by Emerson's opening hymn to the "refulgent summer" (LA 75). It also seems likely that Very would have been sympathetic to Emerson's critique of formal worship as it was commonly practiced among the Unitarians. Though there are few if any direct criticisms by Very of his contemporaries prior to 1838, his commonplace books were showing signs of a clearer critical voice and a more confident consolidation of thought when it came to ministerial practice. Emerson's insistence on the immediacy of spiritual experience and the need for the minister to deal out "to the people his life—life passed though the fire of thought" evoked an image of the preacher as poet-prophet that aligned strongly with Very's long interest in figures like Byron, Pollok, Wordsworth, and Lamartine. All of his thinking in the months leading up to the address closed in on a point similar to Emerson's: a divine Spirit must be allowed to inhabit the self; an immanence of spirit must precede concern for the specifics of worship.

When it comes to Emerson's controversial depiction of Christ and biblical miracles Very's potential reaction is more difficult to imagine. Perhaps surprisingly, there is little surviving evidence indicating that prior to 1838 Very was deeply invested in the traditional image of Christ as miracle worker or supernatural savior. Instead, his sense of spiritual experience, grounded in nature, had always been much closer to the romantic poets' idea of divinity moving meaningfully through creation, the "correspondent breeze" answered by receptive souls. Of course, Emerson's depiction of Jesus as a man who understood the divine potential in all individuals may have struck Very, as it did others, as dangerously self-serving. But given his persistent interest and investment in the prophetic-poetic role, the development of his early desire to "restore epic poetry," it seems far more likely that Emerson's daring vision would have thrilled him with possibility. Emerson's Jesus was one of the "true race of prophets," who saw "the mystery of the soul. Drawn by its severe harmony, ravished with its beauty, he lived in it, and had his being there" (LA 80). For a young man who had already decided on the need to erase his own will, to empty out his personal identity in order to house or embody the Holy Spirit, these lines, heard above the quiet rustling and expiration of the crowded chapel, were more likely electrifying. "He saw that God incarnates himself in man," Emerson chanted, as though intuiting Very's own project. "He said, in this jubilee of sublime emotion, 'I am divine. Through me, God acts; through me, speaks. Would you see God, see me; or, see thee, when thou also thinkest as I now think'" (LA 80).

Commentators and biographers have been correct to claim that the final form of Very's "madness" cannot be understood without the shaping influence of the Divinity School Address. To whatever extent Very himself may have influenced Emerson during its composition, the delivery of the finished lecture, two months before the crucial events of Very's "new birth," provided a specific definition and purpose to Very's spiritual goals. Emerson's essentially kenotic conception of Christ as a vessel for spirit was, as he indicated, transferable to anyone who could understand and enact it. The messianic role, in other words, could be shared, multiplied, evangelized; this was the meaning of "salvation" as such, a new embodiment of spirit within life itself. Emerson's instructions to the new graduates, to "go alone, to refuse the good models . . . and dare to love God without mediator or veil," simply confirmed this radical notion that the individual could, as well as anyone at any time, take on the highest function of "divinity." Speaking even more directly to the graduates, Emerson gave his charge: "Yourself a newborn bard of the Holy Ghost—cast behind you all conformity, and acquaint men at first hand with Deity. . . . I look for the new Teacher, that shall follow so far those shining laws; that he shall see them come full circle; shall see their rounding complete grace; shall see the world to be the mirror of the soul; shall see the identity of the law of gravitation with purity of heart; and shall show that the Ought, that Duty, is one thing with Science, with Beauty, and with Joy" (LA 89, 92). "A newborn bard of the Holy Ghost"—no phrase more accurately describes or predicts Very's dramatic transformation in the months following Emerson's address or his emergence in the autumn of 1838 as a vatic poet and "teacher" of his own version of messianic individualism.

✸ 28 ✸

"The end of all things"

It was precisely in his role as teacher that Very's real crisis began. During the second week of September, fired with spiritual conviction, he began to speak and act oddly in the classroom. Already accustomed to their teacher's habit of interweaving spiritual advice with instruction in Greek language and culture, the students were nevertheless shocked by this new, prophetic manner. Rumors began circulating about Very's behavior; the kind of gentle religious council he had become known for across the small Harvard community had become more emotional—and more strange. His fellow Salemite Samuel Johnson, dazzled at first by his tutor's advice and wisdom, had written his father that "no man" was "more sensible than Mr. Very, whose greatest fault is that he is too frank and open for much communication with the deceitful world."[1] Johnson described Very's "message" to his class with sympathetic clarity: "He bases all these instructions on the submission of our will to that of God: to adapt everything to that: to act, to speak, to move only as it is conformable to his will: then, when we have arrived at that degree of excellence, we shall see God."[2] But Johnson soon realized that something strange was happening when Very began to use "language so wild" and "ideas so startling" that it was hard to believe he was sane. Hearing from other freshmen that Very had "declared to them that he was infallible: that he was a man of heaven, and superior to all the world around him," Johnson quickly backtracked.[3] The Greek tutor appeared to believe that God or the Holy Spirit was speaking through him and came to the point of startling one section by loudly commanding his students to "flee to the mountains, for the end of all things is at hand!"[4]

What had happened? How did the Divinity School student and Greek tutor, the poet who had once wished to "restore epic poetry," come to believe, at least for the moment, that he was infallible, "a man of heaven"? If we can accept Very's own explanation from a few months later, he had at last achieved kenosis, the total emptying-out of the self—the erasure of his personal will. As he explained to Henry Bellows the following December, since the previous spring he had seemed to himself uninterested in the events of his own life,

> and yet I felt very happy for I had so long persevered in this course that it had wrought out for me much peace and content. I began to be happy in simply trying to do and think good. I had nothing more to give up to I had given all I had yet I did not know this then as I do now. . . . But at the beginning of the third that is this collegiate year I meet [*sic*] with another which I will now relate. I had all along as I have said felt a gradual increase of joy and my life was more and more regularly a sacrifice of all things. After having begun my duties at Cambridge this year about the third week I felt within me a new will something which came some time in the week but I could not tell what day exactly. It seemed like my old will only it was to the good—it was not a feeling of my own but a sensible will that was not my own. Accompanying this was another feeling as it were a consciousness which seemed to say—"That which creates you creates also that which you see or him to whom you speak," as it might be. These two consciousnesses as I may call them continued within me two or three weeks and went as they came imperceptably [*sic*]. While they continued I was moved entirely by the Spirit within me to declare to all that the coming of Christ was at hand.[5]

As a retrospective reading of his own behavior, this passage is remarkable both for its frankness and for its Augustinian psychological detail. The increase in joy suggests, on the one hand, a lack of turbulence leading up to this moment and yet, on the other, an increasingly ecstatic state brought about by the "sacrifice of all things." The poems to this point have made clear, at least in part, what that sacrifice meant in emotional terms to Very. Now, fascinatingly, he describes the emergence of a voice or voices within, one of which seems to speak of the unity of all things while the other, the "sensible will that was not [his] own," moves him to declare the coming of Christ. "I had nothing more to give up to I had given all," he told Bellows, implying, however indirectly, that his relinquishment of desire—indeed, his total sacrifice of self—had won for him this compensation: God's voice spoke in and through him.

The letter to Bellows may, of course, be too retrospective a reading of Very's own behavior to tell us why this dramatic turn of events occurred in September; the process was likely to have been more intuitive and emotional than this account indicates. Constructing any sort of immediate etiology of Very's extraordinary leap into prophetic mania is impossible without additional evidence, but there are suggestions of potential catalysts. In November and January of 1838 and 1839, two of his closest friends from his undergraduate days died. Charles Hayward, a young playwright associated with the *Harvardiana* student magazine, had been part of the circle of writers that included Samuel Tenney Hildreth and Very. He graduated in 1837 and began studying at the Divinity School in the autumn of 1838. He seems to have become ill some time in the early months of the term. Charles Stearns Wheeler, writing for the *Christian Examiner*, speculated that Hayward had exhausted himself preparing the "Hebrew Studies requisite for entering his class," and the resulting "typhus fever" overtook him just as Very was reestablishing himself in Salem after his month at McLean Hospital.[6] At the same time, Hildreth, who was arguably Very's closest friend among the writers, had effectively gone blind during his senior year; other students had to read to him, and when he was nevertheless offered a job teaching elocution at Harvard, he was able to continue there until his death, also of typhus, in January of 1839.[7] Despite the fact that Very's ecstatic statements began in September (before both deaths), the tenuous state of his friends' health may well have added tension to his intense desire to rid himself of all trace of personal desire or will. If the need to transcend or overcome grief—or, more generally, to escape the turbulent passions of his mother's willful but anguished life—had brought him to the point of self-erasure, then the fragility of those closest to him could hardly have failed to intensify his surging emotions. Some have taken Very to task for seeming to ignore these deaths that occurred during his mania, and it may be that by the time Hayward and Hildreth had died he was in such a spiritual state that he could simply transcend the pain associated with these events.[8] But if so, this escape from anguish argues all the more for the significance of these timely losses for a young man already convinced that the only way to true peace was through the sacrifice of personal feelings.

In the weeks just after the Divinity School Address and leading up to that fateful September, Very had spoken with William Ellery Channing for the first time at Channing's brother's house in Boston. Though no record of that conversation survives, something of Very's manner can be inferred from the comments of another guest, the elder Richard Henry Dana. Best known for his lectures on Shakespeare, Dana found Very cogent and blessed with a "remarkable mental intensity": the young tutor seemed to Dana "all Love—God was a sort of atmosphere of Love which transfused itself through him and over all things."[9] Others had noticed his peculiar individuality and spiritual certainty. Sarah Freeman Clarke, a friend of Margaret Fuller's and sister to the Unitarian minister James Freeman Clarke, met Very in July and found him "remarkable for always speaking the truth and for believing in an Inward Voice."[10] Even Emerson, as influential as he could possibly be on his younger visitor, recognized Very's note of wildness and idiosyncrasy. Writing on September 1 to his more conventionally religious Aunt Mary, he recommended the "young man at Cambridge" as someone who "would interest [her]," but he made it clear that Very did "not agree to his [Emerson's] dogmatism."[11] This last admission, slightly exaggerated in tone, may have been meant as a reassurance (and a joke), as much to himself as to Aunt Mary. The observation would prove true in many ways, and yet its expression may also have disguised Emerson's sense that some influence had already occurred.

It would have been understandable for Emerson to worry about the effect of his address as the autumn term was beginning at Harvard, and we shouldn't lose sight of the fact that less than two months separated his speech in Divinity Chapel from Very's strange behavior on that same campus. If in fact Very's soul had been roused by Emerson's speech, his reaction combined with the heightened mood of controversy that reigned in the months after the address could account for another dimension of Very's emotional surge. Passions, both for and against Emerson, had been roused; an air of flushed outrage on the part of traditionalists confronted those remnants of messianic elation among their critics, and it would be surprising if Very himself had not engaged in more than one heated discussion about the speech. By September, this combination of his own, long-pursued spiritual and emotional purification as well as the electricity in the air from Emerson's description of the "newborn bard of the Holy Ghost" may have produced in him an accelerated mental energy that tipped him over the thin line that often separates high purpose from mania.

In a defining poem written that September and titled "The New Birth," Very not only announced this spiritual advent; he described the accelerated movement of his excited intelligence:

> 'Tis a new life—thoughts move not as they did
> With slow uncertain steps across my mind,
> In thronging haste fast pressing on they bid
> The portals open to the viewless wind; (*CP* 64)

Slightly breathless, the abbreviated opening moves toward a strange vision of liberation, as though the former life had been spiritually claustrophobic. But the speaker implies more than a conventional image of freedom. The wind is "viewless" because the self has ceased to exist as a subjective entity.

The new life is the result of relinquishing the "crown of pride that gilds each mortal brow," allowing the "heavens and earth" to "fade" (*CP* 64). "Their walls are falling now" (*CP* 64), the speaker insists, suggesting a complete but ecstatic shedding of the structure of identity itself. What remains is the racing Spirit, the onrushing flow of selfless energies that demand expression:

> Fast crowding on each thought claims utterance strong,
> Storm-lifted waves swift rushing to the shore
> On from the sea they send their shouts along,
> Back through the cave-worn rocks their thunders roar,
> And I a child of God by Christ made free
> Start from death's slumbers to eternity. (*CP* 64)

The storm-tossed sea as a metaphor for divine urgency and power recalls the similar embrace of the sublime in "The Voice of God." But here the breakdown of identity in the face of overpowering force is more profound and more complete. The pun on "Start" combines the sudden, visceral moment of awakening with the sense of beginning, though any normal understanding of time is undermined by the paradox of a temporal point that leads to an atemporal "eternity." Thus the new self that wakes to the freedom from death is outside of time itself and, in a sense, not a self at all.

This claim to be, in essence, ego-less, to function beyond the limits of conscious identity, would prove to be one of Very's more radical and difficult-to-maintain conceptions. It can perhaps be accepted as a paradox, but already "The New Birth" points to its necessary contradictions. Most notably, given the events surrounding its composition, the poem raises the basic question of how Mr. Tutor Very, despite his apparent mania and eye-popping claims of infallibility, could produce such controlled and concentrated poetry. Even in its depiction of hurried thinking, "The New Birth" retains its clarity and formal calm: this is no manic gush of semi-intelligible prophecy. If anything, Very's poetry became more rather than less controlled after the events of early September 1838. He had, in essence, become the poet-prophet he had long wished to be, but rather than an epic of Miltonic proportions, he had begun to produce a detailed and tightly bound record—one sonnet at a time—of the transformation of a single soul.

✸ 29 ✸

Madness

Even before Very's outburst in his Greek class, he had set off alarms among the Harvard faculty. On Thursday evening, September 13, he appeared at the home of Henry Ware Jr. and made startling claims: that a "revelation" had been made to him, that "he had fully given up his own will, and now only did the will of the Father—that it was the Father who was speaking thro' him."[1] He asked for a New Testament and explicated Matthew 24, a controversial chapter in which Jesus predicts the destruction of the Temple of Jerusalem and speaks of the signs of apocalypse. According to Divinity School student and Concord native George Moore, who was present and recorded the incident in his diary, Very explained that "Christ's second coming [was] in him," and when Ware refused to assent to the truth of Very's vision, Very "said to him with great solemnity, I had thought that you did the will of the Father, and that I should receive some sympathy from you—but I now find that you are doing your own will, and not the will of your Father."[2]

Ware's immediate reaction to the encounter is not indicated, but the dumbfounded Moore could not avoid the conclusion that Very was "insane."[3] As Moore left Ware's house that evening, he ran into others who had already heard Very's reading of Matthew 24 to much the same effect. The following morning Very continued to deliver his prophetic message in the classroom, and in the evening made an impromptu speech at the regular Divinity School debate. "He told us that we were all men—," Moore later entered into his diary, "that we were all doing our own wills—but that he was doing the will of God—he was no longer a man but the Holy Spirit was speaking in him, and that what he said was eternal truth."[4] Moore was, once again, more than a little unnerved by Very's manner: "It is almost fearful to look upon him, and see his deep earnestness, exhibited in his face, and to hear the tremulous tones of voice as he utters himself—and at the same time to think that he is fully possessed with this great idea that the spirit is revealing itself in him."[5]

That same evening Josiah Quincy, Harvard's president, went to the rooms of Charles Stearns Wheeler and asked him to take over as Greek tutor.[6] Very's younger brother, Washington, who had just started his first year at Harvard, was asked to take Jones back to Salem, and on Saturday, September 15, they arrived at Federal Street. There is no source to tell us what sort of emotional scene met the two brothers when they opened the door of the "old-fashioned" house set above the lakelike inlet of the North River. But we do know from Elizabeth Peabody's later account that Washington "saw & agreed . . . that there was some disease about his [brother's] brain—an intensity of action of the higher intuitive powers suspending those of the common sense" (EP 407). Lydia Very, on the other hand, protective and proud as always, almost immediately accepted her oldest child's explanation of his own exalted spiritual state. If she did have concerns about Jones's state of mind on that first evening, they were likely pushed aside when she realized that others considered him insane and were intent on condemning or confining him.

The vehemence of local reaction, predominantly from the clergy, became clear as soon as the next morning when Very made his way around Salem, giving the same interpretation of Matthew 24 and attempting to "baptize" several local ministers as part of his prophetic office (EP 406). To say he caused a stir is an understatement. Two of them, including the Baptist minister Lucius Bolles, physically threw Very out of their houses. The North Church minister, John Brazer, staring at him with his "very red face . . . [and] very round, china-blue eyes," demanded that he perform a miracle, and when Very refused he accused him of having hallucinations.[7] And Charles Upham, the minister at the First Church who later played a role in Hawthorne's removal from the Salem customhouse, immediately threatened Very with commitment to a mental hospital. Upham was already an avowed enemy of Emerson's, and he leaped at the opportunity to blame the "atheist" from Concord for leading a young divinity student into insanity.[8]

Later that morning, Very knocked on the door of the Peabody house on Charter Street. His face was flushed. His eyes were shining. Elizabeth Peabody opened the door and immediately understood that something strange and possibly "dangerous" was happening: "As soon as we were within the parlor door he laid his hand on my head," she recalled in 1880, "—and said, 'I come to baptize you with the Holy Ghost & with fire'—and then he prayed—I cannot remember his words but they were thrilling—and as I stood under his hand, I trembled to the centre" (EP 406). The rest of her account is the best description that survives of Very in the first rush of his mystic conviction:

> I felt he was beside himself and I was alone in the lower story of the house.—When he had done I sat down and he at a little distance, did the same—and there was a dead silence.—Soon he said,—with a slightly uneasy misgiving said, How do you feel? I replied gently, "I feel no change"—"But you will"—said he hurriedly—"I am the Second Coming—Give me a Bible"—There was one in the room to which I pointed. He went to the table where it was and turned to Christ's prophecy of the Second Coming—and read it ending with the words, "This day is this fulfilled in your hearing." (EP 406)

Though alarmed and increasingly convinced of his insanity, Peabody realized that Very was "gentle & harmless and happy" in his revelation. She was more concerned with how the town was reacting to this peculiar apparition and what sorts of steps were being taken against him. After Very left the Charter Street house, Peabody learned from her friend Mary Foote of his earlier dustups with the ministers and realized the dangerous implications of the moment for both Very and Emerson. She strode purposively to the Very house on Federal Street and was met at the door by Lydia, who had already had a heated exchange with Upham and was in no mood to be friendly to another high-handed visitor.[9] As described earlier, Peabody knew Very's mother by reputation as a "person of great energy," an atheist or freethinker "at odds with the existing state of society," but now she was astonished to find that this intense, vehement woman had not only abandoned her reputed materialism but fully believed that her son "was an *angel* whom God had inspired—and a *proof* that there was a God above us who was Infinite Love" (EP 406; original emphasis). Peabody admitted in her later recounting of these events that these were not Lydia's exact words, but the idea stuck with her that Lydia had, in effect, been converted by her son's mystical experience and behavior. She assured Mrs. Very that she herself "was opposed to all violent methods—and had the greatest reverence for her son," and after learning that Very was "resting in his chamber," Peabody left (EP 407).

We should pause for a moment to consider this account of Lydia's reaction, particularly given its role in the development of the theory that Very's identification of himself as "the second coming" arose from a deep-seated desire to overcome his mother's lack of faith. Though built for the most part on secondhand information, Peabody's description of Lydia is vivid and reflective of her own, obviously heightened experience of their first interview. But was she correct in her reading of the situation, and does this account provide a clear basis for concluding that Very's mission was, fundamentally if subconsciously, to bring his mother to belief? In the absence of other, clearly corroborating evidence, the answer has to be a qualified no. There is no direct evidence that Very's religious experience, though extreme, was fixated primarily on his mother's spiritual state. Nowhere, in his poetry, essays, or notebooks, does he indicate this. What he does clearly express is his own intention to remove from his spiritual life all worldly desire, along with the emotional turmoil that it produces. That Lydia may have been an example to him of this kind of emotional turbulence is reasonable to conclude; that her painful, "severe experience of life," as Peabody described it, could have pushed her son in this direction is likewise plausible, particularly if we remind ourselves that he witnessed and felt much of that history himself. He may well have been pleased that his mother was moving toward a higher, more spiritual vision of her life as a consequence of his vision, but again there is no surviving evidence that indicates his reaction.

Peabody's suggestion that Lydia saw her son's experience as proof of God's existence rings true enough, but this account, by Peabody's own admission, also seems incomplete. "There is something very strange in it all," she explained to Emerson at the time (EP 219). Some of that strangeness may have been her inability to explain how a supposed "course materialist" and "disciple of Fanny Wright" could so quickly accept the idea that her son had become an "angel" or messenger of God. Whatever her reputation, Lydia Very seems from this perspective to have been highly susceptible to spiritual experience. Perhaps she herself wavered between faith and a long-simmered critique of local pieties, and her son's extraordinary claims, bolstered by her own wounded pride, gave her an opportunity to see her struggles in a new light. What we can rely on from Peabody's account is the clear evidence that Lydia, as was often reported, fiercely defended those under her care. That she would take her son's word against the view of others is perfectly consistent with her long history of defensive pride and independence.

Later that evening, Very again knocked at the door on Charter Street, but something had changed. "He came in very quietly," Peabody remembered, "and said, 'I misunderstood the Holy Ghost—the time is not yet for the baptism of fire—Nothing can be done with violence in the Second Coming—You are all in the baptism of John—I only am in the son—and I must speak as the Son—.'" According to Peabody, Very then "unfolded a monstrous folio sheet of paper, on which were four double columns of sonnets." This shift of mood is significant. It remains unclear whether it was in response to the objections of the local ministers or to Very's own uncertainty about the effect of his earlier "baptisms." But it indicates an ability, at the least, to correct or modify his vision, perhaps especially when the high energy of his enthusiasm had partially dissipated. The shift suggested here from prophet to poet, from John to "the Son," also indicates a recovery of sorts of Very's earlier quest to unite the poetic and messianic roles he had long brooded on in his investigations of the contemporary long poem. If his personal acts of prophecy and baptism had failed or proved insufficient, his ability to "speak as the Son" through poetry could fulfill his primary ambition: to eliminate his will via the removal of his personal voice, allowing a direct passage for the words of Christ or the Holy Spirit.

The next day, Monday, September 17, Very was admitted to the McLean Asylum for the Insane in Somerville, Massachusetts. He consented to treatment after consulting with Edward Tyrrel Channing, his former rhetoric professor, in Cambridge. According to Peabody's later account, Very "was persuaded to go to Somerville," and "the considerate and tender manner in which everything was done, took down the excitement" of the past few scandalous days in Cambridge and Salem (EP 407). Contrary to Gittleman's sensationalistic account, there is nothing to indicate that Very was forcibly abducted on the night of September 16. In this telling, Upham and Brazer burst into the Federal Street house and seized Very, hustling him off to McLean. But despite the fact that Upham had threatened such a move, there is no clear evidence that anything of the sort occurred. No existing account describes this event (either at the time or retrospectively), nor does Gittleman cite a source for his dramatic narration. In the December 1838 letter to Henry Bellows, Very explains that he was "placed contrary to my will at the Asylum," which may indicate that some force was applied, but could equally imply that he had agreed to go in order to placate others (it was against his will because it was not his choice) and avoid further conflict.[10] The only hint of possible violence is Peabody's single sentence that simply says Very was "carried off" on the same day he came to her house and gave her his witness. We do know from the McLean records that Very was admitted the next day, on September 17, and in her later account Peabody described the far less dramatic meeting with E. T. Channing that likely occurred that Monday. Her account of Very being "persuaded" to enter McClean is the only surviving description of this event and presents a far more convincing scenario than the supposed abduction.[11] Very would stay at McLean for one month under the care of

Dr. Luther Voss Bell, writing an essay on *Hamlet* and quietly conversing with and encouraging the other patients. His remarkable academic career was over. After his strange behavior at Harvard, he would never be allowed in the classroom again. But he had, in a peculiar and wholly unique way, finally become the poet he had instinctively sought to be—the kenotic poet of God, ready to record, like a devoted copyist, the cries and whispers of the divine.

III
God's Scrivener

✷ 30 ✷
Prince Hamlet

If there is a fundamental scene among the surviving materials of Very's biography, it's the image of the nine-year-old boy, on his first voyage with his sea captain father, treading the stones of Kronborg Slot, "Hamlet's Castle," by the cold blue waters of the Øresund. Merely exciting or strange at the time, this experience may well have assumed greater significance for Very after his father's death and his own later immersion in Shakespeare's plays. Perhaps the strong attraction to the plays themselves, implied by Very's purchase of the complete works of Shakespeare while still a shop boy, began here—with a literate father, soon to be lost, and a few tenuous memories of Captain Very's presence in so distant and legendary a place. In any case, by the time of Very's "change of heart," he had once again turned to Shakespeare, now as a thoughtful reader and critic, brooding on the nature of genius.

As we know from Elizabeth Peabody's account of her first meeting with Very in December of 1837, the essay eventually published as "Shakespeare" was in the works as early as the autumn of that year. Some time later the following summer it was complete enough for Very to share it with Edward Tyrrel Channing, and in September, just as he was dismissed from Harvard, he managed to send it to Emerson. The essay had emerged from the question of Shakespeare's genius in light of his lack of a clear belief in Christian salvation. (Emerson summarized Very's explanation in his journal: "What led him to study Shakspeare [*sic*] was the fact that all young men say, Shakspeare was no saint—yet see what genius. He wished to solve that problem" [*JMN* 7:123]). Very was well aware of the traditional attacks on Shakespeare as too fond of crude humor and too willing to mix the exalted with the mundane, and he wished both to explain this universality and to clarify, as he had with the epic, the difference between pre-Christian and "modern" art. Building from de Staël's distinction between "pagan" and "romantic" literatures (itself closely related to

August Wilhelm Schlegel's contrast of the immediate, sensual poetry of the ancients to the contemporary poetry of *Sehnsucht* or longing), Very argued that Shakespeare, like Homer, was essentially a force of nature, an almost prelapsarian consciousness whose individual will was in complete accord with the world around him: "My object is to show," he declared, "that a desire of action was the ruling impulse of [Shakespeare's] mind; and consequently a sense of existence its permanent state. That this condition was natural; not the result felt from a submission of the will to it, but bearing the will along with it; presenting the mind as phenomenal and unconscious, and almost as much a passive instrument as the material world."[1] In other words, Shakespeare had not overcome or removed his personal will, as Very struggled to do; his mind had simply remained in a state of innocence, open to all before it, much like the romantic conception of the spontaneous child.

This argument, as Very himself notes, provides an "excuse" for "much that has seemed impure in [Shakespeare's] writings," but it also clarifies Very's own conception of what an effectively will-less existence, an immersion in divine spirit, might look like.[2] In this sense, Shakespeare provided a valuable contrast to modern writers like Milton or Wordsworth, who register "the struggle of the child to become the perfect man in Christ Jesus."[3] Without Shakespeare's "childlike state of innocence," they must wrestle against the movement of their individual desires: "Their constant prayer is, 'Not my will, Father, but thine be done.' They are striving for that silence in their own bosoms that shall make the voice that created all things heard."[4] This is the path to virtue, which, if completed, will lead to a state similar to the unconscious purity of Shakespeare's natural mind, freeing "the voice" of God himself to flow unfiltered through the poet: "To become natural, to find again that Paradise which he has lost, man must be born again; he must learn that the true exercise of his own will is only in listening to that voice, which is ever walking in the garden, but of which he is afraid and hides himself."[5]

The essence of Very's spiritual and poetic project is stated clearly here, with remarkable lucidity and coherence for someone who was on the verge of declaring himself "infallible." Shakespeare had become his model of a kind of unmediated expression, a vision so pure and uncorrupted that it had escaped the limitations of modern consciousness. In a curious echo of Keats's "negative capability" letter, Very offered a Shakespeare whose negation of self was inborn rather than achieved through struggle, a romantic child after Emerson's ideal, who had "retained the spirit of infancy even into the era of manhood."[6] In part, this conception provided Very with a sanction for the idea of the pure poetic voice, the spontaneous overflow of divine speech onto the pages of his notebooks. It enacted, in romantic terms, an almost antinomian or "inner light" epiphany of godly presence within. At the same time, it insisted on the possibility of utopian individuality, a heaven-state on earth possible for anyone who might succeed in removing the limitations of personal consciousness. For Very, to approach this condition of redeemed innocence was, paradoxically, to approach the "perfect freedom" of "service": "Let us labor then, knowing that the more we can erase from the tablets of our hearts the false fashions and devices which our own perverse wills have written over them, the more will shine forth, with all their original brightness, those ancient primeval characters traced there by the finger of God, until our whole being is full of light."[7]

At what point, precisely, Very began to believe that his poems were the direct communication of the Holy Spirit is difficult to pinpoint, though by mid-September of 1838 he had begun to understand all of his speech and writing as divine in origin. He declared as much to Emerson, in the letter that accompanied the Shakespeare essay to Concord:

> Cambridge Sept. 1838
>
> My Brother
>
> I am glad at last to be able to transmit what has been told me of Shakespeare—tis but the faint echo of that which speaks to you now. That was the utterance of the soul still in its travail but the hour is past of which I have often spoken to you and you hear not mine own words but the teachings of the Holy Spirit. Rejoice with me my brother and give thanks with me to the Father and our Lord Jesus Christ who have now taken me to themselves and will not let me go any more from them. I feel that the day *now* is when "the tabernacle of God is with men, and he will dwell with them, and they shall be his people." The gathering time has come and the harvest is now reaping from the wide plains of Earth. Here even here the will of the Father begins to be done as in heaven. My friend I tell you these things as they are told me and hope soon for a day or two of leasure [*sic*] (perhaps in two or three weeks) when I may speak with you face to face as I now write. Tell Mrs Emerson that I have the love for her wherewith the Father has loved me and kiss your son for me as my hail in hope to an unborn brother of the kingdom.
>
> Jones Very[8]

As one of the earliest of Very's ecstatic letters, this brief and purposeful note gives us some sense of the kind of language and visionary style

Very had adopted as his prophetic medium. He explains that the essay had been the product of his own voice, that of "the soul still in its travail," but the letter, "that which now speaks to you," issued directly from the Holy Spirit. Very had spoken to Emerson before about his desire to eliminate his will, and now the language of the letter suggested a kind of ventriloquism of the apocalyptic style of Matthew 24. Very was, in a sense, possessed by the voice imagined in its millenarian moment: the "*now*" and "here even here" of a divine immanence that aligned with Emerson's own antinomian-tinged individualism. For his part, Emerson seems not to have been alarmed or particularly surprised by the claims in the letter. He did express concern a few weeks later to William Henry Furness, explaining that he had read Very's "noble paper (MS) on Shakespeare" but was "distressed to hear that he is feared to be insane. His critique certainly is not."[9] Perhaps not for the first or last time, Emerson here seems to underestimate the literal intent of Very's romantic messianism. The Shakespeare essay, as sharply observant and carefully organized as it is, makes clear that the goal of the individual is self-negation, a stripping away of the particulars of desire to make way for the voice "ever walking in the garden."[10] This is the state that Very understood himself to have attained by the time he sent the essay to Emerson. In a remarkable if overweening synthesis, Very had collapsed himself, Shakespeare, and the Holy Spirit into one startling conception of the poet-prophet whose words admit neither question nor doubt.

Despite his confinement at McLean, Very had no intention of slowing down or curtailing his writing. If what emerged on the page was now divine, all the more reason to take down both poetry and prose at speed. While in Somerville he worked on a second Shakespeare essay, this one devoted to *Hamlet,* the play and character he considered most revealing of the deepest being of its author. If Shakespeare was, as Very had argued, "the childlike embodiment" of the natural "sense of existence," then Hamlet dramatized precisely the record of such a mind's encounter with the full consciousness of death.[11] "The great fore-plane of adversity has been driven over him," Very asserted, "and his soul is laid bare to the very foundation. . . . Stunned by the sudden storm of woes, he doubts, as he looks at the havoc spread around him, whether he himself is left, and fears lest the very ground on which he lies prostrate may not prove treacherous."[12] The natural state of Shakespeare's mind, a kind of pure receptor for what he observed and experienced, would have necessarily, for Very, made him more aware and afraid of death. "The thought of death touched him in his very centre," making Hamlet's famous soliloquy the core of the play and the key for understanding its author: "He is contending in thought with the great realities beyond [life]; the dark clouds that hang over the valley of the shadow of death, and float but dimly and indistinct before *our* vision, have, like his father's ghost, become fixed and definite 'in *his* mind's eye;' he has looked them into shape, and they stand before him wherever he turns, with a presence that will not be put by."[13]

In many respects this reading follows paths well trodden by previous romantic commentators. As Jonathan Bate has noted, *Hamlet* was a key text for poets like Coleridge who wished to "move from the realm of action and politics to that of thought and inner feeling. . . . Coleridge's Shakespeare shares the nature of Hamlet, his greatest creation: both the Prince and the poet are 'philosophical aristocrats.'"[14] Hazlitt, whose *Characters of Shakespear's Plays* Very borrowed at least three times from the Harvard library, took the parallels even further, claiming that "Hamlet's thoughts are as real as our own. . . . Their reality is in the reader's mind. It is *we* who are Hamlet."[15] To what extent Very accepted this identification with the character is impossible to determine with any certainty, but we should not dismiss the resonances of the play with his early experiences, particularly given his visit to Helsingør in 1823 and his father's subsequent death. Very's description of Hamlet as a young man, by definition a son, facing the reality of death for the first time seems charged with his own deep and unexpressed memories:

> Was he strongly sensible of a purpose,—it must have been to open to our view that wild tumultuous sea of thoughts which was rolling in the breast of Hamlet, when the idea of death and the presence of things invisible, stood sensible to sight and touch before him. This thought, breaking upon him in so terrible and unexpected a form, tore from life, at one rude grasp, the gaudy and alluring attire with which it is arrayed to the eye of sense; and, blotting out "all trivial fond records, all saws of books," it fronted him in its own grim reality.[16]

Very was eleven years old when his father died. It was not a distant, unwitnessed event but took place in the close confines of the crowded family house at Buffum's Corner. Its effect on him could only have been profound, even, or perhaps especially, if he showed little sign of reaction. If there is a single root that fed the tremendous pressure he felt to transcend the limits of worldly existence—to erase his will, escape affection and desire—it's here: in a young man's stunned confrontation with death and "the mystery of his own being."[17] As he began to announce his mission and his conception of his own role as "the second coming," he also spoke often of the state of "sonship," an idea he never abandoned and explained more fully at times in his later preaching. In an undated sermon on Hebrews 12, he argued that it "is only by this frequent communion with God that we can realize Him as our heavenly parent, who is guiding and blessing us in every event in life. . . . It is thus that we are *drawn* of God, and enabled to do his will in all things. It is thus that we perceive that Jesus is our brother, and that if we be Sons must be like Him" (HS 70; original emphasis [double underscore]). That God the *father* plays so important a role in Very's theology, enabling his own assumption of the role of *son* suggests at the very least the lingering desire to recover or replicate his relationship to his own lost father in the sublimated form of spirit.

Even so, we should avoid applying too schematic a reading of the play onto Very's early experience. There is no evidence to support the theory that he saw his mother as a type of fallen Gertrude who needed to be rescued via his own, Christ-like self-sacrifice. Nor is there any sense that he felt a particular obligation to respond to his father's memory by challenging death itself in his conception of a living "rebirth." That he felt a strong intellectual and emotional connection to the play and character, as well as its author, is clear, if for no other reason than that he himself seems drawn to its depiction of spiritual desolation. *Hamlet* may well have seemed a self-portrait of Very's inner life at the time of his father's death—particularly if he understood his early youth as preceding his embrace of a Christian vision. But his reading of the play could also reflect his observations of others as they encountered grief in ways similar to Hamlet's. Here Lydia Very comes most strongly to mind. Obviously passionate—in her impulsive elopement with her cousin as well as the strength of her emotions in general—Lydia possessed both the sharp vehemence of the wounded, resentful soul and the critical mind unwilling or unable to accept pat consolation for the losses of her children and husband. She was neither quiet nor easy in her grieving and perhaps, to her eldest son, seemed as much a "child of nature" in her garden world as did Shakespeare with his "love of variety and joyous sympathy with all things."[18] Very's reading of *Hamlet* suggests that he may have taken on or deeply sympathized with many of her feelings but at the same time sought an escape from their limits. The desire to quell or transcend emotion, particularly the desolation of grief intensified by passion, defined his essentially quietist determination to vacate his will. Only a few months before, he had made his intentions clear in his commonplace entry on suffering. Asking "how to cure our grief or trouble," he laid the blame clearly on "the *earthly feelings* we cherish" (CB III, 8–9; emphasis added). Whether the emotions he had in mind were his own or his mother's—or some amalgam of the two embittered by family acrimony—Very had found or fashioned his own escape, his own hypothetical suicide, from this sea of troubles.

✳ 31 ✳

Asylum

Despite his apparent loss of everyday reasonableness, Very was well aware that he was writing an essay on Hamlet, whose sanity is so much at issue, while confined to a hospital for the mentally ill. His consideration of this topic took on the manner of the apologist: "Hamlet has been called mad, but, as we think, Shakespeare thought more of his madness than he did of the wisdom of the rest of the play. Like the vision-struck Paul, in the presence of Felix, he spoke what to those around him, whose eyes had not been opened on that light brighter than the sun, seemed madness; but which was, in fact, the words of truth and soberness."[1] The identification could not be clearer: as the world in the play misunderstands Hamlet, so had Harvard and Salem failed to recognize the truth spoken by Jones Very. Both Hamlet and Very, in turn, reflect the prophetic-apostolic tradition of the "vision-struck Paul," hauled before the judge in Caesarea Maritima for preaching a truth as yet unseen by those "whose eyes had not been opened." Defensive though it certainly is, this reading of his own purpose and its relationship to the ordinary world plays an important role in Very's conception of his voice—and of language itself. What people have called "madness," he argues, is the reflection of their own inability to receive the spirit that animates what are otherwise empty sounds: "It is the spirit that quickens what we hear,—the mere hearing is nothing. The words which I say to you, says our Saviour, are *spirit,* and quicken with *eternal* life,—they are not addressed to the flesh, nor are they life-giving to that."[2] Thus, if his auditors have failed to accomplish "the death of [their] own wills," they will be unable to recognize "the divine meaning of that eternal life of which Jesus speaks."[3]

Amid the quiet, wooded eighteen acres that surrounded the former Barrell Mansion (fig. 9) in Somerville, in daily contact with others deemed unable or unfit to function in the outside world, Very may well have found his sense of persecution sharpened. But from what we know of his one month's residence there, he appears to have shown little outward evidence of even mild resistance to his treatment. McLean had been founded in 1816 as an alternative to existing forms of confinement for the mentally ill. Instead of harsh or even brutal measures of restraint, patients were treated respectfully and allowed comparative freedom to walk around the peaceful grounds, engage in crafts or games, or spend their time reading and writing. A magazine article from 1837 describes the daily regimen:

> The patients rise and dress about half an hour before breakfast, which is at sunrise in the winter, and six o'clock in the summer. After breakfast they are taken out to walk, or to ride, or are engaged, so far as possible, in useful labor, as farming, sawing, splitting and piling wood, or assisting their attendants; and a few are engaged in mechanical employments. A large number are occupied, more or less, in the amusements of bowling, quoits, throwing the ring, and in checkers, chess, backgammon, and other games; and in the interval of these amusements, reading books from the library, newspapers, and writing, serve to fill up the time.[4]

In addition there were regular dances in the evening and religious services on Sundays. This new "moral treatment," begun by the Quaker William Tuke at York Retreat in England, suited both the temperament and the interests of Very, who devoted himself to writing poems and completing his *Hamlet* essay. Under the care of Dr. Bell, later one of the founders of the American Psychiatric Association and a proponent of the "healing powers of nature" favored by Benjamin Rush in his *Medical Inquiries and Observations of the Mind* (1812), Very was encouraged to work but also to maintain a balanced, healthy diet and get as much rest as necessary.[5] (Elizabeth Peabody reported to Emerson that Dr. Bell had found Very's "digestive system entirely out of order" [EP 215].) Very also apparently spent a good deal of time talking to and comforting other patients. In a later journal entry, Emerson remembered his delight when Very told him that "the patients severally thanked him when he came away, and told him that he had been of great service to them" (*JMN* 8:299). For his part, at least in retrospect, Very seems to have appreciated the readjustment this time afforded him, telling Henry Bellows a few months later that the "influence of the Spirit" allowed his "usual manner" to return "in all things save that I now obey it as my natural impulse."[6] In 1855, Very wrote a poem praising the institution as a "House of Refuge" for "weary souls, / Trembling on the dizzy heights, mid gloom and shade" (*CP* 294). "A refuge thou from fiery Passion's sway," this "House of blissful Hope!"

was a "home of love, / A blest retreat, to me, . . . / When discord, doubt and fear for mastery strove— / There, first, His bow of Peace shone amid falling tears" (*CP* 294–95).

To those who met him after his release, Very may have seemed calmer and more manageable, but it was clear that his core idea and self-conception had not changed. Dr. Bell had expressed confidence that Very was cured of his "revelation" and advised him to go back to Salem to be "watched over" by his family (EP 215). But Elizabeth Peabody, for one, was not convinced. Very himself did explain to her that he had changed: he had been "intoxicated with the Holy Ghost when he came to see [her] before" but now "he [was] sobered" (EP 215), and she reported to Emerson that Very was thought to be "freed from the delusion of being a prophet extraordinary" and was allowed "to do as he pleased—& go where he pleases" (EP 215). But as far as she was concerned he was "as crazy as ever—" (EP 215). Just three days after his release, Peabody wrote to Emerson to warn him that his young friend was intent on visiting Concord within the week to "deliver his revelation," and she gave an account of Emerson's indirect involvement in the still simmering scandal: "Since he has come home [Mr. Brazer] has been telling him that *you* (from whom Mr. B <he> affects to believe all the thing comes) are now universally acknowledged to be & denounced as an atheist—& measures are taking!! to prevent you from having any more audience to corrupt—& ever so much more nonsense of whose malice or whose utter philisterei as the Germans say—I do not know which is the greatest" (EP 216).

With her typical energy and quick mind for strategy, Peabody could see the danger, despite the self-importance of panjandrums like Brazer.[7] She hoped to insulate Emerson, still under attack for his Divinity School speech, from smears connected to Very's wilder claims.[8] Something of the atmosphere of the moment can be inferred from her emotional reassurance that Emerson had the support of those like her and important Salem patrons such as Susan Burley: "Miss Burley & I spent an hour or two together the other day chiefly talking of you—& our sympathies moral intellectual & religious with you . . . rejoicing to hear that you had said 'none of the dirt thrown upon you sticks to you'—for even *you* cannot make your friends quite so *sublime* as not to feel some degree of tenderness for the man of flesh & blood & part of 'that tissue' so mysteriously called the Human heart—" (EP 217; original emphasis). Peabody feared that Very's intended visit would only provide more ammunition to detractors, and she advised Emerson against allowing Very to stay in his house, "else you may not easily get rid of him" (EP 216). Very himself, she explained, had begun to think of Emerson as an ally, similarly "persecuted" by those who failed to understand his own prophetic revelation. The visit, Peabody believed, was Very's bid for "full sympathy" from someone whose vision aligned with his own.

The following Wednesday, October 24, Very arrived in Concord, carrying his *Hamlet* essay. Having heard from Peabody and others about his behavior and time at McLean, Emerson was fascinated to observe his young friend's behavior and judge his supposed insanity for himself. After two days, he admitted in his journal that Very "gave occasion to many thoughts on his peculiar state of mind and his relation to society" (*JMN* 7:116). Emerson classified his visitor as a "monotone," someone obsessed by a single idea or conviction, and recognized that the critical value of this "telescope's" focus was his ability to isolate and highlight a single evil from the "sphere" of thought and experience. Only in this way can we see "the immense extent of that revolution that must be wrought" toward our apprehension of the "all in all" (*JMN* 7:117). Even though this was their third meeting, it was Emerson's first real opportunity to listen at length to Very's "mission." He was impressed and perhaps even a little flattered by this almost familiar embodiment of his own ideas grafted onto the wild vine of "inner light" enthusiasm. But there were clearly differences. Very had hoped for a complete and sympathetic reaction to his revelation. If anyone were to understand him, it would be Emerson. But according to Emerson's later account, something intervened:

> When Jones Very was in Concord, he said to me, "I always felt when I heard you speak or read your writings that you saw the truth better than others, yet I felt that your spirit was not quite right. It was as if a vein of colder air blew across me." He seemed to expect from me a full acknowledgement of his mission and a participation of the same. Seeing this, I asked him if he did not see that my thoughts and my position were constitutional, that it would be false and impossible for me to say his things or try to occupy his ground as for him to usurp mine? (*JMN* 8:148)

Despite *Nature*'s near-mystical evocations of oneness with nature, Emerson was a modern thinker: his conception of spiritual experience was informed and limited by an acceptance of skepticism. In his foundational essay he had made perfectly clear that he was attempting to recover an individual spirituality from within a philosophy that doubted our ability to perceive the world with objective certainty. Reacting to the empiricism of Locke and Hume—and buoyed by the Kantianism translated by Victor Cousin and Coleridge—he saw intuition and instinct as our personal wellspring of the general truth in nature. But given our individual differences, each expression of those truths must be unique or even strange, their consistency often evident only in retrospect. As he explained to Very, "sincerity is the highest compliment you can pay" to anyone because it indicates a oneness between the self and experience that very likely, if not certainly, gives us a glimpse of truth (*JMN* 7:124). But to demand that everyone see the world only one way—your way—was to ask the impossible and betray the sacred idiosyncrasy of the self.

Despite his wide and intense reading over the previous six years or more, Very had never clearly grappled with the philosophical critiques of epistemology that informed Emerson's thinking. His poetry and few commonplace book annotations suggest that he saw nature as an almost transparent spiritual reality, its truth available to anyone who had sufficiently removed the impediment of the self's interests.[9] For Emerson to evoke precisely those particularities of identity as "constitutional" in the shaping of a version or style of truth was anathema to Very. He had, after all, just erased, to his way of thinking, all traces of his own will, including even normal self-awareness. It was as though Emerson were trying to explain modern subjectivity to Anne Hutchinson or the Quaker George Fox.[10] As sophisticated as Very could be in thinking about poetry or history, his mind was essentially premodern. There were no ironies or indirections in his communication with truth or spirit. God spoke directly to and through him.[11]

Consequently, Very and Emerson struggled to communicate across an unbridgeable divide. They both, however intuitively, understood the problem, Very citing the "colder air" that blew from Emerson's direction, and Emerson noting his friend's remarkable simplicity and purity. (He admitted to his journal that Very's words were "no more disputable than the shining of yonder sun or the blowing of this sound wind" [*JMN* 7:522].) But it's fair to say that, at least at first, Very's unselfconscious directness surprised Emerson, drawing from him intimacies he rarely shared with others. In a remarkable moment in his journals, Emerson confessed to the sort of candor Very was able to elicit:

> I told Jones Very that I had never suffered, that I could scarcely bring myself to feel a concern for the safety and life of my nearest friends that would satisfy them; that I saw clearly that if my wife, my child, my mother, should be taken from me, I should still remain whole, with the same capacity of cheap enjoyment from all things. I should not grieve enough, although I love them. But could I make them feel what I feel,—the boundless resources of the soul,—remaining entire

> when particular threads of relation are snapped,—I should then dismiss forever the little remains of uneasiness I have in regard to them. (*JMN* 7:132)

Commentators have often cited this passage as a foreshadowing of Emerson's similar confession in 1844's "Experience": "In the death of my son, now more than two years ago, I seem to have lost a beautiful estate,—no more. I cannot get it nearer to me" (LA 473). The earlier of two similar entries suggests that this coldness or sense of distance from feelings had been with Emerson for some time, a thread in his inner life that he pulled at from time to time.[12] But it is nevertheless striking that Very, with his unguarded and insistent evangelism, should elicit this moment from someone as personally elusive as Emerson.[13]

Despite these differences—or because of them—Emerson was impressed with his peculiar visitor and not at all convinced that Very was insane. The Shakespeare essays had dazzled him; a few weeks after the visit he listed Very, along with "Coleridge, Lamb, Schlegel, Goethe," and Herder, as one of the dramatist's greatest critics (*JMN* 7:147). And he delighted in Very's ability to upset the social niceties of the parlor. When Barzillai Frost, Emerson's anonymous example of poor preaching in the Divinity School Address, presided over a meeting of local Sunday-school teachers at Emerson's house, Very joined the group only to cause chaos:

> I ought not to omit recording the astonishment which seized all the company when our brave saint, the other day, fronted the presiding preacher. The preacher began to tower and dogmatize with many words. Instantly I foresaw that his doom was fixed; and as quick as he ceased speaking, the saint set right and blew away all his words in an instant,—unhorsed him, I may say, and tumbled him along the ground in utter dismay, like my angel of Heliodorus. Never was discomfiture more complete. In tones of genuine pathos he "bid him wonder at the Love which suffered him to speak there in his chair, of things he knew nothing of . . .—and yet he was allowed to sit and talk, whilst every word he spoke was a step of departure from the truth, and of this he commanded himself to bear witness!" (*JMN* 7:127–28)

Very's ability to usher in social anarchy confirmed the power of his unselfconscious egotism. His performance was just the sort of revolutionary rudeness Emerson would celebrate three years later in "Self-Reliance." Even when Very announced, toward the end of his visit, that today "is with him a day of hate; that he discerns the bad elements in every person whom he meets, which repels him," Emerson, though critical, could not refrain from still more puzzled admiration:

> He would as soon embrace a black Egyptian mummy as Socrates. He would obey, obey. . . . To Lidian he says, "Your thought speaks there, and not your life." And he is very sensible of *interference* in thought and act. A very accurate discernment of spirit belongs to his state, and he detects at once the presence of an alien element, though he cannot tell whence, how, or where to it is. He thinks me covetous in my hold of truth, of seeking truth separate, and of receiving or taking it, instead of merely obeying. The Will is to him all, as to me (after my own showing) Truth. . . . He has nothing to do with time, because he obeys. . . .
>
> He had the manners of a man, one, that is, to whom life was more than meat, the body than raiment. He felt it an honor, he said, to wash his face, being, as it was, the temple of the spirit. And he is gone into the multitude as solitary as Jesus. In dismissing him I seem to have discharged an arrow into the heart of society. Wherever that young enthusiast goes he will astonish and disconcert men by dividing for them the cloud that covers the profound gulf that is in man. (*JMN* 7:122–23)

The language of this final entry suggests that Emerson ended Very's visit after four days, perhaps now in fuller understanding of Peabody's warning that he could be a persistent guest. Emerson drove him as far as Waltham, from which Very likely walked to Cambridge, where he stayed with friends for a few days.[14] On October 30, Emerson wrote to Peabody to give his impressions of the visit, telling her that he enjoyed Very's presence once he "came to understand his vocabulary. I wish the whole world were as mad as he. He discredits himself I think by a certain violence I may say of thought & speech; but it is quite superficial; he is profoundly sane, & as soon as his thoughts subside from their present excited to a more natural state, I think he will make all men sensible of it."[15] To his credit, Emerson showed little sign of concern about Very's reputation or any possible harm that might come from association with him. Considering his reaction to Very's "unhorsing" of Frost, Emerson seems to have relished these signs of friction and disagreement as evidence of a posture more real and truer than social convention typically allows. For his part, Very may well have been disappointed in Emerson's response to his mission, but he showed little sign of real discouragement.

✻ 32 ✻

"In obedience to the Spirit"

Though Concord may have made its peace, for the moment, with the phenomenon of Jones Very, Salem had not. The particular, contesting energies of this community, long riven by political factions and ever conscious of its history of conflict and persecution, made it unlikely that a self-proclaimed Messiah, no matter how harmless, would be left free to spread his message. If Elizabeth Peabody could state quite openly her belief that Very had not been "cured" or substantially changed by his month at McLean, those opposed to Very would have come to the same conclusion. He continued to write and publish poems at an astonishing rate (in November alone, six of his prophetic sonnets appeared in the *Salem Observer*) and to visit anyone he considered open to, or in need of, his mission. (He sent two of the poems to Emerson, who responded enthusiastically: "Do not, I beg of you, let a whisper or sigh of the Muse go unattended to, or unrecorded. The sentiment which inspires your poetry is so deep and true, and the expression so simple, that I am sure you will find your audience very large.")[1] By the latter half of November, largely as a result of Very's continued run-ins with John Brazer, rumors were again circulating that the local ministers, along with Harvard president Josiah Quincy, were intent on removing Very from Salem.

On November 24, while Elizabeth Peabody was away in Boston, her sister Mary was so alarmed by the atmosphere surrounding Very that she wrote to her sister twice that day to inform her of the danger. These letters are among the most revealing and detailed accounts of Very's emotional state during this crucial conflict in Salem and deserve extensive quotation:

> Poor Very came to tea with his eyes full of tears & his face & brow flushed—I saw something was the matter—& I began to tell him how beautiful his sonnets were & how much we enjoyed them—& that I hoped he would write more—He said he hoped to if he was permitted

> to stay, but Mr. Brazer from whom he had just parted, & Mr. Quincy wished to send him away on a voyage or somewhere where they could not hear him or let him be heard—Father said what right have they to send you away? He said they can do it by making my mother think it best—they are men in authority & she can invest them with an authority that will compel me to go—they tell me that the people of Salem think & they think my mind is in a worse state—I can't remember all the words, but he said they thought Mr. Emerson had done him harm—that they had been questioning him about his visit—that they put Mr E by the side of Abner Kneeland & if they could prove the charge of blasphemy against him they would deprive him of his liberty as they had done to A. K.—(can you suppose that Mr. B told him this?) He said a while ago hi[s] [illegible word—ms. torn] might have been called obstrusive, but it certainly w[as not{?}—ms. torn] so now—he had more health too than Mr. B or Mr. Q. I expressed my sympathy & hoped they would not persist in their interference—I said at the same time that I thought they *meant* to do him good, tho' I thought they were mistaken in their measures—but he did not agree—he said he felt anger against them—that perhaps this trial was given him that he might overcome that feeling—& then he smiled very sweetly & said that while he was doing no harm & only good he thought they need not persecute him—All this was told in his gentle way, but evidently in a grieved and wounded spirit.[2]

There are several important elements to take note of here. First, as I discussed earlier in evaluating Elizabeth Peabody's reading of Very during these crucial months, we can see that Mary Peabody and the rest of the family were less critical and less suspicious than Elizabeth of Very's mental state. The Peabodys held a pew at Brazer's North Church but were nevertheless outraged at the minister's aggressive badgering of a young man they all understood as gentle and more fragile than threatening. Second, the letter provides a clear sense of the pressures being brought against Very and the role Emerson was made to play as his imagined evil influencer. The evocation of Abner Kneeland, a former Universalist minister who became a vocal freethinker and skeptic and had been imprisoned for blasphemy in Boston earlier in the year, is a chilling reminder that the threats against Emerson and Very were tangible enough to warrant genuine concern.[3] Finally, we can see clearly for once the emotional register of Very's personality, his unconscious stubbornness in continuing to seek out Brazer and others who attacked him, his buried rage and deference to his mother, whose power to protect him against the town's leading male figures he doubts.

The Peabodys did their best to soothe Very's agitation. He asked Sophia Peabody to show him her drawings and spent time comforting George Peabody, who was suffering from spinal meningitis.[4] They reassured him that notable figures in the town, such as Hawthorne and Judge White, had spoken in support of him. (White, it's important to remember, was the probate judge who had heard Lydia Very's case and overseen her children's estate for many years.) And they were active in recruiting more support around town. Mary, who had written the letter hurriedly to her sister to urge her to write Henry Ware Jr. for help, planned to seek out the local lawyer Frederick Howes on Very's behalf, while her mother made her way that afternoon to see Lydia Very. Some time later that day, Mary wrote a second time to tell Elizabeth that Ware's assistance was no longer needed because Lydia had reassured Mrs. Peabody that she would allow no meddling with her son:

> Mrs. Very told her that Mr. B.[razer] went there yesterday just before Very came here and talked very loud & violently to him in his study—when he came down stairs she opened the door & he came in & *raved* as she expressed it about her son—saying that he was a great deal worse—that his views would do incalculable injury!—!—that he must be sent to sea or to a hospital immediately!—the fact is Mrs. Peabody said she, that my son is better than Mr. Brazer, and he knows it and it makes him *mad*. She told her that he sat there nearly all day with his brother whom he was educating as sane as any man—She declares that he shall not be taken away from her—that he has income enough to maintain him—& so has she—She calls upon no one for assistance & wishes no one's interference.[5]

Agitated as she was by Brazer's intrusion, Lydia was stronger than her son supposed. When Elizabeth Peabody returned a week later, she wrote to Emerson that the "fear of *abduction*" had passed "as Mrs. Very stands guard over his liberty & tranquility" (EP 218–19; original emphasis). Peabody herself had gone to Federal Street to check on Very and was almost unnerved by this "tiger of a woman" who, as Peabody believed, had been converted from atheism to faith by her son's "strange" mission (EP 219). Whether or not this was truly the case—or, as seems more likely, Lydia's sympathy with her son's vision arose from a prideful defense of her family against the pious officials of Salem—it's clear that Lydia was unlikely to be persuaded by anyone simply because they were considered important or influential. She may have been unable to prevent her son from antagonizing the Brazers and Uphams of the world, but she could and would stand on his side and defy these self-important and intrusive men when they threatened one of her children.

The Peabodys' accounts also indicate that the town was largely divided over Very. Aside from those clearly sympathetic to, if not in full accord with, his mission, the reactions ranged from mildly critical to virulently hostile—and it seems as though everyone had a slightly different set of reactions and opinions. Sophia Peabody, for example, less robust and more spiritually inclined than her older sister, was clearly taken with Very's otherworldliness. Somewhat like Lidian Emerson, she was drawn to his gentle, "angelic" nature, and was critical of those, like Susan Burley, who in her opinion failed to "understand" Very's startling claims.[6] But even Sophia, long plagued by physical aliments, could not accept Very's insistence that "there is no such thing as physical evil . . . that perfect yielding of willfulness would produce freedom from the sensation of pain itself," though she clearly took the possibility of such a transcendence seriously (EP 219). Nathaniel Hawthorne, Sophia's soon-to-be fiancé, was more suspicious of Very, but as a student of unusual personalities he could respect Very's conviction without believing his claims. A little more than a year before the encounter recorded by Elizabeth Peabody in December of 1838, the thirty-four-year-old Hawthorne had published the first volume of *Twice-Told Tales,* his initial collection of short stories that included such masterpieces as "The Minister's Black Veil" and "Wakefield." The sort of critical sympathy and imagination required to create such distinctive characters, often themselves local oddities or mild obsessives, is evident in Peabody's description of the meeting: "Did Elizabeth Hoare tell you," she wrote to Emerson, "that I was present when [Very] delivered his mission to Mr. Hawthorne? It was very curious—Hawthorne received it in the loveliest manner—with the same abandonment with which it was given—for he has that confidence in truth—which delivers him from all mean fears—& it was curious to see the respect of Very for *him*—and the reverence with which he treated his genius" (EP 221; original emphasis). Aware of Hawthorne's essentially skeptical intelligence, Peabody was surprised that "in this instance he repressed it & talked with [Very] beautifully—He says Very was always *vain* in his eyes—though it was always an innocent vanity—arising greatly from want of sense of the ludicrous & sanctified by this real piety & goodness. He says he had better remain as he is—however—one organ in the world of the impersonal Spirit—at least as long as he can write such good sonnets—" (EP 221; original emphasis).

Hawthorne's response to Very was complex.[7] He was almost taken aback by how similar Very was to a fictional character he had already created, the preacher in the frame material to the collection he had planned for *The Storyteller* (EP 408). There a young, unmotivated narrator similar to Hawthorne encounters Parson Thumpcushion, who "had an upright heart, and some called it a warm one, [but] was invariably stern and severe, on principle."[8] The storyteller, who feels rootless and lazy, is both drawn to and repelled by this firmer, more committed figure of purpose. As Elizabeth Peabody put it in a later recollection, "These two exceptional Yankees were tabooed by the prosaic community from which they were dissidents; and this brought them into a strange intimacy" (EG 283). This curious reflection of Hawthorne's imagination—as well as the shared experience of being the eldest sons of lost sea captains—may have prolonged or deepened what might otherwise have been a brief set of encounters. On the other hand, Hawthorne was more than capable of maintaining critical distance when it came to Very. In "The Hall of Fantasy" from 1843, he neatly summed up what to him was the essence of Very's dilemma, describing him alone and trapped in a circle of his own making. And in "Egotism; or, the Bosom Serpent," from the same year, he may have had Very in mind when he created Roderick Elliston, the "snake-possessed" figure obsessed with his own, inner sinfulness and eventually confined to a mental institution. Like Very, Elliston is convinced that each person must have one cherished "serpent" inside them, something held to and nursed at the center of their being that required expulsion or erasure, "the type of each man's fatal error, or hoarded sin, or unquiet conscience."[9]

Others saw a similar vanity in Very but lacked Hawthorne's deference to his "innocence" or lack of self-awareness. Susan Burley, according to Peabody, explained that [Very] had "always appeared to her extremely *good*—& with great powers of apprehension on *points*—but naturally excessively conceited—putting the most inordinate value in all his own thoughts—& not capable of complete *views all round subjects*" (EP 220; original emphasis). Apparently sensing a distance or lack of understanding in Burley's circle, Very spoke "a great deal more violently" to those who questioned him there, reacting much as he had on the final day of his visit to the Emersons: "When he goes there," Peabody explained to Emerson, "they argue with him very gently—but he seems driven into extremes that he never uses at our house—they say too that he expresses deep gloom—& looks gloomy & tells them they are wicked—& truth itself is a poison to them—He speaks of the misery of being with people he cannot esteem—& says to them there has been no good man since the apostles until himself—" (EP 220).

Such extravagant statements could provoke rage, puzzlement, or merely gentle reproof, but whatever the response, Very seems to have changed his message little if at all in the months following his time at McLean. The flavor of his language and exalted attitude can be caught in a letter he wrote to Emerson on November 30, in which he continued to preach his doctrine of erasure of the will: "I was glad to hear that my stay with you was improving and that you love that which is spoken by the Word. If you love it aright in the spirit of obedience it shall be unto you given to hear and speak of the Father in Christ. John whom you follow must first decrease in you before you can hear that which is in the beginning. You must pass out of that world in which you are naked (that is willess [*sic*]) as you came in. Then shall you have a *new* will born of the Spirit which also when submited [*sic*] to the Father you shall be one with Him; that is, be prepared to see him as a spirit. Every scribe instructed in the kingdom shall bring John as a householder new and old."[10]

On December 5 Very made his way to Boston to hear Emerson speak "on the doctrine of the soul," and afterward once again challenged his supposed "ally" and his explanation of the subjective nature of experience: "'When I was at Concord,' Very explained, 'I tried to say you were also right; but the spirit said, you were not right. It is just as if I should say, It is not morning; but the morning says, It is the morning.' 'Use what language you will,' he said, 'you can never say anything but what you are'" (*JMN* 8:148). Though he was still unable to adopt Very's vision, Emerson was impressed and fascinated by such oracular statements. In 1844, in his great essay "Experience," he echoed Very's reproof as he meditated on the limits of the subjective in the face of grief:

> Thus inevitably does the universe wear our color, and every object fall successively into the subject itself. The subject exists, the subject enlarges; all things sooner or later fall into place. As I am, so I see; use what language we will, we can never say anything but what we are; Hermes, Cadmus, Columbus, Newton, Buonaparte, are the mind's ministers. Instead of feeling a poverty when we encounter a great man, let us treat the new comer like a travelling geologist, who passes through our estate, and shows us good slate, or limestone, or anthracite, in our brush pasture. The partial action of each strong mind in one direction, is a telescope for the objects on which it is pointed. (LA 489)

Very was certainly an example of a "strong mind" moving "in one direction," and Emerson had earlier used the same metaphor of the "telescope" to describe this effect of Very's "monosania."[11]

While in Boston, Very also visited William Ellery Channing, the great articulator of early Unitarianism. They had met once before, the previous July, but Channing had heard reports of Very's unusual behavior in recent months and had passed along—likely through his close friend and former student and assistant Elizabeth Peabody—an invitation for further conversation. According to James Freeman Clarke, who was present for the meeting, Channing "was always looking for any symptoms of a new birth of spiritual life in the land" and wanted to know "what were [Very's] views on religious subjects."[12] Though firmly established in his position at Boston's Federal Street Church, Channing was known to be sympathetic to, if not in full agreement with, the new ideas emerging from Emerson and others, particularly with respect to individual spiritual experience. In his influential sermon, "Likeness to God," delivered in Providence in 1828, he had gone far in establishing the language of divine immanence that would be extended by Emerson: "The idea of God," he wrote then, "sublime and awful as it is, is the idea of our own spiritual nature, purified and enlarged to infinity. In ourselves are the elements of Divinity. God then does not sustain a figurative resemblance to man. It is the resemblance of a parent to a child, the likeness of a kindred nature."[13] And though he had carefully avoided commenting on Emerson's Divinity School Address, Channing had admitted privately to Peabody that he was largely in agreement with Emerson's vision of the "moral impartiality" of Christ, saying that Emerson's opponents were "fighting with a shadow . . . for Mr. Emerson expressly says, and makes a great point of it, that God is *alive* and not *dead*, and would have the Gospel narrative left to make its own impression of an indwelling life, like the growing grass."[14]

Clarke's account of the conversation between Very and Channing is brief but remarkable, illuminating not only the extent of Very's conception of his will-less state but also Channing's careful and sympathetic investigation of his controversial visitor: "Having listened attentively [to Very's ideas], [Channing] asked him, whether it was in consequence of his invitation or in obedience to the Spirit that he came to Boston that morning. Mr. Very answered, 'I was directed to accept your invitation.' Then Dr. Channing said, 'I observed that during our conversation you left your chair and went while speaking to the fire-place, and rested your arm on the mantel. Did you do this of your own accord or in obedience to the Spirit?' Mr. Very replied, 'In obedience to the Spirit.'"[15] Clarke remarks that "most of us would not think it worth while to consult the Spirit" on such "a purely automatic action as this," but the exchange gives us a clearer sense of just what Very meant by the surrender of his personal will.[16] More than a traditional renunciation of want or desire, his sense of kenosis or the emptying-out of the self extended to the body in all its movements and impulses. A few months later he would put these remarkable ideas into the form of his "Epistles to the Unborn," where he describes "prayer" as the assumption of the body of Christ. To be "born," in his terms, was to come not just into identification with the Holy Spirit but to be a living prayer, a sort of half-conscious marionette moving in frictionless harmony with nature itself.

For his part, Channing was neither shocked nor alarmed at Very's ecstatic claims. Peabody later reported that "Dr. Channing told me of his visit, and was immensely impressed and touched with his union of gentleness, modesty, and yet complete sense of his word being the utterance of the Holy Spirit.—I remember Dr. Channing said—Yes, he had lost his *senses*, but only that part of his mind which was connected therewith—there was an iron sequence of thought—Men in general said he—have lost or never found this higher mind—*Their* insanity is profound,—his is only superficial.—To hear him talk was like looking into the purely spiritual world—into truth itself—He had nothing of self-exaggeration—He seemed . . . rather to have obtained self annihilation & become an oracle of God" (EP 408; original emphasis).

✷ 33 ✷
"Pierced through with many spears"

In the Very files held in Harvard's Houghton Library, there is a large sheet of foolscap paper (roughly 12 ½ × 16 inches) folded into sixteen equal squares. Occupying each square, on both sides of the paper, is a single sonnet, set in close handwriting so as to fill the square entirely. The layout of the poems suggests the formation of a small book, with the bottom eight facing one direction and the top set inverted so that folding the sheet would form consecutive pages. Very may have used several such large sheets to record the outpouring of sonnets that began in September 1838 at roughly the same time as his removal from Harvard. Elizabeth Peabody remembered him returning to her door that chaotic Sunday evening in Salem before he entered McLean Hospital holding "a monstrous folio sheet of paper, on which were four double columns of sonnets—which he said 'the Spirit had enabled' him to write and these he left with me to read as the utterances of the Holy Ghost" (EP 407).

This intriguing piece of manuscript evidence is worth pausing over for a moment as we begin to consider the poems Very was writing during the first months of his spiritual enthusiasm. Though the "monstrous" sheet suggests, as it apparently did to Peabody, that Very was under the influence of a kind of mania, the sonnets it contains—and indeed all of the poems Very would write for the next ten months or so—are remarkably sedate and highly controlled. As Channing had noted about Very's conversation, there is a firm and clear "sequence of thought" throughout, with no raving or overextension of meaning or expression. His premise may be disconnected from everyday reality, but granted his vatic or ventriloquistic conception of his own poetic voice, the poems themselves are lucid and often notably serene. Very's Holy Ghost speaks in meter and rhyme and follows many of the standard conventions of the English sonnet. And the folio sheet of stacked sonnets collects these utterances like substantial blocks of sturdy truth. As a practical expedient, this foldable booklet no doubt made transporting and sharing his message easier, but its assemblage also suggests the desire to incarnate Spirit—the word—into a tangible, material reality. His admission to Channing that his own body moved "in obedience to the Spirit" describes his prophetic and poetic self-conception: the Spirit inhabits both body and language; every act is "prayer." The sonnet, "copied" by a "scribe instructed in the kingdom," as he put it to Emerson in a phrase from Matthew 13, emphasizes formality and containment; the sheet binds them into a literal presence of Spirit.[1]

Though precise dating of many of Very's sonnets remains conjectural, he composed roughly seventy-five between September 1838 and February of 1839. Following "The New Birth," which both announces and instantiates a rush of "Fast crowding," selfless thought, the flood of poems is more various and less strictly monothematic than we might expect. Most significant, given his claims of erasure of will and the transmission of spiritual meaning, there is no single approach in these sonnets to poetic persona or voice. They are, at times, variously personal and dramatic, often leaning on Very's typical persona and favored lyric scenes while increasingly expanding into the voice of a prophet or inspired speaker. In their most dramatic form, they assume specific biblical personae, taking on the identity of John the Baptist, Jesus, or even God. Very's often-present "I" in the sonnets thus suggests an unstable and strangely mutable identity, both more personal than we might expect from the will-less recorder of the Holy Spirit and yet ever more daring in its imbrication with the sacred or divine.

Even in his prophetic strain at its most removed from everyday reality, Very remained a poet of nature. The most common mise-en-scène of his poems to this point might be said to be a path in the fields or woods with the isolated speaker exploring the surroundings symbolically or metaphorically for spiritual meaning. (As an inveterate walker who often made even long journeys by foot along turnpikes and country roads, Very spent many hours in such settings.) And even here, under the burden of his prophetic charge and beset by threatening authorities, he often falls back on the same experiential lyric mode. In "The Violet," for instance, Very's address to a path-side flower picks up the Wordsworthian note of many of his earlier nature poems, praising the truth and humility of the natural: "Thou tellest truths unspoken yet by man / By this thy lonely home and modest look; / For he has not the eyes such truths to scan, / Nor learns to read from such a lowly book" (*CP* 74). The voice is less prophetic than it is observant and receptive. Similarly, in "The Robe" the speaker meditates on the deceptive blanket of snow that hides the "naked" branches and rocks beneath, an emblem of the "corse-like spirit" of man whose guilt cannot hide from "the quick spirit's heart-deep searching eye" (*CP* 79). Between the more dramatic exercises of Very's apocalyptic imagination, the poems written so rapidly over these few months continue to see and respond to nature. The seasons change, and with the settling in of winter, the spiritual eye finds yet more metaphors for those who fail to hear Very's message. "Winter," for instance, evokes the coldness of the "godless heart" whose "blasts are words that chill the loving soul / Though heard in pleasing phrase or learned sound" (*CP* 81). And "The Winter Rain" finds solace in the promise of Spring from the "pattering drops" like "the words of the Holy Spirit" falling "Upon the heart where Winter's robe is flung" (*CP* 86).

Notes too of the personal or autobiographical slip into Very's inveterate generalizing, suggesting that his prophetic identity cannot be entirely abstracted from the scenes of his life. "The River," a prayer for an influx of divine love, gives us a metaphorical river much like the tidal inlet behind Very's Federal Street home: "Oh swell my bosom deeper with thy love, / That I some river's widening mouth may be; / And ever on for many a mile above / May flow the floods that enter from thy sea" (*CP* 90). We know from Lydia L. A. Very's memoirs that her brother often composed his poems while sitting on the shaded bench that looked down on these waters, and in the sonnet "Time" we are give this exact scene suffused with late autumnal, Shakespearean moodiness: "There is no moment but whose flight doth bring / Bright clouds and fluttering leaves to deck my bower, / And I within like some sweet bird must sing / To tell the story of the passing hour" (*CP* 74).

This quiet allusion to Shakespeare's sonnet 73 contains, in its way, a whiff of ambition, suggesting that Very's personal desires and individual will have not been as fully vanquished as he had hoped and proclaimed. And indeed there are poems such as "The Will" that continue to suggest a struggle to suppress the self while paradoxically elevating the role of the inspirited poet: "Help me in Christ to learn to do Thy will, / . . . And gain for me the lyre and martyr-crown / To all who love the praise of men denied" (*CP* 79). Very's youthful determination to "restore epic poetry" could, through self-denial, be translated into this type of ego-less egoism, but his personal romantic feelings—so often the riper target for suppression—could not. The sonnet "Love," published in the *Salem Observer* in November 1838, indicates as much, its poignancy far stronger than its gesture of renunciation:

> I asked of Time to tell me where was Love;
> He pointed to her foot-steps on the snow,
> Where first the angel lighted from above,
> And bid me note the way and onward go;

> Through populous streets of cities spreading wide,
> By lonely cottage rising on the moor,
> Where bursts from sundered cliff the struggling tide,
> To where it hails the sea with answering roar,
> She led me on; o'er mountains' frozen head,
> Where mile on mile still stretches on the plain,
> Then homeward whither first my feet she led
> I traced her path along the snow again,
> But here the sun had melted from the earth
> The prints where first she trod, a child of mortal birth. (*CP* 66)

This complex poem, crisscrossed with seemingly contradictory motives, seems to take shelter in its allegory. Its opening suggests one of George Herbert's distilled conversion narratives, but it moves instead toward something closer to romantic longing. As such it fits less easily into Very's largely consistent and orthodox descriptions of renunciation and spiritual fulfillment and instead suggests a more personal account of his failed pursuit of an intimate relationship. The overriding point that "Love," imagined here as both woman and angel, is "mortal," particularly when indicated by "Time," stands somewhat feebly against the odd power of the half line, "She led me on," amplified as it is by the heavy caesura that follows it. Mortal love draws the speaker forward, perhaps both in the positive sense of motivation and movement toward the realization of a spiritual truth, and in the negative sense of deception. The bitterness and feeling of betrayal are real and registered as such before the last line—augmented by two compensatory syllables—attempts to explain and contain the excess of feeling.[2]

Such residues of emotion are intermittently present even in Very's more prophetic poems from this period. As the sonnets develop into a more full-throated transmittal of divine speech, the personal, Very-esque speaker seems to search for full erasure, not always certain of the relationship between inspiration and inhabitation. In "Labor and Rest," for instance, an address to God or Spirit gives us a traditional image of heavenly afflatus: "And thou dost breathe in me a voice divine / That tells more sure of thine Eternal sway" (*CP* 93). But other poems suggest that the poet is a kind of "son" to a spiritual father who speaks unfiltered through the medium of a cherished disciple. Both "The Son" ("Father! I wait thy word—the sun doth stand, / Beneath the mingling line of night and day") and "The Presence" ("For Thou Thyself, with all a Father's care, / Where'er I turn, art even with me there") seem to domesticate the idea of God the Father and give the poet the privileged role of "sonship," the term Very often used for this state of receptiveness (*CP* 66, 78).[3] Part of that privilege is the sense of righteous justification via persecution—and here again it can be difficult to winnow out Very's resentful reaction to the ministers like Brazer from the poetry's claims to selflessness. The sonnet "Worship," for example, begins with the clear judgment "There is no worship now—the idol stands / Within the spirit's holy resting place," and goes on to show us "The prophet" walking "unhonored mid the crowd / That to the idol's temple daily throng" (*CP* 73). As expected, an apocalyptic justice follows for those who fail to heed the prophet's message.

This mode of frustrated vengeance fantasy emerges often enough in these poems to suggest that it arose in direct response to Very's experiences during the autumn of 1838. We know from Emerson's account of Very's "day of hate" that the poet who preached the renunciation of the personal could not quite rid himself of his own passions, even if they were spiritually directed. Certainly Very understood this anger as the action of the Holy Spirit rather than something specific to himself, but it can be difficult to work through these poems without hearing that unconscious vanity so often attributed to him by observers like Hawthorne. Very was, of course, under duress, and he reacted by seeing himself as closer to God and on a higher spiritual plane than those who disagreed with him. In its most intense moments, his desire for significance and attention, coupled with the long-suppressed emotions of his childhood and youth, moved him to the extravagant point of seeing himself as (the voice of) the Messiah. In less fraught moods he was content to take the role of John the Baptist or merely the prophetic poet à la Milton. Whatever the case, his conception of his own erasure allowed him to assume the historical position of those divine or near-divine figures whose spiritual significance elevated his own. He could, strangely, be both nothing or no one *and* everything or The One, at the same time. He could speak and feel as Jones Very from Salem and still claim that everything he felt and said flowed directly—and without filter—from God.

This strange ambiguity in which the personal and impersonal speak in near unison haunts those early sonnets clearly meant to dramatize divine thoughts. In "John," for example, we might initially imagine that the speaker is a distant historical observer of the career of the John the Baptist: "What went ye out to see? a shaken reed? / In him whose voice proclaims 'prepare the way'" (*CP* 82). And so it continues until the lines "Yet seek ye know now what; blind children all, / Who each his idle fancy will demand; / Nor heed my true-sent prophet's warning call, / That you may learn of me the new command" (*CP* 82). What seemed the poet's voice is revealed as the voice of Christ, particularly the prophetic and minatory

Jesus that Very had seized upon in Matthew 24. The easy slippage between the persona of the poet-prophet most common in Very's sonnets and the dramatic voice of God or Christ suggests a close but not exact identification between the two.[4] Even if we understand such poems as types of dramatic monologue, the blurring of the line between the lyric "I" and the staged speaker is common enough to imagine that Very's own sense of his poetic voice was productively dynamic, the self retreating or advancing as the spirit waxed or waned.

Such a poem as "The Cross," for instance, gives us a clear sense of the *imitatio Christi*, the common exhortation to become more Christ-like, even to the point of imagining the self's sacrifice as a kind of crucifixion:

> I must go on, till in my tearful line
> Walks the full spirit's love as I on earth;
> Till I can all Thou giv'st again resign,
> And he be formed in me who gave me birth;
> . . . .
> Till I through blood like him the prize have bought;
> And I shall hang upon the accursed tree,
> Pierced through with many spears that all may see. (*CP* 91–92)

Again, the note of justification through martyrdom rings clearly, not the least because the voice is close to the persona of Jones Very himself. But it's worth comparing this orthodox, if somewhat lurid, self-sacrifice to the more immediate dramatization of Christ's voice in "Behold He Is at Hand That Doth Betray Me":

> Why come you out to me with clubs and staves,
> That you on every side have fenced me so?
> In every act you dig for me deep graves;
> In which my feet must walk where'er I go;
> You speak and in your words my death I find,
> Pierced through with many sorrows to the core;
> And none that will the bleeding spirit bind,
> But at each touch still freer flows the gore;
> But with my stripes your deep-dyed sins are healed,
> For I must show my master's love for you;
> The cov'nant is witnessed to be just and true;
> And you in turn must bear the stripes I bear,
> And in his sufferings learn alike to share. (*CP* 88–89)

Certainly the opening of the poem suggests a dramatic re-creation of Christ's persecution, and yet almost immediately, the matching and overlapping voice of the poet-prophet, similarly assailed for bearing witness, doubles the scene. This is not an imitation of Christ but an inhabitation of the messianic position. It implies a typological repetition that is more than mere resemblance. "The second coming" that Very claimed to embody became a fusion *in poetry* of his personal voice and the voice of the persecuted Jesus. It may be overly dramatic to say so, but in certain of his sonnets, Jones Very *was* the resurrected Christ—he had fashioned a lyric practice that effectively married his life to the divine.

✷ 34 ✷
"Insane with God"

After his return from Boston in early December, Very continued to deliver his personal testimony to others, though he became somewhat more circumspect about his audience. He no longer pressed his message on local ministers or those who were openly hostile to him, looking instead to former classmates or acquaintances, those of like or nearly like mind, who might be open to his mission. He wrote letters, such as this one on Christmas Eve to Rufus Ellis, a recent Harvard graduate who went on to become pastor of First Church in Boston. It begins: "As I know that you are earnest in seeking the Christ who was promised to the righteous men of old whom the apostles found and who has been revealed unto me at this the time of his second coming I am moved by the spirit to give you this witness within me that you may believe."[1] Though we have no exact transcriptions of Very's oral testimony as given to individuals, this almost formulaic, ritual opening may give the best available example of how he began these encounters. The apocalyptic tone—and extraordinary claim of revelations—must have struck many as both impressive and alarming. Very then sets down his account of John the Baptist's preparation for Christ, clarifying that Christ comes not only by "water" (that is, baptism, via John) but by "blood," or "the suffering in the flesh after you are born of the spirit."[2] This earthly trial joins with the passion of Christ: "You are made a partaker of Christ's sufferings and lay down the life which is given you by the Holy Spirit." The sacrifice of one's life, "the yielding up of every thought and affection to God," is necessary to become "pure as [Christ] was."[3] You must, he exhorts Ellis, follow the difficult path that he himself had followed:

> But that you may see the Lord you need earnestly to strive in the way I have before shown you and which if faithful the Father will always make plain. It is narrow and straight for it requires but one thing, to

> cut down the corrupt tree, to give up the corrupt will gradually and in all things. Live without interest in any thing save as a duty and you will find your reward in peace.[4]

The peace here described and desired was clearly an inner calm derived from a lack of dissonance between the self and God. To attain this level of detachment was to move away from both desire and suffering; what was "corrupt" (that is, temporal, transitory) was "interest" or want, the petty desires of selfhood.

Several of Very's other friends or former students at Harvard received similar letters that December. He explained these efforts to Ellis and urged him to share part or all of this small prophetic sermon with those close to him. A few days later, he wrote the even more revealing letter to Henry Bellows, another of his Divinity School friends. As one of the best sources for Very's own conception of his spiritual experience reaching back to the beginning of his time at Harvard, it remains invaluable and deserves further scrutiny. Roughly the first half of the letter is given over to Very's personal history of faith. Here he explains the "change of heart" during his senior year at Harvard and his inability "to rest in" the discovery that he should eliminate his will (*CP* lvi). He also describes the change that came over him at the beginning of the term in the autumn of 1838 and the presence of a "new will . . . not my own" (*CP* lvii). These two, conflicting wills (that of self and spirit) were matched by "two consciousnesses" that "went as they came imperceptibly [*sic*]," leading to his declaration at Harvard "that the coming of Christ was at hand" (*CP* lvii). He refers to his time "at the Asylum" and his subsequent deeper understanding of his purpose as "one born of God" (*CP* lvii).

Very then offers an account of his current spiritual state similar to the one sent to Ellis:

> I now know by the Spirit of God that my former change and that which is commonly called the new birth, was but the hearing of the voice of John in the wilderness of my heart, and that the purification I experienced, in obeying him, in cutting down the corrupt tree and preparing the way for the One who came after was that of his baptism of water. He, as he said, must *decrease*, he was of the earth;—He whom I now know must *increase*, He is from above. I have been in the heart of the earth obedient to John three days and three nights and am risen in Christ as a witness unto you and all that he comes not by water only but by blood. (*CP* lvii; original emphasis)

This continued emphasis on suffering ("blood") may well have been a product of Very's experiences being dismissed from Harvard, harried by the ministers in Salem, and finally convinced to accept confinement at McLean Hospital. If he was akin to John in his first crying out in the classroom, by December he had more closely identified with the crucified Christ, the prophet unwelcome in his own town, scattering tables in the temple, persecuted by pharisees. Such a transition might well account for the emergence of the voice of Jesus in his sonnets; as Very imagined himself symbolically repeating the death and resurrection so could he rise "in Christ as a witness," a voice that speaks of suffering more than of grace (*CP* lvii). He makes clear to Bellows that his conception of a messianic return is one of individual embodiment rather than historical advent: "As he [John] is imprisoned now in you believe that this is the Christ that is to come and that you are to expect no other. Behold the blind see, the dumb speak, the dead are raised. Believe and go on rejoicing in Johns [*sic*] *decrease* and you shall find him who comes after will thoroughly purge your threshing floor and gather you if worthy into his granary" (*CP* lvii; original emphasis).

If we are to take this kind of language seriously, it's worth asking what Very means by this depiction of miracles upon the "return" of the Christ within. Is this a symbolic language attempting to describe a new sight given to those who suffer the erasure of the personal life? Brazer had, in an early encounter, demanded that Very prove himself by supernatural evidence, and Very had replied that this "revelation would not have miracles" (EP 209). Yet here, still in the midst of the so-called miracles controversy and reaction to Emerson's Divinity School Address, Very seems to echo—and possibly expand—Emerson's contention that the miraculous is everywhere present; we have only to be transformed within to perceive it. In this sense, to be converted into the "Christ within" is to overcome the blindness of our personal desires, to speak in a new voice, and to bring to life those who have not been "born" to the spirit.

What Ellis and Bellows thought of these earnest exhortations and pointed instructions has not survived. As Divinity School students and ministerial candidates, they may well have reacted similarly to George Moore, who concluded that Very was "insane" during his September visit to Henry Ware Jr. Or, after the news of Very's recovery and return from McLean Hospital, they may have taken a more generous approach and come to understand him, as Bronson Alcott notably put it, as "insane with God—diswitted in the contemplation of the holiness of the Divinity."[5] Very had met Alcott, then thirty-nine and running his controversial

Temple School in Boston, the previous May, when he attended his first meeting of the Transcendental Club. In late November or early December 1838, before Emerson's lecture in Boston on December 5, he visited Alcott's home on Beach Street and subsequently spent time in his company when the club met at Cyrus Bartol's house after Emerson's talk. (Henry Bellows also attended this meeting, the topic of which was "Pantheism.")[6] On December 8, Very wrote to Alcott, following up on their conversations a few days before. As he often did with even the most sympathetic friends, he applied his standard of will-lessness to Alcott and found him wanting. He had read Alcott's *Conversations with Children on the Gospels* and identified "curiosity" as the trait to which Alcott remained attached and which prevented "the Spirit of God from creating [him] again in his image."[7] Very then provided an account of "the mission of John" similar to those in the letters to Ellis and Bellows but with a potentially stronger autobiographical resonance: "You have not entirely fulfilled the mission of John within you. He must entirely decrease before Christ can send the Spirit to baptize you into his kingdom, which is not of that world of your own will, in which you still linger a little. John is still in prison; the sensible miracles have been done within his knowledge, but he still doubts whether he shall be raised from the spiritual death which he feels within him."[8] Having found in himself the urgent necessity to remove all traces of his own individuality, Very applied this idiosyncratic template of conversion to almost everyone he met. To be symbolically in the state of John was to feel this "spiritual death" and long for a fuller union with Christ; to leave John behind and move from prophet to the embodiment of Christ required a complete surrender of those traits dearest to the identity of the separate self.

For some, like Very himself, this relinquishment included even thought itself, a radical contention that Alcott clearly recognized as such. "Is he insane?" Alcott asked himself in his journal. "If so, there yet lingers glimpses of wisdom in his memory. He is insane with God. . . . He distrusts intellect; he would have living in the concrete, without the interposition of the meddling, analytic, head. Curiosity, he deems impious. He would have no one stop to account to himself for what he has done, deeming this hiatus of doing, a suicidal act of the profane mind. Intellect, as intellect, he deems the author of all error. . . . This is mysticism of the highest order."[9] Alcott's comments are among the most astute and observant of any recorded about Very's ideas and behavior. Despite his own reputation for sometimes foggy, spiritualized thinking (especially following the publication of his "Orphic Sayings" in *The Dial* in 1840), Alcott was a sharp analyst of personality and a practiced noticer from his time as a teacher. Following the meeting at Bartol's, he recorded his admiration of Very's "interesting remarks on life—will—love, etc. He said much that was true, and expressed himself with great beauty. . . . He is a phenomenon quite remarkable in this age of sensualism, and idolatry."[10] Alcott again deemed Very "a mystic of the highest order; a pietist of the transcendental order," and stated confidently that he "will be deemed insane by nearly every man."[11]

In a later journal entry, on the occasion of Very's death in 1880, Alcott gave an even more detailed and fascinating account of the physical presence of the twenty-four-year-old prophet:

> Very often came to see me. His shadowy aspect at times gave him a ghostly air. While walking by his side, I remember, he seemed spectral,—and somehow using my feet instead of his own, keeping as near me as he could, and jostling me frequently. His voice had a certain hollowness, as if echoing mine. His whole bearing made an impression as if himself were detached from his thought and his body were another's. . . .
>
> His temperament was delicate and nervous, disposed to visionariness and a dreamy idealism, stimulated by over-studies and the school of thought then in the ascendant.[12]

Though this entry was made at an advanced age, it nevertheless provides a type of observation often unrecorded by those who encountered Very. A few who had walked with him in Mount Auburn might describe his long and somewhat stately stride and deeply resonant voice, but only Channing had asked pointed questions about his movements under the influence of the Spirit, and only Alcott thought it appropriate to register Very's strange physical nearness. Alcott seems intent on trying to capture Very's erasure of self as a bodily emptiness, as though his personal presence had been stripped away and what was left was a kind of automaton pulled here and there by invisible strings. This image may have been developed over the years of remembering his relatively few encounters with Very, but the distillation of time also lends it depth and clarity, as though his memory of the younger man "somehow using [Alcott's] feet instead of his own" was the most meaningful remnant of those meetings.

At the gathering of the Transcendental Club on January 29, Alcott again spent time with Very, sharing a room with him in Chandler Robbins's house after the meeting in Lynn, Massachusetts. Alcott continued to find Very impressive, noting his "fine statements" during the group's discussion of "Instinct."[13] But Very's otherworldly distance seemed even more pronounced, and Alcott had begun to believe that so spiritualized a being could not survive much longer:

> He is a remarkable phenomenon. He affects me as a spectre. His looks, tones, words, are all sepulchral. He is a voice from the tombs. He speaks as having once lived in the world amidst men and things, but of being now in the Spirit: time and space are not, save in memory. This idea modifies all his thoughts and expressions, and the thoughts and expressions of others also. It is difficult for those who do not apprehend the state of his Soul to converse with him. . . .
>
> I think he will decease soon. He dies by slowly retreating from the senses, yet existing in them by memory, when men or things are obtruded upon his thought. Nature to him is as a charnel house, and the voices of men, echoes of the dead who haunt its dark chambers.[14]

Anticipating by a few months Emerson's comment that Very's presence in social settings was like having "a corpse in the apartment," Alcott captures more vividly than anyone the deeply strange and alienating quality of Very's manner (*JMN* 7:213). Even for those most sympathetic to his claims, his conscious removal from everyday reality made normal interaction nearly impossible. Alcott also indirectly highlights what must have been Very's intense isolation and loneliness. Despite repeated efforts to reach out to others by sending letters and engaging in long and intense conversations, he had, in effect, locked himself within a conception of his own removal and purification. Each attempt to convert a friend or new acquaintance was essentially a search for an ally, someone who could join him in his experience. But almost by definition such a sharing of self-erasure was impossible. It's as though in an attempt to escape passion—and the painful emotional cost of human love—Very had found it necessary to reject not only romantic feeling but any possibility of friendship. In a curious anticipation of Poe's M. Valdemar or Melville's Bartleby, Alcott's description hints at the logical conclusion of such a thoroughgoing rejection of life. By claiming, essentially, that he alone had relinquished all trace of his personal being—that he alone was alive in spirit—Very had ironically condemned himself to a form of living death.

✹ 35 ✹

"Epistles to the Unborn"

One of the stranger and yet essential texts Very produced in the period leading up to the publication of his essays and poems was likely sent to Emerson not long after the January meeting of the Transcendental Club. The "Epistles to the Unborn" consists of three prophetic or apostolic letters that set out to explain or present Very's vision of his conversion experience.[1] Less a personal communication than a formal statement of Very's conversion narrative and theology, these complex and deeply idiosyncratic letters deserve close attention as the fullest statement of his poetic and prophetic "madness." Though shrouded in biblical language directly mouthed from the Gospels, Revelations, or the letters of the apostle Paul, the epistles can be said to make a few basic claims, stated here in greatly simplified form: first, that our physical births are corrupt and empty (Very uses the term, "*dead*-birth," with emphasis [Cole 176]; the physically born are spiritually "unborn") and must give way to a new birth in spirit; second, that this new being consecrates our actions as "prayer" through our continued self-denial; and third, that the (newly or truly) "born" become "the Resurrection," transforming others inwardly via the "miracle" of "raising" the spiritually dead.

It should be clear from this distillation that the necessary and binding element throughout the epistles is self-denial, particularly the rejection of pleasure. The first, "On Birth," establishes the point with unusual intensity. Very does more than merely reject the indulgence of the flesh; he imagines the erasure of all that we know as normal, physical existence. This total asceticism begins with a removal from the circumstances of our own bodily conception:

> To me, you were *dead* or *still born* into *what you call* the world; that is *your* bodies were begotten in enjoyment; and what you call your spirits naturally, as you would say, seek enjoyment. Your father and mother,

> or that which reminds you of them, this nature which they gave you, you know; and when *your* bodies and spirits are warred with by Him who is begetting you of another nature, you call *them* parents. By your still birth you are by inheritance opposed to the universal relations into which you are thrown, and this opposition continues until it ends in giving you a new body and spirit by which you recognize God as a parent. (Cole 176; original emphasis)

Given the strong likelihood that Very knew of his parents' passionate elopement, it can be hard to read this attempt to remove himself from this moment without reference to his own origins. The disturbing notion that a body "begotten in enjoyment" is necessarily "still born" suggests a kind of revulsion at the sexually driven lives of his young parents, though we should remember that it was Very's own attraction to women that likely led to his shift of feeling during his senior year at Harvard. If God could replace these earthly or earthy parents, Very would be able not only to achieve salvation and glorification as a "truly born" Christ but, in effect, to rewrite the circumstances of his own origin. By removing his own will (which we might sometimes hear as the will to "enjoyment"), Very was rejecting the life of love, pain, and suffering—a life to which he himself was drawn—that took his father at an early age and left his mother the defensive, grieving figure so dominant in the lives of her children.

Conventional though the language of a "new birth" is to Protestant conceptions of salvation, Very's idea of redemption is neither traditionally Calvinist nor specifically Unitarian. While we can find traces of Jonathan Edwards's panentheism and Lockean sensationalism in Very's sensibility, his renunciation of will (as described in his accounts of his own transformation) is clearly a conscious act and therefore distinctly Arminian.[2] That this willful removal of the will makes way for an influx of spirit and "direct revelation" recalls, as I discussed earlier, the "inner light" countertradition of Anne Hutchinson and the Quakers. It similarly suggests a family resemblance to the pietist tradition and, possibly, to the pietist strain that ran through the Unitarianism of someone like Henry Ware Jr. But what makes it truly distinctive is its combination of these near-mystic elements with the romantic Christianity of poets like Wordsworth and Lamartine. As M. H. Abrams famously recounts in *Natural Supernaturalism*, Wordsworth had announced in his prospectus for the design of *The Recluse,* of which *The Excursion* was meant to be a part, "that he had been chosen to be a poet-prophet for his age. He has been granted 'an internal brightness' that is 'shared by none' and that compels him, 'divinely taught,' to speak 'Of what in man is human or divine.'"[3] This vision of a special, prophetic role depended upon a relocation of the drama of Christian apocalypse to the inner life of the individual: "A more important and dramatic phenomenon was the tendency, grounded in text of the New Testament itself, to internalize apocalypse by transferring the theater of events from the outer earth and heaven to the spirit of the single believer, in which there enacts itself, metaphorically, the entire eschatological drama of the destruction of the old creation, the union with Christ, and the emergence of the new creation—not *in illud tempus* [in that other time] but here and now, in this life."[4] If Wordsworth had attempted this secularized psychologizing of an inner apocalypse, Very had seized on almost the same idea much more literally. Adding Lamartine's similar claim, recorded by Very, that "man has nothing great or beautiful appertaining to him that comes from his own power or will; but that all that is supremely beautiful comes from nature and from God," we can see more clearly how his conception of a "new" or true "birth" is focused both on the present ("salvation" as such happens now) and on the formation of a speaker, a voice, and a language issuing directly from the indwelling Spirit.

The second epistle, "On Prayer," dwells upon this fusion of body and spirit with language, transforming the role of the poet from Wordsworthian prophet to messianic presence. Prayer is defined as "that action of the soul which begins at its *birth*" as a result of self-denial (Cole 177; original emphasis). "Prayer" is the erasure of the self by which "you show that you love the brethren, because you cannot love more than *this*, that you accomplish the entire denial of the life you have attained unto by being born" (Cole 177; original emphasis). What those as yet "unborn" think of as prayer is a false and empty speaking because their words can only reflect what they are. The words of the "unborn" are "*not-working*" and "not-quickening" (Cole 178; original emphasis). Only by "dying" to your old self can you truly speak in a way that aligns spirit and body: "Pray always, writes the Apostle, to those in this state; that is bear always about with you, or be you always in that condition of dying, by which your words will make evident, that yours is the *true* body of Jesus Christ" (Cole 178; original emphasis). We might consider, in some respects, this strange fusion of body and word, messianic presence and linguistic power, to be the fulfillment of Very's desire, as a Harvard sophomore, to "restore epic poetry," to take the Miltonic-Wordsworthian tradition of the poet-prophet to its conclusion by imagining a kind of utterance that is at once both voice and flesh.[5] By denying the self, he has purified and unified body and spirit, making speech and action (all exterior signs of self) a direct reflection of the indwelling of Spirit. His actions are thus a divine language; his words, "infallible."[6]

"An Epistle on Prayer" may be the most important document for understanding Very's conception of his religious sonnets and his handling of voice within those "inspired" poems. It explains, for instance, how he can so easily and unselfconsciously move from a general poetic speaker into the voice of John the Baptist and even Christ. To his thinking, there is no poetic personality as such, no "Jones Very" to stand in subordination to a higher being; it's even tempting to say that having erased the self, having become prayer as he imagines it, there is no responsibility, no guilt, no distinction between him and the divine that would create a moral scale for his actions. (This flirtation with anarchy was not dissimilar to Emerson's and no doubt added to the discomfort Very created for the local guardians of behavior.) But the letter also makes clear that despite the alarm at his claims, Very never understood himself to be in exclusive possession of the messianic role. He did think that he had achieved this apotheosis sooner than anyone else, but he also outlined a method by which others could do the same. If Emerson in the Divinity School Address had insisted that anyone conscious of the god within could be what Christ was, Very not only claimed that state but in these letters wrote a kind of vatic instruction manual on how to achieve it. His sonnets enact the reward of that achievement: the self-less speaking of pure "prayer," act and word united in a singular expression of divine will.

The third of the epistles, "On Miracles," takes up two related challenges: the need to comment on the so-called miracles controversy still smoldering in Unitarian circles; and the desire to respond more fully to Brazer's demand for a visible miracle to prove Very's claims. Though no direct response to the miracles question from Very survives, we can sense some sympathy with Emerson's position in this letter. Having internalized the entire drama of apocalyptic return, Very had told Brazer that this "revelation would not have miracles" (EP 209). Here he elaborates on that scene, as though replaying and revising it: "But you will say, 'Let me see you stand forth and exert this power.' I answer I do thus work and in these words declare it" (Cole 179). Similarly to Emerson, Very does not so much deny miracles as redefine them. The miracle as such (what he described as the raising of the dead or giving sight to the blind) is the accomplishment of his words through the embodiment of Spirit as "prayer," and is perceptible only to those who have been "born." Brazer, one of those who pray with "no agency at work benefitting those for whom you speak," had demanded proof prior to faith (Cole 177). But he was unable to "see" because of the interference of his personal will.

True miracles, then, were a result of a revolution in perception rather than a violation of natural laws. In this sense, Very could agree with Emerson. But his sense of how this change occurred was much less secular and much more traditionally theological than Emerson's. If Emerson imagined a fully self-actuated removal of habit or custom to open the mind to the wonder of "the blowing clover and the falling rain," Very saw the removal of the will and the subsequent influx of Spirit as the key. To be "born," in his terms, was to vacate the self, not simply renovate its mechanisms; and though it shared some ground with Emerson's mystic, "transparent" moment in *Nature*, Very's self-erasure made possible a kind of absolute spiritual sight—a "face to face" with others stripped of their deceptive egos:

> *You* therefore shall know *me* not by *this external* semblance of myself which I give you naturally in words by my own growth, but to know me in truth you yourself by a like increase in yourself must see me as I *am* from the eternal image there. As in a glass face answer to face, so will my heart then answer to yours. . . . Now you *make* me what I am to you; then you shall see me as I *am*, for you yourself will be much like unto me. (Cole 180; original emphasis)

It's common to reassure ourselves that Emerson's emphasis on self-reliance was balanced by a sense of the deep unity of all spirit; the individual may (and should) be idiosyncratic, but that particularity will allow one to reach the well of divine spirit shared by all. Paradoxical though it is, the more you are your self, the more you resemble and echo others (*true* others) in spirit. For Very, however, there is no self-reliance, only self-negation. The "born" do not reach a unity of spirit by moving ever deeper into their own instinctive individuality; they deny all that is particular or unique about themselves, remove the "*external* semblance" to reveal the true self as an instance of divinity. Emerson manages, in a very American cultural spirit, to have it all: individuality, unity, and divinity set in a satisfying equipoise. Very's regimen is much starker, less pragmatic, and less obviously self-gratifying: give everything to God, and from that nothingness you will be lifted up, resurrected, as a living truth.

✸ 36 ✸

"Between Very & the Americans"

Following his attendance at the Transcendental Club meeting in late January, Very returned to Salem and continued to write sonnets at an accelerated pace. Though these accumulating verses from the first half of 1839 offer some variety in terms of voice and setting, they remain unwavering in their devotion to the central claims of his apocalyptic vision. There is little if any development of ideas, only the continued restatement or redramatization of the apocalyptic process of conversion explained in his letters. Given the difficulty in precisely dating many of the poems, it can be challenging to determine whether or not Very's mood shifted significantly during this period, but the poems as a whole do give the impression that he had begun to feel increasingly isolated by his ideas. As Alcott had perceptively noted in January, Very's spiritual vision had placed him outside of life itself, and its uncompromising application of salvation via self-erasure meant that he was unlikely to discover any acceptable allies. If even the most sympathetic of his well-wishers—including Emerson, Alcott, and the Peabody family—could be found wanting, how could he find someone to join him in his union of spirit? It may have started to seem, in other words, that Very's "church" would never recruit more than a single member.

Did this failure of full sympathy also apply to his family, gathered protectively around him at Federal Street? Probably so, though the evidence is tenuous. That his mother had fiercely defended him, even to the point of expressing belief in the "angelic" nature of his vision, we know from Peabody's account of the events of the previous autumn. His brother, Washington, two years younger and on an academic path almost identical to Jones's, took a more balanced view, telling Peabody that he hoped his brother would work his way out of his "morbidly excited" views and "become like other people" again (EP 224–25). Of Very's two younger sisters, Frances (then seventeen) and Lydia Louisa Anna (fifteen), nothing can be said, though judging from their later protectiveness of his reputation, it's clear that both revered their older brother's work and character.

Family loyalty was one thing, however, true agreement something else. In the sonnet, "The Rose," published that March, it may be possible to catch a hint of failed sympathy, directed potentially at Lydia Very herself:

> The rose thou showst me has lost all its hue,
> For thou dost seem to me than it less fair;
> For when I look I turn from it to you,
> And feel the flower has been thine only care;
> Though shouldst have grown as freely by its side
> As springs the bud from out its parent stem,
> But thou art from thy Father severed wide,
> And turnst from thine own self to look at them;
> Thy words do not perfume the summer air,
> Nor draw the eye and ear like this thy flower;
> No bees shall make thy lips their daily care,
> And sip the sweets distilled from hour to hour;
> Nor shall new plants from out thy scattered seed,
> O'er many a field the eye with beauty feed. (*CP* 110–11)

This quiet but firm condemnation of the gardener who has failed in devotion to the spiritual world suggests some of the complexities of Very's position in relation to friends and family. Whether the gardener here most resembles Lydia Very or one of the family members—or even an acquaintance showing off a successful bloom—we can sense the isolation of the speaker as he looks from the rose to the gardener and notes the misplaced devotion to the beautiful but transitory flower. Because the gardener is "severed wide" from the "Father," the love of beauty arises from the self rather than the inhabiting Spirit. Only a truly selfless state, as though sprung directly from nature, could make the gardener as beautiful, turning her words into "perfume" or "sweets distilled from hour to hour" and propagating new life via this message. Knowing that Very had identified his own particular weakness as the "love of beauty," we might even hear the poem as a self-rebuke, an attempt to rein in the will by reminding himself not to be too attached to the world of the sensuous garden. The last six lines, in particular, seem fraught with the threat of failure, both spiritual and sexual, suggesting that Very's erasure of his own aesthetic and erotic desires was never complete.

If the ecstatic mood of the previous autumn was in fact yielding to an uneasy and possibly depressed state of mind that spring, the change can hardly be attributed to a lack of attention to Very's writing. He continued to publish poems locally, mostly in the *Salem Observer*; over forty sonnets appeared in its pages between February and May of 1839. And in March, the *Western Messenger*, James Freeman Clarke's liberal Unitarian journal published in Cincinnati, printed a selection of nine sonnets with an extended introduction to and defense of the "young man of much intelligence and of a remarkably pure character" who wrote them.[1] Clarke's preface was the first public defense of Very since his confinement, and it could only be encouraging to see such vigorous praise and protection in print. Aware of the continued controversy around Emerson's address and the attendant charge that this radicalism was responsible for Very's madness, Clarke took time to reassure his readers that he himself had spent time with Very in Boston in December and had found "no evidence even of such partial derangement."[2] Clarke's presence during Very's interview with William Ellery Channing may indicate that this was the meeting he had in mind: "We have heard him converse about his peculiar views of religious truth, and saw only the workings of a mind absorbed in the loftiest contemplations, and which utterly disregarded all which did not come in to that high sphere of thought."[3] But Clarke does more than simply vouch for Very; he attempts to place him in a larger context of religious visionaries who attempt "to introduce to the common mind any very original ideas. . . . He who insists on taking us out of that sphere of thought which is habitual to us, into a higher and purer one, is regarded by us with alarm and dissatisfaction. We must either yield ourselves to him, and suffer our minds to be taken out of their customary routine, which is always painful—or we must find some way to set aside his appeals to our reason and conscience and disarm them of their force. The easiest way is to call him insane."[4]

Such an approach could shelter both Very and Emerson, of course, and Clarke's introduction serves the larger purpose of shifting the definition of sanity away from what is normal and comfortable to what is disruptive but true. He places all such reformers in historical context, citing the "Wesleys, Penns, [and] Foxes" who have "been called delirious by their own age" but "deified by the following one."[5] And he wonders whether this clearer historical vision reveals that anyone's idea of common sense may be a form of shared "delirium." The "man in whose intellect all other thoughts have become merged in the great thought of his connexion [*sic*] with God" may not be subject to "MONO-MANIA" but express instead a form of "MONO-SANIA."[6] And as for "Mr. Very," he clearly falls into the tradition of quietists like François de Salignac de la Mothe-Fénelon, archbishop of Cambrai, and the mystic Madame Guyon, who similarly maintained that "all sin consists in self-will, all holiness in an unconditional surrender of our own will to the will of God."[7] Very is a mystic, in other words, and his messianic claims express the inner conviction of unity with God: "He believes that one whose object is not to do his own will in any thing, but constantly to obey God, is led by Him, and taught of him in all things. He is a Son of God, as Christ was *the* Son, because he *always* did the things which pleased his Father. He professes to be himself guided continually by this inner light, and he does not conjecture, speculate or believe, but he *knows* the truth which he delivers."[8]

Clarke's preface is the clearest and most cogent defense of Very's ideas to appear in print during the roughly two-year period of Very's controversial spiritual enthusiasm. Placing him within the history of quietist mysticism would be unlikely to satisfy conventional Unitarians like Brazer or Charles Wentworth Upham, but it would assuage Clarke's largely liberal readership whose sympathy with Quaker pacificism, abolitionism, and other manifestations of the "inner light" tradition was well established. If Clarke downplayed Very's tendency to blur the line between being "*the* Son" rather than simply "a Son," so much the better for parrying those who would charge Emerson and Very with blasphemous pretentions. Though conservative Unitarians might recoil from the intense spirituality of a figure like George Fox, they could at least appreciate and categorize it as a familiar type of enthusiasm rather than fear it as, in Andrews Norton's formulation, "the latest form of infidelity."[9]

Evidence of what Very thought of Clarke's account and defense has not survived. Given his response to other potential allies, however, we might imagine him both grateful for the support and critical of Clarke's intellectual distance from what Very considered an absolute truth of unquestionable spiritual experience. We do know that shortly after the preface's appearance, Very went into isolation, refusing to see anyone outside his family. Elizabeth Peabody reported to Emerson at the beginning of June that Very had "kept his chamber for more than two months, being not able, and still less inclined to leave it" (EP 224). He told his family that he would emerge from "this state" and "return to the ways of men" in a year (EP 224). Given Very's increasingly strong criticism of those who had failed to understand his mission, some such total rejection of the sinful or hated world followed logically from his isolating vision. Though he imagined others coming to the same revelation and entering into the "state of sonship" as he had, the messianic-apocalyptic structure of his thinking made any real social communion with such another "second coming" unlikely, if not impossible. Purity shrank from impurity, and Very's exalted emotional state (the intense visionary elation he had described to Peabody as being "intoxicated with the Holy Ghost" [EP 215]) was destined to deflate, but how then to reenter a social world so thoroughly condemned? A few years later, Hawthorne would seize on just this sense of self-entrapment when he sketched Very into his satire "The Hall of Fantasy": "In the same part of the hall [as Emerson and other "disciples of the Newness"], Jones Very stood alone, within a circle which no other of mortal race could enter, nor himself escape from."[10]

Whatever the specific causes of Very's choice to isolate himself socially, they did not apply to his writing. The sonnets continued to flow, and his desire to share the words he understood as issuing directly from the Holy Spirit showed no sign of diminished zeal. In late February or early March, he had discussed with Emerson by letter the idea of producing a collection of his poems and essays, and Emerson had in fact invited Very to visit at that time but wrote again on March 19 to push the occasion back to early April because of family illnesses.[11] However, Very had apparently entered his self-imposed seclusion by that time, and it was left until June before he sent a bundle of his poems to Emerson via Peabody. The accompanying letter, written on Very's behalf by his brother, Washington, explained that he would not be able to visit Emerson to help select poems for the volume, that the choice of poems was entirely his to make, and that Very hoped the book could be sold via a subscription paper left at the Cambridge bookstore. No explanation was offered as to why he was unable to write the letter himself or make the trip to Concord; the refusal has the air of a psychological absolute. But roughly ten days later, all had changed. Very was now on his way to Concord, and had stopped in Boston to share a meal at Alcott's house. The perceptive observer who had thought Very destined for an early death in January now found his friend "much better both in body and soul. . . . His interest in man and nature is reviving in him, and he may yet regain his human position and walk about among men as one of them, and not, as heretofore, a spectre."[12] They talked extensively and Alcott was "encouraged," even when Orestes Brownson dropped by and the two contrasting personalities, the mystic and the "proud Philistine," had little to say to one another.[13]

What had happened to bring Very out of his room, out of Salem, and, if Alcott's impressions were correct, out of his antisocial vision of the world's deep corruption? Washington Very had told Peabody his brother had "benefitted by being kept so quietly at home lately" (EP 225), suggesting that the family, still led by Lydia Very, preferred him at Federal Street rather than out creating controversy and emotional turmoil for himself and others. How much was Very's isolation self-imposed and how much the product of Lydia's intense worry that he would harm himself if he continued to evangelize in Salem? Having sent the poems to Emerson under his brother's hand rather than his own, did he then change his mind, resisting whatever constraints he may have put on himself or felt were imposed upon him by town or family? It is, of course, impossible to say, as it is to know whether or not Emerson communicated some unwillingness to do the work without Very's help. Whatever the motives, Very arrived in Concord late on June 14 or early the next morning. He would stay only until the June 17, telling Emerson, who tried to persuade him to remain a few days more, that "he [was] not permitted."[14] Like Alcott, Emerson found Very in a state less extreme than he had been led to believe by the reports of others: "He has been serene, intelligent & true in all the conversation I have had with him, which is not much. He gives me pleasure. . . . His case is unique, & I have no guess as to its issue, which I trust will be the happiest."[15]

In his journal, Emerson recorded a reaction both more complex and less easy, puzzling at the presence in his house of "certain good or evil thoughts masquerading before me in curious frocks of flesh and blood" (*JMN* 7:212). Very's short visit had overlapped with the longer stay of Caroline Sturgis—poet, artist, and close friend of Margaret Fuller—and Emerson wondered at the contrast between the "deep aboriginal thought" of these seemingly representative types as they blended with his busy household:

> And now in my house as I see them pass or hear their step on the stair, it seems to me the step of Ages & Nations. . . . Here is Simeon the Stylite, or John of Patmos in the shape of Jones Very, religion for religion's sake, religion divorced, detached from man, from the world, from science & art; grim, unmarried, insulated, accusing; yet true in itself, & speaking *things* in every word. The lie is in the detachment; and when he is in the room with other persons, speech stops as if there were a corpse in the apartment. Then here is mine Asia [Lidian Emerson] not without a deep tinge herself of the same old land & exaggerated & detached pietism, and so she serves as a bridge between Very & the Americans. Then comes the lofty maiden [Sturgis] who represents the Hope of these modern days, (to) whom the "limits of earth(y)ly existence," "the highest knowledge," "the fairest blessings cannot in the slightest degree satisfy," & whose beautiful impatience of these *dregs of Romulus* predicts to us a fairer future. (*JMN* 7:212–13; original emphasis)

The "modern," progressive Sturgis chafed at the limitations of the age, while Very had seemingly returned, all by himself, to a premodern purity and simplicity. Such otherworldly or "old" world "pietism" had always held a deep attraction for Lidian Emerson, whom Emerson had nicknamed "Asia" because of her emotional intensity and deep attraction to the spiritual. Just as Alcott had found social interaction impossible between Very and the "Philistine" Brownson, Emerson registered the silent space between Sturgis and Very, bridged only partially by Lidian, whose efforts, we can imagine, were not enough to animate "a corpse in the apartment."

There is no reason to believe that Emerson's criticism of Very in this context contradicts his report to Peabody that the visit had given him "pleasure." The two had worked together to choose the poems for the planned book, and though some of Very's demands had seemed ridiculous and astonishingly vain (particularly his insistence that no corrections be made to grammar or spelling), Emerson genuinely admired both the work and the sincerity of its author.[16] But like Alcott in the wake of his January meeting with Very, Emerson had come to recognize the life-rejecting cul-de-sac of his "brave saint's" will-less individualism. Yes, Very had the intensity and visionary clarity of a John of Patmos, the author of the book of Revelation, and his words showed it, but he was cut off from people, from life. Emerson himself had two infant children at this point, Waldo and Ellen, "not yet descended into our sympathy or the world where we work"—other realities, that is, whose existence would not permit Very's purity of "detachment" (*JMN* 7:213).

Emerson refrained from elaborating on Very's insistence that he leave Concord after only a few days. By whom or what Very was "not permitted" to stay remains a mystery, though it seems most probable that this was his way of referring to impulses of the Spirit he believed guided him in all things. His short sojourn outside of his room on Federal Street appears to belie his insistence to his family that he would be in isolation for a year before rejoining the world, but the critical, oppositional feeling toward society generated by his vision of inner apocalypse had not left him. Despite Alcott's more optimistic appraisal, Very had shown no substantial change in vision or purpose, and perhaps the best way to understand his trip to Concord is to see it as a necessary service to the poems he continued to understand as divinely spoken. In this sense, his argument with Emerson over corrections, so often cited as (comical) evidence of his lack of perspective, may have been the primary point of the visit: the outflow of Spirit should not be subject to second guessing. Emerson, for his part, was determined to correct and shape the book into something he considered marketable, though his optimism about any real profit was slight. "I dare not now assure him any pecuniary advantage," he confided to Peabody just as Very was returning to Salem.[17] And the following month, in a letter to Margaret Fuller, he mentioned the small collection of three essays and some sixty-six poems (selected from among two hundred) and asked her to "announce its coming value to all buyers," hoping that "our prophet will get $150" from the sales, a modest enough sum but money Very was eager to have.[18] Despite his otherworldly distance, the eldest son of Lydia Very was never so abstracted as to forget the needs of his mother and siblings, now deprived of his teaching income. Even "a newborn bard of the Holy Ghost" had bills to pay.

✷ 37 ✷

Essays and Poems *by Jones Very*

Though Emerson's motives in editing Very's poems seem to have been largely altruistic, we should not consider his shaping of Very's book without taking into account the previous year's controversy. Just as Emerson was completing the work of assembling the manuscript and finding a publisher, his most vociferous critic, Andrews Norton, was delivering his lecture "A Discourse on the Latest Form of Infidelity" to the newly formed Association of the Alumni of the Cambridge Theological School. What has been described as the long "whispering campaign" against Emerson and Transcendentalism had moved into open combat, and Norton's counterattack began a pamphlet war, chiefly with Emerson's friend and fellow Transcendental Club founder, George Ripley, a former student of Norton's. Emerson remained silent, refusing to engage even with those, like Henry Ware Jr., who had disagreed more cordially. But he did, after all, insist on having editorial control of Very's volume of essays and verse, even though his name would be nowhere on the final production.[1] He was perfectly well aware of how Very's purported madness had been laid at his feet; he may also have understood that Norton was closely allied and in contact with Very's Salem antagonists, Upham and Brazer. Consciously intended or not, Very's *Essays and Poems* could not help but be an answer of sorts to these continuing accusations.

As a consequence, we should consider Very's book as the product not only of his own visionary experience and poetic development but of Emerson's attempt to present that experience in a form acceptable to the audience familiar with both the address and Very's subsequent behavior.[2] Emerson had told Peabody that in editing the whole he had "select[ed] and combine[d] with a sovereign will," and would "'make out quite a little gem of a volume'" (EP 226), an intention and boast that may tell us as much about his attitude toward Very as it does toward those who would demean him. Emerson saw himself as in control, in other words, and felt as much of a boost from overruling Very's scruples about changes as he did from the prospect of showing those chattering ministers that the mad tutor could really write. This is likely why he chose to begin with the essays. In December, Peabody herself had proposed to Emerson that Very be encouraged to "introduce the whole [poems and essays] with an account of his states—psychological autobiography?" (EP 220), and it may well be that the "Epistles to the Unborn" were intended as something of the sort. Given the stakes, Emerson could hardly afford to let the book start with so sibylline and strange a document, but "Epic Poetry," the revised version of Very's senior Bowdoin Prize essay, and the two Shakespeare essays were above suspicion. Emerson himself had been deeply impressed by these performances and considered Very an important Shakespeare critic. What better way to establish the intellectual depth and range of the young poet about whom so many had heard such strange stories?

It was the choice and arrangement of the poems that offered the greater range of decision and opportunity for shaping. If the essays could show readers that this was a serious, enormously well-read intellect, not the mind of a raving religious maniac, the poems could present a narrative of emotional and spiritual development not unfamiliar to readers of contemporary poetry. Moving in mostly chronological order, the volume begins with what might be considered standard nature poems, lamenting the losses of death and time. The first, "To the Humming-Bird," is one of Very's earlier lyrics, from 1835, and though the subject matter is relatively common—a death in nature that the poet "cannot heal"—its placement at the beginning of the volume makes clear not only that the author of the *Hamlet* essay is, like his subject, prone to brood on the "cruel fate" and "Unheard . . . cries" of those who suffer but that the narrative the volume presents begins with death. Death is primary, in other words, and natural, but our response to it reveals our helplessness; against time and change we have little recourse except to suffer and record that suffering. "Eheu! fugaces," the second poem, extends this powerlessness to the preservation of beauty or "All that sense can here enjoy," leaving only a form of spiritual love that feeds off still redolent sensual memories ("soft blue eyes!").

Of the sixty-five poems in all, the first fifteen suggest a speaker struggling to find compensation, in nature and spirit, for what is lost in the material world. Emerson's arranging hand can be seen in the juxtaposition of poems like "Thy Beauty Fades," first published in April 1838, and "Beauty," a similar lyric from the previous autumn. Both suggest an attraction to the sensual world that fails to satisfy or threatens the spiritual life of the speaker. Even an ostensible nature poem like "The Columbine," the last of the opening set, seems haunted by a faded eroticism: "Still, still my eye will gaze long fixed on thee, / Till I forget that I am called a man" (*CP* 62). If not a spiritual crisis, there is certainly a deep dissatisfaction, a mismatch between the yearning, aesthetic self and the world that escapes its embrace.

Having established a soul that seeks, Emerson then placed the most obvious annunciatory poem in Very's oeuvre, "The New Birth," written in the month of his dismissal from Harvard. If Very himself could not be trusted to explain directly to a larger audience the circumstances of his revelation, his poem could work just as well, better even, to create a kind of conversion narrative. Just as Clarke had taken pains to place Very in familiar traditions of religious mystics, Emerson allowed readers to see him less as a newly radicalized disciple of Transcendentalism than as a traditional Christian convert waking to a new spiritual reality. The poem's slightly manic description of thoughts "In thronging haste fast pressing on . . . / The portals open to the viewless wind" and the somewhat apocalyptic final lines ("And I a child of God by Christ made free / Start from death's slumbers to Eternity" [*CP* 64]) might have raised an eyebrow or two, but most would have read the verse as a familiar description of a spiritual transformation. The same is true of many of the sonnets that follow, such as "The Son," "In Him We Live," and "The Living God."

Where Emerson exercised more caution was in allowing room for poems that too clearly broke down the distance between the speaker and the divine. By and large he dodged verses like "The Watchman," likely among the sonnets Very sent from Salem, with its more direct voicing of an apocalyptic Christ: "Prepare ye all my supper to attend! / I have prepared it long that you might eat; / Come in, and I will treat you as a friend," and so on (*CP* 97). But Emerson could not entirely avoid presenting the converted poetic persona in the book as an almost typological reflection of the messianic personality. Poems such as "The War" and "Thy Brother's Blood" give a clear sense of Very's conception of the battle against the will and the reluctance or inability of most to undertake such a conquest of self. But poems of this sort also isolate and sanctify the poet who sees and understands this failure, venting a sense of righteous condemnation at the persecution that comes from the "blind." The poet-prophet is alone, unaided, and, as Jesus pronounced in Luke 4:24, unaccepted "in his own country." "Thy Brother's Blood" begins: "I have no Brother,—they who meet me now / Offer a hand with their own wills defiled" (*CP* 102). The reluctance even to touch the "guilty" recalls Very's "day of hate" at the Emersons' house in November (as well as the reports from Susan Burley and others in Salem). The poetic personality can see through the pretense of the "smooth unwrinkled brow" and know the heart's secrets "untold before" (*CP* 102, 103).

From his own time spent with Very, Emerson certainly understood that such a mixture of messianic pretension and resentful self-defense revealed part of the self-proclaimed prophet's recent experience. In faithfully representing this portion of the struggle, however, Emerson likely found some small satisfaction in letting Very loose on their shared enemies. Just as he had enjoyed Very's "unhorsing" of Barzillai Frost, Emerson may have heard in a poem like "The Jew" a direct condemnation of John Brazer:

> Thou art more deadly than the Jew of old,
> Thou hast his weapons hidden in thy speech;
> And though thy hand from me thou dost withhold,
> They pierce where sword and spear could never reach. (*CP* 111)

Traditional Christian antisemitism cast "the Jew" as the enemy of Christ, particularly the Pharisaic officials of the church depicted as the chief prosecutors of the unwelcome Messiah. Whether or not this poem specifically targets Brazer, it does imagine the enemy of the prophetic speaker as a false-tongued, figuratively crucifying opponent:

> Thou hast me fenced about with thorny talk,
> To pierce my soul with anguish while I hear;
> And while amid thy populous streets I walk,
> I feel at every step the entering spear; (*CP* 111)

Perhaps most convincing, the false "brother" is exhorted to "cleanse the temple thou dost now defile," and cease persecuting the Christ-like speaker, who begs him to "tread with me the path of peace" (*CP* 112).

Lest the whole postconversion section of the volume become an angry brief for the misunderstood, however, Emerson included a number of nature-centered poems that demonstrate the transformation of the youthful admirer of beauty into a deeper, more thoughtful, and not so easily spiritualized voice. Among the more effective of these, "The Song" suggests that spiritual transformation does not preclude a recuperation of the youthfulness of ordinary experience:

> When I would sing of crooked streams and fields,
> On, on from me they stretch too far and wide,
> And at their look my song all powerless yields,

And down the river bears me with its tide;
Amid the fields I am a child again,
The spots that then I loved I love the more,
My fingers drop the strangely-scrawling pen,
And I remember nought but nature's lore; (*CP* 70)

The themes are familiar from romantic poetry in general, and yet the lack of confidence in writing itself strikes an unusual note for Very. Lyric poetry has, of course, even in its earliest recorded examples, worked the conceit of the poet's inability to capture a subject, but Very's version contains little if any knowingness about this strategy. Instead it seems to echo Emerson's own language in *Nature* ("In the woods is perpetual youth") while suggesting that only an immersion in the natural world—and, by implication, a rejection of fallen consciousness (that is, the will)—can return us to a security, as it were, *before* writing:

I plunge in the river's cooling wave,
Or on the embroidered bank admiring lean,
Now some endangered insect life to save,
Now watch the pictured flowers and grasses green;
Forever playing where a boy I played,
By hill and grove, by field and stream delayed. (*CP* 70)

It's plausible to argue that behind Very's intense rejection of mature desire there dwells an imagined childhood both immanent and serene. The poem's final emphasis on "delay" pulls us away from mere nostalgia into a more fraught wish to remain on the other side of knowledge, protected perhaps from the sequence of deaths (Horace's, Franklin's, his father's, his grandfather's) and his mother's angry grief. As part of what appears to be Emerson's attempt to humanize Very's reputation as much as possible, the inclusion of such a lyric amid the more apocalyptic sonnets helps establish an emotional truth at the heart of the work, a poignancy muffled within the strange cloak of Very's ecstatic behavior.

A similarly quiet but unfulfilled thirst haunts the lovely sonnet "The Latter Rain," another nature poem included in the section after "The New Birth" that like "The Song" is substantially less burdened by apocalyptic language:

The latter rain,—it falls in anxious haste
Upon the sun-dried fields and branches bare,
Loosening with searching drops the rigid waste,

As if it would each root's lost strength repair;
But not a blade grows green as in the Spring,
No swelling twig puts forth its thickening leaves;
The robins only mid the harvests sing
Pecking the grain that scatter from the sheaves; (*CP* 72)

By designating an autumn rain as "latter," the opening line gestures toward an end-of-days allegory of sorts, but the attention paid to the action of the "searching drops" on the "sun-dried fields" pulls us away from generalities just enough to let the scene itself quietly rustle. A more natural and fundamental symbolism asserts itself, the deep thirst of all things bearing fruit when the time is late:

The rain falls still,—the fruit all ripened drops,
It pierces chestnut burr and walnut shell,
The furrowed fields disclose the yellow crops,
Each bursting pod of talents used can tell,
And all that once received the early rain
Declare to man it was not sent in vain. (*CP* 72)

Attempts to wrest a parable-like lesson run up against the poem's stark simplicity. We might imagine that the message is meant to suggest that only those who see the truth soonest, early enough to benefit from it, produce spiritual fruit. In that sense, the sonnet could be understood to share something of the apocalyptic hauteur and schadenfreude found in Michael Wigglesworth's *The Day of Doom*. But this type of feeling—undeniably present in many of Very's more strident sonnets—makes little headway against the simple description of a natural moment. The speaker, calm and observant, is held instead by the look (the beauty?) of dry or fruited plants caught in a rain they no longer need. The poem's attempts at allegory thus seem haunted by a mystery of time and timeliness that the speaker cannot quite grasp.

To close the volume, Emerson chose three poems, all apparently new, that employ different forms of the quatrain rather than the sonnet. Since August or early September of 1838, Very had written, with the exception of a few small lines, exclusively English sonnets, well over two hundred by the summer of 1839. He would continue to write in this form through the fall of 1839, after which he used a wide variety of stanzaic forms, much as he had prior to 1838. There is no question but that the sonnet—through its compression, immediacy, formal closure, and Shakespearean aura—embodied something deeply significant about Very's conception of his spiritual project.[3] What he had repeatedly described as the direct voice of the Holy Spirit came to him in this form, and though there is nothing in Very's recorded comments to suggest that the same spirit could not speak otherwise, it is startling nevertheless to see these new poems make use of other formal strategies. Had something changed? Did the isolation of the previous few months alter or reduce the intensity of Very's spiritual commitment and thought? Had the manic phase—if it can be probably so called—of his visionary madness begun to wane, the other "consciousness" he had detected in September of 1838 left him at last?

The final poem in the volume, perhaps chosen by Emerson to suggest such a return or recovery to "normal life," does suggest something of the sort. "The Prayer," a plea for spiritual visitation, is written in quatrains of alternating lines of three to five feet. Built around the question "Wilt thou not visit me?" it gives voice to both prophetic uncertainty and personal loneliness:

> Wilt thou not visit me?
> The plant beside me feels thy gentle dew;
> And every blade of grass I see,
> From thy deep earth its moisture drew. (*CP* 175)

The tension between the presence of spirit in nature and its absence in the speaker governs the plea. The speaker can see God all around him but feels cut off from the "one voice" that pervades the cheerful morning. A note of alienation, unusual for the persona of these poems, suggests a longing for a former state now lost: "Come, for I need thy love; / . . . Come, gently as thy holy dove; / And let me in thy sight rejoice to live again" (*CP* 175). The fault for his isolation lies with the speaker, who pledges to show more courage "When thy storms come, though fierce may be their wrath" and "strengthened follow on thy chosen path" (*CP* 176). With this reassurance the poem ends by predicting that the divine will "visit" again because a spirit "from sin set free" delights God more than "plant" or "tree" (*CP* 176).

Less the record of a failure of faith than a diminishment of spiritual intensity, "The Prayer" records that deflated sense of purpose we have seen before from Very, particularly after his return from McLean Hospital when he told Elizabeth Peabody that he had been "intoxicated with the Holy Ghost" but was now "sobered" (EP 215). "The Prayer" begs again for that ecstatic unity, puzzled that the spirit so clearly evident in nature could abandon a sincerely selfless believer. It may well be that Very found the quatrain a better vehicle for this less confident state of longing. Flirting with both the hymn and the ballad, the poem seems designed formally to reassure but also to allow more room for doubt, lacking the singular force and direction of most of Very's religious sonnets. Whatever Emerson's motives in placing it at the end of the volume, it has the effect of suggesting to its audience that Very's season of prophetic speaking has come to an end—a reassurance, if nothing else, that the volume they held was not the product of a blasphemous lunatic but the sincere record of a searching soul blessed by a visionary season.

✷ 38 ✷

Madness and Meaning

Emerson's concern that *Essays and Poems*—published by Little, Brown in September 1839—would yield Very scarcely any financial reward proved true enough. The book likely sold no more than a few hundred copies. In 1841, Very wrote to Emerson to thank him for a remittance of royalties and mentioned the sale of 110 copies at full price and "the rest" at reduced bookseller rates of 53 3/5 cents or 62 1/2 cents per copy. The print run was just 500 copies, and there was no reprint or reissue until William P. Andrews's larger edition assembled after Very's death.[1] All told, Very likely netted not much more than the $150 Emerson projected, if that, though he continued to push for an accurate reckoning of every copy sold.[2]

Of reviews there was but one until Emerson himself placed a notice in the second issue of *The Dial* in 1841. In the January number of Brownson's *Boston Quarterly Review* for 1840, Margaret Fuller, as Emerson had hoped, brought attention to Very's book in her lightly dramatized omnibus review column, "Chat in Boston Bookstores, No. 1." In this dialogue, a "Rev. Mr. Nightshade" runs into his friend, "Prof. Partridge," in a "Bookseller's shop in ____" and asks for recommendations of new books for "Mrs. N., and the girls."[3] Longfellow's *Hyperion* (1839) is first to be discussed as a "book that every one reads," but the professor finds it "overloaded with prettiness," insincere, and overly Germanic in style.[4] After a more favorable account of Sara Coleridge's *Phantasmion*, the two discuss Very's "unobtrusive" volume, which, though "unfinished in style, and homely of mien," the professor finds filled with "an elasticity of spirit, a genuine flow of thought, and an unsought nobleness and purity almost unknown amid the self-seeking, factitious sentiment, and weak movement of our overtaught, and over-ambitious literature."[5] Less impressed with the essays, particularly the Shakespeare criticism, the professor nevertheless admits that so little "worthy criticism" of the playwright exists that "Mr. Very's observations seem well worth considering. His view, whether you agree with it or not, boasts a height and breadth not unworthy of his subject; and in details, he is delicate and penetrating."[6] The review concludes with a discussion of the sonnet, a form of which both speakers disapprove, despite Wordsworth's well-known defense of the form, which the professor quotes in full. A final quotation from Very's poem "Time" leaves a favorable impression with the ministerial shopper, who ends by purchasing the poems.

Fuller had never been enthusiastic when it came to Very. She found him interesting and his work admirable but limited and yet was suspicious, like many others, of his more expansive spiritual claims. Later in 1839, she summed up her critique of Very's inconsistencies in her journal: "I saw Mr. Very this morning, and was disappointed. His state is imperfect. He thought himself a Son, he should therefore abide in the desert and let the ravens bring him food. But he sometimes uses his human will and understanding, and so falsifies his thought."[7] Very later attended some of Fuller's "Conversations" in Boston but proved too disruptive and single-minded for the discussion. Fuller did, however, prod Emerson into writing a review of *Essays and Poems* for *The Dial*, a year after her own notice.[8] The resulting brief evaluation is in many respects a curious performance: the book's anonymous editor praising the work's "extraordinary depth of sentiment" while distancing himself from the peculiar character of the author: "He [the poet] has apparently made up his mind to follow all [the Spirit's] leadings, though he should be taxed with absurdity or even with insanity. In this enthusiasm he writes most of these verses, which rather flow through him than from him. There is no composition, no elaboration, no artifice in the structure of the rhyme, no variety in the imagery; in short, no pretension to literary merit, for this would be a departure from his singleness, and followed by loss of insight."[9] The backhanded praise may reflect as much Emerson's ambivalent feelings about Very's behavior as it does his desire to contextualize this poet's "insanity," the initial warmth of Emerson's reception having cooled by 1841. Ignoring his own role as shaper and selector of the volume, Emerson acts as if what he has chosen of Very's work is the truest representation of the poet's strengths and faults:

> With the exception of the few first poems, which appear to be of an earlier date, all these verses bear the unquestionable stamp of grandeur. They are the breathings of a certain entranced devotion, which one would say, should be received with affectionate and sympathizing curiosity by all men, as if no recent writer had so much to show them of what is most their own. They are as sincere a litany as the Hebrew songs of David or Isaiah, and only less than they, because indebted to the Hebrew muse for their tone and genius. This makes the singularity

> of the book, namely, that so pure an utterance of the most domestic and primitive of all sentiments should in this age of revolt and experiment use once more the popular religious language, and so show itself secondary and morbid.[10]

An old-fashioned curiosity, in other words, from an atavistic prophet, whose work, praised as one of the reviewer's "favorite books," nevertheless is trapped in a worn-out, biblical language. The review provides a portrait in miniature of Emerson's modernity yet again rubbing uncomfortably against Very's absolutism. Written the same year as the essay "Friendship," this notice is more self-protective and less forthcoming than the often-cited passage in the essay that describes the effect of Very's intense "sincerity" on those around him (LA 347). Whatever Emerson really thought about the anachronism of the verses, he could not (and would not) admit in an anonymous review, as he did in the essay, that the author had forced from him deep personal revelations and "true relations" (LA 347).

What success Very's book did have can be better estimated by following its slow accumulation of respect among significant readers. For a small volume of essays and poems issued in the uncertain context of its author's reputed insanity, it found its way fairly quickly into influential hands. Some of this dissemination can be attributed to Emerson, who, at Very's request, sent a copy to Thomas Carlyle and may have forwarded a second to Wordsworth.[11] Thoreau owned the book and presented a copy to the father of Ellen Sewell, the young woman both he and his brother John hoped to marry.[12] In his journal Thoreau grouped Very's poetry with that of William Ellery Channing (the younger), Emerson, and William Cullen Bryant, verse said to be flowing from "the Pierian spring."[13] Bryant himself chose six of the poems from the book for his 1840 *Selections from the American Poets* anthology, and Rufus Griswold included a remarkable nineteen Very poems in his influential *The Poets and Poetry of America* (1842). From later inquiries by Richard Henry Dana Sr. we know that he too owned a copy of *Essays and Poems* and gave the book to friends, and James Russell Lowell, another admirer, published a Very poem in the inaugural issue of his journal, *The Pioneer*, in 1843 (which also included Poe's "The Tell-Tale Heart").[14]

Whatever the limited commercial appeal of the book, in other words, it certainly had a succès d'estime sufficient to register Very's name in New England literary culture. What it meant to him closer to home, in the circle of his acquaintances and reputation in Salem, is harder to gauge, but his immediate family were certainly proud of the accomplishment. Of the surviving first editions, one bears an inscription from his mother to her sister, Sarah Hazelton (a volume that subsequently collected clippings and other notices of Very's work), and the record of the Very sisters' vigilance and cultivation of their older brother's reputation speaks for itself. But it's unlikely that the book's appearance changed the minds of those already inclined to consider him less than reliable. If even a sympathetic acquaintance like Richard Henry Dana Sr., who had found Very admirable and fascinating in the summer of 1838, could simultaneously recommend Very's poetry to Bryant in 1840 and announce confidently that the author was clearly "insane," those in Salem who had witnessed Very's behavior the previous fall would likely have held similar opinions, no matter how impressive his publications.

The contradiction, in other words, between Very the self-proclaimed "second coming" and the poet presented in the volume was not entirely erased by Emerson's attempted reshaping of his image. As several commentators on Very's work have argued, the image of the poet created by Emerson in *Essays and Poems* was, in many respects, false or misleading. Those whose only exposure to him came from the book were likely to imagine someone both more conventional and less extreme in his views than he really was—and were just as likely to see his poetry as safer and simpler than it had shown itself to be in manuscript. This deception continued with the later editions of 1883 and 1886, the first by Andrews in response to Very's death, the second by Very's sisters in response to alterations they considered improper in Andrews's volume. Not until Bartlett published a large tranche of poems in manuscript in 1943, including those excluded by Emerson and others, did it become possible to consider what sort of poet Very truly had been rather than what others had strategically made of him. The task remained, even as late as the mid-twentieth century, to confront in Very's poetry the central element so assiduously avoided by his editors: his "madness."

For if Very was not precisely the poet Emerson had presented, what sort of poet had he become by the summer of 1839? To put it perhaps too simply, he was exactly what his editors feared and had tried to suppress: an ecstatic writer who pushed the boundaries of accepted religious expression (and belief) and, at least in moments of heightened emotion, believed himself a veritable avatar of Christ. Even now, what remains unique, strange, and valuable about Very's poetry is this movement beyond the boundary of acceptable expression, particularly in those poems that mimic or ventriloquize a divine voice. This unsettling practice combined with a claim of ego-lessness (reflected in the very absence of obvious attempts at "literary merit," as Emerson phrased it) made for a prophetic identity difficult, if not impossible, to process, even for so clear a champion of radical individualism as Emerson. We might recall Emerson's journal entry at the end of Very's first extended visit to Concord in November 1838: "In dismissing him I seem to have discharged an arrow into the heart of society. Wherever that young enthusiast goes he will astonish and disconcert men by dividing for them the cloud that covers the profound gulf that is in man" (*JMN* 7:123). Externalized though it is, such a description reflects Emerson's own experience with Very: he is admitting that the claim of divinity and its attendant directness, Very's "madness" itself, dislodges the careful shroud that constitutes normal social reality. And most people, even Emerson himself to an extent, were unable or unwilling to consider the deeper questions posed by his absolutist and apocalyptic vision.

A few examples from the poems recovered by Bartlett will suffice to show just what Emerson, Andrews, and the Very sisters could not, or would not allow others to, face. The bare, no doubt embarrassing directness of "I am the Way" likely typifies the quality most to be avoided:

> The way is simple for I am the light
> By which thou travelest on to meet thy God
> Brighter and brighter still shall be thy sight
> Till thou hast ended here the path I trod (*CP* 128)[15]

The naked shock of this claim would of course sound preposterously "vain," as Hawthorne put it, to almost any ear. Perhaps less afraid of charges of blasphemy than of this outsized egoism, the editors avoided what was nevertheless the most daring and unusual aspect of Very's poetry. After all, as Lawrence Buell was early to point out, the language here sounds not at all distant from the more famous declarations of Walt Whitman, only fifteen years or so in the future: "Carried to its logical conclusion," Buell argues, "the idea of the self as God means that the 'I' is capable of the same infinite variety as nature and that every thought and act is (at least potentially) significant and holy. The Transcendentalists realized this, but the thought disturbed them."[16] Whitman's "Stop with me this day and you shall possess the origin of all poems" or "And I know that the hand of God is the elderhand of my own" avoids Very's more literal aping of scriptural language but is no less embarrassing in its insistence on the full extension of Emerson's Divinity School Address.[17] Emerson's discomfiture in reaction to Whitman's publication of the famous "wit and wisdom" letter suggests a similar sort of awkwardness: more than just a blush at Whitman's frankness, it implies another confrontation with the prophetic—and slightly improper—"newborn bard of the Holy Ghost" he himself had conjured.

Perhaps even more difficult to digest than Whitman's pansexual messianism, however, was Very's insistence that only through total self-erasure could such a voicing of the divine be possible. Rather than absorb multitudes, Very rigorously purified the self of virtually all trace of life and desire, leaving only the hollowed husk of an identity to echo the voice within. This strand of what was generally referred to as his "morbidity" can be heard behind the ecstasy, as it were, in a poem such as "The Message":

> There is no voice but it is born of Me
> I am there is no other God beside
> Before Me all that live shall bow the knee
> And be as in a fiery furnace tried
> Warn them for I have told thee of my love
> Bid them prepare my supper to attend
> Thou has heard him who cometh from above
> Let them receive thee for I am your friend. (*CP* 150)

The poem here speaks in the voice of God or Holy Spirit, with perhaps the poet as the addressee of this series of commands. Its apocalyptic warning echoes the Christ of Matthew 24, but the all-absorbing presence allows for no ordinary reality, no individual as such, only the remnant, a sort of placeholder for what the self once was. Unlike the poems arranged by Emerson in *Essays and Poems*, it admits of no narrative of spiritual development or poetic growth. To erase the self was, in effect, to make all such perfectionist patterns impossible, irrelevant. There was something, in other words, not merely embarrassing about poems like these but nihilistic with respect to ordinary experience. The editors' unwillingness to include them may indeed suggest that Emerson and others were disguising signs of Very's madness, but it also indicates that they recognized (no matter how intuitively) that the "logical conclusion" of "Transcendental egoism" included not only outrageous claims of divinity but their obverse: modern isolation and emptiness.

Within the contours of this reaction—the mutual embrace and distancing of Emerson and others—we can glimpse Very's historical uniqueness and importance. Far from being an aberration or curiosity associated with Transcendentalism, Very brought to visibility the end point of a certain line of romantic individualism and highlighted one of the ways the deification of the self leads to its eventual loss of agency. Just as one aspect of this messianic poetics made possible the Whitmanic embrace of multitudes (and the conception of the poem as literally divine), another led inevitably to the kind of alienation evident in Melville's characters, particularly the hollowed-out, ironic self-reliance of Bartleby. Hawthorne's description of Very in "The Hall of Fantasy" points clearly to the connection: having followed the fullest implications of his own pursuit of will-lessness, Very had aspired to be, in effect, "the corpse in the apartment" who had eventually tried even Emerson's patience. And just as Very achieved what seemed to be total union with the Holy Spirit, just as his poetry became the word of God itself, he found himself cut off, not merely persecuted as "mad," but disconnected from the social world, unable because of the absolutism of his position to reenter life except as an unwelcome or discomfiting visitor. The effect of such a final position, similar to the disconcertion of the lawyer-narrator in "Bartleby, the Scrivener," was to cast a strong light on the compromises and half-truths of others, to force, as Emerson himself admitted, a kind of truth in everyday situations that most people were unwilling to see.[18]

✻ 39 ✻

"True relations . . . in a false age"

Exactly when Very emerged from the self-imposed isolation begun in the spring of 1839 is difficult to determine with any precision. The visit to Emerson in June had certainly been an exception, and there is no surviving evidence of movement outside Salem until September or October when he again made his way to Concord, probably to consult with Emerson on sales and royalties from the recently released book. A letter to Lidian Emerson, enclosing poems he had written in Concord and read to her there, describes his journey back to Salem via Cambridge:

> My return a few days since from Concord through Watertown, Cambridge, and Boston; was as pleasant as one but little accustomed to travelling and its fatigues has a right to expect. Your *cake* was well supplied by a piece of white bread and a cup of milk and water from a poor yet worthy woman on your turnpike at whose house I rested a little while on my way. Alas, it went to my heart to take it; for I felt I could not as yet give her the true bread in return. I was wearied much by a few days stay at Cambridge, but am now as if with you again and well; waiting for that daily direction which is a path unseen through the world and its visible evils;—in which that we all may walk forever and ever I pray always.[1]

After copying out the poem "This Morn," Very explained that he had stopped at Little, Brown publishers as he "came through Boston" and left an order from Mr. Emerson. He himself had taken four copies of *Essays and Poems* with him but gave one away to his "neighbor," who had given him a ride in his horse and wagon from Chelsea Street bridge.

That Very would write to Lidian Emerson rather than her husband is not entirely a surprise. He had always been closer to her in temperament, as Emerson himself recognized, and she never failed to respond warmly to his speech or writing. Perhaps more significant, Emerson himself left no trace of the visit in his journals, an unusual omission given his lengthy descriptions of Very's stays to this point. It may well be that the stopover was devoted mostly to business, and there was little chance for wider conversation, but the absence of even a notation of the visitor suggests waning interest on Emerson's part. Very may also have been considerably more subdued than in the past; the letter implies physical and emotional fatigue in the still young man who once walked forty miles in one day from New Hampshire to Salem.

The few days' stay in Cambridge probably took Very to old friends as well as his brother, Washington, still at Harvard. In his journal a few months later, Emerson recorded Very describing such a return to his old haunts in suitably prophetic style:

> [Very] said that he went to Cambridge, & found his brother reading Livy—"I asked him, if the Romans were masters of the world? My brother said they had been: I told him, they were still. Then I went to the room of a senior who lived opposite, & found him writing a theme. I asked him, what was his subject? and he said, Cicero's *Vanity*. I asked him if the Romans were masters of the world? he replied, they had been: I told him, they were still. This was in the garret of Mr Ware's house. Then I went down into Mr Ware's study, & found him reading Bishop Butler. And I asked him if the Romans were masters of the world? he said, they had been; I told him, they were still." (*JMN* 7:491)

What Henry Ware Jr. or Washington Very made of this patronizing behavior, if it occurred exactly as recorded, is lost to us. But if Very still entertained any notion of returning to Harvard, such a performance would have confirmed his unreliability (not to mention, unpredictability) now fully one year after his initial breakdown. His condemnations of worldliness, no matter how sincere, were unlikely to go terribly far when they included essentially everyone, no matter how apparently pious, other than himself.

Much of his essential thinking, in other words, had changed little over the last several months of withdrawal from society. The high, bundled energy of his "new life" experience may have diminished, but he had not, as his brother had hoped, "become like other people" again (EP 225). In December, Very again spent a day or two in Boston, this time staying the night with Alcott on Beach Street. Alcott found him "even more preternatural than ever" but not as astonishing or interesting as he had seemed the year before (EG 361). In response to the visit, Very sent Alcott an unusual manuscript. Rather than a set of poems or a hortatory letter, it was a short dialogue between two voices titled "The Morning," and Very urged Alcott to read it aloud to his "friends of a Sunday night and others."[2] The simple scene dramatizes the appearance of a new light, "in the east" but brighter than usual and too early to be the sun. One speaker can feel its presence in his "heart" but cannot see by it. Another can see only "every other step." Others are so insensitive that they are sleeping through the event, unaware of the apocalyptic moment. The partially sighted speaker helps guide his blind friend home before meeting a third figure who is able to see and walk without difficulty. This final speaker has prayed for this event and welcomes it; the new light even casts his shadow on the wall, creating a presence that the first speaker mistakes for another person. The first speaker then attempts to find his way home through the darkness of his partial sight.

Simplistic though it is, "The Morning" reveals important aspects of Very's continued efforts to promote his uncompromising vision. The basic symbolism suggests that there are those further along the path than others when it comes to spiritual illumination. Only by embracing fully the inhabiting presence of the light can we see by it (that is, see what it alone illuminates) and take on sufficient substance to "cast a shadow" (exist, have being). But the dialogue also indicates Very's willingness (or perhaps his need at this point) to make use of other genres, particularly other types of dramatic voicing, in his efforts to transcribe the intimations of Spirit. As such it supports and amplifies the multivocal technique of the sonnets but also implies that Very's poetic energies had diminished in scope and ambition. The copy of *Essays and Poems* he gave away to the neighbor who drove him from Boston to Salem was meant, he said, for one of his children. "The Morning" has something of this elementary quality, as though Very's ambition to reach the heights of poetic expression had given over to a wan simplicity, a repetitive, doctrinal lesson to be shared on a Sabbath night.

While in Boston, likely that same December of 1839, Very visited Samuel Ward at his Boston office.[3] Ward's account of this visit, as we have already seen, is one of the more penetrating descriptions of Very during his early years at Harvard. It was he who recorded Very's intense attraction to women and its related self-imposed asceticism as well as Very's stated desire to "restore epic poetry." Ward's further description of the back-and-forth during the visit itself provides an equally vivid scene of the poet-evangelist pressing his gently imperious and personally apocalyptic vision on a surprised acquaintance. It was three years since Ward had seen Very, likely at their graduation in 1836, and the once thin, pinched scholar had changed: "His face had no longer the hard, thin, anxious look of old,"

Ward noted. "His forehead was fuller—his whole face more smooth. It seemed as if he had left off thinking since he had become so happy as he expressed himself to be. The expression of his features especially the eyes, was peculiarly sweet, and compassionate; but a constant nervous twitching checked his words."[4] Very explained that Emerson had mentioned Ward to him, and he had come "to see where" he was, spiritually speaking: "The husk must be thrown aside as of no value—and I come to bid you if you are ready to come to the feast where we are all assembled—and waiting for you."[5] After a back-and-forth in which Ward attempted to speak in similarly biblical language, refusing Very's invitation, he implied that Very might be deceiving himself, but Very countered strangely that "no one can deceive himself."[6] He then pulled his chair closer to Ward and, as he put it, "laid the axe" at his "door": "I come from the banquet where we are all together. I do not wish to come, for myself. I am happy there—and it pains me to break my repose and come into the world—but I feel that we cannot live for ourselves alone; and so I do come to tell you how sweet the banquet is, and to beg you to come in to it: You are writing a letter—if you are ready, break it off in the middle and follow me."[7] Ward again parried this direct, Christ-like appeal, saying he would come when he was ready. Very left soon after inviting Ward to visit him in Salem, warning him not to look for him "among the best houses" but "in a poor street in a poor house," though he would soon have a "new mansion" for himself.[8]

The visit left Ward more than a little startled. He admitted at one point that the whole experience seemed a bad omen for the business that Very's call had interrupted. That Ward took time to record the episode suggests something of its impact, which he both acknowledged and made light of years later to Higginson: "[Very] sought me at my office one day with his heart in his hands & said he had come to lay axe at my root, to bring me to the Spiritual Life. I was deeply touched to find that he had all the time thought me good enough for the axe!"[9] This mixture of feelings—a genuine impression of sincerity and truth tangled up with uneasiness, strangeness, and a sense of the ridiculous—was common among Very's more sympathetic listeners. Argument, as such, was impossible: one simply witnessed a remarkable manifestation whose effects on the inner life were difficult to gauge and often slow to emerge. Even the clear-sighted Ward, by far the most worldly of those associated with the Transcendentalists, could feel the force of Very's intense sincerity, the "heart in his hands."

This insistence on cutting through social niceties to matters of the deepest spiritual import was the quality that ultimately impressed and stuck with Emerson, even after he had tired of Very's premodern, biblical language and apocalyptic moodiness. The following April Very again spent time with the Emersons in Concord. It was to be his last visit, and this time Emerson did record his thoughts on the strange phenomenon to whom his wife, for one, remained deeply attached. The evening of April 9, he and Very walked "to Edmund Hosmer's & Walden Pond—The south wind blew & filled with bland & warm light the dry sunny woods" (*JMN* 7:491). They sat on the "bank of the Drop or God's Pond" (Goose Pond) and watched the wind wrinkle the water, Emerson so taken with the reciprocal relation between air and liquid that he said, "I declare this world is so beautiful that I can hardly believe it exists" (*JMN* 7:491). To the wilder waves at Walden Pond, Very remarked: "See how each wave rises from the midst with an original force, at the same time that it partakes the general movement" (*JMN* 7:491).

If Emerson meant these two comments to represent a difference of response, he failed to make it explicit. It may be overstating the case to suggest that his own reaction acknowledges skepticism while taking refuge in idealism, while Very's implies a unification of all force within a single impulse. What gulf may exist between the two thoughts—and the two men who uttered them—remains unspoken, though by the next day Emerson had reflected further on Very's effect on those around him: "Very obvious is the one advantage which this singular man has attained unto, that of bringing every man to true relations with him. No man would think of speaking falsely to him. But every man will face him & what love of nature of what symbol of truth he has, he will certainly show him. But to most of us society shows not its face & eye but its side . . . & its back. To stand in true relations with men in a false age, is worth a fit of insanity, is it not?" (*JMN* 7:491–92). In his earlier journal entries from November of 1838, Emerson had described Very as a "telescope," capable of focusing others on higher truths by sheer force of intention. Now he extended this idea to imply that Very's sincerity made deception or misdirection with him impossible. It may well have been that there were some, like Brownson, for instance, who simply could not speak to him, but for those who attempted it, the stark simplicity of mind and attention seemed to make small talk impossible. In his essay "Friendship," written the same year as this final visit, Emerson revised and elaborated on the journal entry, describing Very anonymously as "a man . . . under a certain religious frenzy" who had "cast off this drapery, and, omitting all compliment and commonplace, spoke to the conscience of every person he encountered, and that with great insight and beauty" (LA 347). No false speaking or "chat of markets or reading-rooms" was possible, but "every man was constrained by so much sincerity to the like plain dealing, and what love of nature, what poetry, what symbol of truth he had, he did certainly show him" (LA 347).

What seemed insanity to some, in other words, was a kind of unfiltered interchange, its lack of decorum almost a surprise in its ability to elicit such exclamations as Emerson's at the sight of Goose Pond.

This small summation of Very's surprising influence echoes the revealing journal entry of 1838, the confession that Emerson recorded after Very's first extended visit in the fall of 1838: "I told Jones Very that I had never suffered, & that I could scarce bring myself to feel a concern for the safety & life of my nearest friends that would satisfy them" (*JMN* 7:132). Like the familiar admission in "Experience," the earlier entry underlines a theme for Emerson that is somehow also a personal trait: the world resists us; we are somehow always alone. What stands out with respect to Very, however, is precisely the part he played in bringing out such a revelation. Emerson appears almost taken aback that someone he had met only a few times before could draw something so personal from him. Very may have become tiresome or irretrievably old-fashioned to Emerson by the spring of 1840, but he could still haunt the thoughts of those who had, at whatever cost, worked to take him seriously.

In her 1880 letter to William P. Andrews, Elizabeth Peabody tried to piece together how her friendship with Very had ended: "Our family's leaving Salem to live in Boston in 1840 brought my acquaintance with Mr. Very to an abrupt close—He never came to see me in Boston—As the preternatural excitement of his nerves subsided—I was told that he shunned society" (EP 409). She went on to suggest that she had heard or understood that it might pain Very to be reminded of those days when "he certainly was in a degree *beside himself*" (EP 409; original emphasis). The biographical myth that Very was essentially a recluse for the last forty years of his life may have started here, though it does seem clear that his interactions with notable figures such as Emerson and Peabody significantly diminished as of 1841.[10] In March of that year, Very wrote to Emerson in a tone and manner that suggested he had at last returned to "normal life." In a practical sense he was requesting his publisher's statement of his account, but he first congratulated Emerson on his new volume of essays, filled him in on the latest lectures in Salem, and expressed his thanks to Mrs. Emerson for asking about him, an inquiry passed on by one of his neighbors. Gone is the apocalyptic language and biblical voice; the urgency and avoidance of triviality that Emerson recorded in "Friendship" seems to have yielded to a comfortable acceptance of small talk.

There is similarly no indication that Very considered himself necessarily confined to his room or to Salem. The previous November he had attended the startlingly ecumenical Convention of Friends of Universal Reform at the Chardon Street Chapel in Boston. It was the first of three meetings to consider such topics as the Sabbath, the church, and the priesthood and was attended, according to Emerson's own report in *The Dial*, by "men of every shade of opinion, from the straitest orthodoxy to the wildest heresy, and many persons whose church was a church of one member only."[11] The slightly satirical account gives some indication of the spirit of reform (and religious fragmentation) beginning to take a firmer hold on the era:

> A great variety of dialect and of costume was noticed; a great deal of confusion, eccentricity, and freak appeared, as well as of zeal and enthusiasm. If the assembly was disorderly, it was picturesque. Madmen, madwomen, men with beards, Dunkers, Muggletonians, Come-outers, Groaners, Agrarians, Seventh-day-Baptists, Quakers, Abolitionists, Calvinists, Unitarians, and Philosophers,—all came successively to the top, and seized their moment, if not their hour, wherein to chide, or pray, or preach, or protest. The faces were a study. The most daring innovators, and the champions-until-death of the old cause, sat side by side. The still living merit of the oldest New England families, glowing yet, after several generations, encountered the founders of families, fresh merit, emerging, and expanding the brows to a new breadth, and lighting a clownish face with sacred fire. The assembly was characterized by the predominance of a certain plain, sylvan strength and earnestness, whilst many of the most intellectual and cultivated persons attended its councils. Dr. Channing, Edward Taylor, Bronson Alcott, Mr. Garrison, Mr. May, Theodore Parker, H. C. Wright, Dr. Osgood, William Adams, Edward Palmer, Jones Very, Maria W. Chapman, and many other persons of a mystical, or sectarian, or philanthropic renown, were present, and some of them participant.[12]

Very recalled the meeting to Emerson, whom he must have seen there, but indicated that he was unlikely to go to the second of these, though it was possible he could change his mind. No reports survive that suggest Very took a large part in the gathering or caused any sort of stir with his views. (According to Emerson, Alcott emerged as the dominant force: "Not its least instructive lesson was the gradual but sure ascendency of his spirit, in spite of the incredulity and derision with which he is at first received, and in spite, we might add, of his own failures.")[13] But Very's presence and participation in such an effort do tell us something important about the less studied years of his life to come. Mystic (or "madman") though he may have been—and perhaps still was in 1841—he was not detached from the political, social, and religious movements of his time. He was not, in any real sense, a fully monastic, unresponsive "Simeon the stylite," resistant to political engagement. If others had pulled away from him and found him either too difficult or, possibly, too ordinary now that his "mission" had apparently ended, he had not retreated from the apocalyptic spirit that was now afoot in the region, increasingly energized by abolition and other forms of social change. Quiet he had, in a sense, become—and perhaps quietist, like so many at this moment, in his conception of the method of reform—but his devotion to what such a life devoted to stillness might be continued to find shape from the spirit of sacrifice and will-lessness that had driven him to claims of divinity.

IV

Man of Peace

✷ 40 ✷

Nonresistance

Of those poems written after the summer of 1839 that can be included among Very's religious sonnets, "The Hand and Foot" has attracted perhaps the most commentary over the years. For some readers it has seemed to embody the essence of Very's quiet, receptive spirituality, the erasure of self and full commitment of the body to divine control. In his 1966 selected edition of Very's poems, Nathan Lyons described it as "the perfect inscription to Very's religion," one that clarifies his commitment to "stillness" and the radical passivity of listening for the voice of God. For Lyons, Very was essentially a quietist, the resident of "an upper room," whose "deep quiet encourages a tight marshalling of inner forces."[1] While other of Very's careful readers dispute this label, it's useful to consider how this commitment to stillness and the sacrifice of will—in its most radical forms evoking both Quaker pacifism and Buddhist self-erasure—echoed and participated, directly or indirectly, in the social and political language of the time. As estranged or removed from everyday life as Very's ideas could seem, they were not as purely spiritual or otherworldly as the "mystic" label would imply. Nor did the waning of his apocalyptic personality, evident by 1840–41, diminish his interest in or commitment to the realization of a perfectionist, millennialist vision of heaven on earth. His sermons and poems from the long period after his "madness" had subsided reveal a committed, engaged commentator whose spiritual vision is consistent with, if less immediately intense than, the messianic claims of the sonneteer. Even "The Hand and Foot" can be understood to anticipate this politically engaged pacifism and moral perfectionism that animated the remaining forty years of Very's life.

Published in November of 1839 in the *Salem Gazette*, "The Hand and Foot" describes the passive activity of the inhabited self in terms consistent with Very's description of prayer in the "Epistles to the Unborn":

The hand and foot that stir not, they shall find
Sooner than all the rightful place to go;
Now in their motion free as roving wind,
Though first no snail more limited and slow;
I mark them full of labor all the day,
Each active motion made in perfect rest;
They cannot from their path mistaken stray,
Though 'tis not theirs, yet in it they are blest;
The bird has not their hidden track found out,
Nor cunning fox though full of art he be;
It is the way unseen, the certain route,
Where ever bound, yet thou art ever free;
The path of Him, whose perfect law of love
Bids spheres and atoms in just order move. (*CP* 193)

Built on the basic paradox of action without intention, guided by Spirit, the poem describes the condition of the newly born individual who has overcome his personal will. There is no open conflict as the already calmed voice moves through its quatrains, only a slight intensification of description toward the final couplet. A brief uncertainty in the first two lines—over the implied metaphor of the path ("the rightful place to go") and the need of the body/self to find it—dissipates in the "Now" of line 3, setting the seeker "free" to "labor" on the path "in perfect rest." The remainder of the poem calmly elaborates the paradox of unwilled action, its only disturbance the slight contradiction of natural creatures who cannot find the way, despite God's "perfect law" that motivates all of creation ("spheres and atoms"). Though this is God's path, in other words, it's open only to those who can *consciously* suppress their personal intentions; in this sense Very's passivity is a self-created state, an erasure of will carried out by the will itself.

As others have indicated, this clear registration of choice undercuts those who would claim Very as a strict Calvinist and advocate of predestination.[2] Yet the exalted, decision-less state that follows implies that the otherwise passive self having assented to the erasure of will receives in return an existence free of stress, defined by the ability to live among others without tension or internal conflict. Reflecting Very's understanding of "prayer," defined in the "Epistles to the Unborn" as "the action by which the *living* live and quicken life and happiness in each other," the poem suggests a similar fusion of language and act into a state liberated from either motive or consequence.[3] The only responsibility is to listen and hear and allow the self to be moved by the force that impels it. Such surrender grants a kind of infallibility ("They cannot from their path mistaken stray"), and forecasts a specific mode of being in the world: that of the embodied word, a divinely sanctioned presence that recognizes neither rank nor code. This is another sense in which the convert, though "bound" to the path, is "ever free." "The Hand and Foot," in other words, along with many of Very's sonnets, uses a spiritual experience to establish an exempted *social* status, a way of entering and affecting antebellum society without vulnerability or the need for reciprocity. This state resembles in many respects the unfettered individual Emerson would exalt a few years later in "Self-Reliance" (1841), though in Very's case the self seems more fully erased and the motivating source has not been secularized into instinct or nature's inspiration.[4]

Very's concern with will and its erasure, embodiment and action, reflects a number of persistent antebellum concerns. We can detect resonances with Poe's uncontrolled bodies ("Loss of Breath" [1835]), unruly internal impulses ("William Wilson" [1839]), and seemingly displaced ventriloquistic voices ("The Raven" [1845]); with Hawthorne's persistent worries over personal sovereignty and violations of privacy; and with the continual renegotiation of personhood underway in reformist circles. We could easily make the argument, for instance, that Whitman's claim for the body's equality with the soul ("The scent of these arm-pits is aroma finer than prayer") emerges from the same mixture of poetic and messianic urgencies that almost twenty years before gave us "The Hand and Foot." But more immediately, though perhaps less obviously, Very's interests in this poem share a set of concerns with contemporary debates within the abolitionist movement over the question of active opposition to laws protecting slavery.

Only a year before, in September of 1838, William Lloyd Garrison had organized the Peace Convention held in Boston, at which he presented his "Declaration of Sentiments" for the establishment of the New England Non-Resistance Society. Controversial in its adoption of a pacifism so radical that it precluded self-defense, Garrison's "Declaration" echoed the Declaration of Independence but refused allegiance to any government and all forms of war or "preparations for war."[5] Instead it relied solely on the idea of the imitation of Christ: "The Prince of Peace, under whose stainless banner we rally, came not to destroy, but to save, even the worst of enemies. He has left us an example, that we should follow his steps."[6] Like the Quakers who had influenced him and, to a lesser extent, those liberal theologians such as Channing who were concerned with social reform, Garrison believed that individuals who were "filled with the spirit of Christ" could "speak and act boldly in the cause of God" and thereby "hasten the time when the kingdoms of this world will have become the kingdoms of our Lord and of his Christ, and he shall reign for ever."[7] In such kingdoms, of course, slavery would cease to exist. Passive resistance to unjust laws and peaceful demonstration of the calm moral clarity of "Christ's sufferings" (what Garrison calls "the foolishness of preaching") would work a revolutionary power in others that superseded any need for "jacobinical" violence.[8]

For many, and possibly for Very, the idea of a passive imitation or embodiment of Christ was an end in itself; whether or not reform followed such a conversion was less important than the transformation of the individual into the image of God. Nevertheless, for Garrison and others nonresistance was also clearly a strategy, made necessary in large part by fears of slave revolt—intensified after Nat Turner's rebellion in 1831—and the need to calm concerns about revolutionary violence. Where abolitionists disagreed was in how far to maintain a passive stance in the face of violence. After an increase in attacks against antislavery activists during the 1830s, including the murder of journalist Elijah Lovejoy in 1837, some members of the American Peace Society wished to consider the possibility of self-defense as a justifiable response to such threats. At the 1838 Convention, controlled by Garrison, these comparative moderates hoped to force the issue but quickly recognized their lack of influence and withdrew, leaving Garrison free to propose his "Declaration" to the remaining members, now renamed the New England Non-Resistance Society.[9] The radicalism of the "Declaration" is therefore the product, at least in part, of negation and purification, an attempt to distinguish the otherworldly and Christ-like pacifists from more directly pragmatic abolitionists.

To what extent Jones Very saw himself as participating in one or the other branch of the abolitionist movement in the 1830s is difficult to determine, and the fact that "The Hand and Foot" appeared in the *Salem Gazette* a year after the Peace Convention in Boston does little more than suggest participation in a shared regional perspective and vocabulary.[10] As we have seen, Very did express strong abolitionist sentiment throughout his life. He had witnessed slavery firsthand while exploring New Orleans as a boy in 1823–24 and would continue to write antislavery poems, particularly when current events highlighted the issue. In his sermons delivered after 1843, he often repudiated slavery, though typically while advocating for peaceful change through Christian character and deportment. Here he expressed consistent concern that violence even in the service of a moral cause was inherently corrupting; character and Christian example could bring about change and overcome evil without participating in further evil: "If men would cherish these principles and dispositions," he wrote in an undated sermon, "they would find no great difficulty in overcoming and improving the world. They would carry with them into their daily duties, into political and social life a spirit which would sanctify them all. They would naturally bring forth good fruit, fulfilling with delight every duty to God and their fellow men" (HS 16). Taken together, such evidence suggests that Very would have been highly sympathetic to Garrison's nonresistance platform and suspicious or critical of those who advocated more confrontational methods. While clearly not as radical with respect to government as the Garrison of the "Declaration," Very was essentially a pacifist who strongly supported the idea that the only way to effect true social change was through the transformation and perfection of individual souls.

This pacifism took its most daring form in "The Hand and Foot," which, with a slight adjustment of perspective, can be heard as an echo and extension of the Garrisonian language of nonresistance then in the air: "The hand and foot that stir not, they shall find / Sooner than all the rightful place to go." The question that hovers here is precisely that of 1838–39: what to do, where to go in terms of the available options for all Christian behavior, including social reform. The "rightful place" is the "path" of Christ-like deportment, "found" passively, through a rejection of violence or resistance (products of human intention) that would, in Garrison's words, "ensure all things needful to us, [be] armed with omnipotent power, and . . . ultimately triumph over every assailing force."[11] For Very, this quietist waiting would assure a genuine freedom through paradoxical bondage to the "law of love" that moves all things. Distinguished from the "cunning" or "art" exemplified by the fox, the Christian's refusal to "stir" suggests a strategic rejection of strategy; what Garrison calls the "Jacobinism" of "violence and murder," perhaps implied in the fox's predatory tactics, yields to a quiet freedom that will necessarily abrade the worldly and unjust. In addition, the entire trajectory within Very's poem from bondage to freedom resonates with the abolitionist conflation of spiritual and literal salvation in discussions of slavery. Does the somewhat secretive journey the poem imagines ("the hidden track . . . the way unseen") indirectly reflect the slave narratives that had begun appearing with greater regularity in the 1820s and 1830s? Has Very clarified the soul's journey in a way that deepens the vexed question of action and individual agency within the long tradition of the captivity narrative? Though not overt, such questions seem to lurk just beneath surface of what might otherwise seem to be nothing more than "mystic" verse.

This secondary reading of "The Hand and Foot" also raises an important question about perspective: Is Garrisonian language infiltrating and politicizing Very's otherwise spiritual poetry? Or is Very himself attempting to spiritualize abolitionist tactics, echoing and redirecting the gestures of nonresistance for his own revolutionary purposes? Though Very's poetry as a whole is often more directly political than many commentators have recognized, it is true that the religious sonnets typically describe a conversion or transformation that *precedes* engagement in the social world. Like "The Hand and Foot," these poems concentrate on the movement from willful to will-less states of being and offer no specific description of how the "new life" will manifest itself in society. As is clear from the interview with Channing, Very's absorption in the Holy Spirit appears to preclude any definite foreknowledge of motive or planned action, even of the simplest physical movements. The freedom of bondage described in "The Hand and Foot" thus appears, at least in part, to be a liberation from all forms of choice, from the need to make even the smallest decisions. As such it shares ground with Emerson's ideas about spontaneity, still developing in 1839 and not fully formulated until the publication of "Self-Reliance" in 1841. For both Very and Emerson, the self is subsumed by a larger, benign force (natural spirit; Holy Spirit) that makes possible the "freedom" of unconscious action through the "bondage" to an indwelling, universal power. Where their concept of freedom diverges from Garrison's is precisely in its availability for mobilization as political action. No matter how pure Garrison's Quaker-inspired imitation of Christ, it is formulated with a definite goal in mind: the transformation of society through the elimination of slavery. Neither Emerson nor Very, in the late 1830s and early 1840s, imagined a will-less spontaneity that could be so clearly attached to a specific end. The hand and foot, like Very's arm on Channing's mantel, can be understood in their movements only after the fact, as in Emerson's well-known analogy of the sailing ship: "The voyage of the best ship is a zigzag line of a hundred tacks. See the line from a sufficient distance, and it straightens itself to the average tendency. Your genuine action will explain itself, and will explain your other genuine actions" (LA 266). To see the line is to look back, to add explanation to faith and only then determine the outcome. Goals, as such, cannot be planned or even entertained; they can only be retrospectively revealed.

"The Hand and Foot," through its delicate perch on the edge that divides political nonresistance from pure will-less perfectionism, returns us to Very's descriptions of active "prayer" from "Epistles to the Unborn," in a passage that bears repeating:

> Prayer then is the action by which the *living* live and quicken life and happiness in each other. Its beginning is also that *prelude* to action, too faint and low as yet to be heard and called by the name of prayer,

> by which you, the dead, are becoming, *unknowingly to yourselves*, the living, and drawing along with you those who are around you in your several spheres.[12]

Though the edges of this term remain blurry, for Very those who have eliminated the personal will live a life totally devoted to the impulse of the Holy Spirit; hence, they become "prayer." Those beginning this path move unconsciously toward that pure state in which their actions will speak to others. The emphasis here falls on becoming and being rather than the nonresistant strategy of divine imitation. The distinction is crucial to understanding Very's kinship to the various modes of passive perfectionism in the years leading up to the Civil War. In his "Declaration of Sentiments" Garrison speaks of the desire to participate in Christ's sufferings by analogy: "The ungodly and violent, the proud and pharisaical, the ambitious and tyrannical, principalities and power, and spiritual wickedness in high places, may combine to crush us. So they treated the MESSIAH, whose example we are humbly striving to imitate. If we suffer with him, we know that we shall reign with him."[13] To imitate, to be "like" Christ implies not only a kind of awareness that Very denies to his newly "born"; it also admits a separation from the divine source that allows for a more flexible kind of human agency. The nonresisting imitator of Christ can change, adopt new analogies to meet new needs. Very's will-less embodiments of prayer move without intention or variation; once "born," they cannot choose and cannot change. As is clear in "The Hand and Foot," "They cannot from their path mistaken stray."

Though his gradual loss of zeal and messianic conviction may have softened Very's interactions with the world, his pacifism was not the result of diminished or depressed energies. Despite his ability to create outrage—and, at times, violence—in those who were threatened or offended by his claims, Very himself was consistently a figure of quiet, and his life's development can be best understood as a continual effort to bring peace to the relentless disorder of the passions. If there is a clear psychological origin point for the extremity of his claim to be "the second coming" it is most plausibly found in the cauldron of emotions that surrounded the death of his father and the subsequent struggle between his grandfather and his mother over the estate. To have witnessed these events (a powerful father laid low by consumption; a mother driven to extremities of grief; family avarice, backbiting, public dispute) was to register, as a boy of ten or eleven, the chaotic power of unconstrained human passion. Knowing too—and having the claim publicized by his grandfather—that the legitimacy of his own birth was questionable could only have stirred shame into the mix, driving his pursuit of a higher assurance, a spiritual calm. His mother's personality—often tense, notably and vocally *pained*—likely set a deep aversion to the inner turbulence created by unconstrained passion. At the sign of such feelings in himself, specifically an intense attraction to women, he turned the full force of his inner discipline against the familiar turmoil they produced and began assiduously to suppress his will, to erase all vestige of personal desire in the hope of achieving a Christ-like transcendence. Peace, inner stillness, had always been the goal, whether attained from sitting in the bower he constructed in the garden on Federal Street or through imagining himself as something entirely *other*: removed from human action, his movements the impulses of a Spirit that had absorbed the burden of his being.

Thus if a single strand runs through Very's life after the waning of his visionary energies, it's the more sober and conventional expression of the public pursuit of peace and spiritual perfectionism. Gradually subsiding into a more acceptable form, his ideas about moral perfection through "sonship" changed only in terms of tactics: he ceased making radical claims for his own higher status as "the second coming." The essential conviction that the kingdom of heaven could be achieved on earth through a sacrifice of self to spirit continued to animate many of his sermons and poems, taking very often the more political form of direct appeals for peace or direct application to the affairs of the country. Necessarily, this more conventional mode of expression led him away, though not entirely, from Transcendentalist circles just as it allowed his life to follow a more sedate, less controversial path than it had to this point. However, the notion that Very became something akin to a recluse or that his energies as a writer and thinker diminished to such an extent that the final forty years of his life are essentially "ineffective" is more a function of critical myopia than a clear reflection of the biographical record.[14] Similarly, to ignore his later convictions and commitments as though they had little or nothing to tell us of the remarkable events of 1838 and the person at their center is a clear biographical mistake. To comprehend fully the Harvard mystic, it is as necessary to know the mature person he eventually became as it is to grasp how his early years led to his enthusiasm. Very should be understood—and judged, if he is to be—based on the full account of his life, not just the few years in which he caught the eye of a handful of more famous and better-documented literary personalities.

✷ 41 ✷

"Heaven is a state and not a place"

There are two major repositories of Very's writing after 1841 that survived the culling, both intentional and unintentional, that took place after his death. The poems written after 1841 number in the hundreds and constitute the most significant, and largely unexplored, cache of materials from the last forty years of his life. Though there was no outpouring to match the flood of sonnets he wrote from 1838 through 1841, Very remained a productive poet of traditional lyrics, occasional and ceremonial verse, and of hymn texts. He continued to publish poems in local newspapers and other outlets and sometimes saw his work reprinted in anthologies or religiously themed readers. Over the same period, he wrote and delivered well over a hundred sermons, serving as a Unitarian supply minister for churches in Salem and other nearby communities, ranging as far north as Eastport, Maine, and as far south as Providence, Rhode Island. Given what is likely an incomplete archive of his activities as a minister, we cannot know exactly how many times Very preached over his long tenure as a substitute. Many of the sermons that survive were repeated, sometimes recycled after significant revision. But given the number of manuscripts and the average number of repetitions, we can safely say that Very occupied the pulpit for well over four hundred Sundays, indicating that on average he spoke every three weeks or so over the roughly thirty years of his ministry.[1]

The Cambridge Association of Ministers considered Very's request to be "approbated as a preacher of the Gospel" in March of 1843.[2] Evidence suggests that he had first preached in New Bedford, likely at the invitation of John Hopkins Morison, in November of 1842 and subsequently submitted a formal petition the following February that included recommendations from James W. Thompson, the minister at Barton Square Church in Salem, and Morison, who was then associate pastor at the First Congregational Society in New Bedford.[3] As was typical for such applicants, he was asked to prepare a sermon on a set text, in this case Acts 16:31 ("Believe on the Lord Jesus Christ, and you will be saved, you and your household"). During the meeting at Richard Manning Hodges's house in Cambridge, the letters written on Very's behalf were read to the eight ministers in attendance. Very then delivered his prepared sermon and fielded "various questions" from the panel. His application was approved by vote, and he was issued a certificate.

To what extent this group of ministers may have had concerns about Very's sanity and reliability is hard to say. His case was treated similarly to others applying for approval during this period, though we might imagine that the questions posed after his presentation (which were not recorded in the minutes) were more pointed than usual. All would have known of the events of 1838, including the reason for Very's stay at McLean Hospital, and there is little doubt that they would have wanted to determine for themselves the soundness of both his mind and his doctrine. Even so, this particular meeting of the association included some who were potential allies or who might be considered sympathetic to aspects of Very's reputation. Though fairly conservative Unitarians like Ezra Stiles Gannett from Boston's Federal Street Church might be resistant or suspicious, such figures as Samuel Ripley, Emerson's half uncle, and Convers Francis, a member of the Transcendental Club, may well have balanced the slate.[4]

Whatever the tensions or debates unrecorded in the minutes of the meeting, Very left Cambridge with what he wanted: the chance to preach regularly, to fulfill at least one of his ambitions at the time of his dismissal, and, no doubt, to bring in some form of income for the household on Federal Street. Whether financial pressure or spiritual motivation was the primary factor is impossible to know; there are arguments to be made on each side. It seems significant, for instance, that Very began his ministry shortly after the death of Channing and in the same year as the loss of his teacher and friend, Henry Ware Jr. Upon learning of Ware's death in September of 1843, Very wrote a memorial poem, lamenting the loss not only of his former teacher but of "many of the great and good" who had "passed away" "within this fleeting year" (*CP* 233). Two of his most sympathetic role models, both of whom had treated him with respect and kindness at the height of his visionary experience, had fallen just as he had begun to fulfill their trust in him. "Much have we cause to mourn, whose lights yet burn" (*CP* 233), he wrote, thinking possibly of his own assumption of the pulpit earlier in the year—and of his own responsibilities. In later years, unwilling to venture far from the shadow of the great romantic believer, Very would often describe himself as a "Channing Unitarian." In a poem published during the last year of his life he reaffirmed his devotion to Channing's "growing influence" (*CP* 533). Perhaps some of his desire for licensure derived from the sudden sense that the great light of his time no longer led the way.

At the same time there is little doubt that the family on Federal Street needed money. The sisters, Frances and Lydia L. A., were now teaching in the Salem public schools, but Very's brother, Washington, after working for several years as a clerk and bookkeeper at the Mercantile and Naumkeag Banks, had recently graduated from Harvard and was in his first year at the Divinity School. Though some money remained from Jones and his siblings' inheritance, their regular income was limited, and their mother had little to no cash flow of her own. The fee for substitute preaching (one 1855 letter from William Allen, a Harvard friend and classmate of Thoreau's, offered "six or seven dollars," the equivalent of about $200 today, to preach a Sunday at Bridgewater) could take the pressure off the slim salaries of his sisters or help with Washington's bills in Cambridge.[5] Given Very's eager attention to the proceeds from his book of poetry as well as his later probate request describing his mother's income as no more than $42 a year, we can be sure that all of the Verys lived frugal though not impoverished lives on Federal Street. (Washington Very wrote to a friend in 1848, asking about the price of gloves: "If they should be second-hand & uninjured they would answer my purpose. Cheap, cheap, is, as you know, my failing—a disease, a mania, or whatever you may call it, caused by the want of means more than by anything else.")[6] No longer acceptable, perhaps, as a teacher, Jones could at least be trusted to speak on a temporary basis; and if that went well, perhaps a more permanent role could be arranged. According to a later, defensive statement by his sister Lydia, Very had been offered (at least once) a permanent position away from Salem but "did not wish to leave his home."[7] Over the long years of his preaching career he may well have been in demand at times, but barriers inevitably remained. With the typical Very pride reminiscent of her mother, Lydia L. A. conceded that "many obstacles were placed in the way of my brother Jones' preaching by narrow-minded churchmen."[8]

The reports we do have of Very's style and deportment in the pulpit are generally consistent. According to William P. Andrews's "Memoir," Very was never a "popular" preacher but was ultimately so admired by those who knew him that they were honored to employ him as a substitute. One "singularly eloquent preacher" was said to have told his parishioners that "to see Very for half an hour in my pulpit, and know that such a man existed in the world, was a far greater sermon than any ever preached to them from the lips of an orator."[9] An article published in the *Boston Herald* not long after Very's death claimed he had "failed in the ministry" because "he had no voice, no manner, no presence, to give distinct and forcible utterance to his thoughts. His voice was low, and, at times, indistinct, and his presence clearly indicated that he was not a man for the rough and tumble of this world."[10] Not one to let a slight, imagined or otherwise, pass by, Lydia L. A. responded to this article with a letter that disputed a number of the writer's characterizations. "As to his failing in the ministry," she clarified, "it was not so; as to his having no voice, it was a mistake. He had a loud, clear voice when he chose to exert it, but he preferred the calm, unimpassioned tone and conversational manner of daily intercourse. Then, there was no show-off about him, no self-consciousness, no theatrical elocution and pose to draw attention to himself."[11] Given the mid-nineteenth century's decided taste for histrionic oratory, Very's characteristic inner quiet likely made him seem unusual, if not simply dull, to those less attuned to what one admirer described as his childlike, "transparent" artlessness: "He was," according to William P. Andrews, "the extremest possible distance from pomposity or pretension."[12]

To judge from the style of the sermons themselves, the delivery, if not loud, must have been earnest and charged at the very least with a quiet intensity. Never familiar or colloquial, these manuscripts offer no anecdotes or crowd-pleasing humor; they more or less follow the basic form of the Protestant sermon (text, explication, application) with little real variation other than in the extent of their illustrations. Sober, serious, even at times literary (Very seems to have quoted from poets more often than was typical), the large sample of sermons that have survived remains devoted to his fundamental conception of the immediacy and present-ness of spiritual life.[13] As Andrews put it in his early account of Very's life, "He retained to the last, though he ceased to go about promulgating it, his great idea: that every man who made the complete sacrifice of self necessary to the identification with, the hiding in Christ, would become the voice of the Holy Ghost."[14] What might be surprising is not that Very continued to preach the possibility of heaven on earth *in the present* but that this fervent belief led him to engage closely with and frequently comment upon national and sometimes international events. How might the world move closer to the kingdom of heaven on earth, and why has Christianity not as yet come to its fullest fruition? As he preached through the increasingly strident and alarming era leading to and through the Civil War, this concern for how to embody spirit as an individual and a nation, how to achieve, in Channing's phrase, "likeness to God," never wavered.

As might be expected, Very's preaching in the 1840s was more limited than it came to be in the 1850s and 1860s; some of the resistance cited by Lydia L. A. was likely at its strongest early on, when, as she admitted, the "Unitarians as a body were not as liberal as they are now."[15] Memories of

Very's behavior and reputation in 1838 may still have been fresh enough in the following decade to discourage suspicious congregations from listening to him, even temporarily. Nevertheless, he preached what was apparently his first official sermon as a licensed minister in none other than Salem's First Church, then in the hands of Charles Wentworth Upham, one of Very's staunchest opponents during his visionary period.[16] We might take this evidence to suggest that Very had abandoned all trace of his earlier enthusiasm and reassured ministers like Upham that his doctrinal thinking was firmly in line with conventional Unitarian thought of the time. But the sermons often suggest quiet but significant differences from more cautious Unitarian thinking. In one of the earliest surviving texts, delivered on Fast Day morning at Barton Square Church in Salem in April 1843, Very offered an interpretation of the role of John the Baptist not dissimilar to the visionary claims of 1838. Beginning with Matthew 11:13 ("For all the prophets and the law prophesied until John"), he contrasted the "dispensation of Moses" to the "Appearance of John." John was the prophetic herald of the Messiah, "appointed to give the tide of popular opinion its true direction, and guide it to its natural object" (HS 68). He came to announce a "Second Dispensation" that would remedy the "incompleteness" of the Mosaic law, which was merely external and ultimately enslaving. "From [John] they were not kept back by the remoteness of Forms and Customs, and by the fixed Rites of the Temple" (HS 68). John baptized all in a simple and natural way. He was humble, "not led to self-exultation or ambition. . . . Thus he came, saying, 'Repent ye: for the kingdom of heaven is at hand!'" (HS 68). Very's desire to explain and justify himself cannot be discounted here. Echoing his own notorious command to his students to "Flee to the mountains, for the end of all things is at hand!" he seems intent on returning to clarify his vision and reaffirm, for himself and others, the radical humility and self-erasure of his prophetic conception. Far from shying away from material associated with his apparent madness, he seems eager to reengage precisely those moments in the Gospels that compelled his earlier, stranger behavior.

In this way he also established a set of ideas to which his sermons returned time and again: first, that the "new dispensation" of Christ was an internal transformation rather than an external law; second, that this salvation was therefore universal and applicable to all the world rather than national and restricted to the Jewish tradition; and third, that the "kingdom of heaven" would come into existence not in some future state or afterlife but in the present, now, in the minds and souls of those able to become "sons" of God. In one of his best sermons, an undated explication of Luke 17:21 ("Neither shall they say, Lo here! or, lo there! for, behold, the kingdom of God is within you"), Very makes clear from the first sentence that "Heaven is a state and not a place" (HS 45). It is internal, immediate: "Christ was in heaven while on the earth. . . . It was already *in himself*" (HS 45; original emphasis). Yet again, the convergence of romantic poetics (the Milton-Wordsworth tradition of the internal, Christian epic) with New Light mysticism saturates Very's reading of Christian history. The movement toward spirit and away from forms, the essentially Protestant (and effectively sectarian) conception of the inner drama of salvation, is balanced against the fervent desire for the establishment of a single and united "Kingdom of Christ" in "this world" (HS 45).[17] Though this spiritual rule has yet to occur, "we should strive to realize the kingdom here & now and not live in a vain expectation of its coming in some remote period of earth's history" (HS 45). If "Christ [can] reign in every heart, . . . then heaven will be on earth" (HS 45).

These predominant themes suggest that Very was intent on bringing his own interpretation of Christian history, formulated most radically in 1838, into a language more acceptable and less alarming to his sermon audiences. In this sense, what was remarkable or outrageous about his earlier claims to be "the second coming" quietly adjusted to the more conventional language of spiritual transformation or conversion. At the same time, however, Very became—or revealed himself to be—more conservative in his approach to fundamental theological questions than he may have seemed at the height of his ecstatic experience. For instance, even now his specific reaction to Emerson's critique of miracles remains somewhat unclear. Though we can reasonably posit that Very was roused by the speech, particularly its call for "a newborn bard of the Holy Ghost," he never directly addressed the miracles controversy itself in plain or direct language. In the "Epistles to the Unborn" he does speak somewhat cryptically of miracles and implies that the return of Christ within the individual will allow for the perception of the miraculous, but overall he seems more concerned with refuting John Brazer's demand that he himself produce a miracle to prove his "revelation." The sermons, however, fall back to the conventional Unitarian line—the essential validity of the miracles in the New Testament prove Christ's divinity and purpose—but do so for Very's own, idiosyncratic purposes.

In an early sermon first delivered at the Stone Church in Portsmouth, New Hampshire, in April 1844, Very faced the question directly via a reading of the exorcism in chapter 9 of the Gospel of Mark. The disciples, unable to cast out a "dumb spirit" from a child, watch as Jesus "rebuke[s] the foul" demon and drives him from the boy. Very equates his own audience with those who witnessed the miracle: "When we read the Evangelist's account of the miracles, we are affected in a similar manner. . . . The miracles act upon *our* minds and hearts as they acted upon theirs" (HS 80; original emphasis). The purpose of the miracles is thus to increase our faith, "our faith in Jesus as *the Son of God*; our faith in ourselves as being able to become like Him" (HS 80; original emphasis). We may not believe in the existence of miracles in our time, but reading of these moments in which the laws of nature are transcended raises us "above the impressions of visible things and the regular order of events" (HS 80). We are thus able to approach a "nearer resemblance" to God: "If we have not the power to work the miracles which Jesus worked; yet through faith in them and in his words he has given us a higher and more *glorious Privilege* than that, *of Becoming Sons of God*" (HS 80; original emphasis).

Far from thinking of miracles as a kind of "monster," in Emerson's memorable phrase, Very presents them here as fundamental instances of the elevation of spirit over flesh. In the conventional sense, they aid in faith and are, in a sense, proof of Christ's divinity. But in his unique conception, miracles also provide a modern audience with the inspiring idea that they can rise above the limitations of their own physical existence. They can become, as Very had so starkly claimed to be, "Sons of God," not miracle workers as such but miraculously transformed via the inner presence of Spirit itself. In an undated sermon on John 2:11 ("This beginning of miracles did Jesus in Cana of Galilee, and manifested forth his glory; and his disciples believed on him") Very addressed the modern tendency to see the miracles in the New Testament as "exceptional" or "improbable" (HS 13), arguing instead that nature was created as a moral order and its natural laws could be "suspended or changed" at any time. Nature is subservient "to the moral end of Creation" (HS 13). Almost echoing at times Emersonian idealism ("A fact is the end or last issue of spirit"), Very finds a way to turn secular philosophy into an argument that supports the conventional doctrine of miracles. In Transcendentalist terms, he might be said to be using *Nature* against the Divinity School Address, though ultimately to flesh out his own, unique vision.[18]

This fascinating blend of the new, the old, and the personal is particularly evident in another of the miracle sermons, this one preached in Salem in 1860 and focused on Jesus's healing of the blind man in the ninth chapter of John. It's difficult to read this sermon's opening and not be reminded of Very's experience as a boy watching his brother Franklin:

> Among the wonderful works which our Savior wrought was the restoring of sight to the blind. Many of his countrymen suffered from the loss of sight, and the cure of blindness was one of his most common

> miracles. And on many, says Luke on one occasion, he bestowed the gift of sight. And what a gift was this, second only to the gift of reason itself! How do our hearts rise in gratitude to God, when man through his skill is enabled to [couch?] the curtained eye and to restore the lost sight. . . . But who can describe the wonder & gratitude of the man who had been blind from his birth and sat by the way-side to beg, when such a gift was bestowed upon him by the Savior! With what mingled feelings of anxiety, expectation, and hope must he have groped his way along to the pool of Siloam and descended its rocky steps! (HS 22)

Most of us fail to consider the blessing of sight and take it for granted, he argues. We lose "the freshness of early impression" that once filled and elevated the soul . . . of the boy" (HS 22). We should be like the blind man after his healing, an example and occasion for God's grace: "But he who had been born blind was to manifest the works of God in himself in a far higher than the natural sense, even his works of Grace, Mercy, & Truth which came by Jesus Christ" (HS 22).

"I saw a child, whose eyes had never drunk / The cheerful light of heaven" begins the early poem that seems, despite its moralizing, stunned at the sight of a sibling born to darkness. This image—and its accompanying figures of physical and spiritual light—may in fact return in these sermons that contemplate the possibility of miracles, not merely as physical events but, more significantly, as events of spiritual awakening. Very seems intent not simply on reaffirming the value of miracles as proof of Christ's purpose but on moving the site of the miraculous to the inner plane of existence, just as he had come to see "the second coming" as an internal rather than external event. He never wavered in his conviction that such an indwelling of Spirit came about only after the removal of all trace of personal will or individual attachment. Such a self-scouring would include removing the bruised love and confusion of contemplating a child, his brother, who, though innocent, was in the same state as the man at Siloam. For Franklin, there was no miracle in this material world, but if the true light, the inner sight, were immaterial, if truth itself could be a pure flood of spirit, the "Light of Life" could save us all.

✻ 42 ✻

War, Slavery, and Intemperance

As otherworldly as Very's central message in his sermons typically was, his engagement with the idea of the spiritual life did not avoid or ignore material events or social realities. The surviving manuscripts reveal him to have been intensely interested in national and world affairs, particularly those that reflected upon his central spiritual interests: peace and the development of an immanent Christianity, the coming of the "kingdom of God." As is the case for his later poetry, the sermons offer a moral voice that attempts to maintain an elevated but not abstracted perspective on the turbulent events of the 1850s and 1860s. Keenly convinced that a devotion to earthly desire—perhaps especially the concupiscence of power—lay at the root of the day's evils, he continually pressed the need for an inner renunciation and peace that would translate into a world free of conflict and abuse.

Given the essentially passive, if not quietist, orientation of his religious verse, we should not be surprised that Very's spiritual pacifism became more pronounced as the national debate over slavery heated the passions of reformers and conservatives alike. In April 1849, he, along with several other ministers (including his former student Samuel Johnson), spoke at a meeting of the Friends of the Cause of Peace at Lyceum Hall in Boston. The assembled delegation adopted several resolutions in support of the work of the American Peace Society, including a call for the establishment of a "code of international law, by which . . . disputes may be . . . adjudicated."[1] The participants also "hail[ed] with pleasure" the work of the recent International Peace Congress at Brussels (organized by the "learned blacksmith" from Connecticut, Elihu Burritt) and simultaneously looked forward to the follow-up Peace Conference in Paris in 1849.[2] With the reformist zeal of the times—and following the events of the Mexican War in 1846 and the European revolutions of 1848—the Salem ministers likely wished to counterbalance the increasingly bellicose tone on the national and international scenes. That Very attended along with the seemingly ubiquitous Charles Upham, by this time a state representative, James Flint of East Church, and Alexander Joseph Sessions of Crombie Street Church, suggests a group effort to represent the town in the movement.

Very's extemporaneous speech on this occasion was not recorded, but a few years later he did preach a sermon in Salem, repeated throughout the region six times (with revisions) between 1851 and 1854, that gives us a clearer sense of his pacifist principles. Working from Luke 22:35–38 ("And they said, Lord, behold, here are two swords. And he said unto them, It is enough"), Very addressed the misunderstanding of the disciples as they prepared for Jesus's arrest just after the Lord's Supper. Recognizing that the true difficulty of preaching the "suffering Christ" would come after his death and resurrection, Jesus hoped to prepare his disciples for this "war" by figuratively ordering them to arm themselves. They replied by producing two real swords, revealing their failure to understand the essential nature of Christ's passion: "They knew not that the sword had no place in his kingdom. So little of the spirit of the Prince of Peace, had they received, and so little were they prepared to extend his dominion" (HS 19). Jesus's command to prepare via spiritual armament was also addressed to us, Very continued. We must build strength against the probable difficulties of maintaining the "Christian course" (HS 19). To apply Christianity in a practical sense "to the workings of Society & Government" all must struggle against the "evils" of "War, Slavery, the love of gain, the love of false distinction, intemperance & licentiousness" (HS 19). However, "open violence" should almost never be considered; it is "but one, and that the weakest, most foolish & sinful of all other means of change" (HS 19).

For Very, most of us fail to "elevate & perfect human society" because we lack faith (HS 19). The revolution of the inner individual must precede change in the world: "The New Creation of Righteousness, Peace & Joy within us, must manifest itself, changing & restoring the outward world as it has already done the inward" (HS 19). Christianity may be more powerful in a political sense than ever before, but it cannot rely on immoral methods: "We need more faith in moral means & efforts for overcoming the cruelty & injustice of men, and of human governments" (HS 19). As examples he cites recent efforts to negotiate a peace agreement in the First Schleswig War as well as Millard Fillmore's 1852 State of the Union speech that reaffirmed the American policy of nonintervention in the internal affairs of other countries. In the wake of 1848, many in the US were calling for military assistance to support fledgling revolutions; the 1851 visit by Lajos Kossuth, the former revolutionary leader of Hungary, roused the country into an emotional wave of support (and mania for all things Hungarian) that Fillmore, who had hosted Kossuth at the White House, felt compelled to address. Very, arguing from a more openly pacifist position, agreed with the president that the American tradition had always been noninterventionist. This was the root of American prosperity; its foundation, built on self-government, made it essentially devoted to individual, and thus spiritual, purpose: "Our government is peaceful in its character and ends," Very argued, "and cannot, except in direct opposition to its principles, engage in war" (HS 19). It should instead be "armed" with Christian principles, moving to make peace rather than adding to existing conflicts. To pacify via violence was to make the same mistake as the disciples. Christ's kingdom, we must always remember, is not of this world.[3]

A similar blend of caution, conservatism, and pacifism characterizes Very's approach to the increasing tension in the country in the mid-1850s. Though he would later concede the virtual necessity of the Civil War and its value as the means for ending slavery, his peace principles worked against the increasingly pervasive sense that violence would be required to change the country. In August of 1856, he preached at First Church in Salem on Matthew 5:43 ("Ye have heard that it hath been said, Thou shalt love thy neighbor, and hate thine enemy") and emphasized the lesson of nature: that the rain, like God's mercy, falls on the good and bad alike. It thus commands forgiveness, even though we are still drawn to war: "And alas! an infinitely higher and more affecting witness, the example of the Savior, has not yet prevailed to recall the nations from their dark wanderings and guilty strife to peace and brotherhood and love. . . . Nay, even brethren of the same nation [plan?] with enmity in their hearts against one another. In the present crisis many are tempted to use *violence*, as if violence could ever overthrow the kingdom of Error, and Wickedness; or establish that of Truth, and Righteousness on the earth!" (HS 100; original emphasis). Again, Very argued that the United States was formed in principle as a peaceful nation and claimed that war is "as much, if not more, opposed than Slavery itself" to the guiding ideas that "gave birth to this Republic" (HS 100).

As might be expected, this commitment to peace principles would be tested most strenuously during the war itself. Very's opposition to slavery had been clear at least since 1833, and biographers have reasonably assumed that he witnessed slavery firsthand—and came to oppose it—during his stay in New Orleans in 1824. His near "nonresistance" position on spiritual action implied a familiarity with Garrisonian abolitionism from the late 1830s on, but in his sermons he tends more often than not to gather his critique of slaveholding together with another major cause of the period, intemperance, both terms placed under the general banner of a failed devotion to spirit.[4] If violence, even in a noble cause, was considered an instance of insufficient faith, then war could not necessarily be redeemed by a favorable outcome or other sign of progress. It too was a type of intemperance, its sources mingled with the general cause of other evils, including slavery. In a sermon preached at least seven times from June 1857 to February 1860, Very attributed all "unhappiness, and misery, and sin" to "ignorance of God as a Father"; "this is the root from which enmities, want, war, slavery, and every evil work has sprung" (HS 3). Eager to praise advances such as the movement to emancipate the serfs in Russia and the abolition of slavery in the US, he exhorted his audience to a full embrace of efforts to educate and assimilate this newly liberated population: "Let us hope that the physical bonds of the slaves being broken they will not be still kept in mental & spiritual bondage; but that they will become possessed of all their civil rights and be enabled to read for themselves the Bible and thus be taught the true will & worship of God" (HS 3). The "vast energies & resources of war," he argued, should be redirected to the education of the entire nation to enable it to progress toward a fuller embodiment of the "Righteousness" of God (HS 3).[5]

In other words, even if the changes wrought by the Civil War were positive, war was never to be praised for its own sake or for its potential to generate progress on a particular issue: its spirit should be terminated as quickly as possible and rechanneled into a less compromised good. In a sermon from 1860–61, Very gave his clearest account of what he considered the proper attitude toward the feverish early moments of the Civil War. Working from Matthew 13:27 ("So the servants of the householder came and said unto him, Sir, didst not thou sow good seed in thy field? from whence then hath it tares?"), he explained the parable of the tares in terms of the unfaithfulness of early Christians. Those who continued to believe in elements of polytheism, which generated idolatry, were responsible for the continued existence of worldly attachments. "Slavery, war, intemperance, & licentiousness, tares which have overrun so large a portion of the earth, had their origin in the enmities & luxuries of the ancient Polytheistic nations," he argued (HS 60). In the present, slavery has generated war, one sin compounding itself by another: "Slavery has again involved our government in War. War is never I believe *absolutely* necessary. It is from the neglect and want of faith that it may be said, in any sense, to be necessary" (HS 60; original emphasis). The only "reason which any nation can ever have for engaging in war" is to "put down Rebellion, Violence, & Wrong; and to bring men back to the use of Reason and Judgment" (HS 60). Strength and courage alone cannot "prevail," only "the intellectual and moral powers animating & directing them" (HS 60).

And these could always have been put to greater use to prevent conflict in the first place.

Whatever grudging acceptance Very gave to the need to quell rebellion, his concept of progress remained fundamentally spiritual rather than material. Only by keeping an eye on the concerns of our souls, he exhorted, can we avoid bringing Christian doctrine down to worldly concerns. In a sermon from 1862 on Revelations 4:1, he took the "slave states" to task for using the Bible to support slavery, but was similarly concerned that the Northern war spirit would misuse and diminish the scriptures: "The Bible may be quoted to uphold War as well as Slavery until we have degraded it to our own level" (HS 67). He acknowledged the difficulty of living as a Christian but rejected the notion that the only possible realization of the kingdom of heaven would come after death or in some distant future age: "This is a great, a *factual* error. It must be begun *now*, here in the midst of so many things which oppose & kill it" (HS 67; original emphasis). This duty applies both to the individuals and to states. We must rise to the "duties toward those of our countrymen who have now been declared free forever" (HS 67). And we must simultaneously hear, "in the midst of the tumults of war," the "voice of Ch[ristianity] speaking to us of Peace & Love" (HS 67).

✷ 43 ✷

"I war not, nor wrestle with the earthly man"

Very continued to preach until at least 1873, seven years before his death, though if the existing manuscript record is any indication, requests for his services decreased significantly during the final decade of his life.[1] The sermons collected from roughly thirty years of serving as a supply minister give us some sense of the movement of his interests and the range of his commitments, particularly as they relate to the central issues of his religious thinking. But their scope is necessarily more limited than the hundreds of poems written between 1841 and his death in 1880. Very is rightly known for the ecstatic sonnets that poured forth between September of 1838 and early 1840, and we would hardly consider his poetry remarkable without their peculiar history, association with Transcendentalism, and flirtation with religious "madness." Nevertheless, the poetry of his middle and later life, uneven and perfunctory as it often is, cannot be excluded from a portrait of the man fully drawn. Lives can be read both forward and backward, and the man of fifty, no matter how ordinary, may still have something to say that deepens our understanding of the ecstatic youth of twenty-five.

A full canvas of the hundreds of poems written in the last forty years of Very's life reaffirms his fundamental conception of his poetry as public. Of course, any published poetry becomes, in essence, a public utterance, but Very's work tended from the beginning to take part in a tradition of persuasive statement in which the poet as moral arbiter comments upon a range of current political and cultural topics.[2] As much as we associate his best-known poems with romantic and religious traditions of inwardness, we should remember that even the spiritual sonnets were meant as proselytical or testimonial occasions, the poetic equivalent of those dramatic encounters in the parlors of Salem. Like his sermons, Very's later poems take seriously the idea of the speaker as a "ministerial" or otherwise responsible translator of divine values. Just as he was called upon to preach a sermon for an absent minister or a communal event, he could be—and often was—asked for a hymn or dedicatory verse for a specific occasion. The collected poems register numerous events where Very's poetry was featured, including family gatherings, building dedications, educational conventions, the National Fast Day following the Civil War, the Fourth of July, as well as museum and school openings. At the same time he regularly published verse on specific historical and political events almost as they happened, and generated comment on mundane or, in the truest sense, prosaic topics from the national and local news. Everything from a brawl in Congress to the Quaker peace mission in Russia, the passing of the Kansas-Nebraska Act to mob violence during the strikes of 1877 could be celebrated, criticized, or otherwise pronounced upon. And such lesser but obviously quotidian subjects as the new Salem aqueduct, the Irish potato blight, the telegraph, the telephone, various local weather events, and the camphene lamp (an 1850s fire hazard) were versified with the same direct earnestness as poems on more transcendent subjects. Altogether this mélange of social, cultural, and political commentary combined with what we might now call versified editorials suggests that Very's full body of work is less aptly connected to the tradition of the religious lyric than to the demotic spirituality and theatrical messianism of a poet like Whitman. That a writer who once claimed the direct ventriloquism of the Holy Spirit could also publish verses to warn of a faulty appliance implies something more modern—and more journalistic—than the poetry of, for example, George Herbert. We might be reminded of the Whitman of "A Song for Occupations," a prophetic spiritualist who wrote men's health columns in *The Atlas*, a very American cross-pollination of John the Baptist and John O'Sullivan.

Moving through the forty-year period following Very's visionary season, we can see that his more pragmatic, ministerial voice emerged as the turmoil of the late 1830s slowly settled into a surer set of convictions. In the poems immediately following his surrender of the sonnet as a primary form, a kind of unnamed turbulence remains beneath the surface, the sort of intense emotion often curled inside many of his "will-less" statements. Still reliant, more often than not, on spiritual allegory, Very nevertheless seems most interested at this point in the mysterious actions of time and the need for renunciation when faced with its grip on human life. "The Bunch of Flowers," for instance, presents a straightforward allegory of Time "with withered hand plucking" flowers as "gifts" for those who pass by (*CP* 198). Child, youth, "Man," and "One aged" each receive a flower, each in turn soon losing or discarding "Time's gift" (*CP* 198–99). After observing this instructive parade, the speaker takes his lesson:

Then knew I none could bear away the flower,
That Time on each and all bestows;
Nor would I take this gift when he,
To me in turn held out the rose. (*CP* 199)

The understanding that time slips away, that it cannot be held, is conventional enough, but the speaker's intention to refuse time, in effect to opt out of the emotional framework of temporality suggests something similar to Very's resistance to consciousness in the ecstatic sonnet "The New Birth." There, at the height of his mystical experience in September of 1838, he had claimed a liberation from subjectivity itself; here, the refusal suggests less a divine transformation than a suspicious rejection of the source of pain or loss. Only a firm resistance to the deceptive gift of time can free us from the suffering embodied by the transient beauty of the rose.

Absent at times the moralizing that often rescues Very's spiritual fables from despair, several of these early, postecstatic poems take on the slightly more shadowy film of gothicism. This stylistic flirtation seems limited to late 1839 and the early 1840s, but it suggests a searching out of alternate ways of describing his readjustment to a less exalted state of faith. "The Ghost," for instance, presents a tidy narrative that hovers somewhere between scary story and Christian reassurance. The figure who "passes by at dead of night" is never fully identified and initially seems invasive and threatening, his "hand unheard" trying "every door" for entrance (*CP* 200). But by the third stanza it becomes clear that this "ghost" is a type of divine visitor, seeking out only those who are awake, "watching still," whose houses he will fill "with untold wealth, . . . / For he o'er riches holds the power" (*CP* 200). The gothic figure becomes the "stranger guest," the Holy Spirit reimagined as mysterious visitant, part god in disguise, part Dickensian novelistic convention, bringing spiritual prosperity to the deserving few.

A similar skein of gloom is cast over an otherwise redemptive narrative in "The Watcher," where the nighttime visitor wakes the sleeper and joins him in a perpetual vigil, and "The Silent," whose registration of God's "unheard" and "Silent Voice" suggests a slightly less buoyant form of faith:

And in the speechless human heart
It speaks, where'er man's feet have trod;
Beyond the lip's deceitful art,
To tell of Him, the Unseen God. (*CP* 202)

The paradox of silent speech or unseen presence is common in religious language, and yet these few poems imply a kind of spiritual experience more situated in doubt than is typical of Very's verse overall. We have only to remember that not many months before he had represented God's presence as something more tangible than this "Unseen" figure—and God's voice as anything but "silent."

Perhaps the most suggestive of unease in these early, postecstatic poems is "The Absent," an oblique and difficult sonnet that may reflect something of Very's isolation during the summer of 1839. Similarly tinted with gothic atmosphere, this poem is unusual and suggestive enough to be quoted in full:

> Thou art not yet at home in thine own house,
> But to one room I see thee now confined;
> Having one hole like rat or skulking mouse,
> And as a mole to all the others blind;
> Does the great Day find preference when he shines
> In at each window lighting every room?
> No selfish wish the moon's bright glance confines,
> And each in turn the stars' faint rays illume;
> Within thy sleeping room thou dost abide,
> And thou does the social parlor prefer;
> Another thou wilt in the cupboard hide,
> And this or that's the room for him or her;
> But the same sun, and moon with silver face
> Look in one all, and lighten every place. (*CP* 218)

The opening suggests a return after an absence and a sense of alienation within a family space. The address seems equally applicable to someone other than the speaker—perhaps a sibling—or to the speaker himself, as an act of corrective self-consciousness. The criticism is directed at the figure's isolation, as though the confinement described were self-imposed, a chosen isolation compared bitingly to the act of a "skulking" animal and considered unhealthy and unnatural; the "great Day" and the moon are not so "selfish." There is even the implication that this self-imposed hermeticism contravenes the shut-away's own typical preference: he usually enjoys "the social parlor" but now insists that each member of household remain in separate rooms. The overall thrust of the poem affirms the ideal of a natural communion in the unrestricted, equally distributed light of sun and moon. (There is even a hint of social critique, as though the target could include class snobbery and exclusion.) But its description of a failed or disrupted household suggests other, unspecified dissonances rarely permitted in Very's verse without some attempt at spiritual resolution.

Very wrote and published poems steadily, if not prolifically, during the 1840s. In her edition of the poems, Deese attributes well over fifty verses to the period 1840–49, though many of the dates are conjectural. Spiritual subjects remained common for Very throughout the decade, but his attention also widened, turning outward as his relationship to the everyday world regularized. He took up more common lyric subjects, including landscapes ("The Baker's Island Lights"), light satire ("The Sepulchre of the Books"), elegy ("Jonathan Huntington Bright"), and the romantic lyric of experience ("The Wounded Pigeon"). Likewise, subjects of cultural or political weight began to catch his attention. "The Indian's Retort" and "The Indian's Petition" express typical midcentury critiques of expansionism at the expense of displaced tribes, though couched, as would be expected, in the language of Christian colonialism. "The Man of Science" gives us one of the earliest instances of Very's attempts, increasingly common over the next twenty years, to come to terms with scientific advances; by no means anti-science or suspicious of technology, he worked to reconcile his excitement at the progress of knowledge with the antispiritual encroachments of materialism. And "The Congress of Peace at Brussels" reaffirms his pacifist credentials and willingness to promote social causes via local publication.

Perhaps the most substantial and successful of these more worldly lyrics is "The Evening Choir," published in *The Dial* in 1842.[3] Set in a contemplative blank verse reminiscent of Wordsworth or the Coleridge of the conversation poems, it describes a moment of stilled reflection as the speaker waits on the porch of a local church while a choir sings within. The shadowy, moonlit evening is measured and deepened by "the holy song," a spiritual music analogous to the "Soft soul-like airs" that will come to us "when the hand is mouldered / Of him who sweeps" the organ's keys (*CP* 230). The "restless" crowd "paces" below but fails to perceive this moment of spirit, "when from on high the angels / Listen well pleased, and nearer draw to the earth" (*CP* 230). A blind man seems the "only constant / Listener. . . . with face / Upturned as if he saw, as well as heard, / And music was to him another sense" (*CP* 230). The speaker looks forward to the next day's Sabbath, when the bustling populace will set aside its "thoughts of gain" and "quit their accustomed streets, / And to the temples turn with sober pace" (*CP* 230).

Having acknowledged the value of the spiritual relief provided by the church, the speaker then changes registers; a higher, more critical vision overtakes his contemplative mood, and his language reflects a Miltonic struggle:

> I would not, when my heart is bitter grown,
> And my thoughts turned against the multitude,
> War with their earthly temple; mar its stones;
> Or, with both pillars in my grasp, shake down
> The mighty ruin on their heads. With this
> I war not, nor wrestle with the earthly man.
> I war with the spiritual temple raised
> By pride, whose top is in the heavens, though built
> On the earth; whose site and hydra-headed power
> Is everywhere;—with Principalities,
> And them who rule the darkness of this world,
> The Spirits of wickedness that highest stand. (*CP* 231)

As though defining a position within and yet outside organized religion, the speaker stakes out a realm of more exalted conflict. Pride, the root of all transgression that violates the will of God, is his true opponent, and nature itself, "those bright stars I see that gather round / Nightly this sacred spot," aids him in his fight: "Nor will they lay / Their glittering armor by, till from heaven's height / Is cast Satan with all his host headlong!" (*CP* 231).

The shift of mood in "The Evening Choir" suggests that Very's relationship to the institution of the church remained unsettled, and the poem may have been a way to work out how he would move forward once his prophetic moment had passed. Published the year before he applied for licensure as a minister, it offers a potential explanation of purpose, a way to indicate to those who knew of his recent behavior that he was both committed to the ordinary function of worship and yet still devoted to the higher calling he imagined for himself a few years before. (It's notable that someone thought "vain" or proud by many would dedicate himself to combating the kind of angelic pride associated with divine rebellion.) The poem indirectly invokes his student lecture "Individuality," delivered as part of the commencement exercises in 1836, where he spoke of Milton's Satan as the product of the poet's "breast of flame" and "intensest rage."[4] Here the speaker's "bitter grown" heart carries much the same burden, fantasizing about a Christ-like cleansing of the temple while simultaneously turning back to a spiritualized mission of equally high purpose. It suggests an attempt at the least to resolve a conflict in Very's own mind between the idea of himself as chosen for a specific task and the recognition that the church itself would now be the site of that labor.

✷ 44 ✷

"But still the poet midst the tumult sings"

If a tension did exist between Very's messianic pretensions and his relationship to the official church, it seems to have resolved itself by the later 1840s. After he began preaching regularly following his licensure in 1843, the subject matter of his poetry and the position from which he surveyed personal and public events became more stable, allowing him a steadier eye on external realities. At the same time, national politics—particularly the moral questions of the slavery debate—began to press more acutely on the religious and regional sensibilities of New England. Though no direct comment on the Mexican War (1846–48) survives in his archive, Very's direct engagement with peace activities did increase just after its conclusion. At about the same time, he began to comment directly on national events associated with the debates surrounding the Compromise of 1850. The heated atmosphere in the United States Senate drew his first rebuke. "On the Late Disgraceful Scene in Congress," published in the *Christian Register* on April 27, 1850, excoriates the behavior of Thomas Hart Benton and Henry Foote, who had come near to violence while debating Vice President Millard Fillmore's ruling that Benton had been out of order on the Senate floor. When Benton approached the much smaller Foote in what appeared to be a menacing way, Foote drew a pistol, to which Benton loudly responded, "I have no pistols! Let him fire! Stand out of the way and let the assassin fire!"[1] Horrified at this failure of decorum, Very scolded the "Fools!" who would "waste the hour with highest duties rife" with "folly" and "madness" (*CP* 258). "When millions stand expectant to be free," he scolded, "Is it the time for brawling and for strife[?]" (*CP* 258).

Though focused in this poem more on the senators' outrageous behavior than the underlying sectional issues, Very was obviously animated by his opposition to slavery, now more acutely charged by national politics. The following year he published "Slavery" and "The Fugitive Slaves," followed by a tribute to the eighteenth-century Quaker John Woolman,

"Friend of the slave, and friend of all mankind," the year after (*CP* 274). As he did in the sermons of this period, Very advocated an essentially pacifist, Christian perfectionist approach to slavery, similar to, if not as radical as, the Garrisonians. In "Slavery," he cast "the mighty wrong" as a national sin, arguing that no amount of strife or "blood" could wash away "our Country's guilt" (*CP* 265):

> Not by such means; but by the power of prayer;
> Of faith in God, joined with a sense of sin;
> These, these alone can save us from despair,
> And o'er the mighty wrong a victory win; (*CP* 265)

Committed as he was to the idea of a millennialist spiritual awakening ("Heaven is a state and not a place"), there could be no political change that was not indexed to the state of the national soul. It was a position he would never essentially change, even in the midst of the war, whose necessity he could never completely endorse. Whatever the limitations of this spiritualism for effecting material progress, it had the virtue of an unshakable clarity and consistency, and in its own, more conventional way it replicated Very's insistence that the true path to salvation, whether individual or collective, was through renunciation of the will.

Despite these sentiments, it would be a mistake to argue that Very was a vehement, energetic activist in the cause of antislavery during the 1850s. He remained, first and foremost, a minister and poet whose primary activity was the pursuit of a daily life of reflection and spiritual labor. Aside from religious meetings and some organizational work in the peace movement, he was not prominently involved in political activism beyond statements delivered in his poems and sermons. Nevertheless, his attention was anything but withdrawn from the national scene or from the issues that dominated the news. He maintained a strong civic sense and a ready curiosity that took him often to the Essex Institute or the local news offices, where friendly editors let him read through the out-of-town papers. This habit fed directly into his poetry, where we can find an array of politically engaged topics, as well as thoughtful reflections on civic events. "Voting in the Old North Church," from 1852, suggests something of the seriousness with which Very considered the relationship between country and heavenly kingdom. To vote in a place that was "once a Temple to the Most High" he considered "a sign" of the "freeman's holy trust" in democratic purpose (*CP* 276). Those who would "profane" this place "with passions fierce" or with ignorance fail to recognize "The ends of Government, its righteous ends, / Peace, Order, Industry, and steady growth / In Knowledge, and in Virtue" (*CP* 276). The poem finds significance in the custom of using the Communion table as the site for the ballot box so that those who would approach this sacred duty with anything less than a virtuous heart threaten to corrupt both country and church: "Ye who would serve your Country, serve your God. . . . Do justice, and love mercy. Let not pride / Of country blind you to your country's sins" (*CP* 277).

As much as Very could and did fulfill the role of moral accountant, however, he also understood the limited and lonely role of the poet in a country of increasingly strident political tensions. As the 1850s approached their end and it became more and more clear that the conflict over slavery would require something other than a peaceful resolution, he reflected on the poet's place amid a storm of rising violence. In December of 1859, the same month as John Brown's execution, he published "The Poet" in the *Monthly Religious Magazine* and subsequently in the *Salem Gazette*. Though the sonnet makes no reference to the events in Virginia, its resigned and saddened tone suggests a firm but almost weary response by the spiritualist to what was then a bellicose moment:

> As one who 'midst a choir alone doth sing,
> When voices harsh fill all his soul with pain,
> So that from even a note he would refrain,
> And flee away as with a dove's swift wing,
> Yet for Religion's sake you see him stay,
> And try to raise her service what he may;—
> So doth the Poet live amidst his age!
> Though at the first his lyre he scarce can hear,
> He does not drown its discords in his rage,
> Nor fly where they will not offend his ear;
> But for their very sakes who spoil his song,
> His heaven-taught strain he more and more prolongs;
> Till one by one they with his paean blend,
> And all in one harmonious concert end. (*CP* 319–20)

Hopeful ending notwithstanding, the isolation of the poet whose word is "Religion" and whose "strain" is "heaven-taught" speaks for itself. In a quiet echo of Milton's "When I Consider How My Light Is Spent," Very establishes the poet as the unmoving center of a moral vision, holding fast to eternal truths and waiting for God's time and purpose to be fulfilled.

As the Civil War began, this slight tension between the role of moral commentator and spiritually distanced poet necessarily became more acute. Very published roughly fifteen poems during the war years that commented directly on political issues associated with the conflict: abstract verses such as "Freedom and Union" and "State Rights"; poems related to slavery like "The Abolition of Serfdom in Russia" and "The Freedmen of the Mississippi Valley"; and personal accounts of the emotional toll of war and its threat to belief. "Faith in a Time of War," for instance, gives us a speaker whose "faith grows weak" when he reads about the battles taking place and wonders whether "God look[s] down on us with pitying eyes" (*CP* 357): "I ask, but hear no voice to mine reply! / When tens and hundreds dying strew the plain" (*CP* 357). Predictably, the second half of the poem responds to these worries with chiding reassurance, but the registration of doubt implies, at the minimum, that Very was attuned to the emotionally destabilizing effects of the reported fighting. This shoring up of confidence occupied much of his poetic and ministerial work during this period, but concern over the purpose of such writing never quite fades. "The Poet's Plea"—an elaboration of the worry in "The Poet" over the effectiveness of the lone, irenic voice—once again asks: "Why sing, amidst the strife which reigns around?" (*CP* 343). Will the "poet's heart-felt music" be heard? (*CP* 343):

> Ah no, yet unsubdued men's passions rage!
> The never-ceasing conflict born within,
> Or outward foes, their energies engage,
> O'er which they strive the victory to win.
> But still the poet midst the tumult sings,
> Hoping from war and strife men's thought to gain; (*CP* 343)

That Very would return to this question, continuing to insist on the value of the spiritual refrain, of peace and the stilling of "passions," is neither naïve nor oblivious to what was happening in the country. Though the image drawn is one of isolated idealism in worldly affairs, it remains consistent with his personal and spiritual conviction that willfulness "unsubdued" is what leads both individuals and societies toward destruction.

In other words, the war forced no substantive change in Very's ideas. He accepted that the struggle, no matter how fundamentally objectionable, had brought about the desired end of slavery, and he continued to exhort his audiences to recognize and support the new civil rights of the formerly enslaved. But he remained a pacifist in principle, though now more deeply aware of the gulf between the human instinct for violence and Christianity's promise of a transcendent salvation. In "Man's Heart Prophesieth of Peace," he both faced the inevitable reality of war ("War, dark hateful War, must be") and yet argued that the deeper nature of all, the "mightier need," was to discover "what thou shalt be!" in the spiritual kingdom to come (*CP* 359). And in a poem written a few months after the war's end, he puzzled over the mystery that this same human heart seemed shrouded by worldly desires: "Why cannot I make plain, to sinful men, / The heavenly kingdom that within me lies?" he asked. A veil is on the human heart, "unfelt, unseen / By worldly men, who will not truth receive" (*CP* 393–94). The frustration recorded during his mystic phase (the attitude of the "day of hate") echoes here but blended with a firmer understanding or acceptance of a specific fact of human nature. It's as though the war had made clear to him that even the operation of the spirit cannot save some obdurate souls: "In vain heaven's light would penetrate the screen, / That they might on the truth of God believe; / His glorious kingdom to their souls is near, / They see it not! nor can its welcome hear!" (*CP* 394).

✷ 45 ✷
Knowledge and Truth

Those who spoke of Very during the later years of his life often evoked the image of the solitary man in the fields. Most afternoons in the grassy clearings and woods around Salem, particularly the area known as the Great Pastures, a figure might appear on the horizon of a hill or in the deep of a flowered meadow: thin, dressed invariably in a dark suit, hat pulled low to shade the eyes, his long, deliberate strides halting near a spray of flowers or a bank of ripening vines (fig. 10). (One friend was recorded as joking that "Mr. Very's townsmen had seen him so often they had become perfectly familiar with the *stalk*, but extremely few knew the beauty of the flower.")[1] Those who saw him usually left him to his thoughts, not that he was unfriendly or unwelcoming, but a quiet spell of isolation, from an almost otherworldly devotion to nature, enveloped him. A life-long acquaintance, Charles T. Brooks, sometimes accompanied Very, and he later remembered that his thoughtful companion invariably preferred to head out for the "pastures. Of his conversation at such times, what I remember the most prominently," Brooks later wrote, "is the way in which he would stop, after expressing some thought about nature, man or God, that he seemed to fear might appear commonplace from its simplicity, and then turning round and fixing upon you an earnest look, as if he would show by his piercing glance that there was a depth in his thought concealed from superficial minds by its very transparency. There was something in his manner at such times that I find quite indescribable, but it was very impressive."[2]

There are enough such testimonials to suggest that this kind of exchange—and Very's unusual but admired manner—stuck with most who met him and gave rise to the popular conception of the "brave saint" as an isolated ascetic. But while, as his friend E. A. Silsbee put it, "he [was] as near to God as anybody ever was," Very did not confine his later interests to purely spiritual questions.[3] The later poetry does continue to explore his typical topics, some of which retain traces of Transcendentalist attitudes. A poem like "The Intuitions of the Soul" from 1863, for instance, reaffirms the entanglement of Emersonian ideas and conventional Christian language, while "Inward Direction," published a few years later, criticizes the "outward impulse" that drives "many men with restless minds" (*CP* 380). Obsessed with busyness and bustle, "They hear no other voice within their souls," nor are they aware of "life's highest, holiest end," the registration of God's "Presence" (*CP* 380). But there are also a surprising number of poems from these years devoted to scientific and historical subjects, enough to suggest more than a passing interest in the material, factual world. Often reacting to the midcentury's considerable advances in technology and new knowledge, Very seems drawn both forward and back, attracted to discovery and yet wary of its threat to belief. An interest in history, as it often does for those in middle age, provided a stabilizing force, a way to measure the continuance of eternal truths against the dizzying accomplishments of Victorian progress.

In her correction of the *Boston Herald* article devoted to her brother's life, Lydia L. A. not only denied the writer's characterization of Jones as a recluse, detached from world events, but insisted that he was "intensely interested in all scientific researches, and nothing new escaped his investigation."[4] Neither an uncritical booster of all such achievements nor a scowling critic of newfangledness, Very was both excited by technological improvements and thoughtful about the relationship between material and spiritual "progress." His essentially millenarian mindset and hunger for immediate spiritual advent may well have led him to see the apparently miraculous gains in physical command of the world as a tantalizing symbol of the possibility of divine immanence. (Recall his response to his first train ride in 1837.) "The Triumphs of Science, And of Faith," a sonnet from 1866, hails the laying of the transatlantic telegraph cable and its victory "over space and time" and asks when "Faith, with triumphs as sublime" will "Bind realm to realm and kindred heart to heart" (*CP* 400). Similarly, "The Meteorologists" acknowledges the value of studying "Nature's laws" and revealing "all her hidden mysteries," but makes a distinction between material knowledge of "phaenomena [*sic*] alone" and "higher truth" (*CP* 478). "What profits" this superficial understanding without "wonder, faith," and a "grateful heart"? (*CP* 478). (There is even a moment of science fiction in one of Very's meditations on faith and spirit: "Perhaps in yon fair planet-world there dwells, / A happier race, though mortal, than on earth; / Where death is but a change to higher life, / Without its sufferings and without its fears" [*CP* 339].)

Such enthusiasm only went so far, of course, and Very maintained an important division between ultimate (spiritual) and transitory (material) understanding. The late sonnet "Knowledge and Truth" (1875), for instance, calls knowledge "Too often proud, and selfish, born of earth," while "heavenly" born truth is a "gift . . . , ever young," that fills the "human soul" (*CP* 484). "Increase of knowledge oft doth sorrow bring" to the "restless mind," while the reception of the truth leads to "man's rest" (*CP* 484). No surprise then that he looked on Darwinist ideas with suspicion. In 1875 he produced a pair of sonnets under the title "Evolution" that offers a typical critique of what he considered the humanistic limitations of the theory. Tracing the "gradual growth" of organisms in nature, we "think the origin of things we know," as though "man's narrow thought had Nature planned" (*CP* 493). Only "faith sublime" can lift us above "the encircling bounds of space and time" (*CP* 493). But can we explain our material creation at all? "In vain do we interrogate the past; . . . And who, by natural descent, can know / His origin, or era date in time?" (*CP* 493). But because all are made in God's image, they are "one" and "destined too, as we, / To show the ages of eternity" (*CP* 493–94).

Such a rejection of biological determinism had little effect on Very's interest in his own origins and the background of his family. In fact, it may be that the pressures of forward-looking science and the pace of technological change during his middle life pushed him toward the emotional stability of family and communal history. In 1859 he produced a thorough and densely detailed genealogy of the Very family that was published by the Essex Institute. As part of his research, he once again climbed to the top of Ship Rock and looked out over the land around Cedar Pond that had been his ancestor's farm. Descending into what was even then still known as the "Very lot," he found an "aged man" who could show him the cellar of what was said to be the original farmhouse, now overrun by blackberry vines. A "few old moss-covered apple trees" marked the site where "the early settlers had cleared the land, and made them a home," he wrote.[5] It was a pilgrimage enacted before of course, but now he was serving as the official recorder of the family line, and we can detect that familiar note of Very pride in his careful account of the early presence and subsequent heroism of his forebears. In what must have been months, if not years, of painstaking work, he enumerated seven generations of the family down to his own. The publication of the record in the historical journal of the Essex Institute was likely a source of communal validation of sorts for the sensitive and always defensive family on Federal Street.

What prompted this effort, other than the typical retrospection of middle age, is a mystery, but it did resonate with a strand of his poetry that was increasingly interested in memory and nostalgia. Beginning most notably in the 1860s, there were tributes to Very's early adventures at sea such as "The Barque *Aurelia* of Boston" and "Capt. Samuel Cook"; memories of childhood in "The Hacker School House," "Ship Rock," and "The Youth and the Stream"; and other stray bits of recollection such as "Childhood's Songs" and "Norman's Rocks." Some, like "The King's Arm Chair," respond to changes in the local landscape; the "Steep cliff" from which Very had, as a boy, viewed the "busy streets and houses fair" of Salem had been blasted away by workers. Others, including "Sailing on Cakes of Ice in the North River," evoke an idyllic childhood as the speaker watches the ice break up and remembers his schoolmates' game of riding the larger pieces down the stream: "The merry laugh, the shout, the name, / Still echo from the shore" (*CP* 480). Reflective of the nostalgic wave that swept the nation after the Civil War, these poems evoke the world of Winslow Homer illustrations and *Little Women*, visions of youthful innocence in a world before carnage and loss.

A similar impulse, though couched in terms of regional history, may have driven Very to turn his attention to commemorative subjects associated with New England's past. A note of local pride, as well as typical Protestant bias, had been present in Very's depictions of New England colonists since he began preaching in the 1840s. The original Puritan churches of Plymouth, Boston, and Salem had been for him clear examples of the Reformation's value in allowing direct access to the scriptures and the opportunity to seek a heaven on earth. As he put it in a sermon from 1854, "Here, in the churches & common schools, they laid the foundation of the True Church of God. They built it on the Rock on which the Primitive Christian Church was built, the free, bold, intelligent profession of Christ the Son of God" (HS 96). In "On the First Church Built by the Puritans in 1634" (1861), Very reacted in a similar fashion to the sight of the preserved frame of the original Salem church, then reconstructed on the estate of David Nichols near Boston Street.[6] "Though poor and perishing unto the sight," he recorded, "A glory seems to rest upon the place" (*CP* 344). It's the shrine to "simple worship" and "the heart-felt prayer" and promises a spiritual continuity to the "Church our fathers built to God of old" (*CP* 344). The most extensive of such commemorative efforts was clearly the large sequence titled "A Series of Sonnets on the Puritans" that was probably written as part of the commemoration of the 250th anniversary of the Salem landings of John Endicott (1628) and John Winthrop (1630).[7] The thirty-eight sonnets move from "The Calling," which establishes a divine purpose typologically connected to "Abraham of old," through the sea voyage and establishment of "The Puritan Church and State," to a final exhortation to present descendants: "See that ye tarnish not their honest name, / But add new lustre to the historic page" (*CP* 553). Conventional in thought, except perhaps for the final call to bring about "Her great Millennial Day of Love and Peace" (*CP* 553), the collection is perhaps most interesting for the light it may shed on Very's earlier ambitions with his religious sonnets. The suggestion made by a number of critics that the hundreds of spiritual sonnets may have been meant to form a single, sweeping work—the Christian epic of inwardness that Very had theorized in his essays of the period—gets at least partial reinforcement from his late turn to a deliberate sequence on what was then considered a grand historical subject.

✷ 46 ✷

"The presence of things invisible"

Few notable events shaped the final decades of Very's life. He did in fact live quietly, and though his inner life may have been eventful, we have few reliable records from which to construct a picture of his private affairs. Only glimpses remain: Very at a Unitarian meeting in Salem in 1847, insisting that Unitarianism "should be enlarged by the enlarging disposition of the times" and serve as the "exponent" of other denominations, "showing the power to which they are to be raised"; at the 1852 dedication of the Fowler Street School, a new "Primary and Intermediate" institution to be run by his sisters, Frances and Lydia L. A.; viewing the "Pilgrim's Progress Tableau," a massive exhibition of moving paintings in 1859; and in 1861 replying to a letter from his former student, the poet Frederick Goddard Tuckerman, to say that he was "not engaged in any literary work" at the time and was fully devoted to preaching.[1] What meaningful disturbances there were to his contemplative life came in the form of two significant losses, the deaths of his brother, Washington, in 1853 and of his mother in 1867.

Washington had followed his brother to Harvard, graduating second in his class in 1843. After a four-month trip to Europe, he too attended the Divinity School and became a minister after completing his studies in 1846. His preaching lasted only a year before he opened a school for "young ladies" in Salem at Mechanic Hall, offering to teach "all those branches of study usually deemed necessary for a thorough English and Classical education."[2] From all appearances, this second Very scholar was a steadier version of Jones, a poet (like all the Very children), hymn and sermon writer without the otherworldliness and taint of scandal. Elizabeth Peabody had found him refreshingly normal during the events of 1838, and a friend remembered Washington possessing a "solid mind, tempered too by fine poetical sentiments . . . and remarkably devoid of pretensions of any sort."[3] In 1851, Washington married Martha N. Leach, who was, according to Bartlett, a "member of the socially prominent and wealthy Nichols family" in Salem.[4] And here the story, though extremely threadbare of detail, becomes tantalizingly complicated. Washington brought his bride to Federal Street to live in Lydia's closely guarded household. There the couple had two children, the second of which, a girl, died before she was two. In 1853, Washington himself died of "an enlargement of the heart" after being sick for "little more than a week" (*CP* 588), leaving Martha to carry on with his school and raise their son, Frank. Then in a curious echo of Lydia Very's own experience thirty years before, Martha and the Very women had a serious falling-out. Most of the little surviving evidence of the quarrel comes from Bartlett's description, gleaned from interviews with descendants of Washington (and so, perhaps, one-sided), but there is little doubt that the "dispute" and "violent quarrel" he describes had something of the same intensity as Lydia's battle with Isaac Very in 1824.[5] Martha soon moved out, to 78 Federal Street, where she continued to teach young women for a number of years. According to Bartlett, Jones Very, who took no part in the argument, often visited his sister-in-law and nephew, Franklin Very, whom he "loved greatly" and who grew to become a celebrated astronomer, astrophysicist, and meteorologist.[6]

Once again, we have no way to know what caused this family rift; perhaps the strong-willed Very women simply would not tolerate another Salem outsider in their tightly drawn family circle. If Martha did indeed see herself as part of the Salem elite, there may have been class resentments under the surface that emerged once Washington was no longer there to keep the peace. Could the argument, like Lydia's with Isaac, have been over the estate? It seems possible: Washington died intestate, and the lack of instructions may have left room for different interpretations of his wishes. (This theory could be strengthened by the fact that in their own wills both Lydia L. A. and Frances Very strongly and explicitly disinherited Frank Very from any share in their estates.) But even more suggestive is the possibility that Lydia Very in some fashion may have reenacted her dispute with her husband's father, this time taking Isaac's part, after watching her daughter-in-law lose a young child and experience many of the same hardships she herself had fought so intensely to survive. The empathy we might expect from such a similarity of experience can just as often turn to a dark repetition of suffering. As Elizabeth Peabody said of Lydia's behavior in 1838, there was indeed "something very strange in it all," something that speaks of long years of pain and anger and passions unleashed that her eldest son had wished intensely to constrain. Was it this same intensity, here turned against her daughter-in-law, that had kept Jones from pursuing what were clearly his own attractions to women during his Harvard years?

For Jones himself, the loss of his younger brother may have raised memories of his father's early death at thirty-four. In a poem written shortly after Washington's burial, he described the final moments at the bedside:

> He passed away with morning light,
> Released from every pain;
> For him, the weary hours of night
> No longer could remain.
>
> . . . .
>
> The sun arose; with faith possest,
> He felt his Father near;
> And sunk in peaceful, childlike rest,
> Without a doubt, or fear. (*CP* 282)

It may be too much to suggest that Very's tendency to favor "Father" here over such possible substitutes as "savior" or "maker" suggests a distant invocation of Jones Very Sr., but there is a redolence of deep memory about the idea of Washington reverting to a "childlike rest," gathered back into a spiritual version of his earthly family. The similarities between his death and his father's could not have been lost on the small household, who would have remembered what it was like to be abandoned to their own, slender resources. Jones's reaction, unlike that of his mother and sisters, was to offer some of that care rarely given by family members when he was left fatherless. Memories among the Very descendants place him as a significant influence on young Frank, and it seems quite likely that Jones's enthusiasm for science and technological developments rubbed off on the future director of the Ladd Observatory at Brown University.[7] It may be one of the stranger paradoxes in the history of the American mind that the man known for claiming loudly at Harvard that he was "the second coming" may have inspired a scientist whose name graces craters on both the moon and Mars.

The household remaining after Washington's death changed little after 1853. Lydia L. A. and Frances were running the Fowler School and likely brought in the bulk of the family's income. Jones preached most Sundays and spent his weekdays writing sermons or sometimes poetry while following events in an increasingly turbulent country. And their mother, as she had always done, maintained the garden, sewed, took in strays, and watched over her seemingly threatened household with her typical fierceness. The four survivors each had their own quiet "bower" built in the long, descending garden overlooking what was still sometimes called the Blue Danube of Salem. There they read or wrote poetry or, certainly in Lydia L. A.'s case, made drawings reminiscent of their childhood sports by the river. These creative, intelligent, proud children of a proud mother brought home no more outsiders: none married, nor is there any hint of a flirtation or courtship in the papers that survive.

Another fourteen years, through the war and other signs of the threatening world, this aging household continued, until Lydia's death in 1867. What this loss meant to her children is only partly suggested in the poem Very wrote a few days later. Conventional and sentimental on the surface, it nevertheless reveals the extent to which this small world of the Federal Street house, with its books and plants and needlework, revolved around the willful presence at its center:

> Long did she labor for our good,
> To inform the mind, improve the heart;
> Cared for our raiment, health, and food,
> With all a mother's love and art.
>
> Far into night her busy hand,
> Or thoughtful care our comfort sought;
> With morning's light again she planned,
> And with untiring patience wrought.
>
> To her we came in every ill,
> Whether of body, or of mind;
> Sure in her sympathy and skill,
> Healing and balm for each to find. (*CP* 404)

Though similar attributes were attached to many mothers in this period, we should recall the skills and values implied by the needlework image of Cornelia donated by the family to the Essex Institute at some point after Lydia's death. The image here of the artful mother, fully devoted, "untiring," "busy" on behalf of her children, recalls Cornelia's grand gesture of pointing to her children as her "jewels," but it also implies a restless energy, thin fingers nervously alive to the needs and protection of children, even if those children are now adults. As in the early poem on his brother Franklin's blindness, Lydia is here situated as the sole protector and savior of her vulnerable brood, less a figure of faith than an imagined angel, "A messenger, by night, by day, / Sent by our heavenly Father's love" (*CP* 405).

Very's relationship with his mother—as well as Lydia's complicated personality, intelligence, and changing ideas and beliefs—remains the enduring mystery of his life. Our ability to unpack what was clearly a complex and often unspoken tension between mother and son is severely limited, but the image of a bundled, anxious maternal energy that occupied the center of her children's lives asserts itself clearly enough. Even in death, this quality dominates her son's memories, and we can almost sense, as this poem ends, something like peace descending on the "old-fashioned" house and garden that once bounded Lydia's restless mind. To what extent she was responsible for Jones Very's strange conversion from nervous young Unitarian to messianic pretender we can only imagine. That she played some role is undeniable, just as it stands to reason that her indomitable determination was an unavoidable fact for all of her children. Her death may have eased this burden somewhat, but there is little doubt that the Verys continued to think of themselves as Lydia's children, the extension and expression of her passionate care. At the end of her memoir, written late in her own life, Lydia L. A. was inevitably drawn back to this idea and image:

A REVERIE

A Summer day; a blue sky overhead; the mown grass sending up delicious perfume; it was a day of dream, but—how real.

The Muser in the Old-fashioned Garden. The mother bending over her plants, the elder sister beside her. The brothers examining their trees....

All were together in outward presence and inward union, one heart and one mind, as they always had been—the home unbroken![8]

✷ 47 ✷
"The Book of Life"

On a September day in 1901, Mr. and Mrs. Charles A. Cooper, caretakers for Lydia L. A. Very, went through the house at 154 Federal Street and gathered all the personal papers—letters, notebooks, manuscripts—they could find. The pile must have been large; it was the accumulation of over sixty years by a family of writers. And it would have included correspondence from others, at the minimum communications from Jones Very's known friends and associates: Emerson, Lowell, Whittier, Thoreau, and Alcott. But the Coopers were, according to Bartlett, "illiterate" and unaware of the value of such things.[1] In a society that cherished privacy to the point of repressiveness, they likely thought that what they were doing was proper and customary. And so they fed it all, page by page, into the flames. Their employer and benefactress, the ever formidable Lydia L. A. Very—teacher, children's book writer and artist, amateur sculptor, and family defender—had died just a few days before. Perhaps the Coopers already knew that in her will the youngest Very child had left Mrs. Cooper all of her personal effects; perhaps they wished to show their thanks and complete their duties. It may also be possible that Lydia L. A. had given hints about family secrets she would rather see buried, though likely not in so haphazard and careless a way. As with so much regarding the Very family, it remains a mystery. But as a result of this purge, an entire layer of personal history was quietly erased, its smoke and ash curling out and up above the Very garden toward the high towers of the newly enlarged St. James Catholic Church.

Part of that lost history, whether subject to this auto-da-fé or not, includes any sort of detailed, familial account of Jones Very's death. It was the spring of 1880, and though sixty-seven years had passed since those heady days during the War of 1812 that had witnessed his parents' passionate marriage, there is little indication that Very was in poor health. In mid-April, he had begun to feel unwell, though not seriously so. According to Bartlett, who offers no direct source for these details, Very "was so patient in enduring suffering that his sisters failed to realize his extreme danger."[2] But by the first of May, the peril was clear. Lydia L. A. wrote a hasty note to George Whipple of the Essex Institute explaining that she had no time for business at the moment because her brother was "*very sick*."[3] Erysipelas, the streptococcal skin infection sometimes known as Saint Anthony's Fire, caused fever, chills, and a "flaming" red rash, usually on the face. Before the availability of antibiotics it was a dangerous condition, accounting for a significant number of deaths each year. (Among many others, the English essayist Charles Lamb had died of it in 1834.) It may have been contracted through a cut or other lesion, one of the many reminders of how fragile life could be even as late as 1880. After only a few weeks of symptoms, Jones Very died on May 8, a Saturday, and was buried alongside his father and other family members the following Tuesday in the Old South Cemetery in Peabody.

Responses to the news of Very's death reflect a contradiction in his reputation at the time. Newspaper reports stressed his obscurity, even the perception, as one *New York Tribune* notice put it, that he "was comparatively little known even in the town where he lived."[4] In a similar fashion the *Boston Herald* article that so annoyed the Very sisters a few weeks after the funeral stated matter-of-factly that "few in Salem knew him while living, few knew when he died, few will remember him."[5] And yet, notices and sometimes more fully appreciative accounts of his life were published in all the local papers of both Salem and Boston and in publications as far away as Cincinnati. In an article titled "A Little Known Poet," the writer in the *Cincinnati Daily Gazette*, having learned of Very's death from the *New York Times*, calls him "one of the best sonnet writers in the language."[6] As a cultural figure, in other words, Very was widely known for being obscure, famous for his lack of fame. Certainly he was in no sense a major presence on the literary landscape and never had been, but when the Essex Institute decided to hold a memorial meeting to honor him in December, tributes came in from religious and literary figures throughout the region. Substantial remarks were delivered by William P. Andrews and Edward A. Silsbee, and letters read from George Hosmer, Robert C. Waterston, James Freeman Clarke, Charles T. Brooks, Henry Foote, and others. More testimonials were recorded in the notes to the meeting, including statements from Emerson, Andrew Peabody, Edwin M. Stone, and Thomas Wentworth Higginson. Within the next six years, two editions of Very's writings were published, the first by Andrews in 1883 and the second by the Very sisters with the assistance of Clarke and Cyrus Bartol in 1886.

In his will, Very left all of his property, including his share of the house on Federal Street, to his sisters, and in case of their deaths, to his mother's sister in upstate New York or a cousin in Salem. If none of these family members survived him, the estate would go to the Association for the Relief of Aged and Destitute Women in Salem. Frances and Lydia L. A. continued to live in the house until their deaths, in 1895 and 1901, respectively. In her will, Lydia L. A. bequeathed the house and property to the Essex Institute as a tribute to her brothers with the stipulation that the grounds and garden be maintained as they were at the time of her death. Her hope was that a botanist attached to the institute could live in the house and keep up the cherished trees, paths, and bowers. Both sisters feared more than anything the encroachment of St. James Catholic Church, which had grown to surround the "old-fashioned" property. Frances had explicitly stated in her will that it "is my wish that the estate no. 154 Federal Street should never be sold, let or occupied by Catholics."[7] As is almost predictable when it comes to the story of the Very family, these final wishes were immediately contested: first by Frank Very, who began legal proceedings but apparently did not follow through; and second by the Essex Institute itself, the officers of which claimed there was no money to maintain the house.[8] Lydia L. A. had left a substantial sum to see to the care and upkeep of the family grave, which as a result is now marked by a fairly modern granite memorial. The house, however, remained in ill repair for many years, with only a small plaque indicating it as the former home of Jones and Washington Very. In the 1950s, the lot was finally sold to St. James, the house torn down, and the garden turned into a parking lot. The North River, once the large, sparkling playground of the Very children and others, had by the late nineteenth century been filled in and narrowed to a dismal concrete canal that now resembles little more than a drainage ditch. What trace that once remained of Lydia Very and her children was thoroughly erased, and nothing marks the site today as in any way connected to the man Hawthorne had called the "one organ in the world of the impersonal Spirit" (EP 221).

That so quiet a figure as Very would end up being remembered, if at all, as someone overlooked or left behind is not a surprise. For all of its intense interest in religion, America has never had any real use for "mystics," no matter how close its famous spokesman of individualism might come. In a culture defined by material progress, to insist on the reality of spirit, the possibility of heaven now, has always been to threaten the values of the age—or, what is really the same thing, to be dismissed as otherworldly, impractical, an atavistic curiosity. Very was never so abstracted as not to know this, nor was he so inconsistent as to try to find a compromise between his vision of divine union and the bustling interests of society.

Whatever we might think of such persistent devotion to the idea of otherworldliness, whatever easy criticism of its "foolishness" comes to hand, we should recognize that its presence in our past or our present is fundamental to human desire. Even Very's "madness," such as it was, can stand simply and purely as an emblem of the pursuit of spirit to its mysterious and estranging conclusions. American "enterprise" may never have a use for such a figure, but whether it needs the strange purity of such a voice, despite (or because of) this unworkable peculiarity, remains an open—and urgent—question.

In Very's final years he was certainly more observer than prophet, more collector than creator, the man in the fields, catching at wind-blown flowers to see what their life could say. His inner stillness, gained from a desperate season of love and rage, had left him better able to watch and note than to build imaginative kingdoms. A late poem, undated, describes these final concerns: For what was his life—and those of his parents and family—but passions told and pain remembered?

The Book of Life

My hands have long been busy cutting from each
Day's paper the short tale or verse, that told
To many that around me dwell the shade of grief,
Or note of joy; as to my opening eye
They flitted half-seen by. These pasted in
The blank pages of my unfilled book stand as
Life's true memorial. There every word
The heart unconscious uttered, finding wings,
Has flown to sing of its sweet birth. As birds
From out some thicket scape to tell to the open
Fields and travelled ways the secrets of their
Bower. There live! the record of the Past!
To tell of him who from his labors ceased
Enjoys the goodman's rest forevermore. (*CP* 567–68)

Acknowledgments

Carl Dennis introduced me to Jones Very's poetry many years ago when I was a graduate student. I remain grateful for the seriousness and care he devoted to a poet so seldom taught. My other teachers at the University at Buffalo—particularly the remarkable line-up of Americanists then in place: Marty Pops, Leslie Fiedler, Kenneth Dauber, Robert Daly, and George Hochfield—continue to shape my pursuit of a better understanding of the New England and American traditions.

The debt I owe to scholars of Transcendentalism in general and of Very's writing in particular is, I hope, clearly indicated in the notes and bibliography, but I would add that the books of Barbara L. Packer, particularly her remarkably shrewd and clarifying *The Transcendentalists,* and of Philip Gura, whose *American Transcendentalism* is never far from my desk, have been vital to my larger understanding of the movement.

The work of the late Robert Richardson, author of biographies of Emerson, Thoreau, and William James, has been an important influence on this study. A short, encouraging note Professor Richardson sent while I was writing this book is now a treasured keepsake. I am honored to occupy the same position he once held at the University of Denver.

A research grant from the University of Denver's PROF fund provided time and financial support for travel and archival research. A Dean's Meritorious Sabbatical Award from the College of Liberal Arts allowed for work on this and other projects. Additional support for the publication of this book was provided by the College of Liberal Arts. I wish to thank deans Daniel McIntosh and Rhonda Gonzales.

In a time of pandemic, when many archives were closed to visitors, I was heartened and astonished by the generous assistance offered by librarians and archivists. In many instances, scans of materials were provided at no cost, with little or no staff assistance. I would particularly like to thank the following individuals for their help in locating and duplicating materials: Peggy Keeran at the University of Denver's Anderson Academic Commons; Ruth R. Rogers and Mariana S. Oller at the Wellesley College library; Tal Nadan at the New York Public Library; and Suzanne Inge and Meaghan Wright at the Peabody Essex Museum.

The following libraries and archives provided materials for this study: the Boston Public Library; the Special Collections and Archives of the University of Iowa Libraries; the Wellesley College Library; the New York Public Library; the Brooke Russell Astor Reading Room for Rare Books and Manuscripts at the New York Public Library; the Houghton Library at Harvard University; the John Hay Library at Brown University; the Harvard University Archives; the Harvard Divinity School Library; the Phillips Library of the Peabody Essex Museum; the Peabody Essex Museum art collection; and the Massachusetts Historical Society.

Jan Gorak gave valuable feedback on a draft of early chapters. Robert Gross provided illuminating comments and suggestions for the historical dimension of the manuscript. Laura Walls and an anonymous reader for the press likewise gave valuable advice for improvement and helped identify correctible errors.

Evelyn Hampton transcribed all of Jones Very's letters that remained in manuscript.

Like many families, ours became more concentrated during the pandemic, and I'd like to thank my son, Ethan, and his wife, Miran, for their love and companionship through what were certainly complicated and stressful times.

Finally, this book is dedicated to my wife, Hillary, who not only kept us all moving in the right direction during these few, unusual years, but also performed indispensable, original research in support of this project. Many of the important discoveries in this book regarding the Very family, including the once-lost record of Lydia and Captain Jones Very's marriage, belong to her, and much of the historical texture of this book is due directly to her skill and experience as a researcher and professional librarian.

Portions of two chapters were previously published in different form as parts of the following essays: "Emerson's Telescope: Jones Very and Romantic Individualism," *New England Quarterly* 91.3 (2018): 483–507; and "Very, Garrison, Thoreau: Variations on the Antebellum Passive," *Nineteenth-Century Literature* 74.3 (2019): 332–59, copyright © University of California Press. My thanks to the editors of these journals for permission to reprint this material.

Abbreviations

BPI — "The Practical Application in This Life, by Men as Social and Intellectual Beings, of the Certainty of a Future State." Bowdoin Prize Essay, 1835. Harvard University Archives.

CB I — Commonplace Book, circa 1830s. Harvard University Archives.

CB II — Commonplace Book, 1834 (also known as the "Scrapbook"). Harvard University Archives.

CB III — Commonplace Book, 1837–1850. Harvard University Archives.

CP — *Jones Very: The Complete Poems*. Edited by Helen R. Deese. Athens: University of Georgia Press, 1993.

EG — Edwin Gittleman. *Jones Very: The Effective Years, 1833–1840*. New York: Columbia University Press, 1967.

EP — *Letters of Elizabeth Palmer Peabody*. Edited by Bruce A. Ronda. Middletown, CT: Wesleyan University Press, 1984.

HS — Jones Very Sermons, 1844–1873. Houghton Library. Harvard University. (Sermons are cited by catalogued number.)

JHL — Jones Very Papers, 1833–1886. John Hay Library. Brown University.

JMN — Ralph Waldo Emerson. *The Journals and Miscellaneous Notebooks of Ralph Waldo Emerson*. Edited by William H. Gilman, Alfred R. Ferguson, Merrell R. Davis, Merton M. Sealts, Jr., and Harrison Hayford. 16 vols. Cambridge, MA: Harvard University Press, 1960–82.

LA — Ralph Waldo Emerson. *Essays and Lectures*. New York: Library of America, 1983.

PL — Phillips Library. Peabody Essex Museum.

PVA — Henry Taylor. *Philip Van Artevelde: A Dramatic Romance, in Two Parts*. 3rd ed. London: Edward Moxon, 1844.

VFP — Very Family Papers. Phillips Library. Peabody Essex Museum.

Notes

Introduction

1. Jones Very to Rev. Henry W. Bellows, December 29, 1838; reprinted in *CP* lvi–lviii.

2. Lawrence Buell, *Literary Transcendentalism: Style and Vision in the American Renaissance* (Ithaca, NY: Cornell University Press, 1973), 325.

3. Nathaniel Hawthorne, "The Hall of Fantasy," in *Mosses from an Old Manse*, vol. 10 of *The Centenary Edition of the Works of Nathaniel Hawthorne* (Columbus: Ohio State University Press, 1962), 638.

4. Peter Ackroyd, *Blake* (New York: Alfred A. Knopf, 1995), 238.

5. Phyllis Cole, "Jones Very's 'Epistles to the Unborn,'" *Studies in the American Renaissance*, 1982, 169–83, 178.

6. Bronson Alcott, *The Journals of Bronson Alcott*, ed. Odell Shepherd (Boston: Little, Brown, 1938), 130.

Prologue

1. See "Sound Toll Registers Online," http://dietrich.soundtoll.nl/public/names.php?id=1148374.

2. According to the "Report Concerning Prisoners of War at Melville Island Prison" from the files of John Mitchell, agent for American prisoners of war during the War of 1812, the crew of the brig *Montgomery* was released in a prisoner exchange in July of 1814. See "John Mitchell Papers," Historical Society of Pennsylvania, https://discover.hsp.org/Record/dc-8710. The *Montgomery*'s capture by the *Nymphe* was announced in the *London Gazette* 16762 (August 10, 1813): 1575. The dangerously unsanitary conditions at Melville Island were attested to by several accounts written by prisoners there. See Benjamin Waterhouse, *A Journal of a Young Man of Massachusetts* (Boston: Rowe and Hooper, 1816). "When we arrived here in May, 1813, there were about nine hundred prisoners; but many died by the severity of the winter; for the quantity of fuel allowed by the British government was insufficient to convey warmth through the prison. The men were cruelly harassed by the barbarous custom of mustering and parading them in the severest cold, and even in snow storms" (14). The *Montgomery* fought its most dangerous battle against the much better armed *Surinam* off the coast of Surinam on December 6, 1812. See George Coggeshall, *History of the American Privateers, and Letters-of-Marque, during Our War with England in the Years 1812, '13, and '14* (New York: George P. Putnam, 1861), 69–70. According to Salem minister William Bentley's diary, the *Mont-*

gomery returned to Salem on January 15, 1813, its captain wounded; five crewman were lost in the engagement with the *Surinam*. See William Bentley, *The Diary of William Bentley, 1811–1819* (Salem, MA: Essex Institute, 1914), 145–46.

3. Ralph Waldo Emerson to Rufus W. Griswold, September 25, 1841; in *The Letters of Ralph Waldo Emerson*, vol. 7, ed. Ralph L. Rusk and Eleanor M. Tilton (New York: Columbia University Press, 1939), 472–73.

4. Jones Very, "Shakespeare," in *Poems and Essays by Jones Very* (Boston: Houghton, Mifflin and Company, 1886), 49.

5. Jones Very, "Shakespeare," 49.

6. Jones Very, "Hamlet," in *Poems and Essays*, 60–61.

7. For his son's account of Jones Very Sr.'s life, see Jones Very, "The Father of Rev. Jones Very," *Salem Register*, May 17, 1880.

Chapter 1

1. Bentley, *Diary*, 130.

2. The will of Samuel Very is in the Essex County (Massachusetts) Probate Records. It includes an inventory of his shop at the time of his death.

3. Since the Very brothers lived so close to one another, it's difficult to determine in which house Lydia Very and her children lived during the early years of her marriage. A later Essex Institute report on the estate of Very's sister places Jones's birth "in May Street Court, at the foot of Norman's Rocks," which would indicate Isaac Very's home. See "The President's Address," *Annual Report of the Essex Institute, for the Year Ending May 4, 1903* (Salem: Essex Institute, 1903), 13.

4. The transcript of Lydia Very's suit against her husband's estate is in the Essex County (Massachusetts) Probate Records. It's also reprinted in William Irving Bartlett's *Jones Very: Emerson's "Brave Saint"* (Durham, NC: Duke University Press, 1942), 178–81.

5. Jones Very Sr.'s original will is in the Essex County (Massachusetts) Probate Records.

6. See marriage record for "Lydia Verry" in *Vital Records of Rhode Island* (*Providence Gazette*), 406. The marriage was announced in the *Salem Gazette*, March 5, 1813, 3; and in the *Boston Daily Advertiser*, March 3, 1813.

7. As Robert A. Gross details in his study of eighteenth-century New England, in the years leading up to the Revolution young women had begun to become more independent and "fornication" much more prevalent: "In the twenty years before the Revolution, more than one out of every three firstborn children had been conceived out of wedlock. In the process, young people subverted their parents' authority." Not until the Victorian era did widespread objections to premarital conception take hold. See Gross, *The Minutemen and Their World* (New York: Hill and Wang, 1976), 100.

8. See John Adams Vinton, *The Giles Memorial: Genealogical Memoirs of the Families Bearing the Names of Giles, Gould, Holmes, Jennison, Leonard, Lindall, Curwen, Marshall, Robinson, Sampson, and Webb; Also Genealogical Sketches of the Pool, Very, Tarr and Other Families, with a History of Pemaquid, Ancient and Modern; Some Account of Early Settlements in Maine; and Some Details of Indian Warfare* (Boston: Henry W. Dutton & Son, 1864), 47.

9. See *Salem Mass. Tabernacle Records*, "Church Records, 1783–1833." Isaac's excommunication may also suggest that his personality was less steady and reliable than that of his brother Samuel, who became a governing member of the Tabernacle shortly

after he purchased a pew there in 1803. Samuel Very's will lists a pew at the Tabernacle among his possessions. See Essex County (Massachusetts) Probate Records. Church records indicate that he paid $27.50 for pew number five in 1803.

10. See J. Rixey Ruffin, *A Paradise of Reason: William Bentley and Enlightenment Christianity in the Early Republic* (New York: Oxford University Press, 2008), 84.

11. The full range of documents related to the estate of Jones Very Sr. are in the Essex County (Massachusetts) Probate Records. The deeds for the purchase of the houses on River Street and Federal Street record the children as owners in the care of the estate. A document in the Phillips Library of the Peabody Essex Museum reinforces Lydia's lack of standing. In order to have the house on Federal Street insured in 1837 Lydia had to request power of attorney from her sons, Jones and Washington. See VFP, folder 6.

12. As late as 1858, the Very children petitioned the Essex County Probate Court to allow Lydia to draw $200 per year of the $1,500 principal left to her by her husband in 1823. They noted that the annual interest amounted to only $42 and that she had no other source of personal income.

13. Bartlett, *Jones Very*, 17.

14. Bartlett, 17.

15. Lydia L. A. Very, *An Old-Fashioned Garden, and Walks and Musings Therein* (Salem, MA: Salem Press, 1900), 7.

16. Jones Very, "Hamlet," 54.

Chapter 2

1. "The Father of Reverend Jones Very," *Salem Register*, May 17, 1880.

2. Essex County (Massachusetts) Probate Records.

3. See Essex County (Massachusetts) Probate Records. The records include not only sale prices for the houses but the history of requests made by the estate to the judge. The sale of the River Street house, for example, required court approval of Judge White. The trustee Benjamin Cheever and Lydia argued that the small dwelling was run-down and unsuitable for the health and well-being of the children.

4. Very, *An Old-Fashioned Garden*, 50, 51.

5. Very, 2. According to estate records, $700 came from Jones's inheritance; equal shares of $266.66 came from the accounts of his three siblings. See Essex County (Massachusetts) Probate Records.

6. Very, *An Old-Fashioned Garden*, 1. Notes on the house and neighborhood can be found in Henry K. Oliver, "Reminiscences of Federal Street in 1885," *Essex Institute Historical Collections* 82 (April 1946): 179–85, 182–83. According to Very's poem "Jonathan Huntington Bright" (1844), the local poet who wrote under the pen name "Viator" may have grown up in the house: "I sit within the room where thou once sat, / When half my age, a curly headed boy; / And live beneath the roof where thou once lived" (*CP* 233).

Chapter 3

1. Jerome Curley, "Then and Now: Home Schooling," *Patch: Salem*, Nov. 5, 2011, https://patch.com/massachusetts/salem/home-schooling-89605577. See also Jones Very, "The Hacker School" (*CP* 411).

2. See William Page Andrews, "Memoir," in *Poems by Jones Very* (Boston: Houghton, Mifflin and Company, 1883), 5–6.

3. VFP, folder 1.

4. Bartlett, *Jones Very*, 18.

5. Samuel Very's will is in the Essex County (Massachusetts) Probate Records.

6. See Edwin Haviland Miller, *Salem Is My Dwelling Place: A Life of Nathaniel Hawthorne* (Iowa City: University of Iowa Press, 1991), 12.

7. The manuscript for this story is in VFP, folder 19.

8. The ad for Turrell's auction house is in the *Salem Gazette*, January 21, 1825.

9. See Andrews, "Memoir," 5. C. E. Noyes quotes Thomas Wentworth Higginson on the timetable of Very's early life. See Noyes, "A New England Mystic," *Harvard Monthly* 17 (October 1893): 136–43, 138.

10. Andrews, "Memoir," 5–6.

11. See Jesse H. Jones, "Henry Kemble Oliver," in Massachusetts Bureau of Statistics of Labor, *Seventeenth Annual Report of the Bureau of Statistics of Labor* (Boston: Wright and Potter Printing Co., 1886), 5–12, 41.

12. See Noyes, "New England Mystic," 137–38.

13. Andrews notes that this unnamed uncle "provided what pecuniary aid [Very] needed" to enter Harvard in 1834. Though Very entered Harvard in 1833, it may well have been his father's brother, Nathaniel Very, a well-to-do New York merchant and slaveholder, who was the source of this additional money. In the event of the early death of his son or wife, Nathaniel Very left his entire estate to the Very children in the will he made in 1834. Though this bequest never came about, it does suggest that Nathaniel could have been the source of other forms of support for his brother's children. See Andrews, "Memoir," 6; and *New York, U.S., Wills and Probate Records*, vol. 120, *1857–1868*. See as well Paschal Reeves, "The Making of a Mystic," *Essex Institute Historical Collections* 103 (1967): 3–30, where Reeves notes that Nathaniel Very gave his nephew a copy of *Lord Chesterfield's Principles of Politeness* on the boy's fifth birthday (11).

Chapter 4

1. Bartlett, *Jones Very*, 15.

2. Bartlett, 37.

3. As an indication of how uncertain such anecdotal information can be, court documents of the time detail the case of another Lydia Very, a cousin born in 1812, who was committed in 1833 for insanity by the town council of Danvers. Given the Very family's general presence in North Salem and South Danvers, the possibility of some confusion of reputations is entirely possible. See Essex County Court Records.

4. See Margaret B. Moore, *The Salem World of Nathaniel Hawthorne* (Columbia: University of Missouri Press, 1998), 132–33. Gittleman claims that Wright was with General Lafayette when he made his 1824 visit to Salem as part of his triumphal US tour (EG 383n46). But Wright's biographer indicates that Fanny and her sister Camilla did not reach New York until September 11, and so could not have been with Lafayette on the New England leg of his journey. See Celia Morris Eckhardt, *Fanny Wright: Rebel in America* (Cambridge, MA: Harvard University Press, 1984), 79.

5. Frances Wright, *Reason, Religion, and Morals* (Amherst, NY: Humanity Books, 2004), 135.

6. Eckhardt, *Fanny Wright*, 3.

7. Celia Morris Eckhardt, "Of Fanny and Camilla Wright: Their Sisterly Love," *in The Sister Bond: A Feminist View of a Timeless Connection*, ed. Toni A. McNaron (New York: Pergamon, 1985), 39; quoted in Susan S. Adams, introduction to Wright, *Reason, Religion, and Morals*, 10.

8. *New York Commercial Advertiser*, January 12, 1829; quoted in Eckhardt, *Fanny Wright*, 3.

9. These letters were not published until 1987. See Helen R. Deese, "The Peabody Family and the Jones Very 'Insanity': Two Letters of Mary Peabody," *Harvard Library Bulletin* 35.2 (1987): 218–29, 223.

10. Deese, "Peabody Family," 223.

11. Deese, 225.

12. We should also remember that "atheism" was commonly a shorthand term for any kind of unconventional thinking in relation to traditional Christian belief. Emerson was regularly attacked as an atheist throughout his career by members of the conservative and Unitarian clergy.

13. Very, *An Old-Fashioned Garden*, 7.

14. Very, 67.

15. Very, 32.

16. Very, 3, 5; see also "The Empty Nest," in *Poems and Prose Writings* (Salem, MA: Salem Press, 1890), 94.

17. Lydia L. A. Very, *A Strange Recluse* (Salem, MA: Salem Press, 1899), 45–46.

18. Very, *An Old-Fashioned Garden*, 152.

Chapter 5

1. See Suzanne Dixon, *Cornelia: Mother of the Gracchi* (New York: Routledge, 2007), 11.

2. In 1798, William Godwin, Wollstonecraft's widower, wrote a biography of her that revealed their premarital sexual relationship as well as the illegitimacy of Wollstonecraft's daughter by Gilbert Imlay. See Godwin, *Memoirs of the Author of "A Vindication of the Rights of Women"* (London, 1798).

3. See Paula Bradstreet Richter, "Wollstonecraft and Needlecraft: A Case Study of Women's Rights and Education in Federal Salem, Massachusetts," *Painted with Thread: The Art of American Embroidery* 136 (2000): 141–47, 145.

4. A tantalizing clue, unsupported by any other available evidence, can be found in Candace Wheeler's *The Development of Embroidery in America*, where the piece is cited as having been completed while Lydia Very was at "Mrs. Peabody's School." Elizabeth Peabody's mother, Eliza, started a school for young women in Salem in 1808, the year of Lydia's needlework. Could Mrs. Peabody have been the source, thirty years later, of Elizabeth Palmer Peabody's knowledge of Lydia Very? If so, no trace of such a familiarity is evident in the younger Peabody's letters or in the letters of her sister Mary from the later 1830s. See Wheeler, *The Development of Embroidery in America*, (New York: Harper Brothers, 1921), ix. Also Megan Marshall, *The Peabody Sisters: Three Women Who Ignited American Romanticism* (New York: Houghton Mifflin, 2005), 63.

5. See "Republican Meeting," *Salem Gazette*, May 14, 1804.

6. See Edward Gray, *William Gray of Salem* (Boston: Houghton Mifflin, 1914), 45–46.

7. Ruffin, *Paradise of Reason*, 142.

Chapter 6

1. Compare this reading, for instance, to "Our Dear Mother" (1867), written by Jones after Lydia's death, for a reinforcement of the sense of maternal gentleness and care often emphasized in descriptions of her by her children. See *CP* 404–5.

2. Jonathan Edwards, "Personal Narrative," in *A Jonathan Edwards Reader*, ed. John E. Smith, Harry S. Stout, and Kenneth P. Minkema (New Haven, CT: Yale University Press, 1995), 285.

3. William Ellery Channing, "Unitarian Christianity," in *The Complete Works of William Ellery Channing* (London and New York: Routledge & Sons, 1884), 285. The contrast described in this essay between traditional Calvinist conceptions of God and the tenets of Unitarianism closely matches the contrast in Very's poem.

Chapter 7

1. See Kenneth Walter Cameron, *Transcendental Reading Patterns: Library Charge Lists for the Alcotts, James Freeman Clark, Frederick Henry Hedge, Theodore Parker, George Ripley, Samuel Ripley of Waltham, Jones Very, and Charles Stearns Wheeler—New Areas for Fresh Explorations* (Hartford, CT: Transcendental Books, 1970), 201.

2. See "Samuel Gray Ward's Account of a Visit from Jones Very in 1839," reprinted in L. H. Butterfield, "Come with Me to the Feast; or, Transcendentalism in Action," *MHS Miscellany* 6 (December 1960): 1–5. Ward was later associated with the Transcendentalists and was a good friend of Emerson's.

3. "Samuel Gray Ward's Account," 3.

4. Quoted in "Jones Very" [obituary], *Harvard Register* 1.7 (1880): 130.

5. Quoted in "Jones Very" [obituary], 130.

6. Quoted in "Jones Very" [obituary], 130.

7. Description attributed to Reverend J. H. Heywood, one of Very's classmates; reprinted in "Jones Very's Academic Standing at Harvard," *Emerson Society Quarterly* 19.2 (1960): 52–60, 58.

8. See "Jones Very and the Emersons in Harvard's Official Records," *Emerson Society Quarterly* 10.1 (1958): 46–47.

9. "Jones Very and the Emersons," 46. The Bowdoin Prize included a $40 cash award on each occurrence.

10. Jones Very to Rev. Henry W. Bellows, December 29, 1838.

11. See Samuel Eliot Morison, *Three Centuries of Harvard* (Cambridge, MA: Harvard University Press, 1936), 252–54. Record of Very's appeal can be found in "Jones Very and the Emersons," 47.

12. Very cites an *Edinburgh Review* article from 1833 on page 16. A description of his study schedule for April 25, 1834, appears close to the end of the notebook. The timing for this break coincides with the expulsions for the Dunkin Rebellion.

13. Richard H. Dana Jr., "Biographical Note," in William T. Channing, *Lectures Read to the Seniors of Harvard College*, ed. Dorothy I. Anderson and Waldo N. Braden (Carbondale and Edwardsville: Southern Illinois University Press, 1968), xi–xii.

14. David Potter, introduction to William T. Channing, *Lectures*, xxix.

15. Horace, "Satire II.ii," in *The Complete Odes and Satires of Horace*, trans. Sidney Alexander (Princeton, NJ: Princeton University Press, 1999), 253.

Chapter 8

1. In his remarks to the Essex Institute memorial meeting honoring Very, William P. Andrews is recorded as saying that "'Capt.' Very himself and all the members of his family were fond of verse-making, some of which had shown decided literary talent," a claim that he repeats in his "Memoir." See "Rev. Jones Very, in Memoriam," *Essex Institute Bulletin* 13 (1881): 1–35. In 1878, Lydia L. A. Very participated in a local hospital charity fair that included a book of poetry "autographs" by local and national poets. The list of contributors also includes "Mrs. Lydia Very," suggesting that her daughter had submitted one of Lydia's poems for the event. See "The Fair," *Boston Daily Advertiser*, December 4, 1878.

2. The difficulties of ascribing precise dates to entries in the "Scrapbook" should not be underestimated. In only a few instances in all of the notebooks did Very indicate the date on which he copied a quotation. Though it's possible to correlate some entries with his library charge lists, these conjunctions give only a general sense of when he was reading a particular work. Any narrative based on precise connections between the commonplace books and poems, for instance, can only be highly speculative.

3. See Thomas Wilson Bayne, "Pollok, Robert," in *Dictionary of National Biography* (London: Smith, Elder, 1896), 46:69–70.

4. Robert Pollok, *The Course of Time: A Poem* (New York: Robert Carter and Brothers, 1878), 97.

5. It's possible that Very had Pollok in mind when he wrote his senior essay, later delivered as a lecture in Salem, "What Reasons Are There for Not Expecting Another Epic Poem?" Very's sense that Christianity had moved the external struggle of epic to the internal battlefield of the soul led him to declare that "the struggle of the will" was the true subject of the "modern . . . poetry of sentiment." See EP 20, 15.

Chapter 9

1. See Jones Very to Rev. Henry W. Bellows, December 29, 1838; reprinted in *CP* lvi-lviii. Bellows went on to become a prominent Unitarian minister in New York. For the latter part of his career, he was pastor at All Souls Church, of which Herman Melville was a member. Bellows played a significant role in the controversy surrounding Melville's marital difficulties. See Hershel Parker, *Herman Melville, 1851–1891* (Baltimore: Johns Hopkins University Press, 1996), 629–30.

2. Jones Very to Rev. Henry W. Bellows, December 29, 1838.

3. Butterfield, "Come with Me to the Feast," 1–5.

Chapter 11

1. Jones Very to Rev. Henry W. Bellows, December 29, 1838 (original emphasis).

2. See *The First Centenary of the North Church and Society in Salem, Massachusetts* (Salem, MA, 1873), 194.

3. It's notable that the Verys are not listed as "proprietors or occupants of pews" in the list compiled for the dates 1770–1802, 1820–29, and 1836, though this list is incomplete and the cost of a pew may have been beyond Lydia's means. See *First*

Centenary, 220. None of the Very family is listed as admitted in the years leading up to 1836. Another candidate for an early Unitarian influence is Very's teacher at the West School, O. C. Felton, who was among a group who helped organize and found the Second Unitarian Society of Danvers in 1825.

4. Jones, "Henry Kemble Oliver," 35–36.

5. Unpublished draft of a letter from James Freeman Clarke to the Essex Institute on the occasion of Jones Very's memorial. VFP, folder 12.

6. Elizabeth Peabody and her family were also members of the North Church, a fact that may lend weight to her later characterization of Lydia Very as an "atheist" or "coarse materialist." Curiously, in their 1838 correspondence regarding Very's controversial behavior, none of the Peabody sisters mentions him or his family in connection with their own history at the North Church, and neither Mary nor Sophia refers to Lydia Very in the stark terms Elizabeth uses. See Deese, "Peabody Family," passim.

7. For a detailed discussion of Bentley's Socinian Christology, see Ruffin, *Paradise of Reason*, 79–89.

8. Henry K. Oliver, *Lecture on Teachers' Morals and Manners: Delivered before the American Institute of Instruction, at Keene, N.H., August 1851* (Boston : Ticknor, Reed, & Fields, 1851), 9.

9. Quoted in David Holmes Conrad, *Memoir of Reverend James Chisholm* (New York: Protestant Episcopal Society for the Promotion of Evangelical Knowledge, 1857), 12–13.

Chapter 12

1. Harvard Archives, "Library Charging Records, 1762–1897."

2. See Jane Stabler, "Byron and 'The Excursion,'" *Wordsworth Circle* 45.2 (2014): 137–47.

3. William Wordsworth, *The Prelude, The Recluse, & The Excursion* (Bristol: Read and Company, 2020). Subsequent references will appear parenthetically in the text.

4. Margaret Fuller's comments and references to the play in *Summer on the Lakes* may provide a measure of its popularity and circulation among the Transcendentalist set: "At Chicago I read again Philip Van Artevelde, and certain passages in it will always be in my mind associated with the deep sound of the lake, as heard in the night. I used to read a short time at night, and then open the blind to look out. The moon would be full upon the lake, and the calm breath, pure light, and the deep voice harmonized well with the thought of the Flemish hero." See [Fuller,] *Summer on the Lakes, in 1843* (Boston: Little, Brown, 1844), 103.

5. Henry Taylor, preface to *Philip Van Artevelde: A Dramatic Romance, in Two Parts*, 3rd ed. (London: Edward Moxon, 1844), xi, xii, xiii.

6. Taylor, preface, xv.

7. Taylor, xv, xvi.

8. Taylor, xv.

Chapter 13

1. Quoted in C. M. Lombard, "Early American Admirers of Lamartine," *Études Anglaises* 12 (January 1959): 324–34, 325, 326.

2. Charles M. Lombard, *Lamartine* (New York: Twayne Publishers, 1973), 26.

3. Lombard, *Lamartine*, 26.

4. Alphonse de Lamartine, *On Man. To Lord Byron; Translated from the French of Alph. de Lamartine; with a Letter from the Author to the Translator* (London: T. Hurst, 1827), 4.

5. Alphonse de Lamartine, *A Pilgrimage to the Holy Land*, 4th ed. (Philadelphia: Carey, Lea, and Blanchard, 1838), 9.

6. Quoted in M. H. Abrams, *Natural Supernaturalism: Tradition and Revolution in Romantic Literature* (New York: Norton, 1971), 368.

7. Lamartine, *Pilgrimage*, 25, 38.

8. Lamartine, 25, 37.

9. In his senior Bowdoin essay on epic poetry Very cites Lamartine, and in his senior oration, "Individuality" (1836), he refers to the French poet's conversation with "Lady Stanhope." See Jones Very, "What Reasons Are There for Not Expecting Another Great Epic Poem?," *Emerson Society Quarterly* 12 (1958): 25–38, 31; "Two Harvard Essays by Jones Very," *Emerson Society Quarterly* 29 (1962): 32–40, 38.

10. Lamartine, *Pilgrimage*, 107.

11. Lamartine, 108, 109.

12. Lamartine, 109.

13. Lamartine, 110.

14. Lamartine, 110. Lamartine was minister of affairs and effectively in charge of the Second Republic for a short time during the events of 1848.

Chapter 14

1. Jones Very to Rev. Henry W. Bellows, December 29, 1838.

Chapter 15

1. See David Robinson, "Four Early Poems of Jones Very," *Harvard Library Bulletin* 28.2 (1980): 146–51.

2. See Charles Stearns Wheeler, "Biographical Notices of Mr. Charles Hayward, Jr., and Mr. Samuel T Hildreth," *Christian Examiner and General Review*, September 1839, 114–31, 124.

3. Bartlett, *Jones Very*, 99n64.

Chapter 16

1. The commencement program was reprinted in the *Boston Weekly Messenger*, September 1, 1836, 2.

2. Very, "Two Harvard Essays," 37.

3. Very, 39.

4. Very, 38–39.

5. Very, 39. In his perceptive and detailed reading of Very's relationship to Milton, K. P. Van Anglen argues that Very "recognized something of himself in Milton's moderate puritan dilemma. This was because, like the poet, he too was both of the devil's party and the sect of Heaven." See Van Anglen, *The New England Milton: Literary Reception and Cultural Authority in the Early Republic* (University Park: Penn State University Press, 1993), 166.

6. Very, "Two Harvard Essays," 38.

7. Very, "What Reasons," 28.

8. A more direct source may have been Madame de Staël, whose works Very borrowed from the library in April of 1836. In her *Germany* (1813), de Staël provides the following, widely influential distinction between classical and romantic sensibility: "The ancients had a corporeal soul, so to speak; its feelings were strong, direct, and consecutive. This is not true of the human heart developed by Christianity: modern men have drawn from Christian repentance the habit of turning continually inward upon themselves." See de Staël, *Major Writings of Germaine de Staël*, trans. Vivian Folkenflik (New York: Columbia University Press, 1987), 300.

9. Very, "What Reasons," 31; quoting Samuel Taylor Coleridge, *Table Talk*, August 18, 1833.

10. Very, "What Reasons," 31.

11. Very, 32.

Chapter 17

1. Corydon Ireland, "How Harvard Celebrated," *Harvard Gazette*, September 1, 2011, https://news.harvard.edu/gazette/story/2011/09/how-harvard-celebrated/.

2. See Robert D. Richardson Jr., *Emerson: The Mind on Fire* (Berkeley: University of California Press, 1995), 246.

3. In 1836 alone, Emerson gave five public and six private lectures in Salem, six lectures in Boston, and three in Cambridge. See William Charvat, "A Chronological List of Emerson's American Lecture Engagements," *Bulletin of the New York Public Library* 64.9 (1960): 492–507, 500–501. In December of 1837, after Very's first lecture at the Salem Lyceum, he told Elizabeth Peabody that "he was an enthusiastic listener to Mr. Emerson" (EP 405).

4. Very's copy of *Nature* is in the Parkman Dexter Howe Library at the University of Florida. Though his annotations have faded, it's hardly the case, as David Dowling suggests, that Very "manically annotated" the book and that it was his "bible before his Bible." See Dowling, *Emerson's Protégés: Mentoring and Marketing Transcendentalism's Future* (New Haven, CT: Yale University Press, 2014), 213.

Chapter 18

1. Isaac Taylor, *Natural History of Enthusiasm* (London: Holdsworth and Ball, 1830), v.

2. Taylor, *Enthusiasm*, 63.

3. Isaac Taylor, "Jonathan Edwards' Inquiry into the Freedom of the Will," reprinted in Patrick C. MacDougall, *Papers on Literary and Philosophical Subjects* (Edinburgh: Johnstone and Hunter, 1852), 66–138. Perhaps the best example of a similar passage in Edwards's writings can be found in the early piece "Of Being": "What then is become of the universe? Certainly, it exists nowhere but in the divine mind." See Edwards, *A Jonathan Edwards Reader*, ed. John E. Smith, Harry S. Stout, and Kenneth P. Minkema (New Haven, CT: Yale University Press, 1995), 12.

4. Taylor, *Enthusiasm*, 64.

5. See Jones Very to Rev. Henry W. Bellows, December 29, 1838; Cole, "Jones Very's 'Epistles to the Unborn,'" 176.

6. Taylor, *Enthusiasm*, 67–68.

7. Philip F. Gura, *Jonathan Edwards: America's Evangelical* (New York: Hill and Wang, 2005), 113.

8. Gura, *Jonathan Edwards*, 112.

9. See David D. Hall, introduction to *The Antinomian Controversy, 1636–1638* (Durham, NC: Duke University Press, 1990), 20. The well-known Quaker martyr Mary Dyer, put to death in Boston in 1660, had been a follower of Anne Hutchinson before becoming a Quaker.

10. See Catherine A. Brekus, *Strangers and Pilgrims: Female Preaching in American, 1740–1845* (Chapel Hill: University of North Carolina Press, 1998), 85.

11. Brekus, *Strangers*, 85.

12. Quoted in Brekus, *Strangers*, 97.

13. The announcement of Southwick's wedding lists Lemuel Ostler, the local Adventist minister, as presiding. See *Salem Observer*, March 16, 1850.

14. Emerson's own debt to Quakerism can be gauged by his important essay on George Fox. As Michael Colacurcio argues, "In the end the strikingly unlearned Fox had anticipated far more of what, as a religious reformer, Emerson himself would have to propound, on roughly the same self-discovered authority." Colacurcio, *Emerson and Other Minds: Idealism and the Moral Self* (Waco, TX: Baylor University Press, 2020), 1:146.

Chapter 19

1. For an account of the Divinity School's beginnings, see Morison, *Three Centuries*, 241–43; and Sydney E. Ahlstrom, *A Religious History of the American People* (New Haven, CT: Yale University Press, 1972), 393–95. Conrad Wright's "The Early Period (1811–40)," in *The Harvard Divinity School: Its Place in Harvard University and in American Culture*, ed. George Huntston Williams (Boston: Beacon Press, 1954) also has a very detailed history of teachers and curriculum.

2. See Kenneth Walter Cameron, "Jones Very's Harvard Greek Exposition and Daniel Webster," *Emerson Society Quarterly* 38 (1965): 133–35.

3. One indication of his success is the vote by the Harvard overseers in July 1838 to appoint him as instructor in history to the freshman class and raise his salary to "one thousand dollars per assum." See Reeves, "Making of a Mystic," 13.

4. See Kenneth Walter Cameron, "Jones Very and Thoreau—The 'Greek' Myth," *Emerson Society Quarterly* 7 (1957): 39–40.

5. Unattributed letter, from Bologna, dated April 1880; quoted in Bartlett, *Jones Very*, 36.

6. See Samuel Johnson Jr. to Samuel Johnson Sr., September 6, 1838; PL.

7. Thomas Wentworth Higginson, *Cheerful Yesterdays* (Boston: Houghton Mifflin, 1898), 54.

8. Quoted in Noyes, "New England Mystic," 138.

9. Quoted in Noyes, 138.

10. Quoted in Noyes, 139.

11. Quoted in William Brewster, *The Birds of the Cambridge Region of Massachusetts* (Cambridge, MA: The Club, 1906), 82.

12. Quoted in Brewster, 82.

Chapter 20

1. See Wright, "Early Period," 61.

2. See Very, "Two Harvard Essays," 39.

3. Mackintosh's work was so central to Harvard's culture that when James Russell Lowell was rusticated and sent to Concord, he was required by the Harvard authorities to read the works of John Locke along with Mackintosh's *Review of Ethical Philosophy* under the guidance of Barzillai Frost. See Horace Elisha Scudder, *James Russell Lowell: A Biography* (Frankfurt am Main: Outlook Verlag, 2020), 1:30.

Chapter 21

1. See "Jones Very and Emerson's Friends in College Church Records," *Emerson Society Quarterly* 14.1 (1959): 15–16.

Chapter 22

1. Very's journal identifies his companion only by the initials S. A. This may have been Samuel Archer, a local high school teacher who was the brother-in-law of J. Fox Worcester, Very's former tutor.

2. Scates was one of the editors of *Harvardiana* and later became a lawyer in Pennsylvania. Whitman is best known for his role as assistant quartermaster in charge of national cemeteries after the Civil War. See Drew Gilpin Faust, *This Republic of Suffering: Death and the American Civil War* (New York: Vintage, 2009), 219–23, 224–29, passim.

3. Henry Williams, *Memorials of the Class of 1837 of Harvard University, Prepared for the Fiftieth Anniversary of Their Graduation* (Boston: George Henry Ellis, 1887), 51.

4. Williams, *Memorials of the Class of 1837*, 52.

5. See Thomas Cushing, *Memorials of the Class of 1834 of Harvard College, Prepared for the Fiftieth Anniversary of Their Graduation* (Boston: David Clapp & Son, 1884), 79.

6. See Williams, *Memorials of the Class of 1837*, 102–4.

7. Emerson, *Nature* (LA 20).

Chapter 23

1. Both Bartlett and Gittleman speculate that either Elizabeth Peabody or the Salem literary patron Susan Burley "discovered" Very. There are surviving letters of Peabody's that include invitations to speakers for the ninth series, one of which mentions Very in passing. But she later implied that she went to his lecture simply because the title was attractive, and only subsequently learned about his background. It's also possible that Henry K. Oliver, an active member and later vice-president of the Lyceum, thought of inviting his former student. See Bartlett, *Jones Very*, 41–42; EG 156–58; EP 196, 404.

2. Very, "What Reasons," 28.

3. Very, "Shakespeare," 49.

4. Thomas Carlyle, "Signs of the Times," *Edinburgh Review* 49 (June 1829): 439–59, 454.

Chapter 24

1. Jones Very to Henry W. Bellows, December 29, 1838.

2. Jones Very to Henry W. Bellows, December 29, 1838.

Chapter 25

1. Ralph Waldo Emerson to Elizabeth Peabody, April 5, 1838; quoted in Bartlett, *Jones Very*, 46.

2. Lidian Jackson Emerson to Lucy Jackson Brown, April 5(?), 1838; quoted in Rusk and Tilton, *Letters of Ralph Waldo Emerson*, 7:302 (original emphasis).

3. From Emerson's journals; quoted in Richardson, *Emerson*, 113, 126.

4. Quoted in Richardson, *Emerson*, 119.

5. Quoted in Richardson, 279.

6. From Emerson's journals; quoted in Conrad Wright, "Emerson, Barzillai Frost, and the Divinity School Address," *Harvard Theological Review* 49.1 (1956): 19–43, 22.

7. See Wright, "Emerson, Barzallai Frost, and the Divinity School Address," 27.

8. From Emerson's journals; quoted in Wright, "Emerson, Barzallai Frost, and the Divinity School Address," 30.

9. See Ralph L. Rusk, *The Life of Ralph Waldo Emerson* (New York: Charles Scribner's Sons, 1949), 255. For a fuller description of the relationships between the Emersons and such local families as the Hoars, see Robert A. Gross, *The Transcendentalists and Their World* (New York: Farrar, Straus and Giroux, 2021), 440, 445, and passim.

10. Emerson to Elizabeth Peabody, April 5, 1838.

11. See Joel Myerson, "A Calendar of Transcendental Club Meetings," *American Literature* 44.4 (1972): 197–207, 202; and Larry A. Carlson, "Bronson Alcott's 'Journal for 1838' (Part One)," *Studies in the American Renaissance*, 1993, 161–244, 232.

12. Carlson, "Alcott's 'Journal for 1838' (Part One)," 232–33.

13. Carlson, 233.

14. Lidian Emerson to Lucy Jackson Brown, April 1838, in *The Selected Letters of Lidian Jackson Emerson*, ed. Delores Bird Carpenter (Columbia: University of Missouri Press, 1987), 73.

15. The entry appears on page 126 of CB II. On page 124, Very quotes from Henry McCormick's *Philosophy of Human Nature*, which he borrowed from the Harvard library on March 27. On the same page, he records an extract from George Finlayson's *Mission to Siam*, which he borrowed on April 2.

Chapter 26

1. See Edward M. Griffin, *Old Brick: Charles Chauncey of Boston, 1705–1787* (Minneapolis: University of Minnesota Press, 1980), 4.

2. Channing, "Unitarian Christianity," 285.

3. Richardson, *Emerson*, 125.

4. Emerson to Mary Moody Emerson, August 19, 1832; quoted in Richardson, *Emerson*, 125.

5. Theodore Parker, *Journal, Volume One, July 13, 1838 to December 31, 1840*, 2, Theodore Parker Papers, 1836–1862, Andover-Harvard Theological Library, Harvard Divinity School.

6. See Convers Frances to Frederic Henry Hedge, August 10, 1838, in Guy R. Woodall, "The Record of a Friendship: The Letters of Convers Francis to Frederic Henry Hedge in Bangor and Providence, 1835–1850," *Studies in the American Renaissance*, 1991, 1–57, 34.

7. Convers Frances to Frederic Henry Hedge, August 10, 1838, in Woodall, "Record," 34 (original emphasis).

8. Andrews Norton, *A Discourse on the Latest Form of Infidelity; Delivered at the Request of the Association of the Alumni of the Cambridge Theological School on the 19th of July, 1839* (Cambridge, MA: John Owen, 1839), 11.

9. Quoted in Rusk, *Life of Ralph Waldo Emerson*, 270.

Chapter 27

1. Lidian Emerson to Lucy Jackson Brown, July 19, 1838, in *Selected Letters*, 78.

2. Lidian Emerson to Lucy Jackson Brown, July 19, 1838, 78 (original emphasis).

Chapter 28

1. Quoted in EG 190.

2. Samuel Johnson Jr. to Samuel Johnson Sr., September 6, 1838; PL.

3. Quoted in EG 190.

4. Quoted in G. Bradford Jr., "Jones Very," *Unitarian Review* 27.2 (1887): 111.

5. Jones Very to Rev. Henry W. Bellows, December 29, 1838.

6. Wheeler, "Biographical Notices," 114.

7. Wheeler, 125, 127.

8. Sarah Clayton, for instance, argues that Very "did not even respond" to "attempts to raise money for a memorial to Hildreth in 1839," but knowing this with any certainty would depend on a far more complete record of Very's correspondence than we possess. See Sarah Turner Clayton, *The Angelic Sins of Jones Very* (New York: Peter Lang, 1999), 61.

9. Quoted in EG 169.

10. Quoted in EG 169.

11. Emerson to Mary Moody Emerson, September 1, 1838; in Rusk and Tilton, *Letters of Ralph Waldo Emerson*, 2:153–54.

Chapter 29

1. George Moore, *Diary of George Moore, Friend of Emerson*, in Kenneth Walter Cameron, *Transcendental Epilogue: Primary Materials for Research in Emerson, Thoreau, Literary New England, the Influence of German Theology, and Higher Biblical Criticism* (Hartford, CT: Transcendental Books, 1965), 239–40. Very may have considered Ware as potentially the most sympathetic to his ideas. According to Alan Hodder, "Ware exemplified the pietist strain of early Unitarianism, championing an approach to preaching and pastoral work that blended theological liberalism with a strong appeal to religious emotions, devotion, and self-surrender." See Hodder, "Christian Conversion, the Double Consciousness, and Transcendentalist Religious Rhetoric," *Religions* 8 (2017): 1–19, 4.

2. Moore, *Diary*, 240. For a full sketch of Moore's life, see Gross, *Transcendentalists and Their World*, 413–23.

3. Moore, *Diary*, 239. Ware's sermon, "The Personality of the Deity," delivered at Harvard on September 23, 1838, might be considered part of his response not only to the Divinity School Address but to Very's astonishing behavior.

4. Moore, *Diary*, 240.

5. Moore, 240.

6. John Olin Eidson, *Charles Stearns Wheeler: Friend of Emerson* (Athens: University of Georgia Press, 1951), 17.

7. For the description of Brazer, see Caroline Howard King, *When I Lived in Salem, 1822–1866* (Brattleboro, VT: Stephen Daye Press, 1937), 132–33.

8. This and the following account of Very's movements on September 16, 1838, relies upon Elizabeth Peabody's letters, particularly September 24, 1838, to Emerson and November 12, 1880, to William P. Andrews. See EP 208–9; 404–9. Upham, like his fellow Salem minister John Brazer, was also in contact with Andrews Norton, the vociferous antagonist of the "new thought" who would give the counterstatement to Emerson's address the following July. See Robert D. Habich, "Emerson's Reluctant Foe: Andrews Norton and the Transcendental Controversy," *New England Quarterly* 65.2 (1992): 208–37, 219.

9. There is no evidence that Peabody spoke to Charles Upham that day, as Gittleman claims. It is clear from her account that she heard from Mary Foote about Very's encounter with Upham and later from Lydia Very about her own argument with the anti-Transcendentalist minister. See EP 406, 407.

10. Jones Very to Rev. Henry W. Bellows, December 29, 1838.

11. See as well William P. Andrews's account in his "Memoir," where he describes Very as putting himself "for a while under the care of Dr. Bell" (18).

Chapter 30

1. Very, "Shakespeare," 27.

2. Very, 27.

3. Very, 46.

4. Very, 46.

5. Very, 51.

6. Emerson, *Nature*, 10. There is no record of Very having read Keats, but both were influenced significantly by the Shakespeare criticism of William Hazlitt.

7. Very, "Shakespeare," 52.

8. Jones Very to Ralph Waldo Emerson, September 1838 (original emphasis); Special Collections, Wellesley College Library.

9. Ralph Waldo Emerson to William Henry Furness, October 20, 1838; in Ralph Waldo Emerson and William Henry Furness, *Records of a Lifelong Friendship, 1807–1882* (Boston: Houghton Mifflin, 1910), 7–8.

10. Very, "Shakespeare," 51.

11. Very, "Hamlet," 54.

12. Very, 54, 55.

13. Very, 55, 56–57 (original emphasis).

14. Jonathan Bate, introduction to *The Romantics on Shakespeare* (London: Penguin, 1992), 21, 22.

15. William Hazlitt, *Characters of Shakespear's Plays & Lectures on the English Poets* (London: Macmillan, 1903), 64 (original emphasis).

16. Very, "Hamlet," 60–61.

17. Very, 56.

18. Very, "Shakespeare," 31.

Chapter 31

1. Very, "Hamlet," 61.

2. Very, 61 (original emphasis).

3. Very, 62.

4. See "Treatment of the Insane," in *American Magazine of Useful and Entertaining Knowledge*, January 1, 1837, 4.

5. For information on Bell, see Walter E. Barton, "Bell(wether) of Psychiatry," *Dartmouth Medical School Alumni Magazine*, Fall 1987, 14–15, 34.

6. Jones Very to Rev. Henry W. Bellows, December 29, 1838.

7. The Salem memoirist Caroline Howard King has left a revealing portrait of Brazer: "a dignified figure, who, just at twelve o'clock, slowly stepped along the shady side of the street, on his way to the Atheneum. At that early date the Atheneum was open only between twelve and one o'clock. He held a large black umbrella over his head, and his long black gown floated out behind him. This was not his ministerial gown, as I then firmly believed it to be, but a kind of dressing gown, black or colored, which gentlemen wore on the street in hot weather. In those days clergymen were held in great reverence, and I always watched his stately progress down the street with a kind of fearful interest." King, *When I Lived in Salem*, 17.

8. See Habich, "Emerson's Reluctant Foe," for a detailed account of the connections between Brazer, Upham, and Andrews Norton, the principal defender of the conservative Unitarian view of miracles.

9. In this sense, Carl Dennis is correct to argue that "Very sees nature as a source for the highest laws" and "adopts . . . Emerson's theory of correspondence." See Dennis, "Correspondence in Very's Nature Poetry," *New England Quarterly* 43.2 (1970): 250–73, 251.

10. It should be noted that Emerson admired Fox, possibly in ways very similar to his admiration of Very. Emerson's early lecture on the Quaker visionary suggests a preview of Very's ideas. As Michael Colacurcio summarizes, "For their proclamation, the Quakers made the dangerous claim of 'inspiration'; at the same time, however, they observed the stern condition 'within which that claim may be safely made, the act namely of total self- renouncement.'" See Colacurcio, *Emerson and Other Minds*, 148.

11. This is the somewhat polemical point of Yvor Winters's attempt to restore Very to importance at the expense of Emerson. See Winters, *Maule's Curse: Seven Studies in the History of American Obscurantism* (Norfolk, CT: New Directions, 1938).

12. In fact, he had made a similar entry in 1831 after his first wife's death: "I loved Ellen, & love her with an affection that would ask nothing but its indulgence to make me blessed. Yet when she was taken from me, the air was still sweet, the sun was not taken down from my firmament" (*JMN* 5:19–20).

13. For a wider discussion of the implications of this difference, see Clark Davis, "Emerson's Telescope: Jones Very and Romantic Individualism," *New England Quarterly* 41.3 (2018): 483–507.

14. According to Gittleman, Very stayed in Cambridge for "more than a week,"

while he lobbied to resume his old position. It is more than plausible that Very would have asked for reinstatement, but there is no evidence cited to confirm that such a request occurred at this time. Gittleman's own cited sources indicate only that Very was at Harvard for one day, likely October 31, and spoke with some of his former students, who found him much improved from his earlier mania. See Samuel Johnson Jr. to Dr. Samuel Johnson, November 2(?), 1838, in "Dr. Samuel Johnson Papers, 1815–1876," Philips Library, Peabody Essex Museum.

15. Ralph Waldo Emerson to Elizabeth Palmer Peabody, October 30, 1838; in Rusk and Tilton, *Letters of Ralph Waldo Emerson*, 2:170–71.

Chapter 32

1. Ralph Waldo Emerson to Jones Very, November 13(?), 1838; quoted in Andrews, "Memoir," 19.

2. See Deese, "Peabody Family," 223–24 (original emphasis). Deese's discussion of the letters is perceptive and valuable, and her insights are incorporated in the analysis that follows.

3. The charges against Kneeland were that he had quoted Voltaire's ridicule of the idea of the virgin birth of Jesus, had criticized the practice of prayer, and had written that "Universalists believe in a God, which I do not, but believe that their God, with all his moral attributes (aside from nature itself) is nothing more than a chimera of their imagination." Quoted in Arthur W. Brown, *Always Young for Liberty: A Biography of William Ellery Channing* (Syracuse, NY: Syracuse University Press, 1956), 236. Very was aware of Kneeland's case and sympathetic enough to his plight to sign a pardon petition circulated among members of the Transcendental Club in July of 1838. See Gross, *Transcendentalists and Their World*, 494–95, 755–56n22.

4. See Deese, "Peabody Family," 225.

5. Deese, 225 (original emphasis).

6. See Deese, 227.

7. I have elsewhere compared this incident to Hawthorne's treatment of the similarly eccentric personality of Delia Bacon. See Clark Davis, *Hawthorne's Shyness: Ethics, Politics, and the Question of Engagement* (Baltimore: Johns Hopkins University Press, 2005), 174n8.

8. Nathaniel Hawthorne, "Passages from a Relinquished Work," in *Mosses from an Old Manse*, 406.

9. Nathaniel Hawthorne, "Egotism; or, the Bosom Serpent," in *Mosses from an Old Manse*, 277. For the full development of this reading, see Robert Arner, "Hawthorne and Jones Very," *New England Quarterly* 42.2 (1969): 267–75.

10. Jones Very to Ralph Waldo Emerson, November 30, 1838 (original emphasis); Special Collections, Wellesley College Library.

11. Ralph Waldo Emerson to Margaret Fuller, November, 1838; in Rusk and Tilton, *Letters of Ralph Waldo Emerson*, 2:173.

12. James Freeman Clarke, "Biographical Notice of Jones Very," in *Poems and Essays by Jones Very* (Boston: Houghton Mifflin, 1886), xxv.

13. William Ellery Channing, "Likeness to God," in *Complete Works of William Ellery Channing*, 230–356, 232.

14. Elizabeth Palmer Peabody, *Reminiscences of Rev. Wm. E. Channing, D.D.* (Boston: Roberts Bros., 1880), 379 (original emphasis).

15. Clarke, "Biographical Notice," xxv.

16. Clarke, xxv.

Chapter 33

1. Jones Very to Ralph Waldo Emerson, November 30, 1838.

2. For a more direct address to this still nagging issue of desire, compare this poem's resolution to "Forgive me my trespasses" (*CP* 96–97), where the speaker asks God to "Let me not waste the life my Savior gave, / On the vile lusts that war against the soul."

3. In a letter to her husband, Lidian Emerson includes "Very's state of sonship" as an example of "Divine love" acting "through the human being without effort or resistance." Lidian Jackson Emerson to Ralph Waldo Emerson, March 29, 1840, in *Selected Letters*, 88.

4. In her introduction to *The Complete Poems*, Deese suggests the useful description of a "double or a *layered* voice" (*CP* xliv; Deese's emphasis). The question of how conscious Very was of this technique as a strategy has provoked different responses. Buell finds such awareness unlikely, while Robinson argues that Very "had an intense desire for an audience; his sonnets are far less devotional exercises than calculated attempts to engage his readers in his own religious vision." See Buell, *Literary Transcendentalism*, 323; and Robinson, "The Exemplary Self and the Transcendent Self in the Poetry of Jones Very," *ESQ* 24.4 (1978): 206–14, 206.

Chapter 34

1. Jones Very to Rufus Ellis, December 24, 1838; Special Collections and Archives, University of Iowa Library.

2. Jones Very to Rufus Ellis, December 24, 1838.

3. Jones Very to Rufus Ellis, December 24, 1838.

4. Jones Very to Rufus Ellis, December 24, 1838.

5. Alcott, *Journals*, 108.

6. See Myerson, "Calendar of Transcendental Club Meetings," 203.

7. Larry A. Carlson, "Bronson Alcott's 'Journal for 1838' (Part Two)," *Studies in the American Renaissance*, 1994, 166.

8. Jones Very to Bronson Alcott, December 8, 1838; Houghton Library.

9. Carlson, "Alcott's 'Journal for 1838' (Part Two)," 166.

10. Carlson, 168.

11. Carlson, 168.

12. Alcott, *Journals*, 517.

13. Alcott, *Journals*, 113.

14. Alcott, *Journals*, 113–14.

Chapter 35

1. The exact date on which Very sent the epistles to Emerson is unknown, though it was likely some time between January and June of 1839. For the text of the letters and insightful commentary on their context, see Cole, "Jones Very's 'Epistles to the Unborn,'" 169–83. Subsequent references will appear parenthetically in the text.

2. See my earlier discussion in chapter 18 of Very's comments vis-à-vis the will in Isaac Taylor's *Natural History of Enthusiasm*. In her introduction to the epistles, Cole makes the case for Very as a Calvinist ("Jones Very's 'Epistles to the Unborn,'" 171–72), an argument made earlier by James A. Levernier in "Calvinism and Transcendentalism in the Poetry of Jones Very," *ESQ* 24.1 (1978): 31–41. David Robinson argues that there "are no elect in Very's theology, neither is grace irresistible." Robinson, "Jones Very, the Transcendentalists, and the Unitarian Tradition," *Harvard Theological Review* 68.2 (1975): 103–24, 110.

3. Abrams, *Natural Supernaturalism*, 21.

4. Abrams, 47.

5. Gittleman perceptively suggests that Very could have intended the sonnets to form a more coherent large work, "the only form of epic Very thought still possible in the modern world" (EG 312). However, there is little evidence to confirm the larger claim that the sequence of "more than a hundred poems . . . would depict the prelude and consequences of this manifestation of deity on earth" (EG 323).

6. It's useful to compare this set of ambitions to those outlined by Stanley Cavell for Thoreau's own epic gesture in *Walden*, particularly the prophetic tendency to confuse the "authors' identities with God's." See Cavell, *The Senses of Walden*, expanded ed. (Chicago: University of Chicago Press, 1992), 19–20.

Chapter 36

1. See James Freeman Clarke, editor's note to Jones Very, "Religious Sonnets by Jones Very,—Salem, Mass.," *Western Messenger Devoted to Religion, Life, and Literature*, March 1839, 6, 5.

2. Clarke, "Religious Sonnets," 310.

3. Clarke, 310.

4. Clarke, 309.

5. Clarke, 309.

6. Clarke, 310.

7. Clarke, 310.

8. Clarke, 310 (original emphasis).

9. Norton's speech attacking Emerson, "A Discourse on the Latest Form of Infidelity," was delivered one year after the Divinity School Address. It was printed in pamphlet form shortly thereafter. See Andrews Norton, *A Discourse on the Latest Form of Infidelity; Delivered at the Request of the Association of the Alumni of the Cambridge Theological School on the 19th of July, 1839* (Cambridge, MA: John Owen, 1839).

10. Hawthorne, "Hall of Fantasy," 491.

11. Ralph Waldo Emerson to Jones Very, March 19, 1839; in Rusk and Tilton, *Letters of Ralph Waldo Emerson*, 7:336.

12. Alcott, *Journals*, 130.

13. Alcott, 130.

14. Ralph Waldo Emerson to Elizabeth Palmer Peabody, June 17, 1839; in Rusk and Tilton, *Letters of Ralph Waldo Emerson*, 2:204–5.

15. Ralph Waldo Emerson to Elizabeth Palmer Peabody, June 17, 1839.

16. This anecdote about the Holy Spirit's refusal to be corrected, originally communicated in one of Emerson's letters to Elizabeth Peabody, seems to have had an early life of its own. In 1841, it was related with anti-Transcendentalist relish, in the

Northampton paper, the *Hampshire Gazette*, where Very was held up as the exemplar of the "insanity" of the new ideas. See "Transcendentalism," *Hampshire Gazette*, February 3, 1841.

17. Ralph Waldo Emerson to Elizabeth Palmer Peabody, June 17, 1839.

18. Ralph Waldo Emerson to Margaret Fuller, July 9, 1839; in Rusk and Tilton, *Letters of Ralph Waldo Emerson*, 2:208–9. There are sixty-five poems in the first edition rather than the sixty-six Emerson mentioned to Fuller.

Chapter 37

1. It may be the case, though there is no direct, surviving evidence to indicate it, that Emerson provided the funds for the initial publication, in which case his assumption of editorial control would seem justified.

2. Dowling's observation that "Emerson's liberal gamble on [Very's] eccentric genius gave way to careful career management and responsible mediation" is an apt characterization of the shift of feeling. See Dowling, *Emerson's Protégés*, 208.

3. Jill E. Anderson describes this relationship between containment and expression: "The very rigidity of the form at once contained the otherwise irrepressible sentiment while expressing and then purifying it. If the sonnet form became a device for sublimation, it was also the result of a consciously learned mental process that ultimately served to shape and order Very's increasingly disorderly thought." See Anderson, "'Nothing Done!': The Poet in Early Nineteenth-Century American Culture" (PhD diss., Rutgers University, 2000), 108. We can add Joseph Phelan's sense that the romantic or Wordsworthian sonnet illustrates "the paradoxical relationship between liberty and restriction; its example shows that true rule-governed 'liberty' is different from and superior to mere 'license.'" See Phelan, *The Nineteenth-Century Sonnet* (New York: Palgrave Macmillan, 2005), 4.

Chapter 38

1. According to Gittleman, the original print run was still unexhausted as late as 1865, when Richard Henry Dana Sr. wrote to Very inquiring about copies (EG 408n1).

2. Deese explains how Very's need to track sales of every copy led to a falling out of sorts with Elizabeth Peabody over her mishandling of inventory (*CP* xxiv).

3. [Margaret Fuller,] "Chat in Boston Bookstores No. 1," *Boston Quarterly Review*, Jan. 1840, 3, 1.

4. [Fuller,] "Chat in Boston Bookstores," 3. For a useful comparison of the popularity of Longfellow's works to the reception of Very's book, see Clayton, *Angelic Sins*, 162–65.

5. [Fuller,] "Chat in Boston Bookstores," 3.

6. [Fuller,] 3.

7. Quoted in EG 362.

8. See Deese, *CP* lii, note 32.

9. [Ralph Waldo Emerson,] review of *Essays and Poems* by Jones Very, *The Dial* 2.1 (1841): 130–31.

10. [Emerson,] review of *Essays and Poems*, 130.

11. See *JMN* 7:489; Ralph Waldo Emerson to Thomas Carlyle, May 30, 1841; in *The*

Correspondence of Thomas Carlyle and Ralph Waldo Emerson, 1834–1872 (London: Chatto and Windus, 1883), 334.

12. See Deese, *CP* xxv.

13. Henry David Thoreau, *The Writings of Henry D. Thoreau, Journal*, vol. 1: *1837–1844* (Princeton, NJ: Princeton University Press, 1981), 459. Thoreau also copied several of Very's poems that were published in the *Salem Observer* into his journal in November of 1838. See Kenneth Cameron, *The Transcendentalists and Minerva* (Hartford, CT: Transcendental Books, 1958), 1:272–73.

14. For other indications of the book's influence and distribution among poets, see EG 355–56.

15. Many of these unpublished manuscript poems lack punctuation. For an explanation of Very's manuscript practice, see Deese, *CP* lxvii.

16. Buell, *Literary Transcendentalism*, 324–25.

17. Walt Whitman, *Song of Myself*, in *Whitman: Complete Poetry and Collected Prose*, ed. Justin Kaplan (New York: Library of America, 1982), 28, 30. A more apt comparison might be to William Blake's claims of literal dictation by the spirit.

18. Melville's description of the "original" character in *The Confidence-Man* could also apply to Very: "The original character, essentially such, is like a revolving Drummond light, raying away from itself all round it—everything is lit by it, everything starts up to it (mark how it is with Hamlet), so that, in certain minds, there follows upon the adequate conception of such a character, an effect, in its way, akin to that which in Genesis attends upon the beginning of things." See Herman Melville, *The Confidence-Man: His Masquerade*, vol. 10 of *The Writings of Herman Melville* (Chicago: Northwestern University Press and the Newberry Library, 1984), 239.

Chapter 39

1. Jones Very to Lidian Jackson Emerson, undated (original emphasis); Special Collections, Wellesley College Library.

2. The manuscript of "The Morning" is in the Very collection in the Houghton Library.

3. An accurate date for this meeting is difficult to determine. Ward recorded the incident but did not date it and later indicated that it must have occurred in 1839. Some have conjectured that the meeting took place in January of that year, but Ward was in New Orleans from mid-December 1838 to March 1839. L. H. Butterfield, who brought the account to light in 1960, speculates that the meeting took place in the summer, just before the publication of Very's book of essays and poems. However, a later letter from Ward to Thomas Wentworth Higginson places the meeting after Ward had read "The Barberry Bush," a poem not published until November 16, 1839. It seems most likely that the visit occurred sometime in either September or December 1839, both months when Very was in Boston for short visits. For the full text of Ward's account, see Butterfield, "Come with Me to the Feast," 3–4. See also EG 280 and Samuel G. Ward to Thomas Wentworth Higginson, October 11, 1891, in *The Emily Dickinson Handbook*, ed. Gundrun Grabher, Roland Hagenbüchle, and Cristanne Miller (Amherst: University of Massachusetts Press, 1998), 3. For Ward's movements in 1838–39, see Eleanor M. Tilton, "The True Romance of Anna Hazard Barker and Samuel Gray Ward," *Studies in the American Renaissance*, 1987, 53–72.

4. "Samuel Gray Ward's Account," 3.

5. "Samuel Gray Ward's Account," 3.

6. "Samuel Gray Ward's Account," 4.

7. "Samuel Gray Ward's Account," 4.

8. "Samuel Gray Ward's Account," 4.

9. Samuel Gray Ward to Thomas Wentworth Higginson, October 11, 1891.

10. Deese's explanation of Very's anger at Elizabeth Peabody over misplaced copies of *Essays and Poems* at her bookstore in Boston (*CP* xxiv) suggests that the late letter from Peabody to Andrews is not entirely forthcoming about the context of their lapsed friendship.

11. Ralph Waldo Emerson, "Chardon Street and Bible Conventions," *The Dial*, July 1842, 100–103, 101.

12. Emerson, "Chardon Street," 101.

13. Emerson, 101.

Chapter 40

1. See Nathan Lyons, introduction to *Jones Very: Selected Poems* (New Brunswick: Rutgers University Press, 1966), 34.

2. As Robinson argues, "Yet even if the choice of a 'will-less existence' is only briefly implied in the poem, that choice, and the continual struggle to maintain it, separates Very from Calvinist theology." See Robinson, "Jones Very, the Transcendentalists, and the Unitarian Tradition," 109. For a counterargument on behalf of Very's Calvinism, see Levernier, "Calvinism and Transcendentalism in the Poetry of Jones Very," 30–41.

3. Cole, "Jones Very's 'Epistles to the Unborn,'" 178 (original emphasis).

4. Lyons clarifies this difference succinctly: "Both Very and Emerson would surrender themselves, but for Very this meant abandoning the self, and for Emerson it meant gaining it." See Lyons, introduction, 11.

5. William Lloyd Garrison, "Declaration of Sentiments Adopted by the Peace Convention," in *William Lloyd Garrison and the Fight against Slavery*, ed. William E. Cain (Boston: Bedford Books, 1995), 103.

6. Garrison, "Declaration," 102.

7. Garrison, 104.

8. Garrison, 104.

9. For an overview of the resistance debate within abolitionist circles, see John Demos, "The Antislavery Movement and the Problem of Violent Means," *New England Quarterly* 37.4 (1964): 501–26. For a detailed comparison of Garrison's perfectionism to Emerson's individualism, see T. Gregory Garvey, "Emerson, Garrison, and the Anti-Slavery Society," in *Emerson: Bicentennial Essays*, ed. Ronald A. Bosco and Joel Myerson (Boston: Massachusetts Historical Society, 2006), 153–82.

10. Garrison had published polemical letters in the *Salem Gazette* in the mid-1820s under the pen name "Aristides." However, they predate his engagement with slavery.

11. Garrison, "Declaration," 103–4.

12. Cole, "Jones Very's 'Epistles to the Unborn,'" 178 (original emphasis).

13. Garrison, "Declaration," 105.

14. I agree in this respect with Helen R. Deese, who rightly argues that Gittleman's reading of Very's later years "needs generous qualification. . . . In no sense was he a

recluse or one isolated from fairly normal social intercourse." See Helen R. Deese, "Selected Sermons of Jones Very," *Studies in the American Renaissance*, 1984, 1–78, 1, 2. Paschal Reeves, another student of Very's sermons, makes a similar point in "Jones Very as Preacher: The Extant Sermons," *ESQ* 57.4 (1969): 16–22.

Chapter 41

1. For a full account of Very's activities as a minister, including an index of those sermons with dates and locations of delivery, see Deese, "Selected Sermons of Jones Very," 65–71.

2. See the March 14, 1843, minutes of the Cambridge Association of Ministers, Harvard Divinity School Library, bms 35/1 (3).

3. Jones Very to Ralph Waldo Emerson, November 23, 1842; Special Collections, Wellesley College Library.

4. The other ministers present were Daniel Austin (lately of First Church, Brighton), Artemus Bowers Muzzey (Unitarian church, Framingham), William Newell (First Parish, Cambridge), R. T. Austin, and Richard Manning Hodges (First Congregational church, Bridgewater).

5. JHL 1.1. As a comparison, the average monthly wage for a day laborer with board included in Massachusetts in 1850 was $13.55. See J. D. B. DeBow, *Statistical View of the United States* (Washington, DC: B. Tucker, Senate Printer, 1854), 164.

6. Quoted in Reeves, "Making of a Mystic," 27.

7. See "Jones Very Again," in *Literary Comment in American Renaissance Newspapers*, ed. Kenneth Walter Cameron (Hartford, CT: Transcendental Books, 1977), 103–4.

8. "Jones Very Again," 104.

9. Andrews, "Memoir," 23.

10. See "The Finest Sonnet Writer in America," in *Literary Comment in American Renaissance Newspapers*, 99–103, 102.

11. "Jones Very Again," 104.

12. Andrews, "Memoir," 23.

13. Combining her record of poets and writers referenced in the sermons with Bartlett's and those found by Paschal Reeves, Deese lists Coleridge, Milton, Waller, Wyclif, Tyndale, Luther, Plato, "the ancient Greek tragedies," Ovid, Cicero, Mitford, Homer, Persius, Horace, Samuel Johnson, Sterling, Burns, Wordsworth, Shakespeare, Pope, Longfellow, Tennyson, Gray, Addison, Franklin, Bryant, Goldsmith, Burke, Aeschylus, Richard Henry Dana Jr., Jefferson, Josephus, Neander, Newton, Paley, "Patrick F. Tytler (a Scottish historian), and Luis de Leon (a sixteenth-century Spanish writer)." See Deese, "Selected Sermons," 12.

14. Andrews, "Memoir," 25.

15. "Jones Very Again," 104.

16. Deese points out that Very substituted for a wide range of "Unitarian stalwarts" over the years, suggesting that there may have been less resistance than Lydia L. A. remembered. Upham's early endorsement may have played a role in confirming his suitability. See Deese, "Selected Sermons," 3.

17. Reeves rightly notes Very's anti-Catholicism in the sermons; the interpretation of the Reformation in particular, though not without a critique of the fragmenting force of Protestantism, falls heaviest on Catholic "spiritual tyranny." The fact that St. James Catholic Church was built close to the Verys' house on Federal Street in

1850 and over the next many years slowly consumed much of the land around the property may well have intensified these traditional Protestant complaints. See Reeves, "Jones Very as Preacher," 20–21.

18. Very's general tendency to argue as a spiritualist did not make him open to the new spiritualism of the mid-nineteenth century. In a sermon preached several times in the 1850s, he attacked "spiritualists" who presented "communications" for the purposes of entertainment or idle curiosity. See HS 23.

Chapter 42

1. "Peace Meeting," *Salem Register*, April 26, 1849, 2.

2. "Peace Meeting," 2. The Paris Peace Conference was presided over by Victor Hugo.

3. Very also wrote a poem, published in the *Christian Register* in January 1852, that expressed a similar position: "'Tis ours for Truth to suffer, and to speak; / But not to fight, or warlike trumpet blow." See "Kossuth" (*CP* 273).

4. As Van Anglen argues in *New England Milton*, "Like his earlier 1833 poem, Very's abolitionist sonnets are hardly revolutionary; rather, he consistently takes the heavenly point of view, demonizing those who, by introducing the original sin of slavery in the New World garden, would tamper with his idealized vision of ordered liberty" (173).

5. Very himself took part in meetings and served on committees of the Salem Freedman's Aid Society, which raised money for teachers and other educational expenses for schools in South Carolina. See "Salem Freedman's Aid Society," *Salem Register*, April 8, 1867, and November 9, 1865. It should be clear from these evidences of participation in organized reform efforts that the old notion of Very as indifferent "to institutions," and so "indifferent to reform," as Warner Berthoff claimed in an early essay, is false. See Berthoff, "Jones Very: New England Mystic," *Boston Public Library Quarterly* 2 (January 1950): 63–76, 75.

Chapter 43

1. Reeves plausibly suggests that age plus the retirement or relocation of many older ministerial friends could have meant that "fewer pulpits were open to him" at this point; "but undoubtedly [Very's] pacifism contributed to his unpopularity." See Reeves, "Jones Very as Preacher," 20.

2. See Paula Bernat Bennett's description of public poetry as that "whose expressive and mimetic power is organized explicitly or implicitly for argumentative ends—in order to achieve a practical discursive goal: persuasion." Bennett, *Poets in the Public Sphere: The Emancipatory Project of American Women's Poetry, 1800–1900* (Princeton, NJ: Princeton University Press, 2003), 5.

3. Very complained to Emerson that the poem had been "altered considerably" prior to publication, though no record survives to indicate what changes may have been made. See *CP* 636–37.

4. See Very, "Two Harvard Essays," 38–39.

Chapter 44

1. See United States Senate, Historical Highlights, 1801–1850, https://www.senate.gov/artandhistory/history/minute/Bitter_Feelings_In_the_Senate_Chamber.htm.

Chapter 45

1. "Memorial to Jones Very," *Bulletin of the Essex Institute* 13 (1882): 1–35, 1 (original emphasis).

2. "Memorial to Jones Very," 30.

3. "Memorial to Jones Very," 14.

4. See "Jones Very Again," 104. The assertion is verified by what appears to be a lecture included in the archive of Very's sermons at Harvard. "On Knowledge" (HS 113; delivered in Boston in 1852) presents a detailed case for the value of scientific and technological education as a part of both general and Christian progress.

5. Jones Very, "The Very Family," in *Historical Collections of the Essex Institute* (Salem: Henry Whipple & Son, 1860), 2:33–38.

6. There was some dispute as to the genuineness of the supposed relic from the 1634 building, though a discussion on the topic at the Essex Institute in 1864 concluded that "the arguments adduced seemed to favor the affirmative of the question." See *Proceedings of the Essex Institute*, Monday, January 25, 1864, as well as "Report of the Committee, On the Authenticity of the Tradition of the First Church, Built in 1634," in *Historical Collections of the Essex Institute*, 2:145–48. Later committees determined that the structure was more likely the earliest Quaker meetinghouse, and it was reconstructed and now stands on the property of the Peabody Essex Museum.

7. For more information, see Deese's note in *CP* 672. In 1870, Very delivered a lecture as part of the Essex Institute's "Historical and Scientific" series and concluded his presentation with a poem, "The Settlement of Salem by the Puritans." See "Local Items," *Salem Register*, April 25, 1870.

Chapter 46

1. See "Convention at Salem," *Monthly Religious Magazine*, November 1847, 4, 11; "The Fowler Street School Dedication," *Salem Register*, June 3, 1852; and Deese, "Selected Sermons of Jones Very," 1–2.

2. See advertisement in the *Salem Observer*, May 8, 1847.

3. See Alfred P. Putnam, *Singers and Songs of the Liberal Faith* (Boston: Roberts Brothers, 1875), 373.

4. See Bartlett, *Jones Very*, 120.

5. Bartlett, 120.

6. Bartlett, 120.

7. See Bartlett, 120.

8. Very, *An Old-Fashioned Garden*, 152.

Chapter 47

1. See Bartlett, *Jones Very*, 176.

2. Bartlett, 128.

3. Quoted in Bartlett, 128 (original emphasis).

4. *New York Tribune*, May 18, 1880, 4.

5. "Jones Very Again," 103.

6. "A Little-Known Poet," *Cincinnati Daily Gazette*, May 21, 1880, 3.

7. See Essex County (Massachusetts) Probate Records.

8. See "Contests the Will," *Boston Herald*, January 10, 1902, 7; and "Salem Institute Asks Court to Change the Very Will," *Boston Herald*, November 3, 1903, 14.

A Note on Sources

The primary repositories of Very's papers are the Houghton Library at Harvard University and the John Hay Library at Brown University. In addition, Very's letters and some miscellaneous manuscripts are housed in the following collections: the Brooke Russell Astor Reading Room at the New York Public Library; the Massachusetts Historical Society; Special Collections at Wellesley College, Clapp Library; Special Collections and Archives, the University of Iowa Library; and the Phillips Library of the Peabody Essex Museum. His notebooks and other student work are in the Harvard Archives. Those primary works listed on the abbreviations page are not repeated in the following bibliography.

Bibliography

Abrams, M. H. *Natural Supernaturalism: Tradition and Revolution in Romantic Literature*. New York: Norton, 1971.

Ackroyd, Peter. *Blake*. New York: Alfred A. Knopf, 1995.

Ahlstrom, Sydney E. *A Religious History of the American People*. New Haven, CT: Yale University Press, 1972.

Alcott, Bronson. *The Journals of Bronson Alcott*. Edited by Odell Shepherd. Boston: Little, Brown, 1938.

Anderson, Jill E. "'Nothing Done!': The Poet in Early Nineteenth-Century American Culture." PhD diss., Rutgers University, 2000.

Andrews, William P. "Memoir." In *Poems by Jones Very*, 3–31. Boston: Houghton, Mifflin and Company, 1883.

———. "Rev. Jones Very, in Memoriam." *Essex Institute Bulletin* 13 (1881): 1–35.

Annual Report of the Essex Institute, for the Year Ending May 4, 1903. Salem: Essex Institute, 1903.

Arner, Robert. "Hawthorne and Jones Very." *New England Quarterly* 42.2 (1969): 267–75.

Bartlett, William Irving. *Jones Very: Emerson's "Brave Saint."* Durham, NC: Duke University Press, 1942.

Barton, Walter E. "Bell(wether) of Psychiatry." *Dartmouth Medical School Alumni Magazine*, Fall 1987, 14–15.

Bate, Jonathan. Introduction to *The Romantics on Shakespeare*. London: Penguin, 1992.

Bayne, Thomas Wilson. "Pollok, Robert." In *Dictionary of National Biography*, 46:69–70. London: Smith, Elder, 1896.

Bennett, Paula Bernat. *Poets in the Public Sphere: The Emancipatory Project of American Women's Poetry, 1800–1900*. Princeton, NJ: Princeton University Press, 2003.

Bentley, William. *The Diary of William Bentley, 1811–1819*. Salem, MA: Essex Institute, 1914.

Berthoff, Warner. "Jones Very: New England Mystic." *Boston Public Library Quarterly* 2 (January 1950): 63–76.

"Biographical Notices of Mr. Charles Hayward, Jr., and Mr. Samuel T Hildreth." *Christian Examiner* 27.1 (1839): 114–31.

Bradford, G., Jr. "Jones Very." *Unitarian Review* 27.2 (1887): 111.

Brekus, Catherine A. *Strangers and Pilgrims: Female Preaching in American, 1740–1845*. Chapel Hill: University of North Carolina Press, 1998.

Brewster, William. *The Birds of the Cambridge Region of Massachusetts*. Cambridge, MA: The Club, 1906.

Brown, Arthur W. *Always Young for Liberty: A Biography of William Ellery Channing*. Syracuse, NY: Syracuse University Press, 1956.

Buell, Lawrence. *Literary Transcendentalism: Style and Vision in the American Renaissance*. Ithaca, NY: Cornell University Press, 1973.

Butterfield, L. H. "Come with Me to the Feast; or, Transcendentalism in Action." *MHS Miscellany* 6 (December 1960): 1–5.

Cameron, Kenneth Walter. "Jones Very and Thoreau—The 'Greek' Myth." *Emerson Society Quarterly* 7 (1957): 39–40.

———. "Jones Very's Harvard Greek Exposition and Daniel Webster." *Emerson Society Quarterly* 38 (1965): 133–35.

———. *The Transcendentalists and Minerva*. Vol. 1. Hartford, CT: Transcendental Books, 1958.

———. *Transcendental Reading Patterns: Library Charge Lists for the Alcotts, James Freeman Clark, Frederick Henry Hedge, Theodore Parker, George Ripley, Samuel Ripley of Waltham, Jones Very, and Charles Stearns Wheeler—New Areas for Fresh Explorations*. Hartford, CT: Transcendental Books, 1970.

Carlson, Larry A. "Bronson Alcott's 'Journal for 1838' (Part One)." *Studies in the American Renaissance*, 1993, 161–244.

———. "Bronson Alcott's 'Journal for 1838' (Part Two)." *Studies in the America Renaissance*, 1994, 123–93.

Carlyle, Thomas. "Signs of the Times." *Edinburgh Review* 49 (June 1829): 439–59.

Cavell, Stanley. *The Senses of Walden*. Expanded ed. Chicago: University of Chicago Press, 1992.

Channing, Edward T. *Lectures Read to the Seniors of Harvard College*. Edited by Dorothy I. Anderson and Waldo N. Braden. Carbondale and Edwardsville: Southern Illinois University Press, 1968.

Channing, William Ellery. *The Complete Works of William Ellery Channing*. London and New York: Routledge & Sons, 1884.

Charvat, William. "A Chronological List of Emerson's American Lecture Engagements." *Bulletin of the New York Public Library* 64.9 (1960): 492–507.

Clarke, James Freeman. "Biographical Notice of Jones Very." In *Poems and Essays by Jones Very*, xxiii–xxvi. Boston: Houghton, Mifflin and Company, 1886.

Clayton, Sarah Turner. *The Angelic Sins of Jones Very*. New York: Peter Lang, 1999.

Coggeshall, George. *History of the American Privateers, and Letters-of-Marque, during Our War with England in the Years 1812, '13, and '14*. New York: George P. Putnam, 1861.

Colacurcio, Michael. *Emerson and Other Minds: Idealism and the Moral Self*. Vol. 1. Waco, TX: Baylor University Press, 2020.

Cole, Phyllis. "Jones Very's 'Epistles to the Unborn.'" *Studies in the American Renaissance*, 1982, 169–83.

Conrad, David Holmes. *Memoir of Reverend James Chisholm*. New York: Protestant Episcopal Society for the Promotion of Evangelical Knowledge, 1857.

The Correspondence of Thomas Carlyle and Ralph Waldo Emerson, 1834–1872. London: Chatto and Windus, 1883.

Cushing, Thomas. *Memorials of the Class of 1834 of Harvard College, Prepared for the Fiftieth Anniversary of Their Graduation*. Boston: David Clapp & Son, 1884.

Davis, Clark. "Emerson's Telescope: Jones Very and Romantic Individualism." *New England Quarterly* 41.3 (2018): 483–507.

———. *Hawthorne's Shyness: Ethics, Politics, and the Question of Engagement*. Baltimore: Johns Hopkins University Press, 2005.

DeBow, J. D. B. *Statistical View of the United States*. Washington, DC: B. Tucker, Senate Printer, 1854.

Deese, Helen R. "The Peabody Family and the Jones Very 'Insanity': Two Letters of Mary Peabody." *Harvard Library Bulletin* 35.2 (1987): 218–29.

———. "Selected Sermons of Jones Very." *Studies in the American Renaissance*, 1984, 1–78.

Demos, John. "The Antislavery Movement and the Problem of Violent Means." *New England Quarterly* 37.4 (1964): 501–26.

Dennis, Carl. "Correspondence in Very's Nature Poetry." *New England Quarterly* 43.2 (1970): 250–73.

Dixon, Suzanne. *Cornelia: Mother of the Gracchi*. New York: Routledge, 2007.

Dowling, David. *Emerson's Protégés: Mentoring and Marketing Transcendentalism's Future*. New Haven, CT: Yale University Press, 2014.

Eckhardt, Celia Morris. *Fanny Wright: Rebel in America*. Cambridge, MA: Harvard University Press, 1984.

———. "Of Fanny and Camilla Wright: Their Sisterly Love." In *The Sister Bond: A Feminist View of a Timeless Connection*, edited by Toni A. McNaron, 37–50. New York: Pergamon, 1985.

Edwards, Jonathan. *A Jonathan Edwards Reader*. Edited by John E. Smith, Harry S. Stout, and Kenneth P. Minkema. New Haven, CT: Yale University Press, 1995.

———. "Personal Narrative." In *A Jonathan Edwards Reader*, edited by John E. Smith, Harry S. Stout, and Kenneth P. Minkema, 281–96. New Haven, CT: Yale University Press, 1995.

Eidson, John Olin. *Charles Stearns Wheeler: Friend of Emerson*. Athens: University of Georgia Press, 1951.

Emerson, Lidian Jackson. *The Selected Letters of Lidian Jackson Emerson*. Edited by Delores Bird Carpenter. Columbia: University of Missouri Press, 1987.

Emerson, Ralph Waldo. "Chardon Street and Bible Conventions." *The Dial*, July 1842, 100–103.

———. *The Letters of Ralph Waldo Emerson*. Edited by Ralph L. Rusk and Eleanor M. Tilton. 10 vols. New York: Columbia University Press, 1939–91.

Emerson, Ralph Waldo, and William Henry Furness. *Records of a Lifelong Friendship, 1807–1882*. Boston: Houghton Mifflin, 1910.

Faust, Drew Gilpin. *This Republic of Suffering: Death and the American Civil War*. New York: Vintage, 2009.

"The Finest Sonnet Writer in America." In *Literary Comment in American Renaissance Newspapers: Fresh Discoveries Concerning Emerson, Thoreau, Alcott, and Transcendentalism*, edited by Kenneth Walter Cameron, 99–103. Hartford, CT: Transcendental Books, 1977.

The First Centenary of the North Church and Society in Salem, Massachusetts. Salem, MA, 1873.

[Fuller, Margaret]. "Chat in Boston Bookstores No. 1." *Boston Quarterly Review*, January 1840, 3.

———. *Summer on the Lakes, in 1843*. Boston: Little, Brown, 1844.

Garrison, William Lloyd. "Declaration of Sentiments Adopted by the Peace Convention." In *William Lloyd Garrison and the Fight against Slavery*, edited by William E. Cain, 101–5. Boston: Bedford Books, 1995.

Garvey, T. Gregory. "Emerson, Garrison, and the Anti-Slavery Society." In *Emerson: Bicentennial Essays*, edited by Ronald A. Bosco and Joel Myerson. Boston: Massachusetts Historical Society, 2006.

Godwin, William. *Memoirs of the Author of "A Vindication of the Rights of Women."* London, 1798.

Grabher, Gundrun, Roland Hagenbüchle, and Cristanne Miller, eds. *The Emily Dickinson Handbook*. Amherst: University of Massachusetts Press, 1998.

Gray, Edward. *William Gray of Salem*. Boston: Houghton Mifflin, 1914.

Griffin, Edward M. *Old Brick: Charles Chauncey of Boston, 1705–1787*. Minneapolis: University of Minnesota Press, 1980.

Gross, Robert A. *The Minutemen and Their World*. New York: Hill and Wang, 1976.

———. *The Transcendentalists and Their World*. New York: Farrar, Straus and Giroux, 2021.

Gura, Philip. *Jonathan Edwards: America's Evangelical*. New York: Hill and Wang, 2005.

Habich, Robert D. "Emerson's Reluctant Foe: Andrews Norton and the Transcendental Controversy." *New England Quarterly* 65.2 (1992): 208–37.

Hall, David D. *The Antinomian Controversy, 1636–1638*. Durham, NC: Duke University Press, 1990.

Hawthorne, Nathaniel. *The Centenary Edition of the Works of Nathaniel Hawthorne*. Edited by William Charvat, Roy Harvey Pearce, and Claude M. Simpson. 23 vols. Columbus: Ohio State University Press, 1962–.

Hazlitt, William. *Characters of Shakespear's Plays & Lectures on the English Poets*. London: Macmillan, 1903.

Higginson, Thomas Wentworth. *Cheerful Yesterdays*. Boston: Houghton Mifflin, 1898.

Hodder, Alan. "Christian Conversion, the Double Consciousness, and Transcendentalist Religious Rhetoric." *Religions* 8 (2017): 1–19.

Jones, Jesse H. "Henry Kemble Oliver." In Massachusetts Bureau of Statistics of Labor, *Seventeenth Annual Report of the Bureau of Statistics of Labor*, 1–48. Boston: Wright and Potter Printing Co., 1886.

"Jones Very Again." In *Literary Comment in American Renaissance Newspapers: Fresh Discoveries Concerning Emerson, Thoreau, Alcott, and Transcendentalism*, edited by Kenneth Walter Cameron, 103–4. Hartford, CT: Transcendental Books, 1977.

"Jones Very and Emerson's Friends in College Church Records." *Emerson Society Quarterly* 14.1 (1959): 15–16.

"Jones Very and the Emersons in Harvard's Official Records." *Emerson Society Quarterly* 10.1 (1958): 46–47.

"Jones Very's Academic Standing at Harvard." *Emerson Society Quarterly* 19.2 (1960): 52–60.

King, Caroline Howard. *When I Lived in Salem, 1822–1866*. Brattleboro, VT: Stephen Daye Press, 1937.

Lamartine, Alphonse de. *On Man. To Lord Byron; Translated from the French of Alph. de Lamartine; with a Letter from the Author to the Translator*. London: T. Hurst, 1827.

———. *A Pilgrimage to the Holy Land*. Philadelphia: Carey, Lea, and Blanchard, 1838.

Levernier, James A. "Calvinism and Transcendentalism in the Poetry of Jones Very." *ESQ* 24.1 (1978): 31–41.

Lombard, Charles M. "Early American Admirers of Lamartine." *Études Anglaises* 12 (January 1959): 324–34.

———. *Lamartine*. New York: Twayne Publishers, 1973.

Lyons, Nathan. Introduction to *Jones Very: Selected Poems*. New Brunswick, NJ: Rutgers University Press, 1966.

Marshall, Megan. *The Peabody Sisters: Three Women Who Ignited American Romanticism*. New York: Houghton Mifflin, 2005.

Melville, Herman. *The Confidence-Man: His Masquerade*. Vol. 10 of *The Writings of Herman Melville*. Chicago: Northwestern University Press and the Newberry Library, 1984.

"Memorial to Jones Very." *Bulletin of the Essex Institute* 13 (1882): 1–35.

Miller, Edwin Haviland. *Salem Is My Dwelling Place: A Life of Nathaniel Hawthorne*. Iowa City: University of Iowa Press, 1991.

Moore, George. *Diary of George Moore, Friend of Emerson*. In *Transcendental Epilogue: Primary Materials for Research in Emerson, Thoreau, Literary New England, the Influence of German Theology, and Higher Biblical Criticism*, edited by Kenneth Walter Cameron, 239–40. Hartford, CT: Transcendental Books, 1965.

Moore, Margaret B. *The Salem World of Nathaniel Hawthorne*. Columbia: University of Missouri Press, 1998.

Morison, Samuel Eliot. *Three Centuries of Harvard*. Cambridge, MA: Harvard University Press, 1936.

Myerson, Joel. "A Calendar of Transcendental Club Meetings." *American Literature* 44.4 (1972): 197–207.

Norton, Andrews. *A Discourse on the Latest Form of Infidelity; Delivered at the Request of the Association of the Alumni of the Cambridge Theological School on the 19th of July, 1839*. Cambridge, MA: John Owen, 1839.

Noyes, C. E. "A New England Mystic." *Harvard Monthly* 17 (October 1893): 136–43.

Oliver, Henry K. *Lecture on Teachers' Morals and Manners: Delivered before the American Institute of Instruction, at Keene, N.H., August 1851*. Boston: Ticknor, Reed, & Fields, 1851.

———. "Reminiscences of Federal Street in 1885." *Essex Institute Historical Collections* 82 (April 1946): 179–85.

Parker, Hershel. *Herman Melville, 1851–1891*. Baltimore: Johns Hopkins University Press, 1996.

Parker, Theodore. *Journal, Volume One, July 13, 1838 to December 31, 1840*. Theodore Parker Papers, 1836–1862. Andover-Harvard Theological Library, Harvard Divinity School.

Peabody, Elizabeth Palmer. *Reminiscences of Rev. Wm. E. Channing, D.D.* Boston: Roberts Bros., 1880.

Phelan, Joseph. *The Nineteenth-Century Sonnet*. New York: Palgrave Macmillan, 2005.

Pollok, Robert. *The Course of Time: A Poem*. New York: Robert Carter and Brothers, 1878.

Putnam, Alfred P. *Singers and Songs of the Liberal Faith*. Boston: Roberts Brothers, 1875.

Reeves, Paschal. "Jones Very as Preacher: The Extant Sermons." *ESQ* 57.4 (1969): 16–22.

———. "The Making of a Mystic." *Essex Institute Historical Collections* 103 (1967): 3–30.

Richardson, Robert D., Jr. *Emerson: The Mind on Fire*. Berkeley: University of California Press, 1995.

Richter, Paula Bradstreet. "Wollstonecraft and Needlecraft: A Case Study of Women's Rights and Education in Federal Salem, Massachusetts." *Painted with Thread: The Art of American Embroidery* 136 (2000): 141–47.

Robinson, David. "The Exemplary Self and the Transcendent Self in the Poetry of Jones Very." *ESQ* 24.4 (1978): 206–14.

———. "Four Early Poems of Jones Very." *Harvard Library Bulletin* 28.2 (1980): 146–51.

———. "Jones Very, the Transcendentalists, and the Unitarian Tradition." *Harvard Theological Review* 68.2 (1975): 103–24.

Ruffin, J. Rixey. *A Paradise of Reason: William Bentley and Enlightenment Christianity in the Early Republic*. New York: Oxford University Press, 2008.

Rusk, Ralph L. *The Life of Ralph Waldo Emerson*. New York: Charles Scribner's Sons, 1949.

Scudder, Horace Elisha. *James Russell Lowell: A Biography*. Vol. 1. Frankfurt am Main: Outlook Verlag, 2020.

Stabler, Jane. "Byron and 'The Excursion.'" *Wordsworth Circle* 45.2 (2014): 137–47.

de Staël, Germaine. *Major Writings of Germaine de Staël*. Translated by Vivian Folkenflik. New York: Columbia University Press, 1987.

Taylor, Isaac. "Jonathan Edwards' Inquiry into the Freedom of the Will." In Patrick C. MacDougall, *Papers on Literary and Philosophical Subjects*, 66–138. Edinburgh: Johnstone and Hunter, 1852.

———. *Natural History of Enthusiasm*. London: Holdsworth and Ball, 1830.

Thoreau, Henry David. *The Writings of Henry D. Thoreau. Journal*, vols. 1–8.Princeton, NJ: Princeton University Press, 1981–2002.

Tilton, Eleanor M. "The True Romance of Anna Hazard Barker and Samuel Gray Ward." *Studies in the American Renaissance*, 1987, 53–72.

"Treatment of the Insane." *American Magazine of Useful and Entertaining Knowledge*, January 1, 1837.

Van Anglen, K. P. *The New England Milton: Literary Reception and Cultural Authority in the Early Republic*. University Park: Penn State University Press, 1993.

Very, Jones. *Essays and Poems*. Boston: Little, Brown, 1839.

———. "The Father of Rev. Jones Very." *Salem Register*, May 17, 1880.

———. *Poems and Essays*. Boston: Houghton, Mifflin and Company, 1886.

———. "Two Harvard Essays by Jones Very." *Emerson Society Quarterly* 29 (1962): 32–40.

———. "The Very Family." In *Historical Collections of the Essex Institute*, 2:33–38. Salem: Henry Whipple & Son, 1860.

———. "What Reasons Are There for Not Expecting Another Great Epic Poem?" *Emerson Society Quarterly* 12 (1958): 25–38.

Very, Lydia L. A. *An Old-Fashioned Garden, and Walks and Musings Therein*. Salem, MA: Salem Press, 1900.

———. *Poems and Prose Writings*. Salem, MA: Salem Press, 1890.

———. *A Strange Recluse*. Salem, MA: Salem Press, 1899.

Vinton, John Adams. *The Giles Memorial: Genealogical Memoirs of the Families Bearing the Names of Giles, Gould, Holmes, Jennison, Leonard, Lindall, Curwen, Marshall, Robinson, Sampson, and Webb; Also Genealogical Sketches of the Pool, Very, Tarr and Other Families, with a History of Pemaquid, Ancient and Modern; Some Account of Early Settlements in Maine; and Some Details of Indian Warfare*. Boston: Henry W. Dutton & Son, 1864.

Waterhouse, Benjamin. *A Journal of a Young Man of Massachusetts*. Boston: Rowe and Hooper, 1816.

Wheeler, Candace. *The Development of Embroidery in America*. New York: Harper Brothers, 1921.

Wheeler, Charles Stearns. "Biographical Notices of Mr. Charles Hayward, Jr., and Mr. Samuel T. Hildreth." *Christian Examiner and General Review*, September 1839, 114–31.

Whitman, Walt. *Song of Myself*. In *Whitman: Complete Poetry and Collected Prose*, edited by Justin Kaplan, 27–88. New York: Library of America, 1982.

Williams, George Huntston, ed. *The Harvard Divinity School: Its Place in Harvard University and in American Culture*. Boston: Beacon Press, 1954.

Williams, Henry. *Memorials of the Class of 1837 of Harvard University, Prepared for the Fiftieth Anniversary of Their Graduation*. Boston: George Henry Ellis, 1887.

Winters, Yvor. *Maule's Curse: Seven Studies in the History of American Obscurantism*. Norfolk, CT: New Directions, 1938.

Woodall, Guy R. "The Record of a Friendship: The Letters of Convers Francis to Frederic Henry Hedge in Bangor and Providence, 1835–1850." *Studies in the American Renaissance*, 1991, 1–57.

Wordsworth, William. *The Prelude, The Recluse, & The Excursion*. Bristol: Read and Company, 2020.

Wright, Conrad. "Emerson, Barzillai Frost, and the Divinity School Address." *Harvard Theological Review* 49.1 (1956): 19–43.

Wright, Frances. *Reason, Religion, and Morals*. Amherst, NY: Humanity Books, 2004.

Index